"MY ECCHOING SONG"

"MY ECCHOING SONG"

ANDREW MARVELL'S
POETRY OF CRITICISM

BY ROSALIE L. COLIE

PRINCETON, NEW JERSEY

PRINCETON UNIVERSITY PRESS 1970

Copyright © 1970 by Princeton University Press

ALL RIGHTS RESERVED

Library of Congress Card Number: 69-18053
I.S.B.N.: 0-691-06163-7

This book has been composed in Linotype Granjon

Printed in the United States of America
by Princeton University Press
Princeton, New Jersey

To
Roger and Jessie Hornsby
and
Joan and Murray Krieger,
for light in a dark time.

PREFACE

WITH so many books in print about Andrew Marvell, some of them such good books; with the promise of a modern edition of much of Marvell's prose; with the anticipation of Miss Robbins' study of Marvell's politics, why should anyone be so foolish as to offer another book on this man's poetry? My reasons are, like Marvell's poetry, both private and public: private, in that I have never understood Marvell's verse and, once in the grip of the obsession to do so, found I could not stop trying to get at what he was up to; public, in that a class of very bright graduate students to whom I was trying to teach some new ways—which is to say, some very old ways—of reading Renaissance literature, kept saying, "If you'll just *do* it with some writer, we'll see what you mean." What I "meant" was, merely, to take into consideration as much as possible and feasible about a writer's way of writing and about the ways of writing available to him, to understand as fully as one can, at such a remove, the professional and traditional obligations and observations of a writer to his craft. Although one could write a book about a man's literary work seen against the norms, forms, and patterns of art and thought of his time, against the backgrounds and alternatives of that time, such a book needn't be about Marvell. Why, then, this poet? First, the private reason: because Marvell's work was and remains too hard for me; it has never been easy for me to read any poetry, and Marvell's poems have always seemed to me among the most difficult and elusive I know. Second, a topical social reason: from that class of bright graduate students there were some interesting reactions to Marvell's lyric poetry, reactions which seemed to me relevant to the kind of preoccupation with professional commitment I then had. These young men and women had been highly selected before they assembled; they were being trained by the most alarming bunch of professional scholars, critics, and students it has been my pleasure to observe in a single cluster. These students were, furthermore, cannibals, as is only right and proper in real students; as much of himself as a teacher could give, they ate at once, looking up expectantly for more. Furthermore, they didn't like a continuous diet; a teacher was expected to prepare himself in different succulent ways for them. They ingested their teachers' techniques and ideas, insights and methods; they intended to ingest, if need be, their teachers as well—which is to say, they

vii

had every intention of professionally outsmarting us, of outdoing and overgoing our most beautiful, painful, original achievements. They probably will, too, which is a pleasure to contemplate, if one does not mind being on the wrong end of a little ritual parent-killing. Withal, they were ladies and gentlemen, and they were born into an age that demands the appearance of cool, no matter how engaged they really might be with their studies, their careers, and their lives.

Now, these students waxed violent about Andrew Marvell's lyric poems. He was a cool customer, a smiler in his sleeve, a smiler with a knife—he was all kinds of things of which they disapproved, and which to me they seemed to exemplify themselves, in part of their characters at least. That peculiar situation suggested that there might be some slight purpose, in the present state of academic life, to a book of this kind, which does argue for Marvell's extraordinary professional commitment, but does not deny his peculiar detachment from professional rewards and from professional class-interests. For that group of students, I worked hard to make Marvell respectable if not likeable; I think they rather took to him after a bit—or, at least, came to hide their dislike under their habitual sang-froid, so long as I was there to watch them.

The third reason, my parochial professional one, is the most important—hence the book's title, "My Ecchoing Song," a quotation from Marvell's most familiar lyric poem. His poetry "echoes" in various ways, carrying the overtones of an incredibly rich tradition, these overtones prolonged in our ear and mind by Marvell's miraculous dispositions of sense and sound. Unfortunately, the songs Marvell sang, so familiar to his literate contemporaries, are written in notes almost inaudible to modern ears. We have to work at him, to get him up—and like most things so learned, the Marvellian tradition can seem faint and slack, affected and irrelevant, even to persons like myself, concerned with the tradition's memory. It is lucky, both for us and for the tradition, that Marvell wrote so seductively within it. The sheer beauty of his lines, the result of the order in which he set down his carefully selected words, soothes the ear, as the overtones both satisfy and imply an indefinite prolongation of our satisfactions. In the overtones, indeed, can be heard the sound of the difficulties in Marvell's verse. Ultimately, he is an enigmatic poet—which brings me back to my first reason for undertaking a concerted study of his poems.

The problems of understanding these poems are considerable, and the problems of organizing one's understanding little less taxing. Presenting such puzzles, Marvell not surprisingly has excited and challenged the critics of this century. T. S. Eliot's accolade came early. Professor Empson's love of ambiguity and of pastoral brought him ever back to consider Marvell; many of his remarks on the verse have never been bettered. New critics and post-new critics have tackled the poems, singly and in groups; explicators of every stripe have found ingenuities in Marvell. Scholars like J. B. Leishman, concerned with problems of custom, influence, and decorum, have found innumerable sources and analogues for Marvell's lines. Scholars interested in intellectual content, such as Miss Wallerstein, Mr. Toliver, and Mr. Berger, have greatly illuminated this verse. Mr. Hill's, Mr. Hyman's, Mr. Wallace's, and Mr. Lord's work honors the poet's relation to his trying times. Mr. Allen is concerned with the resources of Marvell's imagery, and Mr. Spitzer devoted himself to the linguistic and syntactical aspects of one major poem, explicated in such a way as to help us with all of them. Miss Røstvig has given us a Horatian Marvell, Mr. O'Loughlin a georgic Marvell, Mr. Holahan a Marvell whose public and private concerns, hitherto held firmly apart by critics, can be seen to overlap and to fuse, even in some of the most "private" poems.[1]

With all this, can one not leave Marvell to chance and to fame, or to

[1] T. S. Eliot, *Selected Essays* (New York and London, 1932); William Empson, *Seven Types of Ambiguity* (London, 1930) and *Some Versions of Pastoral* (London, 1935); Ruth Wallerstein, *Studies in Seventeenth Century Poetic* (Madison, 1950); Harold E. Toliver, *Marvell's Ironic Vision* (New Haven, 1965); Harry Berger, Jr., "Marvell's 'Appleton House': an Interpretation," *Southern Quarterly*, 1966, 7-32; "Andrew Marvell: the Poem as Green World," *Forum for Modern Language Studies*, III (1967), 290-309; "Marvell's 'Garden': Still Another Interpretation," *MLQ*, XXVIII (1967), 285-304; J. B. Leishman, "Theme and Variation in the Poetry of Andrew Marvell," *Proc. Brit. Acad.*, XLVII (1961), 223-41; *The Art of Marvell's Poetry* (London, 1966); John Malcolm Wallace, *Destiny his Choice: the Loyalism of Andrew Marvell* (London, 1968); Lawrence Hyman, *Andrew Marvell* (New York, 1964); George de F. Lord, ed., *Poems on Affairs of State*, I (New Haven, 1963); and "From Contemplation to Action: Marvell's Poetical Career," *PQ*, XLVI (1967), 207-24; Don Cameron Allen, *Image and Meaning* (Baltimore, 1960), Chapters 6 and 7; Leo Spitzer, "Marvell's 'Nymph complaining for the Death of her Faun': Sources versus Meaning," *MLQ*, XIX (1958), 231-43; Maren-Sofie Røstvig, *The Happy Man* (Oslo, 1954), I; Michael J. O'Loughlin, "The Garlands of Repose," unpublished dissertation, Yale University, 1966; Michael N. Holahan, "The Civick Crown," unpublished dissertation, Yale University, 1967; Frank J. Warnke, "Play and Metamorphosis in Marvell's Poetry," *SEL*, V (1965), 23-30; J. A. Carscallen, "Marvell's Infinite Parallels," forthcoming in *The University of Toronto Quarterly*.

the taste and tact of sensitive, educated, or even learned readers? Very likely! But all the same (*vide* that graduate seminar), for some people more might well be said, or some things said differently, to make the poetry more appealing and more accessible. I argue for a kind of reading I think appropriate to Marvell's verse, one which takes into consideration his own habits of learned allusiveness, which compares his poetry with samples of similar verse by his models and by his contemporaries. What were the models Marvell looked to? What did he count on, or hope for, from his audience? For people who find such considerations deadly, this book is not written. It is written for learners, for people who believe not so much in sure methods of interpretation as in preparations for interpretation, who are fonder of forming critical questions than of framing final critical solutions. Here, I try to look at the body of Marvell's lyrical verse in different ways, all of them I hope intelligible to the Renaissance poet, to see how one poet regarded his craft, what he took to be its problems, and whither he looked for their solutions. Another writer might have been chosen for such an exercise—Milton, Swift, Diderot all offer themselves as obvious possibilities. But Marvell was a convenient choice, because his lyrical work, though small, is extremely varied; because in that work he tended to set and solve problems in different ways, so that comparison among his poems is fruitful; because he wrote in the idioms commonly used by his peers, that mob of gentlemen that writ well, comparison with whose verse brings out Marvell's peculiarities of style and spirit.

In this study, I have tried to look at Marvell's verse along lines of vision which, I think, were those of professional poets and serious readers in the Renaissance; to examine, then, Marvell's practice in various ranges sanctioned by his craft. Part I deals with matters of form, genre, and theme, Part II with matters of grammar, rhetoric, and style. Of course these divisions are, in the end, arbitrary, and there is much overlap between my sections. There is another kind of overlap, too, in that I use many of the poems more than once, to illustrate different critical points, so that, e.g., "The Coronet," "The Nymph complaining," and "Damon the Mower," to say nothing of "The Garden" itself, show up again and again in different contexts. For some, this may seem intolerable repetition; its methodological justification lies in the fact that these poems should (and, more important, can) be read in many different ways, squinted at along many different angles of literary vision.

It is axiomatic that any good poet makes something special of the poetic elements he uses. In Marvell's case, I think the poet did still more than what any good poet does, working in and beyond his traditions. Marvell functioned in those traditions not only as creator but as critic as well. It was his naturally double vision, with the irony resulting therefrom, that drove the students to cry out against him as an uncommitted poet. They recognized that his interest in the problems—or, as I prefer to say, the problematics—of poetry often ran counter to his devotion to poetic form and subject. They felt that Marvell was asking for discrepant reactions, and they responded, as primitives do before sophistication, by anger.

They were right, of course; to those students my debt is considerable. Another fundamental debt may be recorded here. For some years, I had the good fortune to be among colleagues (now, alas, largely dispersed) at the University of Iowa, whose fanatical interest in literary criticism and aesthetics, even in literature itself, reanimated at least one of their associates to like enthusiasm. These people organized a conference on modern literature on the theme of "the Poet as Critic," the papers of which were later collected and published.[2] While the conference was being readied, we argued a great deal over the difference between "the poet" and "the critic," and in some cases violent feelings were aroused between delegates from one profession and delegates from the other. More sophisticated querists debated something else—whether it was possible for a great (or even a good) poet *not* to be a critic. I think it is *not* possible, and that all great artists implicitly or explicitly express criticisms and critiques of their craft; but that, nonetheless, some poets are more critical than others— e.g., Virgil than Statius, Milton than Cowley, Cowley than Davenant (in spite of that last man's official status as "critic"), Wallace Stevens than Allen Ginsberg. To say this is not to say, however, that the greater the poet, the greater is the degree of his revisionism or radicalism (though I suspect this is in fact a relevant criterion for literary greatness); rather, the question resides in the use to which literary self-consciousness is put. *Tristram Shandy* is a superb book, the work of a highly self-conscious author; one cannot say that *Jacques le fataliste* is the work of a less self-conscious author, but the second book is considerably less critical than the first. Some men write, in their imaginative work, about or toward critical problems abstractly framed; Marvell is such a man.

This book, then, takes for granted that Marvell is a critic in his poetry, and attempts to justify that assumption by demonstration. Not all the

[2] *The Poet as Critic*, ed. Frederick P. W. McDowell (Evanston, 1967).

poems are therefore good—indeed, I think many of them are flawed, some seriously, by the poet's double preoccupation. When Marvell managed to fuse his poetic and his critical insights, though, his verse takes pride of place in a period remarkable for the multitude and the flawlessness of its lyric poetry. Writing this book has given me an excuse, if such a thing were ever needed, for rereading much sixteenth- and seventeenth-century verse, English and other; for looking at classical texts to which Marvell could have turned for models; for reading many treatises, some quite interesting, on Renaissance poetics, rhetoric, and even grammar; for scouring the emblem-books and for looking at pictures of a grander kind. Upon that accumulation, this book relies.

It has its faults, obviously. One lies deep in the method: when one looks hard at a poet's uses of form, device, and style, one tends to discover that one's poet was "critical"; formalistic preoccupations lead toward conclusions about self-consciousness and criticism. All the same, comparison of Marvell's verse with that of his Cavalier contemporaries, particular masters of form, shows the idiosyncratic nature of his critical investigations, his trick of writing a poem and writing about it at the same time. Marvell's work, I think, cries out for formalist attention. Then, some readers will find parts of the book too skimpy, other parts too full. Some parts are bare of footnotes, others bristle with references. In apology, I can only say that in more than one sense, this is a schematic book—an exercise in schematics and an attempt to indicate something of Marvell's relation to the schemata of his profession; it is also, I fear, often all too schematic in itself. There is more to be said than I had space for about all the topics, all the poems dealt with in Parts I and II; because these sections seemed to me sketchy, from time to time I stopped over a poem, to try to indicate some suggestion of its richness and variety. In Parts III and IV, which I fear cannot be accused of skimpiness, I have tried to read both "The Garden" and "Upon Appleton House" as fully as I could, both to do them some justice and to illustrate this method on poems which do not readily yield their treasures to critical siege. In these sections, though I have certainly dissected and dislocated parts of the poems from each other, I have also tried to show insofar as I could the remarkable harmonies of the two poems.

Happily, the book relies on livelier things than my pedantry and fumbling attempts toward a proper method of reading Renaissance verse. Chiefly, from the generosity of spirit, heart, and mind of Susan and

Michael Holahan and of Harry Berger, Jr., I have drawn so much that I am not sure what is originally theirs and what is my own: what is good is doubtless theirs, the poor things mine own. Alarik Skarstrom, busy with a Marvell of his own making, was relentlessly milked by me, though I buttered him up a little in return. Upon that mob of graduate students sweet and sour, I have reason to dote—particularly upon Carol Christ, Dianne Dumanoski, Judith Kramer, Barbara and Daniel Traister, Stephen Greenblatt, Peter Schwenger, Keith Staveley, and James Thorpe. I have learned much from Harold Toliver, Michael O'Loughlin, and C. E. Ramsey. Bridget Gellert, Maynard Mack, George Lord, Frank Ellis, and Sheldon Zitner all read parts of the book and made helpful suggestions and corrections. W. K. Wimsatt taught me a great deal I ought already to have known. As often before, Julius Held helped me with the sections on visual art and saved me from natural error; from Marie Borroff and A. M. Hudson I got specific help with Marvell's words as well as a great respect for their (very different) uses of linguistics. Joan Webber, to whose work on prose style all students of the seventeenth century are indebted, was kind enough to read the book and to offer advice; the annotations of two readers for the Princeton University Press were extremely valuable in revising the text; George Robinson has proved an exemplary editor. At Toronto, Denton Fox and J. A. Carscallen have greatly helped me. The essay on "The Garden" was written for the Tudor and Stuart Club of the Johns Hopkins University, where it profited from the attentions of the then local Marvellians, Don Cameron Allen, John Malcolm Wallace, and Jackson I. Cope; it was later read elsewhere, to its advantage. The section on the pictorial conventions of "Upon Appleton House" was laid before the students of English at Lady Margaret Hall, Oxford University, with results helpful to me. A man who needs no naming, E. H. Gombrich, left his mark on my simple mind and on this book. J. B. Trapp found much to criticise, expand, and improve; D. J. Olsen made cogent suggestions, and cheered me just when I needed cheering. The book has been several times "finished": I wish to thank Dr. and Mrs. Wijmans (and Roeltje and Diederick and Frans Wouter) for helping me finish it once; and the Governing Body of Lady Margaret Hall, by whose award of the Talbot Research Fellowship the book was in fact enabled to be written. In particular, I am grateful to Miss Lea, Miss Mackenzie, and Miss Hudson for specific contributions and corrections, as well as for general patience. The resources of the Bodley staff, especially the unsung heroism of W. G. Harris, Patricia Brown, and Michael Bull, made it possible for me to learn a little something, for a change; Margaret Crum, as before, was incredibly sympathetic; I. G. Philip helped me with the illustrations. The Beineke Library at Yale, in the shapes of Marjorie G. Wynne and the ladies at the desk, taught me that one American library can make a scholar as happy as European libraries customarily do; Mr. Ludwig, of the Yale libraries, provided many of the illustrations. I thank also the Mauritshuis in The Hague, the National Gallery in London, and the Wadsworth Atheneum in Hartford for permission to reproduce paintings in their care. My greatest personal debts are to Anne Whiteman, generally impatient with "Eng. lit." but tolerant of me and Marvell when I needed it; to Margaret Waggoner, who took time from a busy life to read sharply and constructively; to Willis Lamb, for making me think, as I had not done for many years, about the reasons for poetry. Two people did *not* help me with this project, which taught me how much I have owed them in the past: Philip Long and Arline R. Standley. Murray Krieger is ultimately responsible for this book's existence; and, though they were at work on quite other materials of their own, Roger and Jessie Hornsby and Mrs. Standley set examples to me by their keen attention to literary truth. I have more debts than I can record, but to the Kriegers and the Hornsbys, for determined concentration on important things when the bitterly unimportant threatened to overwhelm me, I owe the most. The dedication is a record that I know that fact, and that the debt is unpayable.

Rosalie L. Colie

Lady Margaret Hall
June, 1968

CONTENTS

Contents

"MY ECCHOING SONG"

INTRODUCTION

THEORETICALLY and poetically, Marvell's lyric poems move upon a very small floor. It is a mosaic floor, delicately worked in intricate patterns of great variety, with a great deal of forethought; within the narrow limits that he chose, Andrew Marvell wrote fantastic variations upon his few themes. No other seventeenth-century poet, not even Marino, did so much in so little. In the last thirty years, Marvell has come into his own—perhaps into more than his own, or more than he deserves; this book adds to the bewildering array of interpretations and polemics clustered around Marvell's name. Not that he really requires our labors. Marvell's poetry is, simply, beautiful to the ear and the mind: who cares what "vegetable Love" is, so long as it grows "vaster than Empires, and more slow"? What difference does it make what "a green Thought in a green Shade" might be, when the line so soothes the ear? All the same, experienced readers, even experienced Marvellians, often find themselves curiously denied thorough satisfaction in the poet's verses, precisely because of an elusiveness and mysteriousness at variance with the apparent precision of the language. Setting and occasion are left unexplained: what are the Bermudians up to? On what errand do the wanton troopers ride? Sometimes a poem ends abruptly where a reader hopes for more, and might legitimately have expected more; sometimes there are disjunctions in a poem which would seem beyond bearing, except that the words are so beautifully said. Merely by their sound, Marvell's lines are often memorable—"And, like *Antipodes* in Shoes/ Have shod their *Heads* in their *Canoos*"; "Yonder all before us lye/ Desarts of vast Eternity"; "The World should all/ Be cramp'd into a *Planisphere*." For these lines alone, a man could have got away with much poetry far worse than any Andrew Marvell ever wrote. In spite of his capacity for striking lines, though, Marvell is not a poet of a few splendid *trouvailles*; rather the opposite—he is a poet of remarkable design, joinery, and finish, a poet of highly polished surfaces. Surfaces: yet no critic has felt him a superficial poet; even to those readers unconcerned with his Platonism, his Puritanism, his republicanism, and so forth, his poetry gives the impression, or the illusion, of great depth—a smooth inviting pool beneath the surface of which are caverns measureless to man.

Marvell wrote at the limits of his traditions, as I shall try to show, but he wrote from well within them. His perspective and his models come

3

from his past, and he does not look ahead to new literary fashions. I would say, joyously, that Marvell is *not* one of those "transitional figures" so beloved of student essay-writers, that he does *not* break new ground in his lyric poetry. Rather, he sums up, examines, and questions the traditions he inherited, without providing either final solutions or prescriptions for a new age in poetry. Though not a transitional figure, he is pre-eminently a mediator: I toyed with the notion of calling this book "The Poetry of Mediation," but decided that the problem for students was too great, with Mr. Martz's classic work on all their reading-lists, and that librarians (some of my best friends are librarians) might not like it. It is useful to keep the concept of mediation in mind, when critical preference seems inclined to deny it so enthusiastically.[1] Marvell's "vision," such as it is, is thoroughly mediated; his was no sensibility laid bare to perception. Everything Marvell wrote came to him somehow prepared, somehow fixed and processed. He examined his literary inheritance with great conscientiousness, rejecting the cliché aspects of tradition, questioning mental set, and checking correspondences between word and thing which had for centuries been taken for granted. Marvell does not open for us—as Shakespeare does, and Milton, another poet who looked back over his shoulder at his own past—immense vistas of new poetic possibility. He does something quite different, boring deep into his own material to discover the concealed, to discard the outworn and useless, to re-animate with his intellectual energy traditions in his day fading into meaninglessness. Chiefly, he accomplishes this by a return to exactness in language, in syntax, metaphor, and image, to display the significances of his tradition. His verse is nervous, cerebral, yet spirited, his detachment is admirable, his precision a delight—why, then, does one sometimes feel disappointed by his verse? Marvell ends a great tradition, I think, with neither bang nor whimper, but with the scrupulous courtesy and grace that had carried the tradition so far, from Greece to seventeenth-century Europe. He looks back at it, studies it, criticizes it, but he neither questions its absoluteness nor offers radically different expressive alternatives. If he were not so good a poet, often an almost "perfect" poet, he might be considered a decadent, for he turns back into his tradition, refining it even as he questions its refinements.

[1] For a discussion of the problems raised by "mediation" and unmediatedness, see Murray Krieger, "Mediation, Language, and Vision in the Reading of Literature," *Interpretation. Theory and Practice*, ed. Charles S. Singleton (Johns Hopkins Press, 1969), pp. 211–42.

Introduction

He was a past master at his art: one miracle of his style is that a man who wrote in so many styles nonetheless could mark verse as unmistakably his own. Stylish though he was, he never took style as his sole aim: for him, stylistic and thematic devices were not part of a wardrobe, to be donned and doffed at will, so much as clothes to wear, which had to be retailored to fit a new body, to suit a man and his personal life. Paradoxes can be formulated about this—that this man by avoiding personal style inevitably formed one; that though so scrupulously undoctrinaire, he nevertheless managed to be remarkably instructive; that by isolating literary elements for examination, he reintegrated them into independent and authentic poems. Insofar as Marvell's disparate work can be characterized as a whole, it is intellectual and critical; his style is "philosophical" in that it is a style of thought—in his case, a skepticism always tempered by common sense and reasonableness. Marvell is critical, but rarely satirical, in the poems treated here: we sense his ridicule, but far more his protection, of the Nymph, of Damon, of the unfortunate Lover. This poet-without-persona, or this poet-with-too-many-personas, turns out in the end to be someone distinguished for his humane understanding of human situations, always aware of the lapse between all appropriate languages and the problems raised by human psychology—or by human beings.

Pushed a little, Marvell's criticism of literature can be seen to be made in terms of life: he was, in a muted way, a moral critic of literature, examining the areas of least fit, where traditional languages seem most to have parted from practical life. He studied literary stress-points and defined areas for repair and research, always in terms of human needs. The tantrums of the Mower-against-gardens are understood, if made fun of; the escapism of the Nymph is made to seem sympathetic if pitiful: underneath these pastoral questions, human problems are seen to lie.

Marvell left us a small body of poems in Latin, in a couple of cases very helpful to our study of his verse, since there are Latin versions to poems written (I think, obviously later) in English. This fact is interesting in itself, not just because it points to his skill in Latin but also because it suggests that he was accustomed to looking at a subject or topic in more than one way. To write "Hortus" simply was not the same thing as to write "The Garden," even if the subject-order of the two poems had been preserved in identical form. Obviously, he liked trying things now one way, now another; liked comparing this with that; liked contrasting one

5

solution with another. All this is typically "critical," indeed, almost scientific in its detachment.

One poem ("On Mr. Milton's Paradise Lost") in particular demonstrates Marvell's critical set. There, one can read his naturally critical bent: when he first looked into the poem—then "slender," in only ten books— he was afraid that so vast a design could not be fitted into the form the poet had chosen. Marvell's opening lines run through the chronological narrative of Milton's poem (itself a feat, since the poem is told out of chronological order), and pell-mell through the other stupendous events of the poem, as if he himself were the poet, judging how to organize these elements:

> *Messiah* Crown'd, *Gods* Reconcil'd Decree,
> Rebelling *Angels*, the Forbidden Tree,
> Heav'n, Hell, Earth, Chaos, All; . . .[2]

With the "All" before the sharp caesural pause, he and we realize what Milton has done—crammed all time and space into the confines of one poem. Marvell's fears are those of a professional, but he thinks of the professional poet also in moral terms: "sacred Truths" are difficult to render in "Fable and old Song," and perhaps ought not to be reduced to classical forms, whose traditional content can seem, for the Christian, so artificial. Furthermore, the poet's motives may not have been pure: he was "blind, yet bold," he may have wished, in his frustration, to pull down old values in revenge for his bitter blindness. But the comparison to Samson (itself perhaps a compliment to the poet's preoccupation with another sacred story of figural and personal significance) makes all well: "*Sampson* groap'd the Temple Posts in spight," but the "spight" was God-sent, and the destruction redounded to Israel's glory.

Marvell must have been a wonderful friend for a fellow-author, his professional awareness giving him immense sympathy with other people's literary problems. As he read on in *Paradise Lost*, he said, his partisanship for the material altered into partisanship for the poet courageously pitted against such an enterprise:

> Yet as I read, soon growing less severe,
> I lik'd his Project, the success did fear;

[2] All quotations from Marvell's poetry are from H. M. Margoliouth, ed., *The Poems and Letters of Andrew Marvell* (Oxford, 1927). Reprinted with permission.

Introduction

> Through that wide Field how he his way should find
> O're which lame Faith leads Understanding blind;
> Lest he perplext the things he would explain,
> And what was easie he should render vain.

Milton might have, like his fallen angels, further confused the mysteries of faith and the paradoxes of doctrine, might have trivialized the moving simplicities of Christian life, though, Marvell saw with relief, he did not. Identified with the poet and recognizing the pitfalls peculiar to the enterprise as defined by the problems of epic writing, Marvell showed his understanding of the moral implications of Milton's technical problems.

Other things about *Paradise Lost* bothered him slightly—the topical matter of "tagging lines," since rhyme was then dominant over blank verse, even so majestic a sample as Milton's; and the local dominance of stage-writing, which could (and did) cause *Paradise Lost* to be bungled into drama or masque. But a whole view of the poem can only indicate its completeness, its literal perfection:

> Thou hast not miss'd one thought that could be fit,
> And all that was improper dost omit:
> So that no room is here for Writers left,
> But to detect their Ignorance or Theft.

In the last line, the moment of wit occurs with the breach of parallelism, characteristic of Marvell's syntax, which here points to the triviality of those rival writers, so impoverished in imagination.

After a long comment about the moral nature of this verse and the particular talents of this prophetic author, whose blindness, like Tiresias', was compensated for by his power to invent "Words of such a compass" and his exercise of "such a vast expense of Minde," Marvell returns to a bantering critical tone which includes his own endeavors. The "tags" of rhyme, likened to the points or tags worn to decorate gentlemen's breeches, he deplores, although, to show definitively his own inferiority to Milton and his own limitation set by the fashion of his age, he himself can write his praise only in rhyme. The first passage of the poem, indeed, is written in a formal Miltonic syntax:

> When I beheld the Poet blind, yet bold,
> In slender Book his vast Design unfold,

7

Messiah Crown'd, *Gods* Reconcil'd Decree,
Rebelling *Angels*, the Forbidden Tree,
Heav'n, Hell, Earth, Chaos, All; the Argument
Held me a while misdoubting his Intent,
That he would ruine (for I saw him strong)
The sacred Truths to Fable and old Song,
(So *Sampson* groap'd the Temple Posts in spight)
The World o'rewhelming to revenge his Sight.

only the rhyme noticeably checks the complicated currents of the lines, flowing in and out in their Virgilian syntax. The sentence is periodic, grand, elevated; the prosodic variation, like Milton's own, is subtle and firm: in this passage Marvell pays Milton the tribute of approximating his "Number, Weight, and Measure," and in the poem as a whole the greater compliment of not daring to dispense with his own support, the rhyme. Only Milton is truly "free" in his verse.

In his identification with the writer's problems, as well as in his recoiling comment on his own place in relation to a greater master, one can read the paradigm of much of Marvell's verse, in which an underlying critical preoccupation deepens the handling of any given subject matter. His critical detachment contributes to what seems the remarkable balance of Marvell's poetry, as well as to the cool but limpid style which more than one reader has observed in his verse. Even in this poem, so conventionally ceremonial, Marvell tries to do two things at once, merely in his metrics—to rhyme according to the current fashion (which meant, to work in couplets), and to imitate the sinuous Miltonic diction and syntax. After the first sixteen lines, the "Miltonic" lines, the poem is designed in epigrammatic couplets, in crisp critical statements and analyses tonally quite different to the beginning. This poem is a remarkable *tour de force*, yet it manages also to be a poem, to say much about poetry, and to demonstrate its own poetic powers.

Marvell's insights into his own practice are even more remarkable than his insight into Milton's poetical problems. I want to look at problems in several ranges, as demonstrated in his verse, at first in terms of the assumptions, techniques, and even the mechanics of the craft, then at the bodies of whole poems. I hope not to reduce Marvell's accomplishment to the level of mechanics; after all, if such an achievement results merely from automatic control over craft, it is odd that no other seventeenth-century poet, similarly equipped, wrote poetry like his. Rather, I hope to move from fairly definable technical problems out into an area far less easily surveyed, that of problematics and the place of problematics in Marvell's verse-experiments. By these means, perhaps, some of the elusiveness of that verse may be understood in terms of Marvell's constant and almost tacit preoccupation, in his poetry, with poetry itself.

Part I
Studies in Theme and Genre

PROBLEMATICS OF THEME
AND FORM

ARVELL's lyric poems have tempted more than one critic to draw conclusions about Marvell the man: his psychology and philosophy have been sketched out from what have seemed to different students the commanding themes and preoccupations of his verse, his character deduced from his imagery and interests.[1] That there are major themes in his poetry is of course undeniable; that he was obsessed by them, or that they have much to do with his life as he lived it, is a more dubious proposition. One does not need to resort to psychiatric caveats that there are not enough data in the conscious and occasional verse of a long-dead man to provide evidence for the course of his inner life, to regard Marvell's poetry as something other than a set of cryptic directions to or from his psyche; one can conclude from the poetry itself that this is so, from the extraordinarily detached view he takes of his materials. Marvell used his poetic alternatives fully but freely, asserting his mastery of them, testing his skill in their development. From his flexible use of themes, his distribution of thematic elements, his combinations of rhetorical techniques, one can only conclude that Marvell's chief reason for writing lyric poetry was an overriding interest in the problems of lyric poetry.

He was certainly much interested in particular themes, but not, I think, committed to any particular theme or obsessed by it. Indeed, the variety of the uses to which he subjects his themes (as I hope to show in later parts of this section of this book) argues for his preoccupation rather with their problematics than with their conventional or single message.

For example, the garden-theme is obviously important in Marvell's work, running through many important poems and governing a principal one.

[1] Among others, Professors Empson, Wallerstein, and Hyman have something to say about Marvell's psyche as they deduce it from his poems; so have Muriel C. Bradbrook and M. G. Lloyd Thomas, *Andrew Marvell* (London, 1940); Denis Davison, *The Poetry of Andrew Marvell* (London, 1964).

13

The gardens, though, are very different in themselves: in "The Nymph complaining," the heroine creates her own garden, constructed for her private needs and covertly contrasted both with the habitat of the footloose Sylvio and with the wild, wanton world of the "Troopers." In "Little T. C." the young girl, still undeveloped, is seen against a background of both wild and cultivated flowers, budding and in full bloom. The disgruntled Mower, dispossessed of some of his domain, denounces the whole gardening-principle, although in Marvell's other poems in defense of gardens there is a magnificent array of arguments against the Mower. "Bermudas" presents an earthly paradise always at spring; "Upon Appleton House" deals with a specific, localized, but fantastic garden marshaled in virtue's defense, and further treats the whole estate, to say nothing of a pristine England, as a near-paradisal garden.[2] "The Garden" itself brings to its height the tradition of Renaissance garden poetry, at the same time refining and exploiting many other traditions not primarily associated with gardens,[3] so as to exhaust the subject, one feels, for other poets coming after.

His capers with the garden-theme were by no means unique in his practice, however; Marvell did the same thing, to a greater or lesser degree, in other ranges of subject and theme: in the musical notions, for example, so delicately handled by Professor Hollander.[4] The rich tradition of ideas associated with "harmony" is hinted at in "Upon Appleton House," and more fully developed in "The Fair Singer," and in "Musicks Empire"; but all these poems speak out in different contexts and tones, so that necessarily the cluster of harmony-ideas is differently exploited in each poem. Closely related to the idea of musical harmony is that of mathematical (especially geometrical) harmony, displayed to perfection in "The Definition of Love," and played on in both the poems on Fairfax's holdings. The theme of the competition between nature and art appears in many of Marvell's poems, sometimes moving forward into view from an originally concealed position.[5] The supposed "vegetable"

---

[2] For a great deal on gardens and garden background, see Marie Luise Gothein, *Geschichte der Gartenkunst* (Jena, 1926), 2 vols. A. Bartlett Giamatti's *The Earthly Paradise and the Renaissance Epic* (Princeton, 1966) is valuable both for its own formulations and for the references it cites. Terry Allen Comito's "Renaissance Gardens and Elizabethan Romance" (unpublished Harvard dissertation, 1968), gives very valuable material on this subject.

[3] See Part III, "The Garden," pp. 141-77.

[4] John Hollander, *The Untuning of the Sky* (Princeton, 1961), p. 303.

[5] See Part I, 2, "Problems of Pastoral."

preoccupation, for which Marvell's psychological structure has been considerably patronized, is in fact an outgrowth of his so deeply and so naturally thinking in terms of literary pastoral, his apparently bizarre images of plant life in fact following the implications of their place in the pastoral mode.

Marvell's pastoralism is, in the modern jargon, both "soft" and "hard," or hardish anyway, although he was careful to reject the extremes of either. Created Pleasure and the nun of Nunappleton are put in the wrong for breaking the rules of the pastoral code, and the granite facts of geographical Arcadia enter Marvell's poetry not at all. Since the pastoral setting, invented by a wish-fulfilling poetic imagination and canonized by literary conservatism, assumes without question a *pathétique* conjunction of mind with landscape, the mind inhabiting a pastoral landscape in fact designs the landscape. The poet chooses whether his pastoral shall be hard or soft, Spartan or paradisal; his thematic choices are assumed to govern whatever scene readers are allowed to see. In pastoral, readers must take what they are given, acknowledging the poet's title to his own projection; nonetheless, it is remarkable to see that projection so naïvely expressed—in "The Nymph complaining," for example, as the girl explains her design for her garden and for her life. For Marvell, the frame of pastoral convention serves as the excuse for a careful examination of many things, including poetry itself, both in very large terms—e.g., what are the public functions of poetry? of the poet?—and in small ones (if technical considerations can ever really be considered "small")—what are the poet's means for expressing this or that? to what extent does theme govern form, and *vice versa*? to what extent can traditional language be detached from particular themes and forms?[6]

Because of his own exploratory tendencies, Marvell's poetry is not so easy to study thematically as at first it seems. On first reading, certainly, the poems seem to cry out for thematic categorization. It is possible, of course, to arrange the poems in various relevant groups—I have tried to do so in this study—but the fact is, I think, that no one's grouping will satisfy another critical reader, and the poems continually and quite properly insist on being shifted from one category to another. Indeed, I hope to show briefly with some of the lyrics how many categories they may involve; the single poems, it is well to remember, are likely to be far richer than at any one time we can take them to be. As in many other

---

[6] See Part IV, 4, "Figures for Theme," and II, 1, "Style and Stylistics."

ranges of Marvell's practice, laid out at length variously in this study, there is a remarkable contradiction in the precision with which he uses thematic and generic designs, and the fluidity and ambiguousness with which he associates them; we can detect similar contradictions and counterpoised balances in his metrical, linguistic, and poetical practices, in his strategy and logic. Altogether, Marvell's poetry displays a consistent specialty in anomaly, indefinition, questioning, and even puzzles. The poems seem to dwell in several areas at once, and even to reach out into areas never clearly marked, but adumbrated or implied in the verse itself and dimly perceived by readers, more apt to know that they have lost their way than to recognize how or where the way was lost. From this, one might think that Marvell was, like Montaigne, say, or like Erasmus' Folly, interested in open-ended vistas; in fact, though, one cannot say of a poet so scrupulously observant of the limits imposed by his craft, that he was interested in amorphousness. On the contrary, his sense of form is so strong as to seem almost formalistic: one of my problems has been to say something about Marvell's peculiar formalism, which constantly challenges formalistic limitation. In the mysteriousness of Marvell's verse, one recognizes a profound intellectual challenge to form and to formalist doctrines, but even that challenge is set in terms of the forms so challenged.

After prolonged exposure to Marvell's poetry, one feels in it more than meets eye or ear; and even after one has worked hard to define this "more," it remains nonetheless elusive, indefinite, recessive. In "The Garden," it seems to me, this device is most successfully exploited. For the reader, the practice makes for uneasiness and even discomfort, but Marvell seems a thoroughly self-confident poet, quite at home with this kind of elusiveness. Some men not only feel comfortable without stating a final position, but choose indeed not to state their ultimate option. Montaigne, for instance, was by no count but his own a cowardly man; he lived quite comfortably with the unsolved and insoluble. Neither was Marvell a cowardly poet, listless or effete. He was no time-server of the Muses, as some people thought he was of the magistrate; but all the same, there is manifest in his poetry an exceptional detachment of the poet from his matter. About poetry, however, he was never detached: he returned again and again, from many different angles of approach, to the technical and moral problems poetry raised for the self-conscious practitioner of the craft.

Problematics of Theme and Form

At first one thinks Marvell's themes displayed at the surface of his utterance, until one begins to deal with them in different poems. Marvell in fact fools us again and again—he leads us into interpretative traps, even about so obvious a topic as "theme." In reading a given poem, one often realizes that although it is ostensibly written in terms of one dominant theme, it conceals another within the first, as "The Coronet" conceals the problem of spiritual regulation beneath the theme of poetical choice; or, in "The Nymph complaining," the theme of art, so fundamental to the poem once it is perceived, hides behind the surface theme of participation and retirement. Sometimes a literary device is offered *both* in its conventional figural function *and* as a metaphor for another literary device; "The Coronet" and "The Garden" eminently illustrate this trick.

Marvell's elusiveness does not characteristically lie in figures of speech and syntax—though I shall have something to say about his idiosyncratic ways with both[7]—nor even in wit's *panache*. Compared with conventionally "witty" poetry, Marvell's verse does not demonstrate Donne's rich, confusing, sometimes bedraggled poetical syntax; though, like Herbert, Marvell is precise in utterance, he does not share Herbert's consistent translucency of sense. Marvell's imagery is sometimes strained, but his conceits are neither so arbitrary as Cleveland's nor so luxuriant as Crashaw's. What is "metaphysical" about Marvell's verse is just its metaphysics, not of expression only, but of subject-matter: his attitude, for instance, to the relation of words to things[8] is in fact philosophical, his experiments with those relations genuinely exploratory. Further, his poetry hints at "more" behind and beyond itself; it seems to front upon an area demanding from readers an enlarged perception and greater intellectual energy than lyric poetry customarily demands. Marvell's philosophical attitude is not really a matter of his mentioning different philosophical positions, nor of his moral assumption that the life of mind and spirit was nobler than the life of body and world (a view which very few contemporary poets, whether or not officially "metaphysical," could be expected to deny); rather, his particular claim upon philosophy is in his experimental attitude toward the fundamental problems of life conceived as a mixed condition of mind and matter, of spirit and substance, of words and things. That the relation between this last pair constitutes the basic problem of his craft is fortunate for us, as mere readers coming

[7] See Part II, 2, "Figures of Speech," and II, 1, "Style and Stylistics."
[8] See Part II, 1; and Part III, "The Garden," pp. 151-52.

so long after, for his odd investigations into the relation of words to things illuminate much about poetry, in very modern terms. Marvell accepted, or assumed, the views of such matters conventional in his time and place, but by the elegant manipulation of the elements of his art, he also managed to offer a critique of the very views to which he himself—probably willingly enough, but also for want of alternatives—subscribed. Marvell does not offer us a philosophical system—as, say, Bruno does, or Henry More—nor even a poetical one; he offers instead something rarer, in poetry at least: a philosophical attitude to poetry scrupulously maintained in poetry.[9]

One result is, as Mr. Toliver particularly has stressed, an extraordinary dose of irony in Marvell's poetry. Irony is not the same as philosophical questioning (though often its by-product), especially when the questioner is less intent upon answers to philosophical questions than upon the processes by which questioning is carried on. Certainly Marvell's verse does not offer us the comfortable fantasies of solution; in this, his attitude to problems of thought and of poetry is, in seventeenth-century terms, "modern": he was interested in method and process, interested in examination and experimentation. His attitude to the finding of solutions is, though, by Royal Society standards, frivolous and uncommitted. Where a Boyle, a Locke, or a Newton, all committed to their descriptive empiricism, all concerned with the open ends of thought, trusted their exiguous data and were willing to risk further experiment on the basis of that data, Andrew Marvell seems remarkably conservative, retreating (as he seems to do) from established certainties, tending not even to close his poems as a proper experiment ought to be closed.[10] In his verse-essays, Marvell leaves uncontrolled variables and inconstants to plague us; he neglects, one feels, more than any sane man would dare. And he intends, I think, just that. The readers seem to happen in on "Bermudas," are tripped into the conclusion of "Mourning," are left to their own conclusions, though by no means to their own devices, in "A Dialogue between the Soul and Body." By the poet's use of professional devices, themes are deprived of conventional definiteness, and are made to open

[9] See Part III, "The Garden," for some discussion of this problem, and "Afterword."

[10] For a discussion of poems' endings, see Barbara Herrnstein Smith, *Poetic Closure* (Chicago, 1968); and below, "Persona," pp. 125-26.

out on vistas of epistemological uncertainty which all before us lie, if we care to look at them.

Committed to the modern attitude but not to the responsibilities of its method, committed as well to the traditions of his craft but not to its absolutism, Marvell managed to balance one against the other, to add to the readers' sense of indefiniteness in both content and theme. "Themes" are difficult to discuss, since they exist on several levels, in verse at least. They can be signaled by *topoi*, the commonplaces of a conventional language; these range from phrases like "rosy-fingered Dawn" through large representational schemes like that of the ideal day, and can be expressed in the formal devices of syntax, vocabulary, and genre. In Marvell's literary vocabulary, there is a great overlap between the language of theme and the language of genre; according to Renaissance poetics, genre was conceived to have been developed for certain thematic purposes and thus to imply theme, just as a given theme often implied certain generic conventions.

"Genre" itself is a tricky term, even in Renaissance usage without the convenience of sharp definition. A genre-critic like Julius Caesar Scaliger offers a superior manual of Renaissance formalism, but even he could not offer genres delimited once and for all. Formal genres are not difficult to identify and to imitate, provided they do not overlap much with a genre bearing another name. An ode, especially if by Pindar, was much like other odes, especially those of Pindar; a tragedy had one kind of shape, an epic another. An epigram was one thing, a sonnet usually something else. At the other end of the scale, there are genres which are more modal than formal. The pastoral is the major example, with its lyrics, its dramas, and its narrative forms, even its dances and masques. The paradoxical mode, another, has a strict physical form only in the discipline of logical argument, but all the same, it managed to invade most of the fixed forms of Renaissance literature, to become an anarchic principle within the *genera*, mixing them in many curious combinations. To subject samples of Renaissance literature to generic study, one has to be fully aware of the theoretical limitations of generic category, to become accustomed to the mixture not of forms only, but also of linguistic devices characteristically associated with any given genre. Genre may afford a system of reference, even of categorization, but it cannot provide a system of interpretation for Renaissance literature, where all

19

kinds of shadings and modulations between genres occur. Some of the richness of major works of art in this period is a result in part of a mixture of thematic genres in substitution for formal genres; "The Garden" is, as I try to show, a classic case of this sort. In Marvell's verse in general, there is a great deal of mixture, the elements large and small, concrete and abstract, rhetorical and thematic, disposed and redisposed into alluring and often baffling combinations. As in his stock of images, Marvell's generic range is not wide; he does not try everything, by any means, but works within strict limits, so that across his work one can read, for all the tantalizing problems of variation it presents, a homogeneity almost as difficult to define. He worked from a palette with a fixed range of rhetorical and poetic colors; what he did with that range is what concerns me here.

Though there are, clearly, impositions and obligations laid upon expression by genre, it is idle to think that the identification of a literary work within a given genre solves many of its puzzles. *Rasselas* and *Candide* belong to the same genre, but they are very different works, and one is manifestly better than the other. The same is true of *Paradise Lost* and *Davideis*; of *Hudibras* and *The Rape of the Lock*. Furthermore, any genre given a name has already had a history before it got its name, and offers a paradigm of alternatives within limitations. Usually, within those limitations, an author tries his skill at imitation and his powers of invention. As a writer in genre, Marvell has been much admired; Joseph Summers has pointed to Marvell's extraordinary achievement in terms of lyric school-genres:

> Sometimes it seems as if Marvell deliberately tried to write a single poem which could summarize and surpass all that had gone before. "To his Coy Mistress" seems to us the culmination of the long tradition of classical and Renaissance persuasions to love in which the lover urged his mistress to "seize the day" before the night of age and death. "The Definition of Love" is one of the best of the "definition" poems. "The Garden" is surely the richest of the "poems of rural solitude." "On a Drop of Dew" follows the practice in which an entire meditative poem proceeds from the meticulous examination of a physical—and symbolic—object. "An Horatian Ode" is the best English heroic ode. The Mower poems summarize and change significantly the large traditions of pastoral love poetry. "The Nymph Complaining for the

Death of her Fawn" draws upon traditions from Catullus, classical elegy, the pastoral, and religious allegory to create a poem so suggestive, so redolent with overtones, that one good reader after another has tried to squeeze it into the form of a strict allegory. "Eyes and Tears" and "Mourning" explore the possibilities of the "lachrymose" poems so definitively that it is hard to imagine the subject's ever being tried again in anything like the same fashion. The "dialogues" "Between the Resolved Soul and Created Pleasure" and "Between the Soul and Body" use the "debate" in differing fashions and with original results. "The Coronet," which owes a good deal to "The Wreath" of George Herbert, is one of the finest "personal" religious lyrics of the century. "On Mr. Milton's *Paradise Lost*" is the finest of the prefatory complimentary-critical poems. . . .[11]

One could extend the list: "The Last Instructions" has had its due praise in comparison with its fellows;[12] "The First Anniversary" is a distinguished political poem, as is the poem on Cromwell's death.

From all this, it is clear that in writing his verse, Marvell was putting himself through his professional paces, exercising himself within the formulaic school-figures of the lyric poet, deliberately testing his capacity, range, and skill. That he repeated so few forms and varied his schemes so radically—two pastoral-lover dialogues, two psychomachic dialogues, two epithalamia, each very different from its mate—suggests the care with which he conducted himself in his discipline, winnowed his work to leave such a professionally dazzling selection of poems for his greedy housekeeper to publish after his death. His small collection of verse is an anthology of lyric form and theme, enriched with heroic poems and satires as well.

Marvell handled generic problems in different ways. Sometimes he works so brilliantly in his expansions that he appears to exhaust a genre: "The Mower against Gardens," "The Definition of Love," "To his Coy Mistress" all seem to me examples of such achievement, in which the limits of genre have been so expanded that once the poem is written, the resources of the whole type seemed to have been used up. Sometimes he

[11] Joseph H. Summers, Introduction to *Andrew Marvell* ("Laurel Poetry Series," New York, 1961), pp. 13-14.

[12] Earl Miner, "The 'Poetic Picture, Painted Poetry' of *The Last Instructions to a Painter*," MP, LXIII (1966), 288-94; and Mary Tom Osborne, *Advice-to-a-Painter Poems* (Austin, 1949).

ridicules generic convention: "The Fair Singer," with its gentle criticism of the artificiality of the "petrarchan" rhetoric, is a case in point; sometimes he compresses a larger genre into a very small compass, as for instance in "The Gallery," where Marino's expansions have been compressed into four pictures and only seven stanzas which manage at once to illustrate and to criticize the *ut pictura poesis* doctrine. "Bermudas" entwines the Exodus theme with the language of earthly paradise and of the psalms of praise, enclosing its ecphrastic vignettes in a frame intelligible to contemporaries, who knew about the pieties expressed by the Virginia Company in offering a haven to exiles "Safe from the Storms, and Prelat's Rage" and were aware of the challenge from idolators "beyond the *Mexique Bay*." An exemplum-poem, its message clear in spite of its spotty explication and indefinite application, "Bermudas" compresses many traditions into small space, and enlarges the spectacle of earthly paradise to include thematic considerations generally foreign to that ideal, encapsulated space. Mixing genres, either *en large*, as in "Upon Appleton House," or *en petit*, as in "Bermudas," "The Garden," "A Dialogue Between The Resolved Soul, and Created Pleasure," to name only a few, was Marvell's *forte*, with the genres handled as a manipulable language, made pliable and portable in the diminished figures appropriate to generic decorum.[18]

At this point I would like to look, not exhaustively but with some care, at two very different poems, to suggest something of Marvell's way with conventions drawn from different literary categories. Since a great part of this book is devoted to long analyses of two poems, I want here only to sketch various possibilities available for reading certain poems, and to suggest a way of reading any of them. Further, I want to consider these poems in different thematic connections within the limits of Marvell's work, to see how variously poems from the canon may be grouped together.

The first is "Upon the Hill and Grove at Bill-borow," a topographical poem about a specific locality belonging to the Fairfax family. As such poems often are, this one is a compliment to a patron, whose virtues are deduced from the morality attributed to the landscape under discussion. The particularities of this hill and this grove are to be read as emblems for Fairfax's character. Thematically similar to "Upon Appleton House," another compliment to Fairfax based on a very different landscape, this

---

[18] See below, Part II, 1 and 2, for further argument and illustration.

poem contrasts the active to the retired life, making plain that the place of retirement can very well be both exemplary and creative. The geometrical imagery of the first stanza

> See how the arched Earth does here
> Rise in a perfect Hemisphere!
> The stiffest Compass could not strike
> A Line more circular and like;
> Nor softest Pensel draw a Brow
> So equal as this Hill does bow.
> It seems as for a Model laid,
> And that the World by it was made

suggests that the Creator is a better geometer than the most skilled human practitioner, and that Bilbrough therefore is properly the model of the larger, less perfect world, as in other terms Nunappleton was the model from which England ought to be reconstituted. One result of created perfection is its social benevolence: the hill acts as seamark to coasting ships, and as a gentle, courteous, inviting, rising slope to landsmen seeking moral elevation (Fig. 1).[14]

Ultimately this hill is awarded the highest spiritual function an earthly thing can hope to perform, namely the exaltation of those lower than itself:

> Nor for it self the height does gain,
> But only strives to raise the Plain.

The hill as a whole celebrated, its crown—those oaks that form its numinous grove—comes to attention. The deforestation of England was a matter of real concern to commonwealth-minded men,[15] so that a stand of trees, for practical as for aesthetic reasons, was highly valued.[16] This grove is "sacred," defended by Fairfax's unseen as well as his visible presence;

---

[14] From Joachim Camerarius, *Symbolorum et Emblematum ex re Herbaria . . . Centuria* (Frankfurt, 1654). On "crowning" a hill with a grove, see Thomas Fuller, *The Holy State* (Cambridge, 1648), p. 155: "But 'tis as well pleasant as profitable to see a house cased with trees, like that of Anchises in Troy. . . . The worst is, where a place is bald of woods, no art can make it a periwig."

[15] John Evelyn's *Sylva* (many editions) is the chief document arguing for the reforestation of England. See also Ralph Austen, *A Discourse of Fruit-Trees* (Oxford, 1643), Epistle Dedicatory.

[16] Cf. Brian Fairfax's poem on his kinsman Thomas Fairfax's groves, "The Vocall Oak," in *Fairfax Correspondence* (ed. George W. Johnson, London, 1848), I, cxxi-cxxv.

visitors to the grove feel the Lord General's greatness in the holy dread proper to sacred groves. The grove symbolizes both the General's success in war (stanza 9) and his domestic happiness; his devotion to his "great *Nymph*," "*Vera*," as Lady Fairfax's name is so happily latinized, is manifest in the grove as well. The trees in this grove are at once heroic and pastoral, inviting comparison to the trees and plants in "The Garden" and "Upon Appleton House." Here, the wounds on the bark are the result of Fairfax's writing on the trees his wife's name, and the trees rejoice in such naming, since they bear her name already written, by their own efforts, upon their hearts:

> But ere he well the Barks could part
> 'Twas writ already in their Heart.
>
> For they ('tis credible) have sense,
> As We, of Love and Reverence, . . .

This use of pastoral name-carving[17] is noticeably different from that in "The Garden," for here Vera's "name" becomes—turns into and adorns—the trees, which the nymphs' names in "The Garden" did not.

These trees grow "streight and green" with the military precision of Fairfax's army, or of the military flower-garden planted at Appleton, or with the military aspiration of the pedigree oaks in the wood at Nunappleton. They are "contented" to grow "fixed," they are "prudent" in withdrawing from "the winds uncertain gust"—from all of which we are to read approbation of Fairfax's withdrawal from the gusts of fortune blowing so wildly to the south. Here, approbation is unqualified; in contrast, the poet's praise of his patron's retirement in "Upon Appleton House" is less than total. At Bilbrough Hill, the winds themselves are transformed from "gusts" to "flutt'ring Breez"; in a wonderfully visualized image, familiar in the iconography of Fame, these breezes swell "the Cheek of Fame" to report Fairfax's exploits in "Much other Groves . . . And other Hills." In the metaphorical militarization of the grove, echoing Fairfax's real military history,

> Through Groves of Pikes he thunder'd then,
> And Mountains rais'd of dying Men

---

[17] On pastoral name-carving, see below, Part III, "The Garden"; Abraham Cowley, "The Tree," *The Mistress* (London, 1647), p. 108; for a short list of classical name-carving, see Evelyn, *Sylva* (London, 1664), p. 341.

the incongruities of Dunsinane are reversed, natural objects presented in military guise, instead of armed men passed off as natural elements. There, men were seen as trees; here, trees are for a moment seen as men. There are topiary parallels to this trick, although not, for once, in Marvell's stiff and formal gardens—trees were cut as bowmen, as cavalrymen, even "Yew-men of the Guard," all in green.[18]

The renunciation of the last stanza, in which Fairfax retires from the battle, bears some relation to Marvell's presentation of Cromwell in "An Horatian Ode" and "The First Anniversary,"[19] in which the victor puts by, out of his natural modesty, the vulgar rewards of fame; obviously, the first stanza of "The Garden" is relevant as well. Fairfax's solution to his problem, both in the record of history and in the assessment of his poet, was very different, of course, from Cromwell's solution to his: Fairfax retired; Cromwell chose to "march indefatigably on." Fairfax's retirement must be balanced, in this poem, against his former active greatness; his fame is properly shaded by trees, as he takes up his civic crown on a country estate. Thomas Fairfax solved his problem of greatness in private, Oliver Cromwell in public.

Like "An Horatian Ode," this poem is written in highly classical terms, the grove and its oaks both elements of the dignified supernatural world of classical myth and sacred story. As in other cases in Marvell's verse, the Latin poem related to this English one is even richer in classical reference: Hercules, Pelion, Ossa, a chorus of nymphs, and Parnassus are all somehow present in "Epigramma in Duos montes Amosclivum et Bilboreum." These are considerably cut back in the English poem: a nymph, "*Civick Garlands*," "*Trophees*," and "*Oracles in Oak*" carry the classical theme of active statecraft, beneath which sounds the merest hint

[18] Henry Hawkins, *Partheneia Sacra* (Rouen, 1633), p. 8, has a fine description of topiary achievement: "I wil not take upon me to tel al; for so of a Garden of flowers, should I make a Labyrinth of discourse, and should never be able to get forth. Cast but your eyes a little on those goodlie Allies, as sowed all over with sands of gold, drawne-forth so streight by a line. Those Crosbowes there (be not affrayed of them) they are but Crosbowes made out of Bayes; and the Harquebusiers, wrought in Rosmarie, shoot but flowers, and dart forth musk. Those beasts likewise, horrible there and dreadful to see to, are but in ieast; as the menace they make, is but a shew only. Al those armed Men with greenish Weapons, and those Beasts al clad in skins of green, are but of Prim, Isop, and Tyme, al hearbs very apt to historify withal."

[19] For discussion of connections of this sort, see Dr. Holahan's dissertation, and Wallace, *Destiny his Choice*, Chapters 2 and 3.

of Christian morality, implied in the charity and humility stressed in the first two stanzas. The same scheme of sentiments is worked out very differently in "Upon Appleton House," and "An Horatian Ode" addresses the same problem, seen the other way on. One would naturally read "Upon the Hill and Grove" with "Upon Appleton House," of course; but it is possible to read it in other connections as well, to see how the poet tackled his problems of theme and diction.

Quite a different sort of poem, "A Dialogue Between The Resolved Soul, and Created Pleasure," artfully intertwines several traditions into its argument; some are discussed in other parts of this essay at greater length.[20] Here, I want to set this poem in different juxtapositions, using it as an example of the ways in which Marvell's poems can be grouped and regrouped for different purposes. First of all, this dialogue offers an entirely different view of the body-soul problem from that of the "Dialogue between the Soul and Body." Now, conventionally, Pleasure is the challenger, tempting the soul with both sense-satisfactions and fulfilled ambitions—almost the same arguments, and in almost the same order, as those offered Christ by Satan in *Paradise Regained*.

In Marvell's poem, two other "temptation" passages seem immediately relevant, one the appeal of Clorinda to Damon, in which the unimaginative "temptress" soon loses her initiative to the proselyte shepherd, who when he takes the lead then dominates the poem's direction heavenward; the other, the nun's appeal to Isabella, rendered in remarkably uncloistral terms of sense-satisfaction. Mr. Berger has noted another progression of this dialogue with "On a Drop of Dew," and "The Nymph complaining," in which the central problem is the maintenance of private integrity against pressures from the world.[21] The dew-poem deals with the dew-drop-soul's hydroptic desire for "the Sphear," as intense as the soul's desire, in this dialogue, to "sup above." The assault of sense-pleasure in the dialogue is expressed in terms of great beauty, of softness and warmth designed to dissolve the soul's resolution. In other poems, though, the poet does not represent himself as so firmly set against sense-pleasures and beauties, although his greatest approval of sense-recreation is reserved for contexts of moral recreation as well: the garden in "Upon Appleton

[20] See Frank Kermode, "The Banquet of Sense," *Bulletin of the John Rylands Library*, XLIV (1961), 68-69, and below, Part I, 5, pp. 57-58, as well as Kitty Scoular Datta, "New Light on Marvell's 'Dialogue between the Soul and Body'," *Ren. Q.*, XXII (1969), 242-55.

[21] Berger, "The Green World as Poem."

House" legitimately assaults the senses because it strengthens and protects them too. Though its recreative powers are less than those of purer ecstasies of soul, the sense-ecstasy in "The Garden" is harmless and light-hearted, a proper preparative for the more crucial ecstasies to follow. From Ralph Austen, a seventeenth-century gardener in prose, we know how seriously the sense-experiences were regarded as recreative;[22] most of Marvell's garden poems take the view that gardens are good. In "A Dialogue Between The Resolved Soul," though, quite another psycho-philosophical schema is invoked, in which the senses are regarded as dangerous precisely because of their attractiveness and beauty; they are seducers. Against even the garden's temptation, where the loveliness of sense-satisfaction is acknowledged in full, the soul remains resolved, does not melt into an epicurean landscape.

In the other psychomachic dialogue, "Between the Soul and Body," the arguments seem to have been selected because they were so different from those between the Resolved Soul and Created Pleasure.[23] In the Body-Soul dialogue, the senses, exacerbated by the strenuous psychological demands of the aspiring soul, are presented entirely in terms of pain or discomfort: no lush ecstatic satisfactions are offered for this body's delight. Indeed, instead of regarding the body with suspicion, we are brought toward pity for it. As for the soul, it is made to sound petulant in its reiterated death-wish, simplistic as Dorinda, wishing for death in another poem. This soul has quite a different psychology from that of its Resolved cousin, or of the drop of dew; the joint-tenancy of body and soul is made to seem thoroughly disagreeable, neither tenant luckier than the other, the conditions and natures of both equally unpleasant. As far as can be determined from these thematically similar debates between soul and sense, Marvell was trying out entirely different conceptual contexts, not just to demonstrate his poetical invention, but to explore the internal problematics of the theme itself, the Pauline imprisonment of the Soul in "the body of this death" (Figs. 2 and 3).

In the first dialogue the soul is and remains "resolved"; in "On a Drop of Dew," the dewdrop-soul is equally firm, self-enclosed, self-defending. Like the Resolved Soul, the drop of dew is impatient with its material

---

[22] Ralph Austen, *The Spiritual Uses of an Orchard* (Oxford, 1653), pp. 35-39, gives an excellent description of the recreations afforded by a garden.

[23] Leishman, p. 212, cites parallels from Francis Davison's *Poetical Rhapsody* (1602) and from Francis Quarles' *Emblems* (1635), as well as from certain continental books in the emblematic tradition.

environment, shunning even "sweat leaves and blossoms green," until it can finally

> . . . dissolving, run
> Into the Glories of th' Almightie Sun.

Resolved or dissolved, the soul is set on paradise, easily rejecting all worldly signatures, even the perfection offered by "roses." In the case of the drop of dew, the speaker's slight disappointment at such rejection shows through his language, since in this poem the world is in no sense rendered as unattractive, corrupting, or harmful; merely, the drop of dew considers it to be so. From its rejection of such loveliness, the perfections of heaven may be read. The confrontation, in the Resolved Soul dialogue so charged with moral meaning, is left curiously neutral in "On a Drop of Dew."

Because of its specific application to poetic problems of principles more generally debated in the Resolved Soul dialogue, "The Coronet" is certainly related to that poem; but it presents the opposing principles, soul and world, not in dialectical agon but in inevitable embrace. The poet's position here resembles that taken in "A Dialogue between the Soul and Body," since both poems record the recognition that on earth the soul can be experienced only through the senses. A pure choice between body and soul is always an illusion, qualified by the context of the human world which imposes such choices. The "flowers" in "The Coronet," worthy of "My Saviours head," are appropriate gifts for Him, it seems, although they turn out to be dangerous to the poet, because of the Edenic (or the Virgilian) snake lurking in their grass.[24] Flowers may be had, perhaps, without snakes, but snakes, the implication runs, must have flowers (Fig. 4).

In argumentative structure, "A Dialogue Between The Resolved Soul" is formally parallel to "Clorinda and Damon," in which the debate is closed by a choral song celebrating the correct moral decision. In the pastoral dialogue, though, the two lovers evidently sing Pan's praise, whereas in the Resolved Soul dialogue, the chorus is assumed to be "heavenly," quite outside the debate itself, something like the great choruses after the agons in heaven and hell in *Paradise Lost*, in which the chorus is uninvolved in the moral competitions but marks its approval of their outcome. Pleasure fades away after her ritual suggestions and does not, as Clorinda does, join in the ultimate decision: Pleasure is an

[24] Virgil, *Ecl.* III, 93.

advocatus diaboli who, having gone through the motions of objection and temptation, is excused further performance.

This coolness stands in contrast to the personal quality of "The Coronet," where for all his technical virtuosity, the poet seems himself deeply involved in working out, as he actually writes, the spiritual problem raised for him by writing a religious lyric. Here, the contrast brings out something about the distance between the speaker and his apparent subject-matter, so schematically presented in both poems, in "A Dialogue" impersonally, in "The Coronet" personally. The formal, epigrammatic language of "A Dialogue" helps to distance speaker and reader from what is going on, and lays stress on the abstract character of the conventional set-problem; the involved syntax of "The Coronet" entwines the reader with the poet's involvement, with himself and with his own problem, the whole expressed, literally, in terms of "involvement" and involution, as the poet winds and twists his flowers into a votive wreath.[25] It takes an apocalypse to solve the problems of "The Coronet," as Christ at last tramples on the serpent's head; "A Dialogue" is solved in the rational conventions of its own debate-form.

The debate itself, set as it is in a curious context of nature and art, is also connected to many other poems on that theme, discussed below under the heading of "pastoral." Stretching a little, one might say that the Resolved Soul dialogue relates to Marvell's other muted debates about the retired and active life, for the Resolved Soul intends to evade and avoid the dissolution, the dissoluteness, of the world. Like the retired and contemplative man, like the pastoral shepherd, the soul keeps away from the hazards of material enjoyment. But for all this bracketing of the poem with others, or with groups of other poems, "A Dialogue Between The Resolved Soul" maintains its particularity, a particularity the more remarkable because we *do* see its theme reiterated in so many of Marvell's lyrics. The poet's experimentalism honors not only its own exploration but the uniqueness of the poem as well: the poem demonstrates the problematics it displays. From how it is made we learn what it says—and because it is so delicately made, it is not always easy to express its formulation of particular insight.

[25] See below, pp. 80-82, for a discussion of this poem's syntax.

❧ 2 ❧

PROBLEMS OF PASTORAL

S o many of Marvell's poems have strong pastoral elements that
it would be idle to try to discuss them all: the four Mower poems,
conveniently enough, provide us with ample material to examine
his ways within a single mode. In the four poems, four different
perspectives upon pastoral are given.

In "The Mower against Gardens," the speaker inveighs against artifice
and artificiality, in terms relevant to both "The Garden" and "Upon
Appleton House." In the longer poems, the poet, though by no means
opposed to meadows, significantly praises the aesthetics of gardening; in
this one, he sets out the traditional arguments against gardening, em-
bellished with some whimsical arguments apparently of the Mower's
own devising. In "Damon the Mower," the innocence of the pastoral
mentality is exposed in the person of the hero, who so openly expresses
his inmost feelings. In "The Mower to the Glo-worms," after some splen-
did conceits on that insect (apparently a set topic for Cavalier poets[1]), a
brief comment on a lady's supernatural beauty is set out. "The Mower's
Song," the lament of a lover spurned and ignored, has an heroic apocalyptic
ring, as in his despair the Mower brings about the ruin of his whole
world, himself included. Linked by the person of the "Mower," these four
poems are nonetheless tonally and thematically inconsistent with one an-
other; indeed, the person of the Mower, I think, cannot be identical in
the four poems.[2] The connective between them is the curious fact that in
each of the four, a different question is raised in terms of and about the
pastoral convention. Making the poet's pastoral figure into a mower per-
mits a deepening of theme by means of the well known comparison
of death to a mower; the theme can then exploit the axiom from
Ecclesiastes that all flesh is grass. The death-theme is kept in constant

[1] For poems on glowworms, see Kitty Scoular, *Natural Magic* (Oxford, 1965);
this book is very valuable for several things—for the relation of emblems to poetry,
for its study of the poetry of minutiae, and for its collection of poems dealing with
the chain of being in the animal kingdom.

[2] One acute reader, Joan Webber, entirely disagrees; she sees all four Mowers as
the same personality.

counterpoint to the simple happiness normally attributed to dwelling in a pastoral environment.

In "The Mower to the Glo-worms," slightest of the set, the four stanzas, in quatrains, pass from the praise of "the living Lamps" and the "Country Comets," tiny insects extravagantly sung for their innocence, beauty, and usefulness, to the Mower's hopeless situation as a lover.[3] The glowworms' light is extinguished by the greater brilliance of Juliana's face, which has so "benighted" the Mower that, as he says, "I shall never find my home," even with the glowworms' helpful guidance. The pastoral hyperbole, first applied to the insects then to the lady's beauty, is simplified somehow to the plainness of the Mower's simple logic:

> Your courteous Lights in vain you wast,
> Since *Juliana* here is come,
> For She my Mind hath so displac'd
> That I shall never find my home.

We have no more data on this Mower than what he gives us, in his innocent confusion: he is left alienated by the power of his love from his otherwise cherishing environment, driven out of his natural context by the violence of love's force.[4]

For love is an emotion often too intense to be permitted entry into a pastoral region of the mind. Some *forms* of love are acceptable there—dalliance is all very well, as Thestylis and Ametas recognize; a Darby and Joan life, with passion past, is also properly pastoral—but passion in its gripping reality tends to rob the pastoralist of "himself," to distract him from going through the rites required in his free but carefully programmed landscape and society. The overriding domination of love destroys the delicacy and detachment of the pastoral artifice; it destroys as well the fundamental, though tolerant, self-centeredness required of a shepherd, who has by the convention agreed to pool his own resonant imagination and fantasy with those of his companions, all sharing in a neutral and pleasant dream-landscape designed to meet all their modest, self-indulgent psychological needs.[5] Pastoral equalizes and generalizes,

---

[3] Pliny, *The Historie of the World*, tr. Philemon Holland (London, 1601), Book X, Chapter xxix, gives a relevant account of glowworms' activity.

[4] For some comment on this, see Renato Poggioli, "The Pastoral of the Self," *Daedalus* (1959), 686-99; and Harry Berger, Jr., "The Renaissance Imagination. Second World and Green World," *Centennial Review*, IX (1965), 36-72.

[5] For the classic statement of this view, see Bruno Snell, *The Discovery of Mind*

whereas love specifies, distinguishes, and dramatizes. Love can destroy shepherds: only by a momentary acquiescence in a love without consequences can a nymph hope to keep her shepherd happy, as Thestylis, for instance, accedes Ametas' desire. The Mower is alienated from his world by his love for the harsh Juliana, as he tells us at length in his beautiful "Song," the refrain of which seems to echo a mower's steady swing. Sadly but gravely, the poem's five stanzas analyze the Mower's state of mind; the pastoral *pathétique* is laid out from beginning to end. Before he had been struck by Juliana's presence, the Mower had experienced the landscape as both reflection and projection of his own emotions, both landscape and his emotions confident, as it were, of their mutual matching:

> My Mind was once the true survey
> Of all these Medows fresh and gay;
> And in the greenness of the Grass
> Did see its Hopes as in a Glass;

"within" and "without" are entirely at one, until

> . . . *Juliana* came, and She
> What I do to the Grass, does to my Thoughts and Me.

The Mower finds himself unable to understand his alienation precisely because his measuring-rods for himself have vanished. His environment fails the pastoral contract, betrays him by growing more beautiful as his grief increases:

> But these, while I with Sorrow pine,
> Grew more luxuriant still and fine;
> That not one Blade of Grass you spy'd,
> But had a Flower on either side;

He has been abandoned by his meadows, who go on with their life without regard to his unhappiness:

> Unthankful Medows, could you so
> A fellowship so true forego,

(New York, 1960); and also, Edward William Tayler, *Nature and Art in Renaissance Literature* (New York, 1964), the last chapter of which is devoted to Marvell's pastoral. Frank Kermode's introduction to *English Pastoral Poetry* (London, 1952), is valuable.

And in your gawdy May-games meet,
While I lay trodden under feet?

He can, however, make them sorry for their ingratitude; he can take revenge on his meadows so that, according to the pastoral bargain, they must once more reflect his feelings, now so unpastoral:

But what you in Compassion ought,
Shall now by my Revenge be wrought:
And Flow'rs, and Grass, and I and all,
Will in one common Ruine fall.

At the expense of the pastoral setting, then, in this poem the pastoral correspondence between mind and landscape is maintained; that is, the perfect peace of pastoral is wilfully destroyed, so that outer can reflect inner world, as the Mower insists on prolonging the beautiful, nonsensical, wish-fulfilling image of a man "at one" with nature by destroying the perfection natural to the pastoral assumption.

Natural man has his moments of violence, forbidden by the civilized pastoral code; caught in such a moment of passionate anger inadequately understood, the Mower forces his localized apocalypse upon the dream-ecology of which he is a part. Insisting upon his rights as a pastoralist, the Mower ruins his environment, destroys the dream, to keep intact the hyperbole to which he is accustomed. The pastoral contract is thus made to recoil upon itself, the tradition's self-destruction made to seem a natural implication of its own convention.

"Damon the Mower" also sings of rejection by Juliana, though in this poem Damon sees his landscape as withered, like himself. His meadows do not reproach him by greenness hardheartedly maintained, nor does he reproach them for faithlessness. Where the Mower in his "Song" had mown the grass because it was green, Damon mows it because, like his hopes, it withers and calls for the scythe. The harmless creatures in his fields have vanished before the crippling July heats, and "Only the Snake" shows to advantage in the grass. In "The Mower's Song," Juliana had cut down the Mower and his hopes, as he cut down the grass; in "Damon the Mower," her beauty, stronger than the sun's exceptional heats, has parched the man and his little world.

Juliana is perhaps a girl from the city, for she does not respond favorably to pastoral innocence, paying no attention to Damon's childlike gifts of leaves and snake. Her sophistication seems naturally adult, and our own: Damon with his gifts remains the pastoral *naïf*:

> To Thee the harmless Snake I bring,
> Disarmed of its teeth and sting.
> To thee *Chameleons* changing-hue,
> And Oak leaves tipt with hony due.
> Yet Thou ungrateful hast not sought
> Nor what they are, nor who them brought.

After such rejection, Damon must regain his identity, proclaiming himself and his empire: "I am the Mower *Damon*, known/ Through all the Meadows I have mown"; he must reassert his former connection with nature, which used, for instance, to cool him so lovingly after toil. He cheers himself up by comparing his riches favorably to those of the shepherds of the plain (upon whom, by implication, Juliana looks with kindness), and by considering his good looks, reflected in his scythe as "in a crescent Moon the Sun." Damon is well within the English pastoral tradition; like Colin Clout, as he says,

> The deathless Fairyes take me oft
> To lead them in their Danses soft;
> And, when I tune my self to sing,
> About me they contract their Ring.

His lovely song enchants the supernature as well as the nature around him. The notion of contraction[6] recurs in this poem: Damon's ideal world is easily manned by one mower and encompassed by that man's mind and personality. His real world, however, is slightly at variance with the ideal one, for labor is not therapeutic, as it ought to be, and in fact does not serve to diminish his grief. Not only is he unable to take pride in his mowing, but he also loses control over his occupation and himself as a result of near-fatal inattention:

> While thus he threw his Elbow round,
> Depopulating all the Ground,
> And, with his whistling Sythe, does cut
> Each stroke between the Earth and Root,

---

[6] See below, pp. 118-23, for comments on diminution and contraction.

34

Problems of Pastoral

> The edge Stele by careless chance
> Did into his own Ankle glance;
> And there among the Grass fell down,
> By his own Sythe, the Mower mown.

With this splendidly sad self-reference, we might expect the poem to end, on a destruction not altogether unlike "The Mower's Song"; but the poet surprises us. The point of view has shifted from Damon's own lament to another standard pastoral theme, the poet's lament for the fall of another singer, with the poet now serving as commentator on Damon's behavior.[7] In the final stanza, Damon springs up from his fallen state to repair himself, out of his infinite identification with natural things. "Shepherds-purse" and "Clowns-all-heal" will "seal" his wound, although no specific can cure the wound from Juliana's eyes. That punishment, that pain, he must bear until a colleague, Death, comes to mow him down in turn. Damon's self-wounding, so easily repaired, is the preparative for the final wound of Death, who also does his job as assigned. The notion of self-destruction in both this poem and the "Mower's Song" helps to blur our impressions of possible pastoral perfection, whose loveliness is threatened always, the landscape for all its beauty presented as unsettled and disturbing.

In both "The Mower's Song" and "Damon the Mower," death and apocalypse are overtly associated with mowing, though schematically, lightly, artificially, almost humorously, against the screen of accepted artifice subscribed to by the pastoral convention. Damon's vigorous, energetic mowing foreshadows death; however, the ease with which he heals himself preserves not just him, but the pastoral setting as well: nature helps nature to live. The seasons' promise of new grass works against the eschatological suggestions of the language. The apocalyptic hints in this poem are not filled out, although the far less overt association of mowing with apocalypse in "Upon Appleton House" makes its warning very clear. In his mowing eclogues, Marvell treats the stylization of pastoral within pastoral terms, which, as he demonstrates, work against resonating seriousness; in "Upon Appleton House," he digs into all his poetical resources to extract even from the delicacies of pastoral the hints of more fearful possibilities threatening the most paradisal landscape, threatening any style or stylization of life.

[7] See below, pp. 129-30, for further comments on persona and poet in this poem.

"The Mower against Gardens" presents a speaker with a grudge, a speaker verging on tantrum. This mower is a moralist, inveighing like a Puritan preacher against the artifices of a materialist, worldly, and producing society: "Luxurious Man," with his "Vice," does "the World seduce," "alluring" the plants from the fields, "Where Nature was most plain and pure." The theology and the morality are orthodox enough: after the Fall, a seduction, nature's perfections were modified and men became vicious. The Eden-*topos* may have flowed together with a passage from Pliny, who inveighed against artificial gardens and praised those "natural" and "useful" gardens planted in the good old days by every Roman freeman; his attack was directed against the self-indulgence of an epicurean and decadent patriciate.[8] What is not orthodox, save within the context of pastoral naïveté, is the transference of such a social attack to an entirely vegetable reference, in which gardens are endowed with the vices traditionally attributed by pastoralists to cities and city dwellers.[9] The Mower, unable to conceptualize beyond his own experience, gives us the pastoral *paragone* of art and nature in terms that he understands, terms which clearly mark the limits of his natural and his intellectual world. It is a matter, in Professor Gombrich's terms, of *ping* and *pong*, of alternatives defined: for everyone, there is some question about the relation of nature to art, of spontaneous to artificial beauty, but the terms of the definition vary considerably. The Mower sees the question in terms of meadows and gardens.

The Mower's argument is, in the context of Marvell's time and therefore according to his audience's expectations, magnificently reactionary and therefore magnificently paradoxical. The long effort of serious-minded agriculturalists to improve plants by hybridization and by grafting got new energies in seventeenth-century England, when a spate of

[8] Pliny, *Historie of the World*, XXI, iv, v; XV, ix, xv.
[9] John Rea, in *Flora: seu de Florum Cultura, Or a Complete Florilegium* (London, 1665), cites so close a parallel to the Mower's tirade against gardens that we may suspect Rea of following Marvell's *topos*: "I have seen many Gardens of the new model, in the hands of unskilful persons, with good Walls, Walks, and Grass-plots; but in the most essential adornments so deficient, that a green Medow is a more delightful object; there Nature alone, without the aid of Art, spreads her verdant Carpets, spontaneously imbroydered with many pretty Plants and pleasing Flowers, far more inviting than such an immured Nothing. And as noble Fountains, Grotto's, Statues, &c. all are excellent ornaments and marks of Magnificence; so all such dead works in Gardens, ill done, are little better than blocks in the way to interrupt the sight, but not at all to satisfie the understanding."

practical works on gardening and cultivation appeared, greatly stimulated by the botanical discoveries in the New World. Bacon's *Sylva Sylvarum* offers many recipes, themselves subject to much later correction, for better growth. The *Sylva*, indeed, looks suspiciously like a "source" for the Mower's topics; the early pages of its Sixth Century describe just such experiments with nature as the Mower despises: recipes to achieve several fruits upon one tree, fruit formed into different shapes, fruit trees with inscriptions or engraving, trees carved into various topiary shapes, flowers with heightened color, flowers made double, fruit without core or stone all occur. Gillyflowers from pinks to carnations are of course prominent in the list of malleable plants.[10] For the Mower, though, "utility" carries no sanction; indeed, he thinks it worse to deal "between the Bark and Tree," to graft, than to sell tulip bulbs for unthinkable prices. (In keeping with the Mower's consistent parochialism, the most unthinkable price for a tulip bulb is "a Meadow".) The prostitution-cosmetic imagery is kept going in the description of the tulip, taught "to interline its cheek" as a woman is taught to paint hers. Plants are adulterated by man's officious interference, the pink, the rose, the tulip all having been wild-flowers originally, growing, as all proper flowers should, in fields. By being tamed, innocent beauty is lost and adulterated.

With cross-breeding, grafting, and other mixes, the social structure of the plant-world has been undone:

> No Plant now knew the Stock from which it came;
> He grafts upon the Wild the Tame:[11]

The Mower's morality speaks out, as in the great Homilies, against popular disturbance, against adultery, against insurrections; in such a context the moral notion of social hierarchy is made ridiculous by its application to the vegetable world. The fruit in the garden is "uncertain," that is, of uncertain birth; "adulterate," immoral itself in turn, evidently; lives in a "green *Seraglio*," i.e., a garden, where there are "Eunuchs," or sterile

---

[10] Francis Bacon, *Sylva Sylvarum* (London, 1677), pp. 107-9; see also Ralph Austen, *Observations upon some part of Sir Francis Bacon's Naturall History . . .* (Oxford, 1658), esp. pp. 22-23, 25-27, 30-33, for Bacon's errors; and John Parkinson, *Paradiso in Sole Paradisus Terrestris* (London, 1629), pp. 22-23, for gilliflowers and other doubling.

[11] For a serious plan to do just such grafting "upon the Wild the Tame," see Samuel Hartlib, *A Designe for Plentie, By an Universall Planting of Fruit-Trees* (London, 1653), pp. 17-23.

plants, as well as the miraculous cherry which can "procreate without a Sex."[12] The Mower is a natural man and a leveler: he speaks against gardens as a political man speaks against a rigid, tyrannical, self-indulgent society where all is, in more than one sense, "enforc't." The Mower laments a pastoral time past, for now

> . . . the sweet Fields do lye forgot:
> Where willing Nature does to all dispence
> A wild and fragrant Innocence:

In fields, no cultivation is necessary, since nature herself has benefit of supernatural aids:

> And *Fauns* and *Faryes* do the Meadows till,
> More by their presence than their skill.

This is true pastoral *otium*: the doctrinaire Mower will not allow even the gentle cultivation of gardens. He yields no point of his program. In meadows, and in meadows only, can a man live virtuously. The Mower rejects art altogether, too; the statues of gods, however ancient, which adorn neoclassical gardens are no substitute for the presence of the gods themselves.[13]

Taken seriously, this Mower is insane: he babbles a' green fields because he cannot consider anything else. He is tense, obsessed, hostile in just the way the classical wish-fulfilling pastoralist considered the negotiating city-dweller to be tense, obsessed, and hostile.

To say this of the Mower, of course, is to grant him a real personality beyond the context of the poem. Really, all that is going on is that, through this mad argument, the poet is again questioning pastoral values and conventions. By making the Mower take elements of the pastoral program absolutely, the poet manages to make us think afresh about a convention in praise of naturalness which is distinguished for its fixedness, its cliché qualities, its artificiality. As we sort out the levels of artificiality involved in this poem, we are drawn to consider conventional thought and behavior in contexts beyond the pastoral. In this poem, the Mower irrationally endorses pastoral life as the only existence rationally conceivable, denounces even the gentle near-pastoralism of gardens. He rejects artificiality, and utility with it as another version of artificiality; only

---

[12] See Austen, *Observations*, p. 42.

[13] See Pliny, XIX, vi, for a lecture against ornamental statues in gardens.

nature "most plain and pure," unadorned, unaltered, unimproved, qualifies as truly virtuous or truly beautiful. Such praise of nature and rejection of art, written in terms of a tradition in which nature is accepted as the self-conscious construct of art, presses to their limits the rules of pastoral conventional competition, in order to bring us back to consider the aesthetic and emotional reasons for those rules, the literary conditions under which they made sense.

The pastoral insists on opposing one kind of artificial nature to another sort of art; Marvell constantly plays between extremes of art and nature, at least as conventionally defined, in ways of which the purist Mower could only disapprove. In common with most poets of the Renaissance, Marvell allows his natural scenes to appear in the dress of sophisticated civilization. In "Bermudas," the "eternal Spring" enamels everything, hangs up the oranges "like golden Lamps," sets within the pomegranates jewels richer than Ormus. In "Upon Appleton House," he conceives of the wood-scene as *"Mexique Paintings"* of feathers; the wood is for him a *"Mosaick."* Later, at the sunset, the landscape becomes a room for the modest Maria, the wood her screen, the sun going to bed behind the clouds. In such transformations of nature into art, Marvell draws upon thoroughly absorbed conventions, in which the spring constantly "enamels," "diapers," and "embroiders," the dew "bejewels" with pearls and other precious stones. Nature sometimes makes mosaics, although not usually in so complicated a sense as in "Upon Appleton House"; feather-paintings are surely rare in English poetry. For Marvell, that is to say, nature can be both a very conventional artist and an extravagant, original one. In the *"Mexique Paintings,"* the elements close in a circle, since though it is highly sophisticated to make pictures of birds' feathers, like those brought back to Antwerp for the great exhibition from the New World, the picture-elements themselves are natural objects. Nature is improved, but offers her choicest products to effect the improvement.

Marvell was capable of transforming real landscapes into imaginary disciplines, as when, in "Upon the Hill and Grove at Bill-borow," the "Groves of Pikes" are assimilated to the natural copse on Bilbrough Hill; he presents us his most inelastic natural scene in the Fairfax gardens at Appleton House, evidently in fact already planted in military design. The severe contrast between the notion of strict military discipline and the notion of a garden (delicate plants, lovely colors, sweet smells, diaphanous insects) is deliberately forced, to demonstrate at its extreme point the interpenetration of the retired by the involved, the fragile by the solid, the evanescent by the concrete.

Taken in conjunction with the Mower poems, these passages offer further comment on the pastoral *paragone*. There is, after all, some artfulness involved in any interference with the natural round, even in any thinking about the natural round. Marvell is playing with a conventional mental set, and by the nature of his games with this particular "set," the pastoral, sends us to consider the controls upon our expectation imposed by any conventional system. In his pastoral exercises, he considers the assumptions of the convention, now in one limited test case, now in another, segmenting one aspect of pastoral from the great amorphous whole, to reveal its literary problems and the moral problems of living for which those literary conventions were designed to stand.

But for all the silliness of Damon or the Mower-against-gardens, readers are not invited to reject them, their position, or their aesthetic preferences without thinking them through. The obvious artificiality of pastoral is by no means silly or repugnant in these poems: the delicacy of the "Gloworms" poem, the beauty of Damon's and the other Mower's meadows are all sincerely offered for our affectionate admiration. Marvell is no Dr. Johnson, rejecting the whole pastoral tradition as empty and false; he does not let us prefer the sophisticated Juliana to the gentle Damon, or reject fields because the Mower's defense of them is so irrational. Damon is a dear; green fields are sweet; we sympathize with the angry Mower whose metrical rationalizations about his total misery help him to get through what is apparently his only annual task. Like the singing oarsmen of "Bermudas," he works better to a song of his own composition. For all the speakers' huge parochialism, so relentlessly exposed by the poet working behind their backs, the mowers nonetheless maintain their integrity. The *naïf* is exposed as such, the limitations of naïveté are criticized, but the values of innocence are honored at the same time. No final positions are taken on the pastoral mode, even in this set of poems, which, precisely as they explore their own premises and push their implications to the limit, exalt the pastoral values as they question them. The beautiful neatness and clarity of the metrics, the sophistication of the underlying ideas of the poems, expressed in such simple and delicate language, all bespeak the poet's sympathy for a beleaguered, sophisticated ideal. Pastoral is cruelly intellectualized in these poems—and to intellectualize is radically to invert pastoral values in any case, which frankly relinquish intellectual burdens for the embrace of a comfortable natural passivity. In his exposé of the *naïf*, the poet manages to make us love the man's innocence; he manages then at once to play devil's advocate and to canonize withal the beauty and the inadequacy of the pastoral program.

If one may draw a moral from Marvell's practice in these poems, it is that the pastoral cannot provide a satisfactory working-model for lives as men and women must live them, complicated beyond help from the pastoral paradigm. Just because the pastoral is so "useless" in interpreting human life, it is important for its recreative, dreaming beauty all the same. In the "Mower against Gardens," the competition is between nature and artifice, between *otium* and *negotium*, between a reduced pastoral and an adumbrated georgic style of life. The poet, one feels, knows the values of both meadows and gardens, and rejects the competition to embrace a world in which all sorts of flowers and plants may grow.

In "The Garden" and "Upon Appleton House," different sorts of plants, different sorts of plantations, grow very well side by side; they are expressed in conjoined literary modes, these in turn standing for conjoined modes or styles of life. Without choosing sides, the poet nevertheless shows that he recognizes what the competition between styles and styles of life may mean: in the longer poems, he himself effects their conjunction. Of course he is not always so eclectic and synthetic. In "The Coronet," another poem in which modes of pastoral are set into opposition, the poet does choose a spiritual over a secular pastoralism. There, a real personal problem somehow shows through the distanced, artificially-developed metaphors of artifice; in "A Dialogue between Thyrsis and Dorinda," emotional and spiritual struggle is barred altogether from the poem. The only problem is the simple one of Dorinda's thoughtless rejection of earthly pastoral pleasures for the joys of the pastures of Heaven. The dialectic of "Clorinda and Damon" does not cut deep: Clorinda is easily converted by her lover to join in praising "Pan." Though the two speakers go through the motions of dialogue, there is in fact no tension in this poem between pagan and Christian innocence.

"The Coronet," though, exploits tension: it is a psychomachia, oddly enough, expressed in terms of pastoral, in terms, moreover, of writing pastoral poetry. It is a professional's poem about a professional problem; a poem written very carefully in two styles, about two styles of pastoral poetry, about religious obligation conceived in terms of pastoral poetry. All this is accomplished without one direct word about "poetry" itself:

fruit, flowers, garlands, chaplet, wreaths, towers, all the paraphernalia of the pastoralist are scrupulously used as a screen for their conventional moral meanings—and for more than their conventional moral meanings.

By his metaphorical substitution, Marvell rigorously maintains his fiction; how, when he is so clearly feigning, dealing so artificially with conventional and artificial counters from a tradition in praise of art, does the poem so manage to move its readers? In part because the syntax at first wreathed and plaited like the garlands he tries to weave, and the confusions of his spirit, later clear but abrupt and broken as he attempts to humble himself, his spirit, and his art, somehow persuade us of the speaker's developing experience, his confusion, shock, and courage. But these are fancifications, after all, and had to be very carefully contrived, as the involutions and complexities of the first sixteen lines are laid aside for a disentangled, flatter, more direct syntax: poetry bends to the spiritual discipline of the soul.

Of course this plain poem is a triumph of artifice, as "set with Skill and chosen out with Care," the official topical language of pastoral poetry is forced to render a "real" spiritual experience in which, for all its peculiarity, the poet remains faithful to his trade of making metaphors. In the simpler syntax of the later part of the poem, the metaphor persists, after all—"Serpent," "knots . . . untie," "disintangle all his winding Snare," "my curious frame," "these wither," "Spoils," "tread," and "crown"— actually *as figure* losing none of its acknowledged artifice but showing us the poet doing what he says he is *not* doing: writing poetry as well as he possibly can. However profound his suspicions of artifice and clear his insight into the artifices of pastoral, Marvell's devotion to art can never be questioned.

This poem examines rival ways of life, like "A Dialogue Between The Resolved Soul, and Created Pleasure," "A Dialogue between the Soul and Body," and "The Mower against Gardens." As in "A Dialogue between the Soul and Body," the poet recognizes that old forms are too limited for modern perceptions: in a fallen world, even pastoral innocence is not innocent enough. Only by experience—such an experience as that rendered in "The Coronet"—can a man recognize the values implicit in the pastoral ideal, the values of conventional artlessness, of language, life, and soul.

❦ 3 ❧

LOVE POEMS

IN A PERIOD so productive of brilliant love poetry,[1] Marvell's love poems are remarkable for their coolness and self-sufficiency. From his love poetry, critics have often been tempted to derive a given poet's attitude to love and psychological involvement generally, and Marvell has not been spared diagnosis from his poems. Precisely because of the detachment of his love lyrics, readers have come to various conclusions about the poet's nature—that he was frigid, impotent, homosexual, capable only of "vegetable" love (whatever that may be). Actually, there is no more need to interpret Marvell's love poetry as autobiographical than so to interpret Herrick's or Donne's or (perhaps the best comparison) Crashaw's. In Marvell's case, the temptation to autobiographize his love poetry is particularly tactless, since the open directives he gives us in that poetry are so clearly to traditions of literary expression, not to immediate experiences. As in his pastorals, Marvell practiced here also in the conventions he received; his love poetry touches on most of the current themes and styles, and, again as in his pastoral poetry, in the lyrics of love too he seems to question and to test most of them. In "The Fair Singer," for instance, the poet plays with petrarchan language, as he sings of his total enslavement to a lady blessed with both a pretty face and a sweet voice.[2] Many different and thoroughly familiar amatory hyperboles are brought together in this little poem: the notion that there is a battle between lady and lover; that the battle is sweet for its very fierceness; that love, though like a battle, is also like harmony in music; that both battle and harmony have their correspondences in cosmic warfare and in cosmic harmony. All these notions, traditional in love poetry, are so intricately intertwined and so trickily played off against one another, that they are difficult to take seriously, the more so because the setting is so clearly just a musical party. The point of this poem is the poet's dexterity with

---

[1] See H. M. Richmond, *The School of Love* (Princeton, 1964), esp. p. 220.
[2] For an appreciation of this poem, see Leishman, pp. 49-56; for its Marinism, see James V. Mirollo, *The Poet of the Marvellous. Giambattista Marino* (New York, 1963), pp. 245-6.

familiar idioms. The extravagance of the developed "petrarchan" rhetoric is here made so intellectually melodious that the silliness of the "curled trammels of her hair," the "Fetters" made of air, or the airs of the lady's breath and her song, seem somehow natural, in so thoroughly and frankly artificial an environment. The lady's voice controls the air, is like the wind; her eyes are like the sun: against an army so favored, how can mere man hope to contend?

Not only are there many concepts in the poem, but conventional conceits are pushed to extremes as well. By their sheer accumulation, the extravagant clichés point to their own nonsense. Against this nonsense-quality, though, something else tugs in another direction, toward composure and sanity. The regular metrics and beautifully counterpoised phrases of

> Love did compose so sweet an Enemy,
> In whom both Beauties to my death agree,
> Joyning themselves in fatal Harmony;

manage to contain and to prolong the image and its meanings. What can this poet not get away with? From curls of hair, which from contemporary usage we expect to signalize wanton irregularity, he manages to move in quite another direction, to cosmic harmony, blending and contrasting the elements in the figures to stress their sweet traditionalism and their literal foolishness.

Quite clearly, the speaker's heart in this poem is left untouched. What concerns him is the nature of the amatory clichés: what can he do with them to make the poem, not the condition of love, interesting? Indeed, it is just the lyricism of the untouched heart that strikes us so strongly in this verse; the poet seems to speak in love's conventional language in order to show its inadequacies, its silliness as applied to an emotion either too stereotyped (as in "The Fair Singer") or too uncontrolled (as in "The unfortunate Lover," discussed below). One might group with "The Fair Singer" such poems as "The Match" and "The Gallery," in which the beloved seems a construct, not a woman, set up for the poet's display of the school-figures of love.

In "The Definition of Love," a poem ostensibly about passion thwarted —the same theme, so differently treated, as in "The unfortunate Lover"— the poet appears to have stretched the possibilities of a love lyric to the utmost: this definition of love is in fact a definition of not-love. A poem called a "definition" may be expected to be intellectual, or intellectually constructed; this poem is surely that. It has an extraordinarily tight logic and consistent argument, rare in any poetry, but the poet's intellectualism lay even more in his poem's plan than in its strategy. Once more, in this poem Marvell has turned a recognized genre on its head, by the simple means of reconsidering and reinterpreting its title. The ordinary "definition" pattern, by which a series of bracketing partial answers to a question offer some approximation of definition, has been abandoned for quite another sort of definition, taken from an entirely different vocabulary, that of Euclidian geometry.[3] As Mr. Hyman's able analysis of the poem has demonstrated, the logic has to be carefully worked out by readers—and, to be successful, had to have been worked out long beforehand by the poet. The "Iron wedges," the "Decrees of Steel," the "Poles," the sphere and the planisphere, the oblique and the parallel lines all maintain their consistency in sequence and in logic, to give an appearance of explanation to the situation in which poet and lady find themselves. What is that situation? Theoretically, an emotional one, the conventions of which are as scrupulously criticized as other conventions are in such poems as "Mourning" and "The Nymph complaining": this poem is about star-crossed love, with none of the resignation or the hope, for instance, of Donne's great valedictions. The lover in this poem is quite content to be separated from his beloved; his geometrical demonstration and his proof of irrevocable parting seem to please him by their implacable logic. Whatever emotion this poem bears comes not from the poet's grief at his situation's hopelessness, but from his satisfaction in having solved his problem intellectually, in having his geometry come out right. In stanza VII, he plays on the geometrical notion of osculation, rather than on the passionate fact of kissing:

> As Lines so Loves *oblique* may well
> Themselves in every Angle greet:
> But ours so truly *Paralel*,
> Though infinite can never meet.

Even the geometry flattens out, as the solid figures become plane. There is a beautiful appropriateness to the last stanza too: certainly the metaphysical bluestocking who could understand this lover's poem is best bound to him by "the Conjunction of the Mind."

[3] See below, pp. 58-59, for further comment.

In these poems, the lover is a cool customer, deliberately distancing himself from the prickly irritations and irrationalities generally attendant upon unhappy love. Though so different in tone, language, and narrative from these poems, "Daphnis and Chloe" has some affinity with "The Definition of Love," in the detachment of the speaker's conclusions about the psychology of love. Chloe loses Daphnis, it seems, because she is coy:

> . . . she neither knew t'enjoy,
> Nor yet let her Lover go.

That is, the thwarted Daphnis has come to the end of his rope and resolves to leave his unyielding lady. At this point, we are on his side; but so, it turns out, is Chloe. Shocked by the possibility of losing Daphnis, she lets down all her conventional defenses, to permit him anything—but by that time, it seems, Daphnis is far too intent on acting his part to take account of her offer of total surrender. For all his passionate utterance, he too turns out to be a very cool customer, enjoying the drama he creates far more than he cares for the girl. At first, his misery seems real enough, even if a little overstated:

> His disorder'd Locks he tare;
> And with rouling Eyes did glare,
> And his cruel Fate forswear.

"Dead," "shrieks," "distracted," "wretched," "torture," "condemned Wight"—Daphnis is torn on the rack of his gothick emotions. We can sympathize, until we realize that in these emotions his pleasure lies. Naturally, he finds his ranting delicious, far too pleasurable to be cut short, or to resolve practically in relation to the girl. He deliberately protracts his suffering valediction, as coy in protesting his love's agony as Chloe had ever been in preserving her virtue. To put it at its plainest, Daphnis does not love the girl—and, if the tenses of the poem can be trusted, he never had loved her. Refusing to be won over by her love for him, he turns out to be much chillier than poor cozened Chloe, coy by convention only:

> Why should I enrich my Fate?
> 'Tis a Vanity to wear,
> For my Executioner,
> Jewels of so high a rate.

Love Poems

> Rather I away will pine
> In a manly stubbornness
> Than be fatted up express
> For the *Canibal* to dine.

Such language might suggest that Daphnis has come to his senses, but that is by no means the case. He is simply using "love" as his excuse for emotional self-indulgence. He enjoys his own part as chief actor in the scene staged; and though Chloe tries to make some part in it for herself, he consistently upstages her in his determination to act out his part. Daphnis maintains his integrity, all right, but it is the integrity of histrionics rather than of a "self":

> Joy will not with Sorrow weave,
> Nor will I this Grief pollute.

"Pollute"! One must grant to professional emotionalists their rights to live in perpetual crisis, however disruptive the crises may be of other people's peace and quiet; Daphnis is indeed a familiar psychological type. But such people do not, or cannot, love: their satisfactions come from the climactic display of their passions, and their release comes not from the unions of love but from the lonely pressures of their dramatic drives. Daphnis exists to criticize not only the extravagant gestures of lovers, but also the use of "love" as a screen for other kinds of self-indulgence and self-expression, regardless of social cost.

The poem makes no bones of its morality: had it ended at the twenty-fifth stanza—

> At these words away he broke;
> As who long has praying ly'n,
> To his Heads-man makes the Sign,
> And receives the parting stroke.

—we would have had a commentary on the imaginary, fantastic, unreal, beautifully private nature of renunciation, with all its selfishness gentled in its sentimentality. Daphnis might then have been the male counterpart of the complaining Nymph, who after all does no one any harm; or he might have been another renouncing lover, in a different style, like the speaker in "The Definition of Love," proud of his iron control over his behavior. But the poem does not end with the twenty-fifth stanza, with the dramatics of Daphnis and the revealed concealments of Chloe.

47

Rather, the poet mercilessly undercuts his chief character, to show him at last a crude sensualist. Chloe's refusal has, in a way, lasted just long enough to justify Daphnis' systematic promiscuity with the other nymphs in the neighborhood:

> But hence Virgins all beware.
> Last night he with *Phlogis* slept;
> This night for *Dorinda* kept;
> And but rid to take the Air.
>
> Yet he doth himself excuse;

In the last line, there is a wealth of observation of real life: pastoral convention does not yield young men like this one. By allowing Daphnis his "cause" for sleeping around, the poet comments on the brutality underlying the conventional relations of lovers:

> Nor indeed without a Cause.
> For, according to the Lawes,
> Why did *Chloe* once refuse?

One of the ironies in this poem is entirely literary: its title. Those original pastoral lovers, so gentle with one another, so devoted through all difficulty and trial, are the exact opposite of these unfeeling creatures, quite out of tune with one another and with their pastoral environment. Like "The Definition of Love," which undercuts the conventions of passionate love lyric, this poem stretches the pastoral, that sentimental mode, quite out of shape. Really, this poem is emotionally anti-pastoral and anti-love. The ranting lover is an unfeeling calculator, a sensualist denying sentimental rights to anyone else. This love lyric turns out to be about quite different emotions masked under the name of love.

Daphnis has some kinship with the hero of "The unfortunate Lover," a poem very difficult to explicate,[4] which also deals with the psychological impasses, the self-frustrations of an unfortunate lover. The first stanza begins with a picture of happy lovers unharmed by their passion, the beautiful picture smudged by the stanza's first word:

> Alas, how pleasant are their dayes
> With whom the Infant Love yet playes!

---

[4] An attempt at such explanation is made below, pp. 109-13, 125.

48

Love Poems

Sorted by pairs, they still are seen
By Fountains cool, and Shadows green.

The tonal interloper, "Alas," ushers in, in the fifth line, its reliable "but":

But soon these Flames do lose their light,
Like Meteors of a Summers night:
Nor can they to that Region climb,
To make impression upon Time.

About another exhibitionist and compulsive lover, this poem is, how-
ever, written from quite a different point of view, that of an almost
material figure who sympathetically tries to understand and explain the
passionateless and unsuccess of the lover, who raves, like Daphnis, but has
not Daphnis' capacity to resolve his dilemma in brutality. The lover's
emblematized birth was of course unfortunate: he was born in a storm
characteristic of his nature and his behavior in later life:

The Sea lent him these bitter Tears
Which at his Eyes he alwaies bears.
And from the Winds the Sighs he bore,
Which through his surging Breast do roar.
No Day he saw but that which breaks,
Through frighted Clouds in forked streaks.
While round the ratling Thunder hurl'd,
As at the Fun'ral of the World.

The image-structure is clear enough, the familiar likening of human
temperament to the elements of the physical universe, winds turned to
sighs, rain to tears, thunder to groans and cries. But the correspondence-
pattern in this poem is also stretched beyond conventional limits, to
bring the convention to obvious absurdity. The incredible, emblematic,
mysterious nature of this poem's figures flaunts the conceitedness of the
hyperbolical notion in the first place, comments on the clichés of this
particular hyperbolical style—but it does not merely reduce to absurdity
an over-used set of psychological clichés; it leaves us wondering, also,
about the problems of compulsive behavior. This language, though so
deliberately stilted and deformed, has the advantage of matching the
poor lover's spiritual tumult. His quality as unfortunate resides in his
having been born into his temperament. This gloomy Promethean figure

49

characteristically overreacts, struggling against his life with the froward stubbornness of a King Lear:

> . . . he, betwixt the Flames and Waves,
> Like *Ajax*, the mad Tempest braves.

The ridiculousness of this poem does not lie wholly in the sad but inevitable foolishness of the lover; it lies as well in making a lover like this the inhabitant of a lyric poem. This man was born to tragedy, not lyric; like Daphnis, his real occupation is not in being a lover, but in being something else—in his case, an unfortunate. He must be self-frustrated, even before he can fix on an object of desire. Furthermore, like Daphnis, he loves his own role:

> See how he nak'd and fierce does stand,
> Cuffing the Thunder with one hand;
> While with the other he does lock,
> And grapple, with the stubborn Rock:
> From which he with each Wave rebounds,
> Torn into Flames, and ragg'd with Wounds.
> And all he saies, a Lover drest
> In his own Blood doth relish best.

His own quibble turns him into food; his appetite feeds on himself. The speaker in "The Definition of Love" and "The Nymph complaining" certainly "relish" their conditions, too, and enjoy their own sense of deprivation; they too stage their emotions to suit their temperaments. But what they do with taste and tact, delicacy and grace, this lover does at the top of his voice, farcically exaggerating gesture and word. Indeed, the controlling "voice" in "The Definition of Love" is very like the anonymous speaker of "The unfortunate Lover," who seems by understanding the hysterical subject to distance him, even from his own passions; who seems to accept the Lover's violence without judging his personality or requiring him to alter his behavior in any way. Unlike the desperate Chloe or the hypersensitive Nymph, the cool voice speaking "The unfortunate Lover" is an art critic, enjoying the lover's turning into a heraldic pattern, ending the din, ending the story. Dying, the Lover is far prettier, to say nothing of more manageable than when alive. He

> . . . dying leaves a Perfume here,
> And Musick within every Ear:

Love Poems

And he in Story only rules,
In a Field *Sable* a Lover *Gules*.

On the face of it, Marvell's love poetry also seems to rule in story rather than in anything like real life. The kind of amatory fiction the poet deals in is neither lyrical nor dramatic, though cast in those modes; it is critical. No lover could of course linger with Chloe; before long all the nymphs of the environment will have had enough of Daphnis, as he of Chloe. No lady could get a word in edgewise with the unfortunate Lover. Really, no lady exists, in effect, in "The Definition of Love": the lady is so abstracted by the predestining geometry that she relinquishes all claim to flesh and blood. These poems are not about love between persons, with its overwhelming intensities, its painful misunderstandings, and its peaceful satisfactions and boredoms. They are about the literary languages of love, about poses struck by lovers, about love as an excuse for emotional and poetical play. They are studies in feelings masked, disguised, concealed, repressed; they consider emotions detached from situations and from personality. They are about behavior loosed from its normal emotional sources. As such, these poems comment not only on the language poets are assigned to "express" their conventional and their real notions, but on the social and psychological states to which such languages are assumed to correspond. Therefore they reach out to say something not in their mandate, or in the mandate of lyric poetry—they say something definite about love itself. To be real, it cannot be like this; the conventions by which love is expressed, like the psychomachic conventions of the Body-Soul dialogue, must be revised to bring love's language into line with psychological actuality. Such ironic comments on literary love as these say something important about life as well—that lovers who fit such patterns are mutilated human beings.

CARPE DIEM POEMS

ONE GREAT topic in western love literature is the *carpe diem, carpe florem* theme, so common in Renaissance poetry that one cannot expect a poet coming so late in time as Marvell to have made much of it. Normally, *carpe diem* poems are love poems, although in Marvell's hands the theme is not so limited. He manages to try the hackneyed subject now this way, now that, to explore its possibilities and to reanimate some of its stiffened motifs. His *carpe diem* poems range from love lyrics to meditative poetry, from "Young Love" to "The Garden."

In "The Coronet," the poet quite literally gathers flowers to weave the garlands for his Saviour's head, a straight and direct form of *carpere* generally rare in verse. In "Thyrsis and Dorinda," flowers—poppies, significantly—are plucked, this time to carry the pair to Elysium. In "The Garden," the flowers of experience as of rhetoric are gathered to extraordinary effect. In "Young Love" and "The Picture of little T.C. in a Prospect of Flowers," the poet offers slant-examples of *carpe diem, carpe florem,* different comments on the theme of the young budding girl. "Young Love" owes most to an epigram in The Greek Anthology (V. iii) and to Horace, I, xxiii, and II, v, all involving the seduction of a "green" girl, a girl by convention too young for sexuality; an older and experienced man plucks this "bud," both the girl and her virginity. In Marvell's first stanza, the speaker makes clear how experienced he is, as he takes his customary care to fool the *senex,* the girl's defending father:

> Come little Infant, Love me now,
>   While thine unsuspected years
> Clear thine aged Fathers brow
>   From cold Jealousie and Fears.

The speaker reinforces a radical contrast between innocence and experience, between love and lust, as he permits his persuasion to turn on the oldest of *carpe diem* arguments, an appeal to the girl on the basis of her own transience:

Carpe Diem *Poems*

> Now then love me: time may take
> Thee before thy time away:

She is likened to a sacrifice of lambs and kids; he assures her that if love is a good thing, then to "antedate" love, to enter into its initiations early, will simply be to enrich her yet more. What the speaker says is conventional enough; that he says it to so young a girl gives the poem its peculiar twist. This speaker is an honest sensualist, quite aware of what he is doing. His love is lust; the "plucking," that seems so delightful between young lovers of equal age, is simply self-indulgence at a child's expense. In "Little T.C." the same situation prevails, in that an older man observes a young girl, like the child in "Young Love," "too green/ Yet for Lust," and (it seems) for love too. She is a figure in the pastoral scene, herself *carpens*, picking the flowers of transience all about her, but a flower-element herself as well, in the "prospect of flowers."

These two poems demonstrate something quite interesting and, once one has grasped the problem, quite obvious: that *carpe diem* is a fundamental element of the pastoral love code as well as of the sensualist's code. We can tell a virtuous shepherd from Comus, or an innocent from an experienced lover, not by what each says, since each uses the same language, but by the context in which he says it. In "Little T.C.," the speaker remarkably "cleans" the poem of any suggestion of the girl's, or his own present, sexuality; as the poet in "Upon Appleton House" sees an unblemished sexual future for Maria, so does the poet foresee no wantonness in T.C.'s future:

> Who can foretel for what high cause
> This Darling of the Gods was born!
> Yet this is She whose chaster Laws
> The wanton Love shall one day fear,
> And, under her command severe,
> See his Bow broke and Ensigns torn.
> Happy, who can
> Appease this virtuous Enemy of Man!

The speaker here, then, is the exact opposite of the speaker in "Young Love"; here, entirely without prurience, he watches a mode of *carpe diem* appearing emblematically before him. He himself is not tempted, denies temptation, retires from competitive *carpere*: as he images T.C.'s future triumphs over love, he himself becomes steadily more passive, watching

53

the child, as the poet watches Maria in the Nunappleton evening go about her business. T.C. is not free from danger, but this speaker is on her side against what threatens her. Though he warns her that she will be plucked in the end, like all things, he advises the same self-control in her that he asks of Nature on her behalf; there is certainly real love for the little girl in this poem, but as opposed to "Young Love," a protective rather than a predatory love. Like Horace, Marvell writes one poem of seduction, another of renunciation of too-young love.

In "Ametas and Thestylis" the sexual theme is presented in yet another way, this time as entirely without consequences, emotional or social. Here, sexuality is for once simple, and simply treated, with neither the sidelong libertinism of "Young Love" nor the protectiveness, of girl and self, of "Little T.C." The only odd note in this dialogue is that Thestylis insists on the transience of her relation to Ametas, consenting to "kiss within the Hay" not because all youth is transient and must be seized before it is gone, but because Ametas promises her that their relation shall not build into a complicated future. Her reasons for "coyness," then, are just the opposite to the received reasons; she extracts from her lover the promise of infidelity. These two are guileless naturalists, not sophisticated libertines like the speaker in "Young Love." Their love is designed for and from psychological uninvolvement, accepted by the two as an equal experience, an equal irresponsibility. Theirs is "plucking" at its most agreeable, and its most natural.

"To his Coy Mistress" is obviously Marvell's most remarkable poem of carpe diem, his most remarkable love poem in any form. The speaker speaks out of a desire that may be transitory; he promises nothing beyond an experience of shared joy. This poem plucks the day, laying immense stress on the day itself, a point in all time; it promises nothing beyond that day except the night of endless sleep to which all mortals must go down. Further, there is no shred of flower imagery in the poem. Rosebuds are not gathered; the lady does not put on her foliage, is never seen in a prospect of flowers—rather, surrealistically, she stands against a background of desert sand stretching to infinity. The implications of carpe diem are explored in the poem; the lady, and by implication all love, are threatened by time; the speaker is as aware of his imminent death as he is of hers. Whereas most poems on this theme tend to intensify the poet's desire at the expense of other aspects of life, this poem prolongs fulfilment, stretches out the courtship to make more intense its short, powerful consummation.

Further, the poem examines its own official premises, following their implications to their logical conclusions. Time threatens love, so the poet takes a long look at all time and all space, made "endless" in the literary hyperbole of compliment. *Adunata* serve to praise this lady, imaginatively seen in a prospect of all time and space, her beauties measured off against slices of time. The secondary sense of love as "value" is explored and set forth; love is accounted for and appraised, in the commercial sense[1]— and, as usual, Marvell has managed to literalize the concept in an idiom proper to the environments of the poem, the customary overpraise of lovers looking for physical love. The Ganges, so romantic and exotic, alternates with the Humber, the local stream; the scriptural-historical Flood alternates with the never-never conversion of the Jews. The millennium, "the last Age," shows the lady's heart, concealed till then— and yet, and yet, all that compliment turns into "worms" trying, as the poet hopes to try before them, the lady's "long preserv'd Virginity." Preoccupation with the flesh in life suggests the career of the flesh after death.

The time which all *carpe diem* poems exploit is here extended to eternity, and eternity is spatially presented ("Desarts of vast Eternity"). *Nox una perpetua dormienda* is made actual in an intensely imagined, intimate tomb scene, to frighten the living lady into taking comfort in her lover's arms. The elements are purely literary, but the poet's psychology is sound. This poem shows how to accomplish a seduction, to pluck love's day, made bright against the dark night of death. And, to stress that it is *day* that is to be plucked, the lover and his lady challenge the sun itself, hastening their day by loving proudly and professionally. In this poem, unlike so many of Marvell's other love poems, passion and criticism seem to support one another: for all the poem's acute examination of its own sources, it finds new resources to affirm the intense experience of life that love can be. The speaker, for once, is committed to an act and to affirming that act. This poem is analyzed in another context below; here let it stand, simply to show some of the expansions possible of a hackneyed theme, which the poet transforms into one of the most imaginative of all formal persuasives to love.

"The Garden," also discussed at length later, is Marvell's subtlest and

[1] See T. Hawke, " 'Love' in *King Lear*," *RES*, NS X (1959), 178-79 and Richmond, pp. 15-18, 36.

most obvious *carpe diem*, a *carpe florem* concealed beneath an obvious display of plants. Here, the subject is not love, although it is commitment. The speaker may be literally detached, ec-static in the word's etymological sense, but he cares intensely for his subject and the morality implied in the experience dealt with in the poem. By returning to the non-amatory simplicity of *carpe diem*, the poet strips the injunction of its customary implications, to urge us to pluck our day of experience in whatever form we may receive it, as the bee plucks sweetness from the flowers, or the poet plucks his lessons from the remarkable garden of eloquence in which he dwells. In "The Garden," *carpe diem* is one of many themes, but its lesson of life, transposed to the plane of intellect and emotion, is no less compelling than the usual delightful commands to pluck the flowers and fruits of experience. The commitment of this poem is the more striking when we see it against its thematic fellows in Marvell's corpus of verse, most of them so cool and detached from the mood habitually dictated by the *carpe diem* theme. This theme, too, Marvell manages to transform into something new, just as he seems most to be exposing its triviality and outworn use.

GENRE: EXPANSION, EXHAUSTION,
AND TRANSCENDENCE

MARVELL's examination of the implications of theme and genre led him to make different kinds of tacit comment on them: sometimes he noted the failure of a genre to fit even conventional and stylized behavior; sometimes he noted the limpness of conventional generic literary utterance, no longer interesting for a poet concerned with the limits and problems of his craft; sometimes he explored the possibilities implied in generic convention, developing its internal implications beyond their received limits; sometimes he analyzed the reasons for the failure of a genre or theme, occasionally offering new alternatives to a failed type. As in "To his Coy Mistress," Marvell could expand a genre remarkably; it is a point of theoretical interest that generic "expansion" and "exhaustion" are in fact difficult to distinguish, that formal limitations do not allow of much "enlargement" before they seem "exhausted,"—or, better, to have been transformed into something else, with other boundaries of sense and expectation. Taking as test-cases several familiar poems dealt with elsewhere in this study, I want to explore Marvell's analytical attack on generic conventions and see what alternatives he could offer.

"A Dialogue between the Soul and Body" is one example of Marvell's exhaustion of a genre. His inspection of the psychological meanings of the form led him to question the simple Manicheism underlying its structure. The poet not only overturns the usual expectation of any well-read reader by making the soul and the body into whining complainers instead of aggressive advocates for exclusive programs of life, but also presents them so that their traditional independence and opposition are seen to be illusory. Neither soul nor body is a sympathetic figure in the poem: the paradoxes uttered by both—"manacled in Hands," "mine own Precipice I go," "Shipwrackt into Health again"—seem to express not their considerable detachment from their plight, but the parochial ignorance of their views of each other. Even in theological terms, the Soul ought not to speak so disparagingly of life; the Body's rejection of psychology—Hope, Fear, Love, Hatred, Joy, Sorrow, Knowledge, and Memory—denies human potentiality altogether. The blindness of these two, their failure to recognize their interdependence, alienates them from the readers to whom they make their appeals for sympathy; their childishness points to the simplistic conceptual ground of the psychomachia, and its irrelevance to questions which, in seventeenth-century terms, demand new formulations and new solutions.

In this particular poem, Marvell has examined the intellectual implications of a literary form, found them wanting, and supplied a pair of antagonistic personas to demonstrate the nature of the conceptual inadequacy. In "Ametas and Thestylis," quite a different sort of poem, he allows himself one image—binding the hay and the binding of love—to show at its purest one aspect of pastoral love, its naturalism, its lack of complication. "Daphnis and Chloe" and the Mower's laments for Juliana demonstrate other aspects of pastoral love, as we have seen; in this poem, the poet simply points to the transience (like the transience of grass, or hay) of a love which must fit this artificial convention. There is an oddity in the poem: this love-contract consists in rejecting the contractual bonds of love.

In quite a different sense from the example of "A Dialogue," which points to complexities in real life not covered by the convention, "Ametas and Thestylis" exhausts a convention by emptying it even of conventional drama and climax. The simplicity of naturalistic love is the subject of the poem: the poet brings out the meaninglessness of this sort of love in the pseudo-dialogic form.

"The Definition of Love" presents a different sort of love doctrine and attacks the problem of genre and convention in still another way. By its title, this poem declares itself to be a member of a class, the definition-poem.[1] When we examine those poems, full of formal anomaly, contradiction, and paradox, we find them interesting in that they do not define meaning, so much as encircle it. This poem is quite other—in the usual definition of love stated contradictions point to its "impossibility," or at least the impossibility of uncomplicated love. The emotion itself is experienced and defined in terms of contrariety and irreconcilability. In Mar-

[1] See Frank Kermode, "Definitions of Love," *RES* NS VII (1956), 183-85, where the suggestion is made that the wrong title has been affixed to the poem. His article, together with that of Denis Davison (*RES* NS VI [1955]), provoked a lively discussion: *RES* NS XI (1961) (D. M. Schmitter and P. Legouis) and XVII (1966) (Anne E. Berthoff), as well as L. W. Hyman, *Andrew Marvell*, pp. 54-59.

vell's "Definition," the method of other poetic definitions is rejected, and a new mode of defining is undertaken—love here is "impossible" because

> It was begotten by despair
> Upon Impossibility.

What follows then is a demonstration of its impossibility, given in a language of a non-literary discipline, geometry. Geometrical definitions must demonstrate and delimit: they must in short actually define and prove the limits of their definition. So far as I can discover, this use of geometrical definition is original, in English anyway, with Marvell. It is as if in his brooding on the literary term "definition," he came upon the brilliant notion of assimilating another language of definition to the poetic language, to prove the impossibility of the conventionally impossible premise. By so doing, he rewrote the definition form altogether; that he managed by the by to outdo the geometrical imagery of other seventeenth-century poets is simply another example of Marvell's competitive elegance. One might further hazard the notion that the tidiness with which he managed to make consistent two such different forms of thought may owe something to the economical principles involved in geometrical expression, and that the spareness of the sense-imagery in this poem may be a compliment to, or experiment in, geometrical language.[2] The poem is "scientific" in its matter; it is, also, "scientific," in that it is an exercise carefully planned. In its generic context, it demonstrates the inadequacy of the existing form of poetic definition. The poet certainly points to a generic failure, but reanimates the exhausted form by reconsidering the potentiality of its name: he produces a definition designed, by very conceited means, to be *about* definition and to define the nature of unrealizable love. By so doing, he translates the convention into terms new to it.

"To his Coy Mistress" is, literally, an expansion, expanding even the poem's setting to include all space and all time. Matching time's measurement, the poet undertakes to measure his values in terms of time: his accounting is amusing because it is temporal. As he runs through, in *blason*-manner, the lady's otherwise uncharacterized physical charms, we realize how he has pushed the *blason* too, beyond its customary limits. The harshness of the talk about worms and lust, characteristic of poems

---

[2] The book which seems to have most to do with this imagery is Euclid, bks. 3 and 12; I used *Euclidis Elementorum Libri XV breviter demonstrati*, ed. Isaac Barrow (Cambridge, 1655).

on "coyness," is sweetened by the undeniable intensity of the poet's particular passion. This lover is no Daphnis, cruel to his lady for her coyness; he does not reject her, but confidently sets himself the job of persuasion. That he does so in terms of worms and lust, dust and ashes, with a realism surprising after the first twenty lines of compliment, honors the tradition, recorded in the title, in which coyness habitually rouses frustrated lovers to crude language; but even in this relatively courteous passage of threat, the poet's irony is present. He admits his own limitations on knowing, his agnosticism before the mystery of death:

> The Grave's a fine and private place,
> But none I think do there embrace.

"I think" marks the finite individual man, set against the vastness of conceivable time and space, looking out on incomparable vistas of unknowing.

The harsh language modulates into something else: from the long, slow prospects, the hyperbolical courtesies of the first section, the last section bursts into life in a far franker sexual joy than is normally encountered in poems like these, sensual and libertine though the tradition is. In the teeth of impersonality and death, the poet knows how to affirm life and living; knows that in life, lovers can embrace. Strength joined to sweetness can intensify life and for a little bring time's passage under lovers' personal control. This lover is utterly confident that he can make the love-experience mean much to his mistress.

Masculine in vocabulary and tone, this lover monopolizes such personality as there is in the poem. The lady, like so many of the ladies in Marvell's love poems, remains curiously impersonal, a stock figure for whom the poet's personality displays its ingenuities and originalities. In literary persuasions to love, though, this is normally the case; intent on physical joy, the lover has little energy to spare for a lady's fears or hesitations—especially if, as in these generic situations, he knows that she is only conventionally coy. In such a poem, to endow a lady with personality would break the tone, turn the argument into dialogue, make dramatic a rhetorical moment. By expanding the genre as he has in this poem, Marvell observes its conventions too: he does not press it to another form. And yet the form seems exhausted by the display: after this, very little new can be said in terms of *carpe diem*.

As is more fully discussed below, "The Garden" ranges over and exhausts the possibilities of retirement poetry, but at the same time the poem manages to charge the theme with a great deal more than its usual burden. "To his Coy Mistress" brings all its extra-generic materials to focus on the function of seduction; "The Garden" expands beyond the imaginative limits of the normal garden theme, to open out upon its remarkable speculative purposes. The intricacies of the poem's argument reach from rejection of the active life to enlightened acceptance of it, embrace literary modes of life, express various psychological states from an ecstatic experience of sublime understanding to a willing entry into day-to-day existence. Every element in this poem—even its ecstasy—is somehow heightened, so that the poem seems inexhaustible. It manages to include so much of life's possibilities, always given in terms of literary expression, that it is difficult to explicate and impossible to paraphrase. The poem brings to a triumphant close the whole genre of garden- and retirement-poetry, so that one wonders why anyone ever again thought to write an English poem on the subject.

These poems compress a great deal into a small compass—it is difficult for me to remember that "The Garden" is only nine stanzas long. A glance at some of the poems less successful in compressing many themes into one whole, may indicate the difficulty of the task of diminution: "The Nymph complaining" is another poem in which many traditions, many themes, many genres have left their trace—the pastoral, for instance, and poems of lament for a pet's death, poems of retirement, of the creative imagination, of innocence, and so on. Herrick's poems on whiteness have some relation to the whiteness of this one; Niobe and Galatea have, in different ways, left their mark on the poem, too. This too (in spite of some masterly commentary by Mr. Berger, Mrs. Williamson, and Leo Spitzer[3]) has proved a poem difficult to find a single satisfactory interpretation for; some of its difficulty lies, I think, in the enigmatic way in which the themes are deployed. We are not quite sure of the relative weights to assign the different elements; and yet these elements call attention to themselves, even though the poem's structure does not greatly "explain" their mutual relations. *Something* is exhausted in this poem; but I am not quite sure what it is.

[3] Berger, "The Poem as Green World" and Karina Williamson "Marvell's 'The Nymph Complaining for the Death of her Faun'," *MP* LI (1953), 268-71; Spitzer, "Marvell's 'Nymph Complaining'." See also Earl Miner, *The Metaphysical Mode from Donne to Cowley* (Princeton, 1969), p. 259, for a religious interpretation; pp. 262-66 for a "Virgilian" political interpretation. In "'The Nymph Complaining . . .' A Brief Allegory" (*Essays in Criticism*, 1968, 113-35), Geoffrey Hartman makes some illuminating remarks on the epigrammatic traditions exemplified in the poem; but see below, p. 88, note 6a.

To many critics, "Upon Appleton House" has seemed to suffer from a similar failure of fusion. There is no denying the poem's disjunctions: the elements are confusing, and in spite of the poem's length, apparently offering room for transition and gradation, they remain obstinately separated. Although, in my opinion, this disjunctive quality is very important to the poem,[4] many critics find it a major flaw. The incongruity of the elements from different sorts of poetry—the pastoral eclogue, the epic similes, the biblical references—strikes us sharply in "Upon Appleton House," and sets us to thinking about what the poet is up to. In both "The Nymph complaining" and "Upon Appleton House," we are forced to give some consideration to this disjunction of elements, this "failure," if it be that, of fusion, precisely because, in so many other poems, Marvell was so masterly a mixer of modes and genres.

"An Horatian Ode upon Cromwel's Return from Ireland" is a poem which draws attention to itself as a member of a class. The title itself directs our study, proclaiming its affiliation to Horace's Augustan odes, as John Coolidge's essay beautifully demonstrates.[5] However much it relies on Horatian models, subject, and style, the poem gathers to itself more than that: "Pindaric spirit," as Mr. Hardison has said, has been infused into an Horatian form in this ode,[6] and John Wallace has stressed the immediate and applicable poetical content of the poem.[7] In another kind of reading, Joseph Mazzeo has stressed the poem's Machiavellianism,[8] and although Hans Baron has questioned Mazzeo's interpretation of Machiavelli,[9] there is no doubt that providential expediency is one element of the poem's ethos. Mr. Holahan has beautifully related this poem to the Protectorate poems written later, and to Marvell's retirement-poetry in general;[10] others have made valuable contributions to our knowledge of the poem, not the least of them Cleanth Brooks and Douglas Bush, in an enlightening exchange.[11] Obviously, this is a major work, rich in resonance

---

[4] See below, Part IV, pp. 142, 146, for "disjunction."

[5] John C. Coolidge, "Marvell and Horace," *MP* LXIII (1965), 111-20.

[6] O. B. Hardison, Jr., *The Enduring Monument* (Chapel Hill, 1962), p. 101.

[7] Wallace, *Destiny his Choice*, Chapter 2.

[8] J. A. Mazzeo, "Cromwell as Machiavellian Prince in Marvell's '*An Horatian Ode*,'" *JHI* XXI (1960), 1-17.

[9] Hans Baron, "Marvell's 'An Horatian Ode' and Machiavelli," *JHI* XXI (1960), 450-1.

[10] Holahan, "The Civick Crown," *op.cit.*, is excellent on this poem.

[11] Douglas Bush, "Marvell's 'Horatian Ode,'" *English Institute Essays* (New York, 1947), pp. 127-58; Cleanth Brooks, "A Note on the Limits of 'History' and The Limits of 'Criticism,'" *Sewanee Review* LXI (1953), 129-35. See also R. H. Syfret,

and content, rewarding to the careful student in a number of ways: I want to consider it in some of its generic relations.

Here, as elsewhere, Marvell has managed to make a generic form do an extraordinary amount, both what it "ought" to do, within the expectations of the genre, and much more than that; he has managed to fill the poem to its brim, without making it seem clogged or complicated. The "ode" was by no means restricted to a public subject: Lovelace's "The Grass-hopper" is an ode, so also are "Corinna's going a-Maying" and "The Canonization," formally, at least; "L'Allegro" and "Il Penseroso" are odes celebrating private psychological states. The public events of private persons—marriages, births, deaths—habitually found celebration in odes. In its treatment of the King's death, this poem of course draws on the conventions of funerary odes. Religious ("On the Morning of Christ's Nativity") and, most commonly, public events were proper subjects for odes.[12] One particular topic for the ode, for which Horace provided the model, was a ruler's "return" from a campaign or a progress; Pindaric triumphal language was often adapted to such celebrations. Wotton wrote "An Ode to the King. At his returning from Scotland to the Queen, after his Coronation there,"[13] and, of course, many odes were written for Charles II when he returned to his kingdom in 1660. Charles I was a king who particularly called forth poetry on his "returns"; when one glances at the immense number of poems written for him on this theme, one might well wonder if Marvell were not seeking a little to redress the balance in favor of the underprivileged Cromwell. In 1623 a volume of poems, chiefly in Latin, was published by the Cambridge laureates to celebrate Charles' safe return from Spain, where he had attempted to betroth himself to the Infanta;[14] another Cambridge volume, called *Rex Redux*,[15] was published after his return from his Scottish coronation; still

---

"Marvell's 'Horatian Ode,' " *RES* NS XII (1961), 160-72; Ruth Nevo, *The Dial of Virtue* (Princeton, 1963); and Patrick Cruttwell, *The Shakespearean Moment* (London, 1954), pp. 193-196.

[12] Carol Maddison, *Apollo and the Nine* (London, 1960); Robert Shafer, *The English Ode to 1660* (Princeton, 1918); George N. Schuster, *The English Ode from Milton to Keats* (New York, 1940).

[13] Henry Wotton, *Reliquiae Wottonianae* (London, 1651).

[14] *Gratulatio Academiae Cantabrigiensis De Serenissimi Principis reditu ex Hispanijs exoptatissimo* (Cambridge, 1623); an oration on the same subject was delivered by the University orator, George Herbert.

[15] *Rex Redux, sive Musa Cantabrigiensis . . . De Incolumitate et felici redi Regis Caroli . . . Scotia* (Cambridge, 1633).

another in 1641, with poems by Cowley, Cleveland, and Cudworth, cele-
brated his return from the Scottish war.[16] There was an Oxford effort as
well, to which Jasper Mayne and Henry Vaughan contributed, to mark the
King's return from that war.[17] One can see that Cromwell's returning—
from a successful war, after all—might well call forth an ode of praise,
especially since the King's less successful returns had elicited such ful-
some response. The King's death was celebrated in many poems too, and
odes were common among the outraged laments on that bitter subject.
Monumentum regale, Or a Tombe, erected for . . . Charles the First
(1649), is a collection of such pieces, several of which share elements
with Marvell's poem.[18] Cromwell's career was not so studded with vol-
umes of verse as the King's had been, but he had his share; a notable
example is *Musarum Oxoniensium* ΕΛΑΙΟΦΟΡΙΑ (Oxford, 1654), cele-
brating the conclusion of the first Anglo-Dutch war, to which among
others the young John Locke contributed both Latin and English verses.
Within Marvell's own work, "An Horatian Ode" must be taken in con-
junction with the other poems on Cromwell, since it is one stage in the
poet's complicated tribute to that complicated man.

"An Horatian Ode" is officially a panegyric to Cromwell, but a pane-
gyric, as critics have pointed out, seriously qualified by its praise of the
King and its clear expression of the country's peculiar legal plight. Com-
parison with the poems to Charles in *Monumentum Regale*, or the poems
in praise of Cromwell by Waller, Dryden, and Sprat,[19] readily indicates
the subtlety of Marvell's understanding, and the difficulty of the task he
set himself. In Waller's "A Panegyrick on Oliver Cromwell, and his
Victories," many of the same themes occur, but in that poem, Cromwell is
a static, posed figure to whom conventional and unqualified praise is
offered; Cromwell is identified, really, with England and English po-

[16] *Irenodia Cantabrigiensis* (Cambridge, 1641). There were other poems written
to the king on this occasion, among them one by Alexander Gill, *Gratulatoria dicata
Serenis. et Potentis. Carolo Regi, e Caledone ad Trinobantes suas reverse* (London,
1641).

[17] *Eucharistica Oxoniensa* (Oxford, 1641).

[18] This book would repay study; taken with the various epitaphs, elegies, and
obsequies for Prince Henry and for the Duke of Buckingham, as well as with those
for Strafford, these poems tell a good deal about the poetry of public events.

[19] Edmund Waller, *A panegyrick to my Lord Protector* (London, 1655); John
Dryden, *Heroick Stanza's, consecrated to the memory of his Highness Oliver, late
Lord Protector of this Commonwealth* (London, 1659); Thomas Sprat, *A Poem to
the happie Memorie of the Most Renouned Prince, Oliver, Lord Protector* (London,
1659).

litical expansion, not, as in Marvell's poem, with a classical-providential power above the reach of "mere" politics. "An Horatian Ode" praises Cromwell, of course, but with a difference: as Mr. Coolidge has pointed out, pure panegyric is absent from the poem; rather at every point the poem indicates the problematics of Cromwell's own situation. First, the hero was not born to heroism; he chose it, and was chosen for it, emerging from his private life ("the Bergamot") to the public stage. His partisan life was not easy; the hero had to "inclose" "the Emulous or Enemy" on his own side, before he could defeat the kingdom's enemies without and, finally, could "cast the Kingdome old/ Into another Mold."

The hero behaves in different ways; in the wars, he was among the bravest; he organized the civilized "chase" by which the King was captured; after that incident, so curiously neutralized in the poem, he turned back to warfare, subduing the Irish and turning to subdue the Scots. This man of Caesarean powers, however, behaves like an idealized Julius Caesar in refusing the crown or its equivalent; obedient to "the *Republick's* hand," he puts aside the possibility of a kingdom, handing over his spoils to the Parliament he served. Combining the powers and virtues of Julius and Augustus Caesar, yet refusing empire, Cromwell simply acts as an agent of the Republic and of the Lord, accomplishing one conquest and undertaking the next. The "return" from victory can hardly be enjoyed by the victorious warrior, who in the poem at least is not presented personally, who unemotionally and "indefatigably" moves from one duty to the next.

In the poem, all this is rendered in providential, if not in predestinarian, terms. Cromwell

> . . . like the three-fork'd Lightning, first
> Breaking the Clouds where it was nurst,
>   Did thorough his own Side
>   His fiery way divide.

As the poet says, " 'Tis Madness to resist or blame" this sort of man, equated with "The force of angry Heaven's flame"; through all the difficulties, he is "The Wars and Fortunes Son," destined to lead the country to its inevitable "*Clymacterick*." But however selected by heaven, war, and fortune, however inexorable his march, Cromwell is foreseen as moving into a future of difficulties and problems; like Milton in his great sonnet to Cromwell, Marvell enjoins him to prolong both his readiness and his courage:

> And for the last effect
> Still keep thy Sword erect:
> Besides the force it has to fright
> The Spirits of the shady Night,
> The same *Arts* that did *gain*
> A *Pow'r* must it *maintain.*

In this passage, as particularly in the "chase" passages also, Mazzeo has seen Marvell's recognition of Oliver's Machiavellianism; a simpler view of these lines is that, in the Puritan sense, always "much remains to conquer still." A "calling" is for a man's remaining lifetime: once having left the bergamot and the private gardens, the public man is committed to public duties, a lifetime of activity, a lifetime of watchfulness. From Horace derives the topic of the problematics of public life, although, as Mr. Wallace has shown, Marvell's way of expressing these matters brings the poem close both to the contemporary political situation and to contemporary political subliterature about it. That is, the general literary problem has been taken specifically in this instance. The minatory tone at beginning and end is Horatian, and Pindaric as well: a victor's morals must be kept in order, as well as his skills.

Interestingly enough, the seriously problematic nature of public life is assimilated in this poem to the professional problems of the poet. Horace affords the most obvious model for this device, but the strenuous metrical and formal exercises of Pindar's odes may owe something to the athleticism of his subjects as well. Marvell's risks in this poem introduce and grade into the tremendous risks of the public figure in general, and the peculiar riskiness of the career of Oliver Cromwell. The note of caution or warning so stressed in this poem carries over from Pindar's cautions to his young victors; Horace translated and heightened this topic in applying it to political victors. The poem is oddly impartial, and even though many explanations have been offered for its being so, the fact remains that for a poem which celebrates a highly controversial figure deliberately to deal with the most unpleasant aspect of the hero's career, his place in the King's execution, and in that episode to deal so favorably with the King, is a remarkable exercise in detachment. The example of Horace has often been noted, another poet given to singular exploits in

66

balance, impartiality, and inclusive justice.[20] Horace's ironies no doubt served Marvell well, in his remarkable qualifications of the greatness of both Cromwell and the King: the poet's recognition of the uniqueness and cruelty of the political situation is part of what allows his even-handed distribution of praise to both antagonists. Though "the Wars and Fortunes Son," Cromwell has been cast into an extraordinarily bitter position, in which no act taken can be without some guilt; the poet cleans the regicide as best he can by the asepsis of his language, but the harsh and bloody fact of the regicide is not shirked in the poem. Charles' "perfect" performance is beautifully praised, but the King's ineptitude, though gracefully put ("That *Charles* himself might chase/ To *Caresbrooks* narrow case"), is also made quite clear. That the capture and death of the King are made to seem formal and ritualized is in part an adaptation of Horatian detachment, in part a borrowing of Pindar's regulated competitive subject, an athletic contest. From the formal aspects of a game, the poet finds much to use: both the King's capture and the battle against the Scots are rendered in terms of hunting. The Irish are, simply, "tam'd." Further, the King undergoes his last ceremonial appearance formally as the "*Royal Actor*" on the "*Tragick Scaffold*"; though it is true that his death did become the subject of tragedies, this poem does not rely on that literary fact. Rather, its poet chooses to present the event in those terms, to praise the King for his performance in a role. Around him, "the armed Bands/Did clap their bloody hands": even the soldiers set to guard the King to his death and to check any public demonstration were so moved by the performance that they applauded it. Lest, though, we forget the significance of the execution, their hands—which, literally, were not so—are called "bloody." Marvell scours the scene clean of the emotions we might expect, and just as the reader has taken in the poet's neutralizing the very controversial and affective event, "bloody" comes to remind of all that its violence meant.

From the Irish, violence is also cleaned away. They confess "How good he is, how just"; Cromwell himself appears as the impersonal instrument of God's providence, returning from his victories modestly and dutifully, innocent of Caesarean ambition to rule in his own right. The extreme impersonality of Cromwell's behavior to Parliament is characteristic of the detachment in the whole poem. At the beginning, the poet tells us, he "must" write another kind of poetry, "must now forsake his *Muses* dear,"

[20] Maddison, *Apollo and the Nine*, p. 34; Coolidge, *passim*.

the private, contemplative, lyric poetry thitherto his choice, for a more heroic style and subject. Like the hero-subject of the poem, the poet is under compulsion; in a brilliant maneuver with generic metaphor,[21]

> Removing from the Wall
> The Corslet of the Hall

he makes the transition from his poetic persona to his subject's action. In this image, expressive of poetic endeavor, a "Virgilian" metaphorical reference to poetic subject and style, the poet begins by referring to his own risks in beginning an ode; but suddenly, the image is literalized, unmetaphored, and we see Cromwell, the country gentleman, issuing from his ancestral home, clad in the ancient family armor with which a gentleman might be expected to emerge into his country's battles.

In this poem, to borrow a phrase from another, both poet and Cromwell have made "their *Destiny* their *Choice*," have been moved as by something other than their own will. They accept their role as their duty. So with the King, captured to be beheaded—or, rather, captured to take the part of a man beheaded, in a play about royal power. The King knows his part, too; behaving beautifully "Upon that memorable Scene," he does not, for instance, speak out of turn, "To vindicate his helpless Right," since, evidently, no such speech was written for him. By such means, the actual violence of the event is gentled, the soldiers becoming an applauding audience of the King's gestures. At the end, he merely

> . . . bow'd his comely Head,
> Down as upon a Bed,

in a simple and domestic image. Indeed, that domesticity is carried over into the poet's language about Cromwell as well, who like a dutiful child brings home his Irish victories, "A *Kingdome*, for his first years rents." The language for that triumph is consistent with the ritual hunting imagery, too: Cromwell is a falcon willingly caught by the falconer, as the bird rests on "the next green Bow" after its kill. No more than that. Thus the poet empties the wild and sanguinary events of 1648-50 of their horror: Cromwell shows no personal rancor or ambition, the King no resentment, the Irish (!) no bitterness after defeat. The agon, undertaken according to the rules of civilized competition and poetry, makes it seem that all the figures in the poem understand their parts and abide by them.

[21] See below, Part III, "The Garden," pp. 146-47, for a fuller discussion of "generic metaphor."

The Pindaric theme of athletic competition becomes, then, a metaphor for politics; Horatian tone and understatement, without any loss of subtle understanding, have neutralized a situation in which passions ran dangerously, and understandably, high. From just this deliberate denaturing of actual events, one may infer Marvell's thorough awareness of the threat to the Republic implicit in Cromwell's success and his power. In this poem, the events of the Interregnum have been given the status of an inexorable and providential play, written for men to act in and to act out. They must "both act and know"; that is, they must take upon them whatever role has been assigned, and must know their parts fully before they appear upon the public scene. Again and again, the poet's insistence upon docility—the King's at his execution, Cromwell's before Parliament—draws attention *away* from the threats implicit in the actions in question. Marvell is not without nostalgia, even real sadness, for what is going on: the King's death, however ritualized in the poem, is an act of violence, and even the benevolent "bleeding Head" that augured well for Rome cannot turn Charles' severed head into an omen unequivocally good. The monarchy was not, surely, for the poet in this poem, politically repugnant, strong Republican though he later became; it had to be "ruined," as the poem acknowledges, but its ruin was all the same "the great Work of Time." Its "ruin" is not allowed to stand alone in the poem, either; "the Kingdome old" must be cast "Into another Mold," into a republic. As Miss Syfret put it, Marvell drew from Horace the language to express his hopes for the Republic, and from Lucan the language to express his fears;[22] even the Republic is seen as problematical within the poem. Indeed, one might hazard the guess that the poet deliberately attempted here as many devices for achieving detachment as he could find, precisely in order to intellectualize catastrophic and violent events naturally difficult to accept or to arrange in some coherent order. His task was to diminish affect, to neutralize legitimate passions, so that, for instance, even the prophetic role open to the ode-writer has been greatly reduced, an invocation at the poem's end the remnant of that role. The last lines, with their injunction and invocation, are formal, detached, impersonal: Cromwell's gesture is part, one is made to feel, of an inexorable process, his indefatigability something superhuman and the gift of God. However "forced" the power he represents and enforces, that power must prevail, as it has hitherto with the King and with Ireland,

---

[22] Syfret, pp. 163, 172.

both of them submitting to inevitability with extraordinary grace. The poem's peculiar slow motion, from the first lines in which poet and country gentleman sally forth together through the stylized regicide and the wars in Ireland and Scotland, adds to that objectified, impersonal inevitability, with which the poem, like its hero, marches on. Impelled and guided by both divine providence and classical fate, Cromwell goes as if by ritual through the motions of his extraordinary and iconoclastic career.

The simplification of the violent events in the poem naturally owes much to literary forms which permitted such neutralization; but all the same, the events are not made unserious thereby. In fact, the ritualization and formalization impart a peculiar mysteriousness to the poem, as if its events were supposed, by their peculiar impulse, to pass our understanding. By simplicity and formality, the poet controls the radically disturbing subject of his poetic occasion; but by his even-handed distribution of praise and blame, he maintains our sense of the huge complexity of both the persons involved and the historical situation in which they find themselves. By stressing what was problematical in his literary form, the poet at the same time succeeds in keeping constantly before us the problematics of his historical subject.

The "Ode" is, then, heavily loaded, more heavily loaded than any comparable public poem of the period, perhaps of any period in English literature. Though it is true that Marvell modeled his ode chiefly on Horace's practice, as Mr. Coolidge has stressed, nonetheless he drew in a single poem from several sorts of Horatian odes; other critics have shown how much else, from other sources, went into the poem. The generic ode-form certainly can bear all this: one does not feel, after reading this poem, that there is no more to be said in the form, as one does after reading the Body-Soul dialogue or the "Coy Mistress" poem, or "The Garden"; but one must doubt that anyone could ever produce another ode so subtle and so grand. The hints of *genera mixta* are present in the poem, as the ode itself moves from private to public to providential preoccupations; we are protected from feeling the possible exhaustion of the form by its faintly-marked frontiers shared with other sorts of verse. *Genera mixta* is no absolute hedge against generic exhaustion, either; one cannot perk up a limp type merely by grafting bits of other types on it. "To his Coy Mistress" and "The Garden" are remarkable because although they scrupulously examine and exhaust the conventions in which they are officially cast, they raise those generic themes to a higher plane by fusing them with the themes, conventions, and implications of other generic forms. Poetry is made richer by the manipulations of its technical elements, because those technical elements point to other associations, other feelings and considerations. Indeed, *genera mixta* requires at least as much skill on the poet's part as a single genre does; even Marvell could fail in his exercises in mixed forms, as "The Nymph complaining" seems to me to fail. But to work in several genres at once translates the technical problems into something else, rises out of specific conventions in a deliberate effort to transcend those conventions. The poet engaged in exercises like these is vulnerable to criticism because he proclaims his professional commitment and his professional daring, because he tries to outdo the limits his profession sets on him.

Part II

Stylistic and Rhetorical Devices

STYLE AND STYLISTICS

THE PLACE conveniently assigned to Andrew Marvell among seventeenth-century poets may be a generalization for the convenience of teachers, but it is also true. He does sum up in his practice most of the major idiosyncratic styles of the period; his work provides traces of the major "schools" of poetry into which late-Renaissance English verse is often divided. He shares something with the metaphysical school, with the classical school, and much with "Miltonic" moral poetry. Marvell is a mediator in lyric style, as in much else: from the *concettismo* of Cleveland and Crashaw to the smoothness of Carew, from the understatement of Herbert to the brilliant emblematism of Vaughan, from the wit of Donne to the metaphysics of Traherne, examples may be found in Marvell's work. As in so many other literary areas, Marvell experimented with stylistic alternatives, and—miraculously—managed in spite of his eclecticism or his virtuosity, his mimicry or his imitativeness, to make a style of them recognizably his own. To the trained ear and eye, Marvell's poems cannot be confounded with the verse of any other of that mob of gentlemen that writ well.

Unquestionably, Marvell's experimentalism led him to play with language and syntax as he played with traditions, conventions, and generic modes. From Mr. Leishman's painstaking examination of Marvell's poetical habits, it is clear that he shared with his literate contemporaries, readers and writers, a common education in the modes and decorum of literary expression; some of these rhetorical and syntactical devices are treated in this section of the book.

In some very obvious ways, Marvell's language clearly "belongs" with Jonson's, in Mr. Winter's and Mr. Trimpi's pious plain-style category;[1] in other ways, equally obvious, it does not. Marvell was given to test-situations, and he tested plain-style writing as he tested decorative and

[1] Yvor Winters, "The Sixteenth Century Lyric in England," *Poetry*, LII-LIV (1939); Wesley Trimpi, *Ben Jonson's Poems. A Study of the Plain Style* (Stanford, 1962); Douglas L. Peterson, *The English Lyric from Wyatt to Donne* (Princeton, 1967).

ornamental styles; he worked with images in all kinds of ways, intellectually as well as sensuously. In "The Definition of Love," for instance, Marvell experiments with the intellectual working-out of imagery in the manner of Donne: he outdoes the geometric imagery of "A Valediction: Forbidding Mourning," in his own poem more fully explored and consistently developed than in Donne's. He manages his argument in terms of remarkable "logical" consequence, as Donne did in "A Valediction: of Weeping." In other poems, he stretched that "untruthful" decorative device, the pastoral hyperbole, beyond its customary bounds, as Mr. Leishman's analogues show us; his games with pastoral are extraordinary, both in content and in style. His antipodeans, tortoises, and hemispheres; his swelling houses and metamorphosing meadows are, perhaps, Clevelandisms, but if so, they are also explorations of the conceited style itself which not only outdo Cleveland's habitual talent, but also demonstrate how even an outrageous conceit can be used to integrate thematic elements of a poem. "The Match" perhaps provides a better example of the conceited style than the imagery of "Upon Appleton House"; there, the major image is extended to absurdity, and the poet is forced to "save" himself by the abrupt simplicity of the last line.

Marvell's range is astonishing. At one end of the scale, the simplicities of such a line, from the "Horatian Ode," occurring amid passages in the grand style

> And, if we would speak true,
> Much to the Man is due.

are the more moving because of the distant, formal, hyperbolical praise which it immediately follows, sums up, and "corrects"; at the other the beautifully elaborate "petrarchan" language of "The Fair Singer" reminds readers of the sheer loveliness of conventional decorative language. To dismiss that poem as "merely" petrarchan is to do it serious injustice, for the middle stanza magnificently demonstrates the harmonizing conventionally introduced in the first stanza, as it twines the artificialities into a careful counterpoint ("dis-intangled," "curled trammels of her hair," "Slave," "subtile Art invisibly can wreath/ My Fetters"), only to resolve them all in the simplest involuntary act of life—"the very Air I breath." As genres were characteristically mixed in this author's work, so are styles. Sometimes language pulls one way and syntax another, as in the pastoral poems, where the plain style and syntax is set against the sense of whole pastoral "myth" made in praise of artefaction and contrivance.

Marvell's ways with imagery vary, and so do his ways with syntax, by no means consistent or programmatic. Mr. Leishman finds Marvell's inversions stilted, careless, and unprofessional, many of them forced by the simple exigencies of rhyme. Marvell's solecisms of this sort (if that is what they are) are less obvious to me than to Mr. Leishman, and furthermore, I find similar usage everywhere in seventeenth-century poetry. It was, I think, by Marvell's time, a little archaic to use "do" and "did" to fill out the metrics of a line, although vernacular usage still sanctions it. Marvell did go in for inversion, though not significantly more than his contemporaries. What is more important than this kind of habit, I think, is the question of obscurity in Marvell's syntax: there, it seems to me, he permitted himself more syntactical ambiguities than most of his contemporaries. Some of these ambiguities may be the result of his strong latinity; he learnt from Ovid, from Virgil, and especially from Horace to hinge two quite different phrases or clauses on a single word. Of this, more below: the trick is connected with Marvell's power to pun.

A glance at a few passages may show some of the anomalies in his practice. His tendency to epigram, for instance, naturally reinforces the tendency toward simple syntax:

> I sup above, and cannot stay
> To bait so long upon the way.

> A Soul that knowes not to presume
> Is Heaven's and its own perfume,

says the Resolved Soul, whom one would expect to speak plainly. The *style*, though, in which Created Pleasure speaks, is no more complex:

> Welcome the Creations Guest,
> Lord of Earth, and Heavens Heir.
> Lay aside that Warlike Crest,
> And of Nature's banquet share:
> Where the Souls of fruits and flow'rs
> Stand prepar'd to heighten yours.

Pleasure is in fact no less epigrammatic, no less plain, than the Soul is:

> Wilt thou all the Glory have
>> That War or Peace commend?
> Half the World shall be thy Slave
>> The other half thy Friend.

The linguistic difference between the two speakers in this dialogue lies not in their syntax, but in their imagery, their terms of argument. Pleasure offers "Nature's banquet," "the Souls of fruits and flow'rs," "downy Pillows," "charming Aires," and so forth, all elements which, even when so simply stated as this, inevitably call up affective sense-associations. Created Pleasure is an Epicurean, but her sentence structure is stoically plain. In "The Coronet," as often remarked, the wreathing, writhing, serpentine complexities of worldliness are expressed in an involuted, gordian syntax made sharply to contrast with the moralizings of the poem's final ten lines, these written in a direct and limpid syntax. In the involuted first sixteen lines, though, there are relatively few figures of speech which cannot in some sense be regarded as dictated by the poet's choice of fictional environment:

> When for the Thorns with which I long, too long,
>> With many a piercing wound,
>> My Saviours head have crown'd,
> I seek with Garlands to redress that Wrong:
>> Through every Garden, every Mead,
> I gather flow'rs (my fruits are only flow'rs)
>> Dismantling all the fragrant Towers
> That once adorn'd my Shepherdesses head.
> And now when I have summ'd up all my store,
>> Thinking (so I my self deceive)
>> So rich a Chaplet thence to weave
> As never yet the king of Glory wore:
>> Alas I find the Serpent old
>> That, twining in his speckled breast,
>> About the flow'rs disguis'd does fold,
>> With wreaths of Fame and Interest.

The poem is written from within the pastoral fiction, as if the poet were in fact a shepherd, in fact gathering flowers. He used to gather flowers to make garlands for his lady love, but now seeks them to make soothing, sacrificial garlands for his God. As he picks the flowers, he finds a snake: Eve, Eurydice, any child has had his experience. So far, everything in the poem is well within possible naturalistic experience, once one has accepted the limits of the pastoral mode. The "pastoralism" is so natural, indeed, that the pastoral images are barely figurative; in this context, oddly enough, the *moral* statement seems the most figurative element—"wreaths of Fame and Interest."

The figures, then, are so naturalized within the pastoral as to lose their figurative power: the poet mocks their cliché quality by taking their fiction literally. Such "unfiguring" and "unmetaphoring" characterizes much of Marvell's practice and is, I think, a function of his critical analysis. He turns back, as it were, to actualize the charged language of poetic traditions.[2] In many ranges of his practice, Marvell tends to unfigure—to "unpun," for instance, in a phrase like "The *Nuns* smooth tongue has suckt her in"; or to literalize metaphor, as in the assumption in "The Garden" that, plants being better than humans, the gods deliberately metamorphosed girls into laurel and rushes; or, to show the transfixing force of mourning and grief, to turn a bereaved girl into a statue. Again and again, he pushes against the devices of his craft to find the literal truth they contain. He cleans them of their conventional metaphorical associations to begin anew. This trick manages at once to maintain the advantages of accrued traditional meaning, the literary "charge" of the device, and to return us to the source of the figure, so that by apparently negating the figurative content, the poet actually enlivens what was so conventional as to be a cliché or near-cliché, forcing the reader to take the conventional image seriously, to give a sharp look at an old custom. In terms of style, the process of unfiguring is very interesting: while it certainly seems to make style "plainer" or "straighter," it also points to the fact that pseudo-plainness, the "poetry of statement," is in fact a form of figure, too, this time an intellectual figure. The area of fictionalization has been removed from the decorative or figurative level to the level of thought and theme. As the poet discusses his intentions in "The Coronet"—to find appropriate flowers and to plait them into appropriate garlands—he makes his unmetaphored figure stand for something made

[2] "Unmetaphoring" seems to me one of the marks of a poet critical of traditions, attempting to see into their meaning some basis in actuality. I have dealt with the subject at considerable length in this book, as well as in my forthcoming study of some formal aspects of Shakespeare's art.

out of metaphors, or makes his figure stand for the writing of poetry. Further, his "garlands" signify the *paragone* between sacred and secular writing, which in its turn is made to stand for the struggle of soul and body, or for the contest between ways of life sacred and secular.

The first sixteen lines of "The Coronet" are written in what Morris Croll[3] has called the loose periodic Attic style: phrases and clauses are crossed and thwarted by other phrases and clauses, the principal verb so delayed as to make us unsure of the parts of speech in the first line. Does the poet also "long" for thorns, or does he long for them for too long a time, or both? What does the verb "seek" govern, "for the Thorns" or "to redress," or both? The sixteen lines are two sentences of eight lines each, both sharply broken up, wedged, and qualified by their various elements, to represent on the one hand a gradually unfolding experience which, as Croll has taught us, so much of the loose grammatical structure of the attic prose seeks to impart; and on the other, to "match" the grammar to the "wreathing" of the subject. The experience itself is, first, one of recoil, of self-deception, of self-deception uncovered; the wreathing syntax can be seen, finally, to conceal the thematic serpent within as well as the serpent we expect to find *in herba* (Fig. 4). Compared to the long sentences of Montaigne's prose, or Browne's, or Donne's, often grammatically very complex, this poetic sentence manages yet another layer of complication, since it achieves the double object of presenting a developing experience as if it were actually taking place, and of criticizing the experience's moral mode. By its syntax alone, this kind of poetic sentence presents and corrects naïveté, the while appearing spontaneous and natural. To achieve such a natural poise, the poet has had to think hard beforehand.

The second part of the poem, ten pentameter lines rhyming aabcdbcdee, manages, like the first part, to do several things at once, but quite different things and by quite different means.

> Ah, foolish Man, that would'st debase with them,
> And mortal Glory, Heavens Diadem!
> But thou who only could'st the Serpent tame,
> Either his slipp'ry knots at once untie,
> And disentangle all his winding Snare:
> Or shatter too with him my curious frame:

[3] Morris Croll, *Style, Rhetoric, and Rhythm* (Princeton, 1966), Essays 2 and 4.

And let these wither, so that he may die,
Though set with Skill and chosen out with Care.
That they, while Thou on both their Spoils dost tread,
May crown thy Feet, that could not crown thy Head.

The sentence structure is clear, often even epigrammatic, more or less what Croll has christened the "curt period." Compared to the first part, metrically and syntactically so much more various, the second part offers a simple and moralizing message. It is not, however, without ambiguity: "my curious Frame," for instance, certainly refers to the garland being made (or, as some have thought, the complicated poem at that moment being written), but may also refer to the poet himself, to his body. "So that he may die" requires "the Serpent" as its antecedent if sense is to be satisfied, but structurally makes us consider "my curious Frame" as a possible antecedent as well. "These" must mean the flowers, the poet's coronet-in-the-making, although no actual antecedent is given us in the grammar. "Both their Spoils" seems to involve the coronets and the serpent's achievements, again with no pure grammatical signature; "Spoils" is a pun, forcing at least two alternative readings of the passage. The relative pronouns alone, often in Marvell's syntax elliptical or hinge-like, produce some of the twining by which the garland-idea is given even grammatical expression.

In this poem, though, the theme relies on the "attic" notion that elegance is deceit; the maxim is, in the poem itself, both illustrated and questioned. Within the conventions of attic-naturalistic, or rambling, syntax, the poet points to his own self-deception, experienced in a mode, the pastoral, officially designed to express sincerity, honesty, and truth. That the involutions of thought can be rendered also in the plainer style of the last ten lines is an example of the poet's virtuosity, of his presenting us with a grammatical "ping" and "pong" in which, nonetheless, the same general message is conveyed.[4] In his involution, the poet first shows the connection between fame and interest, then between sin and salvation, and also manages to disentangle them. That disentanglement does not make for simplicity, however: the poem's garlands, whether sacred or secular, must exist in a world flawed and even upside-down; the garlands, when they are properly made and properly offered, can "crown" only the Saviour's feet, though they were designed to replace the crown

[4] E. H. Gombrich, *Art and Illusion* (London and New York, 1960), pp. 370.

81

of thorns on His head. There is no simplicity in this poem: where the poet might have achieved it, he chose complexity—and this he managed although in mode and in the syntactical contrast, he *seems* to assert simplicity. The conventions of frankness are used, then, to demonstrate the impossibility, in the fallen world, of personal sincerity; the styles officially labelled "sincere" are used to demonstrate complexity, duplicity, and double-dealing. If eloquence is deceit, then here at least the converse is not true. Plain speech has its means to deceit as well as eloquence.

In other places, Marvell can illustrate, and illustrate beautifully, the more conventional literary notion that eloquence is deceit, as the nun's speech to Isabella so magnificently demonstrates in "Upon Appleton House." There, false logic and glozing rhetoric shamelessly conspire in thirteen stanzas of persuasion. Even in this speech, though, a sharp glance at the syntax shows how grammar pulls against imagery as well as against logic and rhetoric. The syntax itself is extremely simple: such ambiguity as exists in the nun's long aria comes from her sly way with images, not from her sentence structure. In the nun's first stanza, there is considerable handy-dandy:

> "Within this holy leisure we
> "Live innocently as you see.
> "These Walls restrain the World without,
> "But hedge our Liberty about."

The last line carries its double meanings; the nun means to say that the cloister's "liberties" are defended by the walls, although the reader, oriented another way, quickly gathers that it is Isabella's liberties that are curtailed by these wicked walls. Later in the poem, Fairfax's garden is turned inside out in something the same way;[5] but the garden (if one may say such a thing about so extravagant a conceit) seems earnestly and actively to be engaged in its offensive and defensive actions, as if it were in fact doing what the nun had claimed for the cloister:

> "These Bars inclose that wider Den
> "Of those wild Creatures, called Men.
> "The Cloyster outward shuts its Gates,
> "And, from us, locks on them the Grates."

> (stanza 13)

[5] See below, pp. 232, 274-75.

The nuns behave oddly: they weep, not from grief but from "Calm Pleasure," or from a needless sort of pity; they are ornamental and think in terms of ornaments—"Our brighter Robes and Crowns of Gold," "*Altar's Ornaments*," "the *Angels* in a Crown . . . the Lillies show'ring down," "for the Clothes, The Sea-born Amber," "Pearls," "Chrystal pure with Cotton warm." Certainly the nun's discourse is extremely sensuous; for all her abhorrence of "those wild Creatures, called Men," one feels the sensuality of her imagination. Her similes are ostentatiously "ornamental," in the pejorative sense of stylistic purists such as Mr. Winters, because she speaks in terms of adornments and decorations—but she does so in a syntax of remarkable plainness. Her couplets have a claim upon that epigrammatic neatness characteristic of the plain style, although again and again her sentences turn out to have their own enigmas, their own puzzles and tricks of compression:

> "What need is here of Man? unless
> "These as sweet Sins we should confess."
>
> (stanza 23)

One must think hard about what this means: that a man is needed only because a priest can hear confessions, and a priest can only be a man; but also, the nun implies that her cloister has no need for confession itself, since these are the only things they do which might be construed as confessable sins. From the syntax, "these" appear to be the conserving of cool jellies, the preparation of sachets, occupations called "sweet" because of the taste and odor of the things worked on; in the nun's mind, such things can be regarded as sinful only by the most puritanical standards. She banters, of course, not only with confession but with sin and virtue as well: anyone who says that such things are the worst "sins" of which she is guilty is self-evidently guilty of self-deception, at least.

"These as sweet sins" is also an example of the literalizing of figure. By strict standards of convental behavior, all this sweet-making for a proudly proclaimed "Delight" and "Pleasure" is improper; the nun's ironical tone, designed to make fun of puritanical critics of their life, turns back on her in an enveloping irony shared by writer and reader. By calling a spade a spade, the poet manages to suggest that it is in fact, in the nun's mind, something quite different; again, Marvell experiments, in quite a different way from that of "The Coronet," with the deceits possible in plain speech. By the nun's way of speaking, we are led to suspect the truth of her argument.

These games with plain speech, or with one kind of plain speech overlaid by another kind of speech far less plain, force us back to Marvell's curious ways with language. He was able to adjust language in many ways: in "On a Drop of Dew," he managed to "elevate" the second half of his poem by the simple device of making the rhyme scheme more regular (a modification of Herbert's trick in "The Altar"). In "Clorinda and Damon," he demonstrates the agon by breaking up the lines, so that the speakers cannot speak whole couplets as they debate their positions. The poet only allows them to return to full lines when they reach agreement and find the moral solution to their problem, thus "solving" the poem as well.

Marvell was a poet of enormous precision; his vocabulary is remarkably exact, and in his short lines, he manages to honor sense, metrics, and subtlety in a way few poets in English have. By his very exactness, the limitations upon language he accepts and sets, he often points to linguistic duplicity. The trick of unmetaphoring is allied to this: Marvell directs attention at once to the absurdity and the reality of figure itself, relinquishing neither the one nor the other, insisting that readers experience anew not only the highly figurative nature of poetic language, but the figurative nature of all language. His strong sense of etymology ("fetters/feet," "manacled/hands," *acies* as both "glance" and "edge") brings to a focus his concern for the manifoldness of single words: he seems to have understood the historical and psychological connotations surrounding the official denotations of any given word, and to have set himself to exploration of the problem. Though he so often rejects a conventional phrase, a conventional association, a conventional theme, he does not do so, I think, so much out of repugnance for its "untruthfulness," as some simplifying critics would have it, as out of a desire to understand the reasons for the convention. So he redefines figures, or transfers a figure or device from its customary range to another; because he thinks so much about figures, he gives us, literally, figures of thought, figures for thinking about.

An element of Marvell's style, now much discussed in the critical literature, is his *argutia, acutezza,* sharpness of image and conceit, recently defined as a major element of the metaphysical style.[6] Obviously, one way

[6] For some discussion of this, see J. A. Mazzeo, *Renaissance* and *Seventeenth-Century Studies* (New York, 1964), pp. 29-59.

to achieve sharpness is grammatical, in the "curt period" of epigram, which may be either extremely clear or, though verbally extremely precise, ambiguous by reason of that conciseness. Syntactical hooking is another means of compressing two things into one, chiefly accomplished by hinge-words, or link-words; that is, by the use of a single word bearing a different relation to its dependent grammatical units. "Nip in the blossome all our Hopes, and Thee," for instance, in "Little T.C.," would not escape the freshman-English teacher's red pencil, sinning as it does against parallelism; Marvell's use of relative pronouns with no absolute antecedent has been referred to. The "their" and "these" of "The Coronet" are cases in point; "Whose Columnes," in the first stanza of "Upon Appleton House," is a syntactical pivot, "whose" referring both to "a Model" and to the "Forrain *Architect*," who in turn appears as both "that" and "who" in otherwise parallel relative clauses. In stanza 10 of that poem, the last word of the first couplet requires some search to be properly attached to its antecedents; "Frontispiece," "Furniture," "House," and "Inn" all recommend themselves.

> Him *Bishops-Hill*, or *Denton* may,
> Or *Bilbrough*, better hold then they:

this couplet is noticeably vernacular, informal, awkward, with Bilbrough as it were added late to the list. Its informality may make it seem natural, but it does not noticeably clarify meaning. "Him" is Fairfax, or, more exactly, "Its *Lord*," of stanza 9. Since the last line of that stanza—"Its *Lord* a while, but not remain"—recoils to deal with the quality of the house, not of Fairfax, the "Him" by which the next stanza must be hooked to "Its *Lord*" is odd: the sense seems to be shifted once again in yet another direction. In stanza 62, the relative pronoun joins two different grammatical and referential elements: the heroes of the families of Vere and Fairfax and the oaks of Appleton's wood, which are fused into a single image:

> Of whom though many fell in War,
> Yet more to Heaven shooting are:

The first line seems to refer to soldiers, since trees do not customarily go to war; the second plays on "shooting" to return to the notion of trees, which certainly are the "they" of the next couplet, governing both verbs.

At other times, pronouns are ambiguous: in "An Horatian Ode," the lines

> Did thorough his own Side
> His fiery way divide,

have never been glossed to everyone's satisfaction. Did Cromwell like the lightning break through *himself*, or through his group of partisans? Later, in the lines

> And *Caesars* head at last
> Did thorough his Laurels blast,

it is not altogether clear who is Caesar—the King, as monarch in some sense a "Caesar," whose "head" somehow makes Cromwell's wreath imperfect; or Cromwell properly crowned by the laurel. Still later in that poem, we come upon graver difficulties with "he," who becomes "the Royal Actor," Charles I. "He" can be no one else:

> *He* nothing common did or mean
> Upon that memorable Scene:

but the strict antecedent is lines away. In "An Horatian Ode" in general, one comes up against shifts in point of view which Croll regards as typical of a style he finally (confusingly) labelled "baroque," and which Leo Spitzer has called "perspectivism." An example is this famous passage:

> Then burning through the Air he went,
> And Pallaces and Temples rent:
> And *Caesars* head at last
> Did thorough his Laurels blast.
> 'Tis Madness to resist or blame
> The force of angry Heavens flame:
> And, if we would speak true,
> Much to the Man is due.

The "he" of the first two lines is certainly Cromwell, and the "his" of the fourth probably also; the fifth and sixth lines turn into a moral axiom, spoken in a different tone and breaking the speed of the narrative thitherto; in turn, this modulates into a pair of lines assuming great intimacy between writer and reader, thoroughly in each other's confidence. The passage moves from highly formalized and hyperbolical ritual action to extraordinary vernacular, as for the reader's private ear the poet were willing to drop his official heroics for an honest assessment of a situation obviously very difficult for both reader and writer to judge.

Indeed, much of this poem's difficulty lies in its presentation of the *situation*'s difficulties: Charles is a true king, like Richard II. Cromwell, like Bolingbroke, is a true ruler. One way in which the problematical situation is kept so problematical is by the shifts in point of view through the poem; the speaker shifts his own point of view, now speaking as if divinely appointed to characterize events, now probing them and testing them, revising his judgments on historical events, revising his rhetorical perspectives upon his subject. Perhaps the regular shift from tetrameter to trimeter encourages rapid shifts of other kinds. In the four lines

> Nor call'd the *Gods* with vulgar spight
> To vindicate his helpless Right,
>> But bow'd his comely Head,
>> Down as upon a Bed.

for instance, the public and political vocabulary of the first pair of lines alters into domestic privacy; public exhortation gives way to private prayer, as the head is "bow'd" in ritual submission. In another place, the moralized objective description of a falcon's typical behavior, given in a rather stiff syntax

> She, having kill'd, no more does search,
> But on the next green Bow to pearch;

changes into colloquialism as the falcon is recaptured, quite naturally: "The Falckner has her sure."

One can interpret the syntactical and tonal shifts of the "Ode" in terms of its problematical subject; tonal shifts have many other effects in Marvell's poetry, too. In "The Nymph complaining," for instance, the girl's innocence is in part communicated by the childishness of some of her sentences:

> I'me sure I never wisht them ill;
> Nor do I for all this; nor will:

> . . . nay and I know
> What he said then; I'me sure I do.

> And when 'thad left me far away,
> 'Twould stay, and run again, and stay.

> O help! O help! I see it faint:

> O do not run too fast. . . .

Against this naïveté are set other stylistic elements which call into question the speaker's attitude to the Nymph's innocence, the place of such innocence in the world, even in the sheltered world she creates for herself. Occasionally a single word, rare in poetry (in this case rare even in technical usage), breaks upon the fiction of innocence to make clear how the speaker manipulates the little nymph. "Deodands" is such a word, clean out of the girl's possible vocabulary. In quite another way, the sophisticated caesural variation gives away the poet's experienced detachment, so much greater than the girl's:

> Ungentle men! They cannot thrive
> To kill thee. Thou neer didst alive
> Them any harm: alas nor cou'd
> Thy death yet do them any good.

The word order manages to suggest the girl's unpremeditated sorrow, its twisted grammar the "attic" result of her sincerity and spontaneity; at the same time, the word order stresses the exigencies of meter and rhyme, perforce altering the normal speaking order in obedience, not to the girl's spontaneity, but to a prior contract between the poet and his work of art. In the word "alive" especially, rhyme manages to shift stress so that meaning is refreshed, as also in the couplet

> There is not such another in
> The World, to offer for their Sin.

The stress on the word "in"—which makes the object of that insignificant preposition, "the World," so much more important just *because* of the unimportance of "in"—is not, I think, accidental: ending the line on "in," which then rhymes with the important word "Sin," shows the girl's naïveté in the very unpoetical quality of the couplet. One could go on, to the substance of the couplet: the fact that so many people have read the white fawn as a figure for Christ is an indication, it seems to me, of their mis-reading the Nymph's utterance for the poet's. What is sad, if sweet, about her bereavement is that she expresses it in terms which ought to be reserved for the Saviour.[6a]

In this poem, point of view is established in very simple ways. The nymph refers everything to herself: we start with a description of an

---

[6a] In reference to this, Hartman's interpretation of the poem, in particular of the fawn (*Essays in Criticism*, 1968), not only ignores the tonal implications of the nymph's and the speaker's voices, but also radically reinterprets both the structure and the function of the Trinity.

event, the death of the little animal, which remains unmotivated, described only by the word "wanton." The girl cannot and does not conceive of any reason for killing casually; it never occurs to her to analyze either behavior or motive. Like a child, she reacts to events as they take place, looking neither before nor after. We must infer the troopers' motives, or habits, as we must infer Sylvio's: their acts are inconceivable in the nymph's world, even though they happen into that world, and she does not attempt to consider *why* such acts take place. The peculiarly distant narrative objectivity with which the poem begins shifts, as we read, to something else: the nymph's overriding effort to express her feelings. What might have gone into analysis is all used up in merely speaking out of her tumultuous state of mind; only her own feelings can command her attention. The first person pronoun clusters in lines 7-12, as in other sections of the poem (e.g., lines 26-30, 44-48, 60-61), to demonstrate the innocent welling-up of her young ego. It is worth noting that where there are several "I's," this word is not always metrically stressed, though it normally is:

> But I am sure, for ought that I
> Could in so short a time espie,
>
>   I have a Garden of my own,
> But so with Roses over grown,
> And Lillies, . . .
>
> Among the beds of Lillyes, I
> Have sought it oft, where it should lye; . . .
>
>   I in a golden Vial will
> Keep these two crystal Tears; and fill
> It till it do o'reflow with mine;
>
> O do not run too fast: for I
> Will but bespeak thy Grave, and dye.
>
> For I so truly thee bemoane,
> That I shall weep though I be Stone:
>
> For I would have thine Image be
> White as I can, though not as Thee.

The effect of all this is certainly to show the narrowly confined emotional vision of the nymph, myopically self-regarding; her garden and her pet are, in the end, projections of herself and her own strongly aesthetic needs. She is as candid as her own preference for whiteness; but this endearing candor, so openly expressed, is limited by her total failure to conceive of more complicated motives than those she can identify in herself. Again, a simple rhetoric, delicately varied, points to simplistic self-concern; or, points to the fact that plain speech is no guarantee of self-understanding.

Two points of comparison immediately offer themselves: the one, Damon's speech on himself, a set-piece encased within what seems the poet's objective view of the total Damon-world; the other, the use of the first person pronoun in "The Garden." In "Damon the Mower," the first-personal words are often in stressed position:

> Tell me where I may pass the Fires . . .

> To what cool Cave shall I descend,

> I am the Mower *Damon*, known
> Through all the Meadows I have mown.
> On me the Morn her dew distills. . . .

> This Sithe of mine . . .

> Yet am I richer far in Hay.

As in "The Nymph complaining," where several first-person pronouns cluster, the pronoun here does not need always to stand in stressed position; the egocentric point is made by frequency rather than by stress.

In "The Garden," the word "I" is never in stressed position, and occurs in only three stanzas of the nine (2, 3, 5). One result of this is, I think, to emphasize the retired literary place of this speaker. In stanza 6, the most famous stanza of the poem, "I" does not appear; "the Mind" is the subject of the sentence as of the stanza. In stanza 7, "my Soul," liberated from "the Bodies Vest," is called "it," and referred to as if the poet's personality were not identified with that soul, but rather remained in the "vest," temporarily left on the ground. The detachments of both modes of ecstasy, then, are faithfully rendered in the language. Part of the coolness of "The Garden" lies in this curious detachment of the speaker from "himself," as in "The Nymph complaining" and "The unfortunate Lover," the coolness derives from the detachment between speaker and suffering subject.

In "Upon Appleton House," the nun's speech, so often exploited in this book, serves to illustrate something else in Marvell's verse, the manipulations of pseudo-logic. As Croll puts it, there are many conjunctions with no logical *plus*-force, which simply reinforce a statement or idea with several examples or variants. Sometimes the elements of the argument are arranged in logical sequence, the conclusions effected by tense-indications:

> "Your voice, the sweetest of the Quire,
> "Shall draw *Heav'n* nearer, raise us higher.
> "And your Example, if our Head,
> "Will soon us to perfection lead.
> "Those Virtues to us all so dear,
> "Will straight grow Sanctity when here:
> "And that, once sprung, increase so fast
> "Till Miracles it work at last."
>
> (stanza 21)

At other times, the semblance of logic is given to alogical statements by means of conjunctions: "For," "unless," "Yet," "But." In stanza 25, the odd repetitiousness of "but" in two entirely different grammatical uses sets the teeth on edge:

> "But what is this to all the store
> "Of Joys you see, and may make more!
> "Try but a while, if you be wise:

A more famous example is a couplet (in stanza 71) from the wood-episode in "Upon Appleton House":

> Or turn me but, and you shall see
> I was but an inverted Tree.

The reader's attention is caught by the solecism, but somehow not altogether displeased with it: the doubling of "but" increases the peculiar contrary-to-factness of the fancy, operating grammatically to qualify the statement, as in quite a different range of literary language, the double-inversion ("Antipodes" etc.) in the last stanza serves to stress upside-downness and also to deny it.

The nun of course uses pseudo-logical conjunctions to weave her fragile dialectic into a net to catch the coney Isabel: a semblance of, or substitution for, logical construction recurs throughout Marvell's poetry, in many places where deception is not the aim. "The Definition of Love" has "And yet," "For," "And therefore," "Unless," "As," "But," and "Therefore"; "To His Coy Mistress," "Had we," "We would," "For," "But," "Now therefore," and "Thus." In "The Garden," the careful progression of points is not marked by such traffic signals of logic;[7] the method of hiatus in that poem leaps over official connective and conjunction, to permit us only at the end to see how "logically," or anthologically, a series of tableaux, exemplifying alternative modes of perception, has been offered us, in strict progression of the soul's ascent and return. In "Upon Appleton House," the pseudo-logical conjunctions—especially "but" (st. 3, 4, 10, 29, 32, 33, 34, 36, 40, 41, 43, 44, 45, 46, 47, 48, 51, 61, 65, 66, 68, 69, 70, 71, 78, 82, 86, 88, 89, 90, 91, 95, 96, 97), "For," "Yet," "Therefore," "So," and "Thus"—are sprinkled across the poem, making another connective net to hold together its thrashing elements.

That the conjunctions express connections made on the basis of perception and emotion, rather than on the basis of logic, is really irrelevant, is an example of Marvell's peculiar translation of ideas and philosophical structures into purely poetical terms. If anything, this "false" net of connectives is another pointer to the instability and disruption stressed throughout the poem; here, logical expectations remain unfulfilled, although the pseudo-logical words have a connective value of their own. Translation of the expressive language of one discipline—in this case, logic—into the language of poetry is consistent with Marvell's general attitude of experimentation; in the case of "Upon Appleton House," this pseudo-logical linguistic experiment is parallel to many different kinds of experiment and expression of problematics. In this particular case, logic was simply one conventional range of expression which he distorted from its traditional function to serve poetic purposes of his own.

One of Marvell's characteristic habits was to shift the grammatical position of a word so that one sentence or one line must be read in two quite different ways; his sleight-of-hand with relative pronouns is one conspicuous example of this maneuver. " 'Tis not, what once it was, the World" presents a problem of paraphrase;[8] so does, in "Upon Appleton House,"

> Dark all without it knits; within
> It opens passable and thin;

(stanza 64)

[7] See J. V. Cunningham, *Tradition and Poetic Structure* (Denver, 1960), pp. 40-58.
[8] Berger, "Marvell's 'Upon Appleton House.' "

What part of speech is "without"? And, related to that, the first "it"? In both cases, the wood turns out to be "it"—that is, the wood knits, and the wood opens; but "Dark" too makes its claim to be taken, for a moment at least, as the subject, not the object, of "knits." "Dark all without," furthermore, seems to be parallel to "the Night within" of the preceding line (at the end of the preceding stanza), so that one expects a guide from stanza to stanza which in fact turns out not to exist. The grammatical trick effects not a connective but a reversal; we discover that the "Night within" will become the light of the wood's "passable and thin" interior. Sometimes grammatical ambiguities are not important: it would be foolish to argue for deep significance in each and every syntactical oddity in Marvell's verse, some of which must be the result of simple carelessness on the poet's part, or the proofreader's, or of the state of the manuscript posthumously published. Furthermore, the images of the former world as chaos and of the wood are clear, even if the syntax is not. Nor does it much matter whether the poet speaks of three different flowers or of two different colors in the line "That of the Tulip Pinke and Rose"; with or without commas, the line makes sense.

"Nip in the blossome all our hopes and Thee" plays with degrees of metaphor as well as with "nip" as a syntactical pivot: the line begins as a cliché, and gains power as we realize that T.C. is taken, throughout the poem, as a "flower," and that both girl and flowers are symbols of transience. A simpler example of a grammatical pivot is the line in "Tom May's Death," "By this *May* to himself and them was come," another striking failure of parallelism which allows a rather doggerel wit, fitting the kind of inferior accomplishment Marvell attributes to May. Such grammatical pivots are often in effect puns: "sound" in "And not of one the bottom sound," from "Mourning." In the line "Since this ill Spirit it possest," of the "Dialogue," there are several double meanings (ill, Spirit, possest) to make this one of the most notionally complicated lines of all Marvell's verse. "It" is either the subject or the object of "possest"; by either reading, the line makes sense.

Marvell's puns are difficult to avoid discussing. Sometimes a grammatical pivot is indistinguishable from a pun; sometimes a quibble focuses several meanings in a single word—and, in "The Garden," a series of puns seems to keep alive a consistent series of different meanings;[9] sometimes the poet "unpuns," as he unfigures and unmetaphors. Frequently

[9] See below, pp. 147-51.

there is a late resonance to his double meanings: their implications follow at some distance from the words themselves. "Fly from their Ruine," in "Upon Appleton House," stanza 28, is such a phrase: the nun's plan would "ruin" Isabella; the nunnery ultimately becomes a "ruin" on the estate. "*Virgin Buildings* oft brought forth" seems to make a figure about the provenance of the new Appleton House from the stones of the old; only later do we realize that Marvell was getting his licks in at the Roman Church. Still later, we realize the thematic connection between this remark, about the Cistercian nunnery, and the swelling house honoring its master and designer. "A Dialogue between the Soul and Body" plays on "possest"; "Upon Appleton House" plays on "dispossest." "Dispensed" is a quibble, as is "imbark"—and so on, and on. Sometimes a pun echoes another denotation, as in the questionable "quaint" of "To his Coy Mistress" or "The Scales of either Eye" in "Eyes and Tears." Occasionally Marvell may have made a mistake, so to speak, suggesting a double meaning not actually present, as in the word "scale" in the line "And Fishes do the Stables scale," from "Upon Appleton House."

Sometimes a play on a word extends a figure, or a common locution, as in stanza 40 of "Upon Appleton House," where the "guard stars" around the North Star are called "the vigilant *Patroul*/ Of Stars [that] walks round about the Pole"; or in "Eyes and Tears," where the word "captivating" leads the poet to his figure of the Magdalene's tears as "liquid Chaines." These chains "fetter her Redeemers feet"—that is, they captivate, or make captive. In "A Dialogue between the Soul and Body," the fetters-feet, manacled-hands plays extend the notion in "Eyes and Tears," exploring etymology to end in unpunning. The metaphorical meanings are collapsed back into their literal origin: so Damon "discovers" the meadows as he strips them of their protective grass, or the nun's tongue "suckt" Isabella in. In the "Horatian Ode," the sense of *pictus*, painted, in "Pict" may have suggested the word "party-colour'd" for Scots. Because of their tartans, of course, and their outspoken political partisanship, "party-colour'd" is an apt pun even without the notion of "pictus." The tortoises are encased "In cases fit of Tortoise shell": that is, of their natural condition, a metaphor seems to be made, although in fact the poet tautologically describes their shells. Nonetheless, because of his wording, which applies to the artificial cases for other things made of tortoiseshell, he succeeds in confounding for a moment the natural with the artificial world. By these means, the process of metaphor is exposed to the reader's examination; we see how metaphors are made.

There are anomalies in this practice, too, as I need hardly say—the poet who can do so many different things, can so maneuver styles of diction, syntax, and imagery, who can so manipulate persona and tone, obviously chooses to be associated or connected with no one style, no one school of verse. A reader might be forgiven for assuming that Marvell donned and doffed styles as if they were garments hanging ready for him; for assuming, perhaps, with a school of modern American stylistic critics distinguished for their own stylishness, that all there is to Marvell's verse is its capacity to assume styles. For such critics, the style of a literary work—its language, its tone—is its whole substance. "Style" is simply—or complexly—a shimmering screen on which an illusory reality is made to appear, is, indeed, the only reality attributable to a work of art. Certainly in a crude sense, this is always so—in a literary work, all we have is words, those chosen and those not chosen, separated by intervals of silence, by intervals of space. There was no Anna Karenina, no Hamlet; still less was there a Nymph or Maria, as the poet conceives her in his poem. Art *is* illusion. But some illusions are more illusory than others; or some illusions direct us at once to considerations of reality (Rembrandt, Goya, Cézanne) even when they are "about" illusion, inevitably constructed of materials and conventions having nothing specific to do with the "reality" to which the painters seem to point.[10] We know what "betrayal" means from Rembrandt's "Saint Peter" in the Rijksmuseum although the trick with the maidservant's candle is technically *chic* beyond measure—the technical trick does not detract from but rather manages to enhance the moral meaning of the painting. We know what gratuitous violence "means" from Goya's pictures of the French wars, what rocks are, in all their hardness, from Cézanne's extremely stylized geology. In Marvell's "style," both the precision of some of his images—the Nymph's garden, say, or the emblematic environment of the unfortunate Lover—and the diaphanousness of others (in particular, the middle stanzas of "The Garden") relate to a context of ideas, even of morality, to which they unmistakably direct the reader. The "concreteness" of these ideas and impressions, the concreteness, then, of the most elusive elements of our life, forces

[10] Sigurd Burckhardt, "The Poet as Fool and Priest," *ELH*, XXIII (1956), pp. 279-98.

us through sensory perception to intellectual perception. We are set to think about the range, even about the decorum, within the conscious concept of style; we are asked to consider the reasons for style, and for choosing any particular aspect of style over any other. Even at the level of individual words—"Deodands," "Corslet," "green"—Marvell acts as critic of his poetic materials, reexamining the elements which make up style and asking us, as critical readers, to examine them too. The poet-as-critic forces the job of criticism upon his readers, involves his readers inextricably in his own professional problems.

❦{ 2 }❧

FIGURES OF SPEECH

M<small>R. LEISHMAN</small>'s book demonstrates beyond question what Marvell had in common with his contemporaries: a good classical education, a store of rhetorical commonplaces deriving from antiquity and enlarged in the Renaissance, a lively professional interest in the technical possibilities of verse and of poetry. Like more poets than we realize, perhaps, Marvell used his stock of images with considerable economy, even, one occasionally thinks, niggardliness. A figure is likely to occur more than once in his work, adapted to different needs; some tendencies in his use of figure can be identified. His language often naturalizes the artificial or artificializes the natural; he tends to pastoralize or, at least, to psychologize, nature; he tends to use old figures with an arch novelty. His references to classical myth and story are, relative to the work of contemporaries writing roughly the same kind of verse, sparse; in this respect particularly his work differs from that of the French *libertin* poets to whom he has so often been compared. One remembers "the brotherless *Heliades*," Apollo and Pan hunting their vegetable loves, Danae, Narcissus, Alexander, but there is little else directly drawn from handbooks of classical myth. Many of Marvell's references are perfectly standard: perfume, ambergris, amber tears, trees, blossoms form a familiar sequence; others seem strikingly "invented": "Caesarean Section," "Shipwrackt into Health," "*Antipodes* in Shoes," "*Amphibium* of Life and Death." Sometimes the sequences of images can be matched in other poets' works—the clouds, fountains, floods of "Eyes and Tears," for instance, occur in many "tear-poems"—but the same language is less frequently applied to drops of dew. Another cluster, as in "Musicks Empire," seems the poet's own *trouvaille*, as he presents in musical terms the social generations of natural law, from solitude to cities, from virgins to "Progeny," thence to "Colonies" and finally to "Empire," requiring all the stages of human development for its validation. The notion is clever, but as Mr. Hollander's book indicates,[1] it relies on a very

---

[1] Hollander, pp. 309-15; for an interesting discussion of Marvell's imagery, see Klaus Hofman, *Das Bild in Andrew Marvell's lyrischen Gedichten* (Heidelberg, 1967).

97

old cliché that music has power to organize human passions and human lives. This is not Marvell's only use of the notion; he exploited it again, of course with a difference, in his "The First Anniversary of the Government under O.C.," where the extended simile occurs, its elements in much the same order, but with Cromwell as the composer-musician of the forming state. This comparison, in a poem of clear and unequivocal praise, is lightened from time to time by puns, such as the one on the "Instrument of Government" of 1653:

> Such was that wondrous Order and Consent.
> When *Cromwell* tun'd the ruling Instrument;

In "The First Anniversary," Cromwell's musical powers raise a state, this state given in architectural terms, as "No Note he struck, but a new Story lay'd," and "the *Theban* Tow'r arose," as well as "a Palace" and "Temples." Often the uses to which the same figure is put vary more radically than in the last example: the Body complains of architects who "square and hew/Green Trees that in the Forest grew"; but Fairfax as an architect (and an architect notably devoted to trees)[2] is praised without question for his accomplishments in building and in forestry. Trees, of course, occupy an important position in Marvell's poetry:[3] the Body loves nature, and likens itself to a green tree; the poet in "Hortus" and "The Garden" recoils from the notion of defacing trees with the names of girls, however much they are beloved; in "Upon the Hill and Grove at Bill-borow," as in "Upon Appleton House," the trees stand for the union of Fairfax and Vere. In "Upon the Hill and Grove," Lady Fairfax's name is written on the trees, not by her husband's doing, but by the trees themselves, who wish to bear her name. In both poems, the Fairfax trees manage to "shoot to Heaven" and at the same time to rest content with their limited stature on earth. Like the trees the Body approved of, those on Bilbrough Hill are "streight and green"; but unlike the trees of "The Garden," debased by ladies' names written in their bark, they spontaneously produce on their bark the name of a true nymph. In "A Poem upon the Death of O.C.," the sacred oak, which in "Upon Appleton House" had been an emblematic equivalent to a falling figure of greatness, falls

---

[2] Cf. Brian Fairfax, "The Vocall Oak." For a criticism of "squaring" and "hewing," see Seneca, *Ep. mor.* xc.

[3] Those who consider Marvell's "vegetable" preoccupation psychologically telling should consider Abraham Cowley's exceptionally large poetic output on the subject of plants.

heavily at Cromwell's death: the oak had been the Protector. The tainted oak at Nunappleton had seemed to fall painlessly, almost willingly; by contrast, the Cromwellian oak goes down very hard:

> (It groanes, and bruises all below that stood
> So many yeares the shelter of the wood.)

Fallen, though, it is even more impressive than when it had stood straight:

> The tree ere while foreshortned to our view,
> When fall'n shews taller yet than as it grew:

That is, Cromwell's fallen tree could be measured at last and its greatness taken. It is difficult not to compare this image with that of the stage-prop oak the hewel brought down by his "tinckling."

"Daphnis and Chloe" plays with another conceit of lopping, this time with beheading. Daphnis leaves Chloe only after long preparation:

> As who long has praying ly'n,
> To his Heads-man makes the Sign,
> And receives the parting stroke.

In "Daphnis and Chloe," the beheading is metaphorical; in "An Horatian Ode," of course, it is all too real. The execution image in the first instance is designed to show the violence of Daphnis' behavior and his conception of love; for the King, the poet softens the actual blow, until the subject simply

> . . . bow'd his comely Head,
> Down as upon a Bed.

Such horror as is allowed to remain in "that memorable Scene" is transferred from Charles' neatly subsiding head to the "bleeding Head" found on the Capitol at the foundation of the temple in Rome, a head interpreted as a sign benevolent to the Republic.

Marvell's "fetters" are famous. He plays generally with ideas of entanglement, in "The Fair Singer" (hair, voice); in "The Coronet" (wreaths of fame and interest); in "The Garden," stanza 5, and in "Upon Appleton House," in the wood-scene. In "Eyes and Tears," the notion led to the "fettering" by the captivating Magdalene of her Saviour's feet, evidently with the chains of her tears, perhaps also with her hair; in "A Dialogue between the Soul and Body," the unpunning of "fetters" and "feet" reaches the extreme of possibility. All these plays have a family resemblance: one can conceive of the poet continually working his variations on the metaphor.

Other metaphors occur in different places, too; the divers dive in "Mourning" and dive again in the meadows at Nunappleton; the tears bend upward in "Mourning," and the drop of dew does the same thing in its poem. "Upon Appleton House" collects and recapitulates many themes and figures used, more scantily, in other poems or touches lightly on themes and images more highly developed in a shorter poem. The garden enclosed of "The Nymph complaining," the earthly paradise of "Bermudas," the ecstatic landscape of "The Garden" itself are all present in "Upon Appleton House"; so are the mowers and the grass of the eclogues, the halcyon of "The Gallery," as well as the quails and manna of that poem and the manna of "On a Drop of Dew," the "hemisphere" of the Bilbrough poem, the geometry of that poem and of "The Definition of Love." Like "The unfortunate Lover," "Upon Appleton House" has its masques; like "An Horatian Ode," its "scenes"; like "Musicks Empire" its "mosaique"; like Bilbrough Hill, the Nunappleton estate is a model for the world. The nightingale studies in "The Mower to the Glo-worms" and is instructed in "Upon Appleton House"; tears seem pregnant in "Eyes and Tears," the house in "Upon Appleton House." Heraldry marks "Clorinda and Damon," and memorially closes "The unfortunate Lover," as well as "The Mower's Song." Again and again, indeed, the poems end on a work of art, stiffen into heraldry or sculpture —"The Nymph" is the most striking example, and Clora of course is fixed into one of her portraits at the end of "The Gallery." The statues of "The Mower against Gardens" have a place within the poem, as has the contrived flower-dial of "The Garden."

Other forms of art have the fixative ecphrastic effect, of which Murray Krieger has written;[4] for example, the formal songs ending the Resolved Soul dialogue and "Clorinda and Damon," as well as the liturgical hallelujah of "Musicks Empire," all signalling art's transcendence over time. In both "Bermudas" and "Damon the Mower," work is performed to the rhythm of a song; the same relation between work and imagination, or

---

[4] I borrow the term, as well as the interest in the problem, from Murray Krieger, "The Ekphrastic Principle and the Still Movement of Poetry," in *The Play and Place of Criticism* (Baltimore, 1967). See also Rensselaer W. Lee, "*Ut Pictura Poesis*: The Humanistic Theory of Painting," *Art Bulletin*, XXI (1940), 197-269; Jean H. Hagstrum, *The Sister Arts* (Chicago, 1958); and my *Paradoxia Epidemica* (Princeton, 1966), pp. 273-99.

between *negotium* and imaginative *otium*, is suggested in the bee-figure in "The Garden," where the living, moving bee animates and recreates from the perfection of the zodiacal garden. Tears soften hearts in "Mourning," and wear away stone in "The Nymph"; in the cloister of Nunappleton, tears merely clear complexions—as, in fact, they do in "Mourning" too. Whether in a trivial worldly context or a spiritual one, Marvell's tears must be closely examined to see what they imply.

Sometimes a figure shifts from one usage to another: the divers in "Mourning" do not "sound" the bottom of a lady's tears; the divers in "Upon Appleton House" cannot sound something more significant: that is, themselves and their environment, not just the depth of a "dive." As they "fall" or "go" through the "unfathomable grass," the Nunappleton divers experience the problem which the poet poses throughout the whole poem; they and their action demonstrate that unknowing which is the poem's principal condition. One could go on and on: little T.C. is, like Mary Fairfax, a slightly stern virgin, and both girls are destined to present problems to glib lovers. Little T.C. lies "in the green Grass" as she names and tames the "wilder flow'rs"; evidently in her "naming magic," she has something of the *logos'* power over nature, as has Mary Fairfax, young mistress of "Heavens Dialect." T.C.'s indolent admirer, the poet, watches her from the safety of the "shades"; the many meanings of that wonderful word throng "The Garden," and the shade in the Appleton wood is important, too. "Sliding foot" offers a pretty play on a Latin cliché: a river *labitur*, glides with regular pace. This phrase was, legitimately enough, transferred to the rhythm of water, so that, in "The Garden," the fountain has a "sliding foot" as well. In "Upon Appleton House," though, the figurative "foot" is simply realized: the poet's own foot "slides" on the bank as he lies next to the river, so that he and the river, like a classical river god, are almost identified. The phrase by this means is at once literalized and made figurative in a new context, as the poet melts into the river and the scene of which he is a part. Marvell raises figure from one plane, that of conventional quotation, to a very different one, the poet's own refiguring, as he creates a new poetic language out of old poetic idioms.[5]

Among so very much else, "The Garden" is an extraordinary exercise

[5] From conversations with Marie Borroff, I have derived some of the notions and methods used in this section; she is in no way responsible for my irresponsible use of her stylistics.

in just this problem—the conservation, exploitation, extension, and even transformation of old poetical forms into new ones. In the poem, the poet reduces poetic traditions to highly charged and telling figures, then plays upon those figures detached from their traditional environments, so as to modify the traditions from which they come and for which they are made to stand. As Mr. Leishman, Professor Kermode, and many others have noted, Marvell works by figure, develops his arguments by means of figure; by these tricks, he seems to us such a sharp and unscrupulous manipulator of poetic logic. An example of the gradation from a fairly simple figure to an analytical one is, I think, demonstrable in his use of colors, the "Red, the White, the Green" in "Eyes and Tears," and those same three colors as they appear in "The Garden." In "Eyes and Tears," the colors simply stand for flowers and leaves; in "Hortus," they are associated with their poetical environments, but they are secondary and decorative: red belongs with purple dye, white with snow, green with branches. An entirely different intellectual environment has been entered with "No white nor red was ever seen/ So am'rous as this lovely green," in which all the ecological elements have been sheared away, leaving us with the naked colors alone, which are forced to stand, all by themselves in their simplicity, for an enormous, varied affective world; this world the reader must fill in, from his own experience of life and of poetry.

In the opening lines of "A Dialogue Between The Resolved Soul, and Created Pleasure," we can see the curious juxtaposition of stock literary elements: again, figures are recognizable enough, but the environment from which they come and to which they refer must be supplied by the reader if he is properly to follow the argument between the soul and its tempter. The shield, helmet, and sword are Paul's Christian armor; the army with banners is an hyperbole from Canticles; the quarrel of nature and art is the pastoral formula. By these quick references, great themes are reduced, diminished, abstracted, and can be readily manipulated and shifted by the poet, once he has established their economical importance. The images are counters, standing for much credit behind them: we must know what they mean to see why they are as they are in the poem.

Though Marvell's tricks with figure are lovely, all the same one cannot say that he organized his figures in a purely logical relation to one another, or that he makes one-to-one substitutions of figural for logical elements. In poetry, after all, one cannot make such systematic alterations—what a poet does is to give the illusion of logic by poetic means. In the long sections which follow, on "The Garden" and "Upon Appleton House," I argue that by reducing great traditions to brief phrases, deeply laden with their literary associations, Marvell manages to sum up, even to emblematize, such traditions; his reducing whole traditions to convenient smallness permits him to chuck the "reduced" verbal elements about, so it seems, in a remarkably cavalier fashion. Since he can realign his reduced and diminished elements, he seems to be using them "logically"; so, then, the assumption that since gardens are better than girls, the gods must have chased their girls in order to turn them into plants. In "The Garden" there is a great deal of revision going on—of Ovidian myth, of Scriptural didacticism, of libertine self-indulgence—all in terms of very brief but fully allusive phrases. Traditions are distilled and compressed into typical figures, so that a small figure may stand for an enormous background of thought and of emotional association.

An analogy may be made to musical structure: a pavanne calls up one world of reference, a tarantella another; a "peasant" cantata involves musical motifs and styles quite different, say, from those of a "coffee" cantata. The meanings of *contredanse* and *alla turca* cannot be exhausted by pointing to country fairs or to Turks: historical conceptions and misconceptions are involved in understanding these apparently simple phrases. Nonetheless, behind these phrases loom large sets of musical ideas and forms to which the names refer. In much the same way, we recognize from titles, first lines, names of characters, styles, and syntax what "order" a poem belongs to. We remember, for instance, the original Daphnis and Chloe while we read of Marvell's pair; we remember the traditionally unsolved *débat* as we read Marvell's psychomachias. In "Upon Appleton House," for instance, the effect of Maria upon the "loose" disjointed landscape is a pastoral commonplace; the extraordinary stillness which she creates surpasses, however, the "normal" poetical supernatural effects upon a natural scene of a lovely girl's arrival. By comparing this scene with its analogues, its particularities can be recognized and its author's peculiar ingenuity identified: Marvell here raises pastoral to a higher power— literally divinizes the pastoral supernatural. Maria's *"Discipline severe,"* inculcated by her dutiful parents, introduces a stern morality into the beautiful perfection of her landscape, and introduces an alien element into the literary area of pastoral, normally untrespassed upon by rigors of any sort.

In the same way, the curious pastoral of the Nunappleton mowers grades into epic seriousness with the references to Alexander, tumuli, and the exodus from Egypt; it is here not just the thematic atmosphere of the specific references that is invoked, but their formal literary habitat as well. "An Horatian Ode" offers a remarkable—and remarkably obvious—example of a generic metaphor: because in the first "Servian" lines of the *Aeneid*, Virgil had written about the *themes* of his earlier works as if they were *styles*, had used, then, a stylistic term as a metaphor for a certain kind of subject, he made it easier for other writers to use subject matter as an image for genre and mode. "Arms and the man" means "epic"; "georgic" refers not just to fields and techniques of cultivation, but also to cultivation in the broader sense, education and spiritual development as well; "the pipe" is pastoral, pure and simple. In "An Horatian Ode," then, when the poet "explains" his emergence from "the Shadows," where he wrote the poetry of retirement ("Numbers languishing") into the world, where he had to relinquish his private pursuits for a public idiom, he puts it in thoroughly literary terms:

> 'Tis time to leave the Books in dust,
> And oyl th'unused Armours rust:
>> Removing from the Wall
>> The Corslet of the Hall

What does it mean? Simply, that the apprenticeship is over, and that the poet must now turn to old heroic themes, must "oyl" the unused armor—or, must refurbish the language of epic in his own terms, to suit his own purposes. It comes as some surprise when this conventional image, developed traditionally in terms of the speaking poet, is literalized and applied to the poem's subject: "So restless *Cromwel* . . . ," the poet's metaphorical behavior becoming the actual behavior of the country gentleman taking up the cause of his ancestral rights. By forcing one image to do both metaphorical and literal service in the poem, the poet not only identifies his own issuing into public poetry with Cromwell's entry into the public world, but also points to the highly moral and social view of poetic language which this poem, as others, demonstrates. Marvell's readers are given no quarter: they must consider the significance of the poet's writing in a particular form, genre, mode, or style, and the seriousness, for the poet, of his choice.

Some of Marvell's elusiveness lies in his peculiar perception into the meanings of poetic techniques: even as he uses a device, an image, a form, a figure, he appears to be analyzing it for his own purposes, and to incorporate into his poem his own thinking about its problems. Poetry so conceived is experimental, exploratory, discovering; its end, often, is experiment, exploration, and discovery, with the result that for a reader, the poem becomes an experience of what a poet does, how a poet works his materials to make something new of his traditions.

Marvell's use of figure provides us with material for comparison; we are allowed to see him select from his stock, polish his old image to a new gloss or a new reflection. There is considerable *sprezzatura* in this display, of course, and much of what Marvell does certainly seems effortless, fluent, natural; but there is another kind of confidence, too, which permits a reader to see how that *sprezzatura* is achieved—what work, what play, must go into the art. Marvell shows off, surely, but he instructs us too, forcing us to think about the ways in which figures of speech are and are not decoration, about the ways they can express thought and even truth. From highly figurative and conceited imagery to radical colloquial statement, Marvell demonstrates not just his versatility as a craftsman, but the range and limits of language as well. His poetry is to a high degree "intellectual," because of his own preoccupation with poetry's problems; it is, though it seems not to be so, a didactic exercise of a challenging sort.

3

PICTORIAL TRADITIONS

OBVIOUSLY, figures involve imagery, and imagery has something to do with pictures visible to the eye or the mind. Marvell's use of visual tradition is remarkable, even in an age when "iconography" was one material reservoir for a poet. Many of the poems he wrote fall into standard forms accommodating ecphrasis, or poetic rendering of a work of art, and follow the Horatian maxim that poetry and painting are alike, *ut pictura poesis*. "The Gallery" is an obvious example, as are the various Instructions to a Painter, both forms common in late seventeenth century poetry, and both of them dependent upon visual traditions and visual crafts. Into its short length "The Gallery" compresses the form Marino made famous,[1] though Marino's collection is obviously more various, rambling, and diffuse than Marvell's remarkable exercise in diminution.[2] "The unfortunate Lover" animates a series of love-emblems to raise for us serious questions about the translation of traditions from one art into another. "The Picture of little T.C." is an exact poetic parallel to pictures of children ringed with emblematic flowers indicating the transience both of childhood and beauty; "On a Drop of Dew" provides in verse the moralizing meditation upon a small, commonplace, and—in this case, at least—beautiful object, the descriptive nicety of which is related to the technique of the illustrated emblem. Marvell conspicuously uses art objects as metaphorical elements: Fleckno is "This *Basso Relievo* of a Man"; "The Gallery" is about pictures; "The Nymph complaining" designs her own tomb; "Upon Appleton House" utilizes landscape traditions and emblem traditions with remarkable sophistication and skill.[3] As we might by now come to expect, Marvell's use of visual traditions provides useful hints toward his poetic practice as a whole.

"The Gallery" belongs in a traditional type, dominated by Marino's anthological *La Galeria*, in which it was "fair" to depict in words real pictures (such as Titian's great "Maddalena"), conventional pictures on

[1] Giambattista Marino, *La Galeria.*   [2] For diminution, see below, pp. 118-23.
[3] See IV, 2, below, pp. 192-96.

106

themes so common as to need no particular model, and pictures sheerly imaginary. Marino's gallery was an "ideal" one, for all its occasional actuality of description; the poems derive as much from the perfecting imagination as from real visual experience, but both rely heavily on visual conventions and traditions. Marvell's "Gallery" is something else again: it celebrates an act of the imagination, since the poet chooses as a metaphor for his mind, literally preoccupied with his mistress, a gallery of pictures. He makes up an ideal collection, but only for himself—no other man could be expected to value this collection as he did, intent on a particular beloved. Furthermore, his collection is ideal in the literal sense of the word, since it is of his ideas of her, these figured forth as hung on the inside walls of his mind. He "furnishes" his mind with her; perhaps the poem is a memory-poem, more likely a parodied memory-poem, in which his lady's moods are forever recorded.[4] This is a love poem, extravagant but distant, introspective but unpersuasive; this lover meditates on the facets of his lady's character, as in another poem he meditates on the various aspects of a drop of dew. A love poem, this poem observes and presses various conventions of metaphoric utterance about ladies. Clora is a "Murtheress," killing her lover by tormenting him with her weapons, which are, of course, "Black Eyes, red Lips, and curled Hair." At another time, in another mood, she benevolently enchants him, as Aurora, as Venus; then again, she is a witch. She is *la belle dame sans merci* as well as the perfect love-object, naked asleep or naked awake on her shell. Last of all, she is "a tender Shepherdess," designated as artless, like so many other graceful, disorderly ladies in seventeenth-century poems—Julia, Eve—by her "Hair . . . loosely playing in the Air."

The poem is courtly not in its reference to courts (Whitehall and Mantua), but in its deliberate artificiality and sophistication. The poet is up-to-date as a connoisseur; in his interior decoration, tapestries are put away to make room for a display in the modern kind:

> And the great *Arras*-hangings, made
> Of various Faces, by are laid;

to be replaced by

> . . . a Collection choicer far
> Then or *White-hall's*, or *Mantua's* were,

4 For material on memory and mnemonics, see Francis A. Yates, *The Art of Memory* (London and Chicago, 1966).

that is, by a display of paintings finer than the King's own, purchased from the Gonzaga cabinet at Mantua. The mental cabinet of the poem manages to be "choice" by its careful, exclusive concentration on one subject; since all the paintings are of one sitter, they offer a kind of consistency, and since they are all different, they offer variety as well. The "Inhumane Murtheress," who examines her engines of war and instruments of torture is like an Italian picture of dark gardens and mysterious flickering lights; this one image can be connected to the bizarre, grotesque image of horror common in the work of the French *libertins* to whom Marvell is so often (I think unduly) likened. Here, Clora is a night-witch. Aurora asleep, in the third stanza, is like the nymphs of Titian and others, or like Giorgione's sleeping Venus,[5] with Venus' attributes of doves and roses around her; the "*Venus* in her pearly Boat," save perhaps for her posture, is familiar to everyone, with her airs, halcyons, ambergris and other perfumes somehow depicted. Marvell solves the problem of sweetness in a way different from Botticelli, but both this stanza and Botticelli's great picture catch the peculiar freshness of windborne odors.

The first four pictures in this gallery alternate a lovable with a cruel mistress, a decorous confrontation prescribed in literary versions of love affairs. This love affair, though, is of the mind and therefore undramatic; the poet simply surveys Clora's moods or, rather, her decisions to adopt moods each fixed in a mental picture. He does not, like the sonnet-lover faced with the same variation in a lady's behavior, embark upon the tortuous self-investigation characteristic of more analytical love poetry. The compliments to this lady increase stanza by stanza, though hardly the intimacy between poet and lady; in the end, he is as distant from her as at the beginning. First she is a murderess, then Aurora, next an enchantress who, however demented, nonetheless gives herself over entirely to preoccupation with love. Finally she is Venus, the unspoilt goddess of love rising from the sea. In all these "pictures," the lady is promisingly and tantalizingly displayed; the poet has yet to be awarded the full delights of this mistress, and simply dwells on their possibility. There is a curiously aseptic quality to this poem, as if the situation were in fact only mental, as if there were no real lady, no real love affair. The poet offers no invocation, no plea, no persuasive, as he enjoys his ideas and his art, his ideas

[5] For a useful article on this type, see Millard Meiss, "Sleep in Venice," *Akten des 21. Internationalen Kongresses für Kunstgeschichte*, Bonn, 1964 (Berlin, 1967), III, 271-79.

of art. There is an affinity between the connoisseur-speaker in this poem, delighting in his artefacts, and the Nymph in her poem, delighting in her pretty garden and her candid statue; both are satisfied with the beautiful, objectified constructs of their own minds.

Even in this poem, there is a pastoral undersong. Against the manifest artificiality of high art and the grandeurs of two courts, against the artifices of magicians, against even the superb stylizations of Aurora and Venus, the poet sets over his preferred picture of his beloved as she seemed when he "first was took":

> A tender Shepherdess, whose Hair
> Hangs loosely playing in the Air,
> Transplanting Flow'rs from the green Hill,
> To crown her Head, and Bosome fill.

As in Marvell's other pastoral poems, there is the bulge here of the poet's tongue in his cheek. He recognizes that a lady must play roles; he knows what those roles are; by fixing her in them himself, then choosing among them, he can fix her in ways that no flesh and blood lady can be fixed. If she persists in her varying theatricals, then his art can always stay one jump ahead of her imagination:

> These Pictures and a thousand more,
> Of Thee, my Gallery do store;
> In all the Forms thou can'st invent
> Either to please me, or torment:

He can turn her into an object, even if it is an object of art; he can denature her moods, reduce all her emotions, real or acted, to mere pose. In his view of her she is beautiful and rare; but she is not even unique. She is artificial, and she is his artifice. Customary artifice is brought up against the open sublimation of the artist; it doesn't matter who the lady is, or whether she is real or not: the poet's imagination can do without her, can satisfy itself alone. The lady actually is not really "in" these pictures; rather, at the beginning of the poem, the poet invites her to go around his gallery with him, to appraise his taste; the poet's idealism turns out to be as thin as the lady's poses. This courtship is merely "courtly," an artefact of the imagination, even down to the suitor's stylized affectation of preference for pastoral innocence.

"The unfortunate Lover" is a different arrangement of tableaux symbolizing emotional states. Where the pictures of "The Gallery" demonstrated the facets of Clora's behavior, however stereotyped, the images so carefully depicted in "The unfortunate Lover" are all directed to show a single personality. If one can say this of so compulsive a character, the images of this poem are analytic of his psychology. This lover demonstrates the complicated manifestations of a single mode of reaction, a personality emotionally violent and consistently self-frustrating. Clora was forever being fixed in "The Gallery"; the unfortunate Lover is ever in motion, although involuntary motion, it seems. She is fragmented by the poet's devices; he is given in full, studied from every side.

At the outset, the Lover is distinguished from those happy pairs who play so sweetly with one another through the pages of Otto van Veen's *Amorum Emblemata*[6] or of Herman Hugo's *Pia Desideria*,[7] or of Quarles' *Emblems*.[8] There, pairs of child-lovers, sometimes two *amorini*, sometimes an *amorino* with a little girl, play together, struggle over a palm, diagnose and cure each other's pains, cover a torch with a barrel or otherwise enjoy their childhoods together (Figs. 5, 6, 7).[9]

> Alas, how pleasant are their dayes
> With whom the Infant Love yet playes!
> Sorted by pairs, they still are seen
> By Fountains cool, and Shadows green.

"Alas," so inappropriate to the perfection described in the stanza, sets the tone for the whole poem, for to our unfortunate Lover such idylls are denied. This lover's difficult nature is revealed in a series of emblematic scenes to which parallels and analogues can be found in the emblem books, especially those dealing with the subject of love. In this poem, Marvell is up to something quite complex, attempting a mediation between verbal and visual arts. Love emblems on the whole derive from literary sources, which they illustrate, depicting the metaphorical extravagances of the Anthology, the Latin love lyrics, and the petrarchan tradition. In many cases, emblems reversed the *"ut pictura poesis"* dictum, picturing poetical forms, some of them very bizarre, in visual shapes. In "The unfortunate Lover," Marvell points to the origins of emblems by reversing the normal

[6] Otto van Veen, *Amorum Emblemata* (Antwerp, 1608).

[7] Hermann Hugo, *Pia Desideria* (Antwerp, 1624).

[8] Francis Quarles, *Emblems* (London, 1635).

[9] Quarles took many of his illustrations, with the plates reversed, from Hugo's book: for these particular subjects, see Quarles III, IV, and Veen, pp. 177.

emblematic procedure, which was to make extravagant pictures form hyperbolical metaphors. In this poem, he extends the usual range of metaphor and conceit by borrowing from the extravagant and conceited pictorial tradition, itself based on figures of speech. This is the opposite procedure from his demonstration in other poems of meaning in metaphor by seeming to unmetaphor, to take the metaphors in their own terms. Here, he starts from the heightened fantasy of emblem, to take their overstatements literally, as the "real" setting of this lover's life.

The lover is a mariner, his life and love likened to a ship. Veen's emblem (Fig. 8) shows an *amorino* gazing after a ship heeling over; the epigram accompanying the picture celebrates the safe return to harbor of the endangered vessel. Born into a tempest and from a "Shipwrack," his poor mother having

> . . . split against the Stone
> In a *Cesarian Section*.

this lover can only turn out stormy within himself. Our lover does not make port. His love is pointless and futile: the winds of love not only blow this lover, as they do the little love in Veen's picture (Fig. 9), but also they "become" him. He is a wind and a generator of winds. "Sunt Lacrimae Testes," Veen's emblem assures us;[10] this lover is by his own reflective behavior a constant witness to his own internal state:

> The Sea him lent these bitter Tears
> Which at his Eyes he alwaies bears.

He is like Clora in her wicked moods, a night-lover, which is normal enough, according to the emblematist, for lovers take to night;[11] our lover never looks on day unless it is darkened by storms. There is no cure for this lover (stanza 5; Veen, 155); he chooses to prolong his life without repose (Veen, 95), chooses then to remain frenetic.

His upbringing was deficient, too: "Corm'rants black" attended him, feeding "him up with Hopes and Air,/Which soon digested to Despair," one bird feeding him while another billed at his heart. This is a version of "Quod nutrit, exstinguit,"[12] (Fig. 10) the constant torment of a man

[10] Veen, p. 188.   [11] Veen, pp. 112-13.

[12] Veen, pp. 190-91; the English version (tr. Richard Verstegan, Antwerp, 1608) gives the following verse:

> *Quod Nutrit, Extinguit*
> The torche is by the wax maintayned whyle it burnes,
> But turned upsyde-down it straight goes out and dyes,

kept alive only to go on suffering, as for instance the Body and Soul feel they are, in their "Dialogue."

After such a birth and such an education, it is hardly surprising that the lover is thrust upon a life of violence. Veen's "Fit Amor Violenter Avi," seems to illustrate the whole of Marvell's poem;[13] other emblems serve to support the same theme: "Est Miser Omnis Amans," for instance, and "Quod Enim Securus Amavit?"[14] Cupid piles fire on his own flame (Veen, 143), or is crucified and burnt (Veen, 185, 229); whatever happens, he is always committed to the excruciations of punishment and pain in exchange for loving. As in Alciati's emblem (Fig. 11),[15] our lover is an Ajax, insanely taking on forces no man can withstand and most men do not dare to attack. The naked lover in Alciati's picture "cuffs" the air, as the heavens rain fire down on his body. Our lover is "betwixt the Flames and Waves," braving the "mad Tempest," "Cuffing the Thunder with one hand" as he clings to his rock with the other. Each wave threatens to dislodge him, and he is "Torn into Flames, and ragg'd with Wounds." "Flames" figure large in love emblems; Veen's *amorini* play with fire, one sustaining the flame that consumes him, another blowing up his candle as it gutters.[16] For another, the wind blows up the fire; another says like the salamander, "Mea Vita per Ignem" (Fig. 12).[17] These are emblematic fires, of course: the little lover fans his flame or blows up his candle, but always, because he is only a baby, he does it symbolically. Our lover has poignancy, if no more actuality, because we watch him grow up in years if not in wisdom, watch him suffering for his obsession. Love shoots him through, not once but many times

> And Tyrant Love his brest does ply
> With all his wing'd Artillery.

as Veen shows his little amor shooting at a target fastened to the breast

---

Right so by Cupid's heat the lover lyves lykewyse,
But thereby is hee kild, when it contrarie turnes.

See also Andrea Alciati, *Emblematum libellus* (Paris, 1535), p. 32, Prometheus with the eagle; and Geoffrey Whitney, *A Choice of Emblems* (Leiden, 1586), p. 75, same subject.

[13] Veen, pp. 224-5.   [14] Veen, pp. 125 and 139.

[15] Alciati, Emblema CVII; I think this is the picture referred to by J. Max Patrick, *Explicator* XX (1961-2), item 65.

[16] Veen, 139, 137.

[17] Veen, 229; this may relate, too, to "Th' *Amphibium* of Life and Death."

of a man looking hopelessly into the distance out of the picture,[18] and another poor man shot full of arrows, prone on the ground (Fig. 13).[19] This kind of love is too violent to last—even the poet cannot torture the lover past the point of sufficient unreason, and must eventually save his figure by another means. This means is the transformation of the lover into a heraldic device of himself, of his behavior and his temperament, the colors marking him once and for all: "In a Field *Sable* a Lover *Gules*."

Marvell plays again and again with artifying nature, and naturalizing art; he even turns people into works of art, as particularly illustrated in "The Gallery." In "The Nymph complaining," there are levels of artification: the girl constructs her garden, first, which is given in thoroughly visual terms; the fawn's death has its counterparts in the emblem-literature, as it gently dies, weeping balsam and leaking its life away; white deer, stags, and even unicorns (habitually associated with virgins and the Virgin) appear collared and chained, domesticated in the service of a particular lady, in heraldry, tapestry, and emblem. The final statue, designed by the girl for us, recalls the Niobe story and reverses the Pygmalion one. In Ovid's narrative, the artist's creation became animate; in Marvell's poem, an animate artistic girl opts out of life for the beautiful irresponsibilities of a detached work of art.[20]

"On a Drop of Dew" is another poem of cool self-sufficiency, told in impersonal terms, the only emotion the dewdrop's worried yearning to return to the peaceful, quiet heaven whence it came. "Dew" is a subject treated in emblems and emblem poems; Marvell lengthens the form, so to speak, in this poem, to unite the visual elements with a religious meditation, extended over considerable time. Noticeably, many visual elements of this poem have their counterparts in still life painting; indeed, the meditation and the still life, in particular that sort called "Vanitas," share the theme of seeing through the emptiness of materiality into the permanent spiritual meanings of religious value. Dewdrops or drops of water challenged painters' skill, as also the tears to which they are (in this poem, too) inevitably likened. The painter's task is to render the crystalline quality of water-drops against its background of color and form,

---

[18] Veen, 153.   [19] Veen, 215.

[20] For another lady mourning a slain deer, see J. S. Held, "Rubens and Virgil: A Self-correction," *Art Bulletin*, XXIX (1947), 125-26, a discussion of an oil sketch showing Sylvia and her stag, with hunters and farmers in combat around her; Nicholas Guild, "Marvell's 'The Nymph Complaining for the Death of her Faun,'" *MLQ*, XXIX (1968), pp. 385-94, gives the Virgilian reference.

showing the texture of the background through the surface, at once transparent and reflecting. Marvell's dewdrop lies on a rose leaf, where

> it the purple flow'r does slight,
> Scarce touching where it lyes. . . .

> Restless it roules and unsecure,
> Trembling lest it grow impure:

The play of light and shade on the little globe is precisely explained, and that explanation moralized:

> So the World excluding round,
> Yet receiving in the Day.
> Dark beneath, but bright above:

"Exhaled" from the heavens, the dewdrop remains on earth only for a little while before being returned to the sky by the sun's power; in this, like the Resolved Soul, it yearns for and aspires to its original state. This figure, the dewdrop, is "right" in form, properly crystalline and clear, properly transparent and translucent, properly spherical. For a moment on earth it captures and recapitulates all the perfections of the sphere whence it descended:

> . . . recollecting its own Light,
> Does, in its pure and circling thoughts, express
> The greater Heaven in an Heaven less.

Its perfect sphericity means that it balances on a point, scarcely touching the rose petals at all:

> How girt and ready to ascend.
> Moving but on a point below,
> It all about does upwards bend.

In this poem the dewdrop maintains its purity, even to the extent of shunning "the sweat leaves and blossoms green," and "the World excluding round." The spherical shape of the dewdrop corresponds to the "sphere" whence it came, and expresses also the necessary inward attention and self-concentration of pure virtue. It mourns while on earth, is "its own Tear," keeps itself uncontaminated by the world, even though the world of its environment is so lovely. Its virtue is distilled, white, "intire," congealed, and chill; world-rejecting and emotion-rejecting, it exists until it can

. . . dissolving, run
Into the Glories of th' Almighty Sun.

In some respects the notion on which the poem is built is common-
place enough; this is a characteristic descent and ascent of the soul, its
theme worked out without doctrinal or moral idiosyncrasy. What is im-
pressive is the way in which, circling around his spiritual object-subject,
the poet manages to give the impression of the integrity, the totality of
this water-drop within the material world. He places his dewdrop between
one kind of language—"orient," "bosom," "blowing roses"—and another—
"white," "intire," "congealed," "still," the languages themselves of psy-
chomachia. The beautiful world is a real threat to this sensitive and
scrupulous emblem for the soul; like the Resolved Soul, the dewdrop
desiring dissolution must resist the secular preoccupations, even when they
are as little "sinful" as the rose and garden of this poem. In the word
"dissolving," profane and divine love are allowed for a moment to run
together, as one realizes the likeness between religious and secular rapture.
Only to secular suit is the dewdrop "coy"; it yearns, weeps, waits, hopes
for unification with the deity.

Marvell made use of iconic sources open to him, of course adapting
them to the poet's general needs and to his own needs in particular. In
other cases, he manages to exploit emblematic or graphic traditions: the
conceits of "Eyes and Tears," for instance, the notion of tears as "Lines
and Plummets," or the notion of tears weighed against joy, are illustrated
in emblems. In "The Match," the extended conceit of love's arsenal owes
as much to visual as to literary analogues. In both "The Garden" and
"Upon Appleton House," there are important adaptations from the em-
blem books; and "Upon Appleton House" makes complex use of many
optical and visual techniques. In the Mower poems, the mower has his
symbolisms, and the glowworms theirs, both figures emblematized too;
the landscape of "Upon the Hill and Grove at Bill-borow" is thoroughly
emblematized (Fig. 1). One of Marvell's major preoccupations, the gar-
den itself, is an important emblem-topic. One literary picture book, Henry
Hawkins' religious meditation on the Virgin, takes a garden as its frame;
several elements in that book offer useful comparison to Marvell's tech-
niques.

Hawkins' *Partheneia Sacra* is a little book of Catholic devotion, and an
excellent example of the confluence of the literature of meditation and

emblem literature. Generally speaking, it is for the use of "Parthenes," virgins or nuns, and deals with the *hortus conclusus*, literally and symbolically. Some of the elements of the garden which Hawkins elects to treat are very conventional, others seem more matters of his choice. In structure, each topic or "Symbol" has several sections, as is characteristic of "emblem" form—in this case, the "Devise," a picture; the "Character," the "Morals," the "Essay," the "Discourse," the "Poesie" (with a second picture), the "Theorie," and the "Apostrophe," or prayer to either the Virgin or to God. In all these, Hawkins manages to say a great deal about his garden, the flowers, the dew, the house, the birds, and so forth, that make it up: not surprisingly, some of his elements are like elements in Marvell's verse. Hawkins' "The Deaw," for instance, has many similarities with Marvell's poem, although a comparison of the two "dews" serves to show how little theology and doctrine Marvell used in his poem. Hawkins' dew-meditation, like his other meditations, tends toward panegyric of a specifically Catholic kind. Something in Hawkins' language is more akin to Crashaw's usage than to Marvell's, which is to say, not that luxuriance of language is a Roman Catholic stylistic device, but that Marvell's language, even in his most sensuous passages, tends toward the spare. Hawkins' "Character" of the dew begins:

> The *Deawes* are the sugred stillicids of Nature, falling from the Limbeck of the Heavens, as so manie liquid pearls, and everie pearl as precious as the truest Margarits. They are liquified Cristal, made into so manie silver-orbs as drops. They are the verie teares of Nature, dissolved and soft through tendernes, to see the Earth so made a Libian Desart, which she supplies a meer compassion with the ruine of herself. . . . They are the *Manna* of Nature, to vye with those Corianders, food of Pilgrims, made by Angels: with this unhappiness, they could not be congealed, to make a food so much for men, as a Nectar for the plants to drink.[21]

In Hawkins' discussion of the dew, he repeats Pliny's remark about its "compliance" with everything it meets, its manner of "temporizing" with its earthly environment, so that it takes on the character of its background. This is precisely what Marvell's dewdrop does *not* do: for the commonplace of the dew's protean, mirroring, rainbow qualities, Marvell substitutes the theme of its integrity, independence, and rejection of all other

[21] Hawkins, *Partheneia Sacra* (Rouen, 1633), pp. 59-60.

things in its earthly environment. Marvell's drop is exclusive, self-contained, self-reflecting, an emblem for rejection of *res creatae*. Though Hawkins' passage offers verbal parallels to Marvell's poem—"dissolve," "recollect," "congealed"—it points in a different direction. Hawkins' eye and mind wander from the dew to other things; his meditative technique is expansive. Marvell concentrates ever more fully on the single, self-concentrated object; he narrows his meditation inward. Though certainly very graphic, Hawkins' visual imagery does not compose a single picture, but stresses the different units; the lovely engravings illustrating his book (Fig. 19) are of single elements: one carefully drawn rose or lily, one elegant bee. Marvell keeps our attention on one thing, but all the rest of its environment is depicted in relation to it, the rose leaf, the way the light falls, the motion of the dew on its "point." Marvell's meditative way, in this poem, rejects visual *copia*, which so often inspired contemplation and vision, to concentrate on one precise, meaningful object, self-contained but existing in a world of other things. Hawkins gives a more generous universe than Marvell's in this particular poem. In Hawkins' enclosed garden, all things are free and interchangeable; certainly in the poem, this is not so: the poem is about demarcation and separation. The rigor of Marvell's poetic discipline reinforces our sense of the dew's, or the soul's, need for rigor in a world full of distraction and dissipation.

That Marvell's visual imagination could be prodigal also is apparent in "Upon Appleton House," with its abundant translation of different pictorial conventions, different emblematic modes. There, the poet worked both in the large and in the small, impressionistically and emblematically, fantastically and with a magnifying glass, to give us a world of great visual plurality, a world as wide as imagination can make it. In many ways, "Upon Appleton House" is the climax of Marvell's experiments in poeticizing pictorial modes—but that is another story, told in another place.[22]

[22] See IV, 2, below, pp. 192-218.

4

DIMINUTION

MARVELL'S use of visual traditions leads one to consider his tendency to miniature, so beautifully exhibited in a poem like "On a Drop of Dew," or in the bird-emblems of "Upon Appleton House." Emblems have a tendency toward diminution, but there are other kinds of diminution illustrated in several ranges of Marvell's practice. In his epigrams, the poet achieves compactness and fullness at the same time, a compactness which opens out, as the epigrammatic couplets of "The Garden" do, like Japanese paper flowers. Very often, Marvell's formal diminutions relate to thematic points: he wants to present, for instance, the mysterious self-sufficiency and self-absorption of "Bermudas," and so frames his psalm of praise in a quiet introduction and conclusion that we "see" the vision of paradise compacted between. The "Picture of Little T. C." is frankly ecphrastic, and the scene is a delicate one, a "little" one, like the girl herself. To "frame" as Marvell does sets limits to scenes and to themes; framing makes us concentrate on the things framed, tends to present subjects neatly and tidily. So we are invited to look at the series of tableaux in "The unfortunate Lover," studying the poem's central character now in one psychological phrase and situation, now in another; so we are invited to see the girl in "The Gallery," clad one by one in her social roles. We progress through the stanzas of the poem looking at one picture after another, as if the gallery were "real": but, we learn, the gallery is an image for "my Soul," as the poet tells us, where

> . . . several lodgings lye
> Compos'd into one Gallery;

His mind is enclosed, the gallery is enclosed; both concentrate upon a single thought, a single obsession, Clora. The image of the mind is one of encasement, its contents reduced to a manageable size.

In the idyll, or little picture, "The Nymph," the subject of the poem deals with the correspondence between the external world and the internal mind: as in "The Gallery," a work of art, this time a garden, is formed to match the Nymph's inward needs. Still, the accomplishment is overtly criticized in this poem—like many of Marvell's figures, the Nymph retreats from the world to a garden of retirement, where she redesigns her environment to suit herself and her needs. Sylvio turns out to have been the reason for her withdrawal, his rejection having sent the girl back into an early stage of arcadianism, where no wilful emotions may trespass. Sylvio returns to his wild forest; he is a wild creature, then, as "Men" are considered in this poem, and as they are characterized also by the nun in "Upon Appleton House." The Nymph cultivates her garden, which is informal, "a little Wilderness," a manageable projection of her fears and her attempts at controlling them. At the same time, her garden is distinctly enclosed; that is, it is her effort at a self-sufficient emotional economy, a projection of her favorite side of her personality. That the poet presents these scenes—"I have a Garden of my own"; "The Tears do come"; "In fair *Elizium*"—in perfectly visual terms, inviting illustration from analogous pictures in contemporary art, stresses their peculiar quality of fixedness; in the Nymph's poem, the different scenes are gallery-pictures too, ending in the great tomb of marble and alabaster.

The poem is a manifest ecphrasis, or is manifestly ecphrastic; save for the final statue, however, the scenes are pictorial but not about works of art, pictorial but not about pictures. The Nymph frames mental pictures to isolate herself from the cruel world outside, though her creation cannot, as the troopers' behavior demonstrates, protect her at all. The Nymph is a real pastoralist, an isolated artist, who must give way before the world: the troopers did not honor her integrity, did shoot her fawn. Unsophisticated men from a different profession and a different world, they missed the autonomy and delicacy of the pastoral mode, perceiving the fawn merely as game or prey. The pastoral mode postulates some correspondence between inner and outer worlds; much of Marvell's poetry concerns itself with examining that Platonic view of epistemology, and therefore deals with the notion of diminution, since by that psychology all that is can be enclosed in one small mind. Damon the Mower finds that

> . . . ev'ry thing did seem to paint
> The Scene more fit for his complaint.

and the other Mower laments the breakdown of that consistency between inner and outer worlds:

My Mind was once the true survey
Of all these Medows fresh and gay;
And in the greenness of the Grass
Did see its Hopes as in a Glass; . . .

But . . .

now all is altered. He is emotionally destitute, and his landscape, hitherto
faithful to his mood, nonetheless continues to bloom. Psychology breaks
down, as the correspondence between inner and outer worlds fails.

Properly speaking, the mind accurately reflects the world, and the world
reflects the mind in a comforting tautological mutuality which manages
at the same time a conveniently reductive model for the world. This cor-
respondence, assumed in the Platonic epistemology, is very important in
Marvell's techniques of diminution: though vastly overworked, the term
"microcosm" is here for once exact. The mind is a tiny cosmos, a tiny
totality, a tiny universe, its finiteness managing to enclose everything
in pattern, whatever it may be. "All that's made" can be reduced to the
measure of a man's mind, and in "The Garden" is so reduced:

The Mind, that Ocean where each kind
Does streight its own resemblance find;

Annihilating all that's made
To a green Thought in a green Shade.

This Mind encapsulates all the kinds, which find their "resemblance"
reliably filed therein; such a mind is passive, its realizations dependent
upon presentations from the world without. The Garden-mind is also
active, though, capable of immense acts of creative power; this mind
expands and contracts beyond the normal, or even the actual, limits of
created things. I am concerned here only with the mind as an image of
reduction, not of expansion, though the other subject is important too;
here, though, everything is reduced to a single, whole thought. The mind
is an envelope of possibilities, enclosing within itself all conceivable to
any mind, even that of the deity.

The soul also contains much: the drop of dew in Marvell's poem is
another inviolate microcosm, a little globe in which "all" is reflected:

See how the Orient Dew,
Shed from the Bosom of the Morn
Into the blowing Roses,
Yet careless of its Mansion new;
For the clear Region where 'twas born
Round in its self incloses:
And in its little Globes Extent,
Frames as it can its native Element.

And, recollecting its own Light,
Does, in its pure and circling thoughts, express
The greater Heaven in an Heaven less.

This drop of dew not only is self-contained, but intends to remain so; the drop's anxieties about its contamination are part of the poem's tension. In other contexts, emblematic drops of dew tend to be more promiscuous than this cool example: unlike Hawkins' reflective drop, Marvell's deliberately excludes the rest of creation:

In how coy a Figure wound,
Every way it turns away:
So the World excluding round,
Yet receiving in the Day.

As the Nymph tries to be, the dewdrop *is* self-sufficient, until it is allowed to dissolve "Into the Glories of th' Almighty Sun." In it, then, are those virtues necessary for salvation, uncontaminated even by the beautiful roses. The Garden-mind is self-sufficient too, but in a different mode, since it reaches out to enclose all things, and to imagine for itself. If the Garden-mind rejects the world, it is to return to it purified by its experience of retreat. The world as well as the mind is bettered by that retreat. The garden universe of "On a Drop of Dew" and that of "The Garden" are poles apart, really; one locates the morality of rejection, the other the morality of involvement.

But both dewdrop and Garden-mind are, in their own terms, sufficiently endowed to merit "grace," as that quality fits those two universes. Spatially limited though both are, their significance is increased for us by their very concentration, their smallness. "Sufficiency," as a norm and as an ideal, preoccupied Marvell through his poetic career; the problems and values of sufficiency are discussed overtly in "Upon Appleton House," where bee-like cells and tortoiseshell are praised for their minimal size and maximal function. Roman simplicity and Horatian sufficiency make up Appleton's moral world. It is, certainly, Horace who made model statements about sufficiency; the retired poet on his Sabine farm provided European literary men with their chief example of plain living and high thinking. The sufficiency-topos, as this recurrent theme may be called, is a regular statement of georgic literature and the literature of retirement and solitude. It may well be, simply, another version of pastoral, for an ideal of sufficiency has affinities both with the economic rigors of hard pastoral and the self-satisfying ideals of soft; certainly the correspondence between the shepherd's and nature's pathos offers one way of presenting great things in small.

At Appleton, his smallest house, evidently Fairfax did live on a small scale, for a grandee at least; he certainly had several more ostentatious holdings in which he could be more spaciously housed. Though his other dwellings may have satisfied Fairfax's more heroic tastes, Appleton testified, in the poet's fiction anyway, to Horatian economy. Like the dens of beasts, the shells of tortoises, the nests of birds, the cells of bees, this house seemed to fit his owner as part of him; as Romulus' bee-like cell was the proper house for a great founder, so this house's scale was the proper one for real heroism. In the poem, though the counterpoint of abundant imagery often suggests another theme, the melodic line comes out strongly against extravagance in architecture and in life, praises the sufficiency of the microcosmic estate as well as the moral self-sufficiency of the members of the Fairfax family. Things greater are in less contained; in the emblematic vignettes of the wood-episode, in the frozen still life elements of the vitrified stream, in the curious close-ups of rail and grasshopper, one realizes that far more is implied than the poet ever mentions outright. In Maria herself, a diminutive figure for magnanimity, the bearer of continuous custom, of virtue, of wisdom, civilization is compressed: this green girl, not yet marriageable, is the container of far more than her real self. She is the estate in epitome, and the estate is an epitome of the world: through her, the traditions of her "house" and of all holy living must be carried on.

"Upon Appleton House," which Kitty Scoular has characterized as a "tissue of epigrams," naturally offers many examples of compression:

Diminution

Humility alone designs
Those short but admirable Lines,
By which, ungirt and unconstrain'd,
Things greater are in less contain'd.

(stanza 6)

The extraordinary neatness of the verse is made, like Appleton House itself, to "answer Use"; as Horace did for his farm, Marvell insists upon a functional economy for the estate. When we come to look at it, that most expansive of episodes, the poet's near-magical experience in the wood, manages to compress and to compact even his heightened consciousness. "What *Rome, Greece, Palestine*, ere said"—in short, all significant human utterance—is displayed in a pattern of light through figured leaves, to be read by the poet in his ecstasy. The emblem-scenes of the birds, too, contain far more than they seem; their very enigmatic qualities assure us of their trim significances. In the implication of his imagery, in his epigrammatic passages, and even in his neat syntax and vocabulary, particularly in his puns, Marvell tends to apply the principle of sufficiency. That he could pare down his utterances—and also that his control over his native language and his formal vocabulary was so masterly—is demonstrated by comparing the Latin to the English versions of "The Garden" or "On a Drop of Dew." Where a single word could work for several, that word is used. The puns, the hooking syntactical devices, the sentences full of ambiguity, manage to compress more than is quite proper into one "set," and at the same time to focus upon meaning from two very different angles of vision. It is worth noting that where Marvell has to be vague (as, for instance, in the sixth stanza of "The Garden," where his material left him no choice), he hedges and protects his meanings by different precisions in different ranges. Where the puns are confusing, the images are clear; where the syntax forces questions, the meanings suggested are separately clear, confusing only as they overlay in our reading minds; where an epigram is too full of ideas for comfort, its syntax is comfortingly limpid and free. Marvell's diminutions are, I think, never made for their own sake alone, although he was certainly interested in the poetic limits of a principle of parsimony. He was not, however, parsimonious: he allows for expansion even in his most considerable exercises in tightness.

123

5

PERSONA

SINCE Marvell so often used the same theme to many different ends, or looked at an idea from many different perspectives, it is not surprising that the poet himself seems to some readers remarkably uncommitted to his poems and their "message." Many readers react sharply to what seems a cold-bloodedness they feel inappropriate in a lyric poet, a cold-bloodedness absent from the work of, say, Donne, Herbert, Crashaw, and Vaughan. In this respect, Marvell is more like those Cavalier poets whose conventions permitted and even required that poetical persona be detached from the feeling poet: one would never guess from his elegant verse that Suckling committed suicide. Though their personalities were surely not easy, Lovelace and Herrick speak, insofar as "they" speak at all, with remarkable consistency throughout their poetry—and Marvell does not. One reason why "he" seems so absent from his lyric poems, taken as a whole, is that the point of view changes so radically from poem to poem—the speakers come, as it were, from very different backgrounds of assumption about themselves and about life.

The Mower poems offer a good case in point: there, four quite different speakers speak, one with a name, the others nameless. We are not told whether or not the gentle Damon is the same person as the gentle Mower singing his "song," or the benighted Mower who appeals to the glow-worms, though it seems pretty certain that Damon is not the cranky Mower who hates gardens. In the love poems, the poet tries many modes, in consequence assuming many personas, but rarely does this poet, even in his love poems, seem to be in love, or to care much about loving. "To his Coy Mistress" demonstrates awareness of desire, but doesn't say much about love; "The Definition of Love" scrupulously avoids all questions of either desire or love.

It is difficult to feel autobiography in Marvell's lyrics. In "The Match," for instance, though that "he" who builds, tends, and ignites the confla-gration of ardent love for Celia's sake is the speaker, officially, nonetheless it is quite clear from the poem's tactics that there is no question of either "real" lady or "real" love in the poem. There is a peculiar irony in the distance between the chilly speaker and the ardent lover; when in the last stanza the speaker assumes the mask of the lover, no reader for a moment is fooled by the "poet's sincerity." Indeed, there is a detachment about this poem which may properly, given the imagery, be called "scientific": the conceit is presented in terms of a chemical experiment, so that the lines

> None ever burn'd so hot, so bright;
> And *Celia* that am I.

come as a conclusion to what had hitherto seemed an entirely intellectual exercise and therefore are not designed to convince anyone of the emotional commitment of this "I." Furthermore, the tone of the speaker of this poem is exactly opposite to what is implied by the figure of ardency; one must assume that the poet was attempting limits, this time the limits of disjunction between tone and subject.

Certainly in many of these poems, the poet manages to keep a feeling self at a considerable distance. When such a self *is* involved, as in "The Mower against Gardens," then the speaker's and poet's voices sing in quite different keys; "The unfortunate Lover" and "The Nymph complaining" show a similar discrepancy between speaker and feeling self. In poems where a feeling self is more integrally involved with the poem, the poet's voice seems to sing in the same key: in "The Garden," for instance, or in long passages from "Upon Appleton House," poet and speaker seem genuinely at one. But in other poems, those mentioned and "The Mower against Gardens," poet and speaker seem to sing in quite different keys. In general, in such cases there is a suggestion of monomania, obvious in the case of the anti-gardening Mower, apparent also in the Nymph's limited psychological perception; the poet seems to be showing the strong limitations of a point of view, in particular of a point of view dictated by literary tradition. So the unfortunate Lover is reduced to just that, and to no more than that; or, to take a "better" poem and a more sympathetic speaker, for all its marvelously understanding presentation of sexual desire, "To his Coy Mistress" does not suggest that its speaker has a fuller awareness of love than of the kind he is talking about in the poem. Sometimes the speaker's voice and the poet's radically diverge, "Damon the Mower" is one example, the interruption of Thestylis in "Upon Appleton House" another.

In other poems, the speaker seems to refuse to give sympathy to his subject; in "Mourning," for instance, much of the same language of imagery used in "Eyes and Tears" appears in the diction, but undoubtedly the poet wants readers to feel quite differently about its meaning in the two situations. In "Eyes and Tears," the poet was content in his image-spinning conceits, professionally engaged, at the very least, in making the most of the conventional cluster of images. In "Mourning," something else is going on, the poet beginning by sympathizing with the conventional hyperbolical language about grief, then subjecting it to scrutiny which entirely undermines that sympathy: the girl weeps in all kinds of impossible ways (her eyes "Seem bending upwards") because her Strephon is dead. At first when other people suspect her, casting doubt on the sincerity of her tears, the poet seems to "protect" her against such malicious gossips, who claim that she loved loving more than she loved her shepherd, that her pleasure was in her emotion, not in another person. Then, suddenly, the poet begins to join her detractors, with his image of the girl weeping alone, seeming both Danae and the shower. The fusion of the two, Danae and shower, underlines the weeper's narcissism, and indeed one realizes that she can dispense with the lover in her satisfaction in her tableau of bereavement. Such a girl is self-absorbed and self-satisfied by her own sentiments and deserves the sharp couplet at the end, a generalized rejection of the notion that a woman can be sincere:

> But sure as oft as Women weep,
> It is to be suppos'd they grieve.

In "A Dialogue between the Soul and Body," something else is going on. There, the poet's voice strengthens neither speaker in the dialogue. If a ruling tone can be established for the poet, it is one of impatience with the childish complaints of both parties. In contrast with the other dialogue, "The Resolved Soul," where the poet's sympathies are clearly with the soul, the body-soul dialogue leaves us hanging because the poet refuses engagement with either side. The result is a thorough rejection of the terms of psychomachia; but the means by which a reader is brought to that awareness are tonal and personal, not doctrinal or dogmatic. Here, part of the point lies in the fact that the poet does *not* express his point of view: there is, so to speak, no poet present in the poem. "Bermudas" is another such poem, curiously neutral and undirected because a poet seems absent: "the listening Winds" hear the song, which cannot be expected to express an opinion on it. In the appearance of contextlessness, this poem brings us up sharp against the problem of speaker and persona, who seem to have been entirely deracinated from the poem itself.

In these cases, the poet seems to be practicing at the edge of poetic likelihood. In poems like "Mourning" and "The Match," he plays with reversals, by which the poet's irony has the last word, dominating the poem by a *tour de force*, robbing by means of wit such passion as the poem might imply. In "A Dialogue between the Soul and Body," he does away with "himself" altogether; an even greater *tour de force* is "The Definition of Love," in which the speaker, doomed to eternal frustration, rationalizes and accepts that frustration, denaturing by his reasonable "explanation" the human emotion which, above all others, naturally passes the bounds of reason. To compare "The Definition of Love" with "The unfortunate Lover" is to observe the gamut of frustration, and to be offered totally opposite solutions to the problem. At the same time, the first of those poems seems to be consistently written in one voice, whereas in "The unfortunate Lover" the poem's speaker seems to understand and to forgive the violence and unreason of the afflicted lover, or in "The Gallery," the speaker seems at the last ironic at his, not his lady-love's, expense.

Beginnings and ends of poems are often slightly out of tune with the rest. "The Nymph complaining" begins *in medias res*, as the girl in the simplest possible way explains what her situation is, and demonstrates how little of it she understands:

> The wanton Troopers riding by
> Have shot my Faun and it will dye.

By the end of the poem, she has managed to resolve herself and her pretty pet into a permanent, hard, chill work of art, commemorating (as is appropriate) her life and love in a sepulchral statue. The poem moves from the nymph's lack of emotional control to her establishment of a fixed control over her future, a future empty of life, but preserved in art. Many of Marvell's lyrics end on some kind of ecphrastic event, a metamorphosis into art, as in "The Nymph complaining," or a paean to art, as in "Musicks Empire" or "The Fair Singer." Such solidification of psychology, by definition a motive and emotive set of conditions, into art is in some cases a real "resolution" to a poem, in others a mere twist.

At the beginning of "Clorinda and Damon," a nymph seems bent on a shepherd's seduction—and a seduction to which, from her openness in the poem, we must assume that not only the pastoral convention but this particular shepherd has acquiesced. Clorinda's uncomplicated offering of her own body for pleasure is what, in another poem, the crude Daphnis thought he wanted of his shepherdess; but, as if to Clorinda's surprise, the poem develops another way, into a dialogue between her environmental naturalism and Damon's proselytizing morality. Pagan and Christian pastorals conduct a decent agon, variously interpreting the landscape elements according to quite different *pathétiques*:

> C. Seest thou that unfrequented Cave?
> D. That den? C. Loves Shrine. D. But Virtue's Grave.

Leaving aside Clorinda's understandable surprise at the overturning of what she must have assumed to be their common ideology, we must admire this method of presenting the rival claims of love and spirituality, in terms of emblematic interpretation.

In "A Dialogue Between The Resolved Soul, and Created Pleasure," different symbolic elements appeared in the two arguments; in this poem, the two debaters offer different interpretations of the same elements. As in the "Dialogue," spirituality here promptly purifies the pleasant carnality of Clorinda, who agrees to join with her beloved in a hymn to Pan; that is, she agrees to substitute his pastoral for hers.

"A Dialogue between Thyrsis and Dorinda" treats the problem of Christian pastoralism too, but the poem is a different one altogether. Here, the pastoral lovers are well into their companionship, far beyond concerns of dalliance or seduction, but rather interested in their spiritual relation to one another. Dorinda worries about what will happen to them after death; that separation, so painful a subject for any pair of lovers, proves a difficult idea for her. Thyrsis provides instruction on the afterlife, which takes a beautiful, innocent, pastoral form:

> Oh, ther's, neither hope nor fear
> Ther's no Wolf, no Fox, nor Bear.
> No need of Dog to fetch our stray,
> Our Lightfoot we may give away;
> No Oat-pipe's needfull, there thine Ears
> May feast with Musick of the Spheres.
>
> . . . There, sheep are full
> Of sweetest grass, and softest wooll;

Persona

> There, birds sing Consorts, garlands grow,
> Cold winds do whisper, springs do flow.
> There, alwayes is, a rising Sun,
> And day is ever, but begun.
> Shepheards there, bear equal sway,
> And every Nimph's a Queen of *May*.

When Dorinda hears this, she falls ill from longing for such a paradise. What is interesting is that, from the dog Lightfoot to eternal sunrise, Thyrsis offers her a heaven in terms of pastoral orthodoxy, which the girl can be expected to understand; he is, so to speak, a Jesuit proselytizing for heaven offered in terms of his hearer's highest cultural expectations. By implication, then, these two need a heaven; their pastoral life is somehow not quite pastoral enough, not quite perfect. Dorinda shows all the marks of the convert, immediately wishing for that paradise and deciding with her Thyrsis to die at once, in order to achieve it. Pastoral means are available to her—like Damon acquainted with the local pharmacopeia, she produces opium so that they can "smoothly pass away in sleep" to Elysium. Such a solution, so grossly and yet so innocently submissive, so negligent of all life-problems, sends us unexpectedly to reconsider life and death from a context apparently far too casual and conventional for such problems. In life, Marvell seems to say, received opinion can be an opiate, for, if one took the promises of heaven seriously, why should anyone persist in living? The pastoral naïveté with which Dorinda faces her new knowledge throws us back on what is *not* said in the poem: the all-too-real difficulties of holy living and holy dying. A comparison with the Soul-Body dialogue is useful; here, all is incredibly simplified; there, all is reduced to an irresolute question between wretched and ignorant protagonists. The simplicities of Christian teaching are in both cases called into question: there are no home remedies for life or for death.

In this poem, the poet seems to back off from both speakers, as he does in the Soul-Body dialogue too. In "Damon the Mower," something similar happens: Damon mows his meadows, sorrowfully brooding over his unrequited love for Julia. His environment reflects, as pastoral landscapes prescriptively do, his mood:

> While ev'ry thing did seem to paint
> The Scene more fit for his complaint.

Like her fair Eyes the day was fair;
But scorching like his am'rous Care.
Sharp like his Sythe his Sorrow was,
And wither'd like his Hopes the Grass.

He sings of his little world, of the "unusual" heats, of the silent grass-hoppers, the "hamstring'd Frogs," the cool snake. He laments Julia's care-lessness of his gifts, the toothless snake, the chameleon, the oak leaf. He is, certainly, an innocent, a *naïf*, a sweet if parochial man, all that the pastoral hero is supposed to be.

The poet does not merely leave things at that, at mere conformity to the pastoral prescription. Suddenly, he strips Damon bare of defenses, makes him appear foolish, precisely at his point of greatest self-pride, in his self-proclamation: "I am the Mower *Damon*, known"—known where? "Through all the Meadows I have mown." In that local scene, large to him, negligible to all others, Damon the mower can count on his reputa-tion. There and, we assume, there only, is he safe. In the competition between him and another group of pastoralists, with different occupations, shepherds, he believes himself the victor:

And though in Wooll more poor then they,
Yet am I richer far in Hay.

One does not need the traditional worthlessness of "hay" to realize Da-mon's poverty in the world's eyes.[1] Damon is frighteningly vulnerable; his world is alarmingly open to attack. The poet throughout the poem is disposed, one feels, toward his speaker, but at the same time some-how pities him, recognizes the beautiful fragility of the pastoral ethos, and so, at this point, withdraws his support to let poor Damon trumpet out his foolishness.

Something of this same near-betrayal by the poet of his principal speaker happens in that great and enigmatic poem, "The Nymph com-plaining." Mr. Toliver and Mr. Berger[2] have commented on the poor

[1] See O. Kurz, "Four Tapestries after Hieronymus Bosch," *JWCI*, XXX (1967), p. 154 and note 21.

[2] Toliver, *op.cit.*; Berger, "The Poem as Green World." See also Peter Dronke, *The Medieval Lyric* (London, 1968), pp. 103-04, where various Galician lyrics are cited, in which hinds are addressed by young girls. The hinds, Dronke says, are the symbolic confidantes of a girl in love and embody "all that is *farouche* and ardent in her nature." Certainly neither Nymph nor fawn is *farouche*, but there may be a thematic echo in the topic.

nymph's "character," upon her self-protections and the poet's shattering of them; I must borrow from them to make my point. Like the girl in "Mourning," or like the unfortunate Lover, the Nymph is sensitive and self-centered. She is, I think, more attractively delicate than either of those others. Then, too, some of her exaggeration lies in the genre Marvell has set her. Skelton's young girl spoke in mightily exaggerated terms of the loss of Philip Sparrow. The Nymph, like Jane Scroup, enjoys her sensations and emotions even more than she suffers the experiences calling forth those emotions. Something like Chlora in "Mourning," but far more sweetly, she enjoys her bereavement and enjoys expressing her delicious unhappiness. The girl professes not to hate "the wanton Troopers" who have so needlessly destroyed her pet, although she reckons their sin so great that she seems to assimilate the murder of the creature to the death of Christ.[3] Some critics are convinced that the fawn is not simply *surrogatio amoris* in the girl's mind, a substitute then for Sylvio, but *surrogatio Amoris*, a substitute for Christ Himself.[4] To assume this is to simplify needlessly, and to skew what the poem says and does; the point is that for the Nymph, the loss is incomparable, and therefore she uses language which, in the ordinary world, is suitable for a far more important sacrifice and death.

As Mr. Berger has suggested, the loss of the fawn means more to this girl than the loss of her lover; there is a certain comfort and relief manifest in the nymph's speaking of her life after Sylvio's defection. Then, she was free to order her own life her own way—to make a boudoir, really, of her plot of ground; to bring up her pet, an undemanding creature who laid no tax on her real personality. Such demands as the fawn makes seem all the nymph can cope with, otherwise why such a tremendous demonstration of grief? Niobe after all lost *all* her children; this girl has lost a single white deer. In the garden of her own construction, planted to suit her own style, her fawn is so "fit" that it could mingle with the roses and the lilies. The girl, the garden, and the fawn all blend into one virginal scene, white, cold, and still. As Dorinda and Thyrsis had done, the nymph interprets Elysium in terms private to her own experience and aesthetics, of virgin candor and integrity:

> Now my Sweet Faun is vanish'd to
> Whether the Swans and Turtles goe:

[3] Williamson, *op.cit.*   [4] Spitzer, *op.cit.*

In fair *Elizium* to endure,
With milk-white Lambs, and Ermins pure.

Like Dorinda, the Nymph cannot endure to linger on earth:

O do not run too fast: for I
Will but bespeak thy Grave, and dye.

The shepherdess, then, orders her tomb, herself to be hardened by grief into a stone (marble), the fawn to be turned into even whiter alabaster. Her tears, though, will continue after the metamorphosis, like those of "Mourning," to wear away her breast. The girl and fawn are their own monuments, she like Niobe all tears commemorating the self she has so carefully guarded against violation. The Pygmalion theme is reversed as the girl opts against love and the flesh, to turn the flesh to stone.

One might feel a certain cruelty in the poet's exposure of his characters: Damon is after all lovable, the nymph, in the word's best sense, pathetic; but the shock, such as it is, is always muted. The poet may mock, but he does not satirize. The splitting off of the poet's persona from that of his speaker, however abrupt, just misses cruelty. Clearly, though he deplores the nymph's narrowness of vision, he appreciates her sweetness and her taste, and makes us acknowledge the power and appeal of her aesthetic sensibility. Damon may be a bumpkin, but he is a delicate bumpkin; his pliable sweetness is the more manifest when he is compared to the ill-tempered Mower against gardens. Marvell may expose his characters' limitations, but he protects them, too, by the same means by which he exposes them—by his detachment from them. He judges, but mercifully; he can understand the nymph, both her genre and her personality; he can understand the unfortunate Lover—and, even, himself or "himself" in "Upon Appleton House."

Such detachment is extraordinary in lyric poetry, of course; in real life, this speaker's detachment from his own emotions in "The Definition of Love" would classify him in our categorizing world as a psychiatric case; so would the violent behavior of the unfortunate Lover, though one would expect a different diagnosis. "Bermudas" offers another kind of detachment, a Berkeleian situation, where no hearer is present to record the song of the rowers. The distance of the speaker of "An Horatian Ode" is an even more miraculous achievement, considering how the poet's task at the outset modulates into Cromwell's; but just as the even-handedness of the poet permits his readers to see the *monarchomachia* as ritual, not as bloody scene, the tragic involvements are brilliantly skirted. We need not weep over the dead King—pity and fear, proper reactions to tragic events on the stage or off it, are sponged out by the poet's magnificent effacement of a reacting, or over-reacting, sensibility. The poet and the poet's subject are made somehow impersonal, are moved by "forces," professional, historical, and providential, beyond their private wills and beyond the readers' full comprehension as well. What happens in that poem—like what happens in "Bermudas"—fulfills a questionless destiny overriding manifest personal problems.

"An Horatian Ode" begins with a conventionally apologetic commonplace and ends upon formal injunction and invocation. The poem is closed, hieratic, accomplished. For not all of Marvell's poems can the same claims be made. "Bermudas" slides into being and out again; "A Dialogue between the Soul and Body" stops but does not end; some readers have felt significantly let down by the last stanza of "The Garden." Though that last stanza seems to me thoroughly proper, and to provide a proper closed ending to the poem,[5] it cannot be denied that it is disjunctive from what goes before. "Upon Appleton House" at least appears to begin hieratically, formally, in annunciation, but its end is both ambiguous and abrupt, with a problematic image of hemispheres and an informal injunction, "Let's in." The poem's great weight rests on a small final point, as under the cover of the dark the actors, the speaker and others, leave the outdoor scene. Another way of saying this is that the tone shifts, and we are not quite sure how, or from what to what it shifts. Who says "Let's in," and to whom? To Maria? To his readers? Persona, in other words, is bound up with theme and tone in these poems; like them, persona is a device treated as a problem, and presented problematically. Some poems have little or no "speaker" in them; others have several; others, apparently united but later divergent speakers; still others, of which "Upon Appleton House" is the chief example, a multiplicity of voices, speakers, tones, personae.

It is no wonder "Andrew Marvell" seems a detached and uncommitted poet: he leaves his poetical characters in the lurch, he is not faithful to his

[5] See pp. 174-77.

poetical subjects, he offers allegiance and withdraws it from his styles and his tones. But in all this, one attachment, one commitment is very clear— to the poetic craft itself. A man who can speak with more than one voice at a time is a man of detachment and control, certainly, but a man remarkably dedicated to the exigencies of his art.

Intersection

Preface to III and IV

IN THE SECTIONS which follow, I have tried to provide a reading for two of Marvell's most substantial poems, "The Garden" and "Upon Appleton House." Because the two poems share a good deal and draw upon a common store of resources, some of my observations may seem to overlap. What I say about the emblematic method, for instance, applies to both poems, or to parts of both poems, but I have laid it out most fully in the chapter on "The Garden." Much of what I say about mixed genres applies to both poems, too; indeed, I think the poems in major part quite different kinds of exercise in *genera mixta*. The two poems are, however, very different in technique: "The Garden" is a staggering triumph of compression, and "Upon Appleton House" is loose, disconnected, inconclusive, often chatty. In many ways, the two poems represent opposite solutions to many of the same problems of structure and style; both poems are remarkably eclectic and, at the same time, unpedantic. Both poems are anthological, I think, but neither is an anthology merely; both poems are traditional, but what they do with traditions is immensely inventive. Without in the least sacrificing the supports of their own past, these poems throw out bridges to new slopes of idea and expression.

Marvell is a remarkable pontifex of traditions, and could design both the precise, exact, economical bridge that "The Garden" is, tight and yare, and the strong loop of rope and vines of "Upon Appleton House," cast over an abyss of literary depth. In the first poem, one must walk delicately; in the second, one must dare to swing out across the spaces the poet leaves his readers to traverse alone.

Though the poems are so unpedantic, there is a good deal of pedantry in the pages that follow: Lucan, Livy, Valeriano, Alciati, and Scaliger are not, on the whole, the most exciting reading imaginable, though Plato, Philo, Pliny, and Virgil cannot be dismissed as worthless authors. These writers and many more are adduced to help identify the languages and modes of literary tradition in which Marvell wrote so fluently. Though of course I think they help us to think with something like the poet's own professionalism, I also know very well that all these aids to understanding cannot add a jot to the poems' simple beauty—these poems appeal at many levels, and to many kinds of readers. Read aloud, Marvell's poetry is sufficient to most men's needs, and the intellectual and craftsmanlike questions set here fade into insignificance as one listens merely to the words. But all the same, I hope these pedantries may add some overtones and undertones to the lovely sound; that by knowing something of his own preoccupations with his art, we may prolong his echoing song in our minds and in others'.

Part III

"The Garden"

❦ 1 ❧

"THE GARDEN"

[i]

T HE GARDEN" presents a primary puzzle, because though its language is clear as glass, the *sfumato* of its meanings seems to belie the beautiful precision of vocabulary and syntax. However we read the poem, it seems to hold "more" the next time; it must, then, withhold something of itself from us at each reading. It shares its mysteriousness with other poems in Marvell's lyric collection, although its idiom of mystery seems to me to be its own.

Among other poems, "Bermudas," oddly unexplained, is a case in point. We know a great deal about the poem and its content, perhaps even its occasion; we know about Bermuda itself, about the sense of election fostered in its colonists by the Virginia Company, about the great whale that "threatened" the islanders; a great deal, also, about the tradition of a paradisal garden planted to the westward, and about its language of *locus amoenus* and *locus amoenissimus*.[1] What we do not know, though, is what is going on in this poem. What are the people up to, in that "small Boat, that row'd along"? In a seascape seen from a great distance, "the remote *Bermudas*" ride on a map of "th' Oceans bosome," where the rowers keep their significant secret. We seem, like the "list'ning Winds," simply to overhear the oarsmen's psalm of praise about the island's supernatural wonders. Though in this poem the themes of withdrawal and emergence, characteristic of so much of Marvell's poetry, are clear enough, and we think we know something of the specific reasons for withdrawal ("the Storms, and Prelat's rage"), the reasons for and the direction of emergence remain concealed. These singing oarsmen go about their business, perhaps also about their Father's, but they do not tell us just what their errand is.

In the Mower poems, as we have noted, another kind of suspension results from the poet's explorations of the meanings, for poetry and for ethical life, of the pastoral convention, which he presents so variously in

---

[1] See Josephine Waters Bennett, "Britain among the Fortunate Isles," *SP*, LIII (1956), 114-40; for Marvell, p. 131.

the poems that he seems not to favor any particular interpretation over another, but offers them all for *our* option. We are distracted by having, in the specific poems, to choose between fields and gardens, by not understanding how even glowworms can light benighted lovers home—whatever that "home" may be—and by not understanding the real or the symbolic Damon, or what he makes of himself in his song. In the "Horatian Ode," we are not permitted to guess what the poet really thinks of Oliver, what of the King, but are forced to accept his acceptance of a situation fundamentally qualified. What this poet gives, evidently so generously, with one hand, he contrives to take away with the other; the apparent exactness of his language is belied by the elusiveness of the verse. Such elusiveness cannot be accident: our view of "Bermudas" has been carefully arranged, after all. If we do not catch more than a hint of the social and spiritual measure of that island, it is not wholly our fault.

But what is one to make of hiatus like this in poems written before the twentieth century? Nowadays, space is regularly left in works of art for us to provide our own psychological cadenzas; we are assumed to be sensitive collaborators in a given work of art. In Marvell's traditions, such a thing was unthinkable: the work of art was the unmistakable point of contact between artist and reader, artist and beholder; it legitimately focused attention upon itself, made demands upon both creator's skill and beholder's responsiveness. Decorum did not allow for cadenzas, and space in literary works was not left to be filled by random and idiosyncratic associations or daydreaming. When space is left, then, in such a poem as "The Garden" one is required to see why this is so, to follow the directions given within the work itself for filling that space. In Marvell's case, we are not lacking for fill: industrious bees, ants, caterpillars, and bulldozers have amassed huge slagheaps of material, from which we have been politely invited to stuff the felt gaps in the poet's work. Bonaventure,[2] Canticles,[3] Plotinus,[4] Horace,[5] hermetica of various sorts,[6] St.

[2] Ruth Wallerstein, *Studies in Seventeenth Century Poetic*, esp. pp. 181-277. Since Miss Wallerstein's study has been so much cited in Marvell criticism, it is perhaps appropriate to note that her texts from intellectual and theological traditions appear to have been chosen with some disregard for the directions given in Marvell's verse. Miss Wallerstein's problem is mine, or anyone's who works on the difficult question of the relation of ideas to literary texts: how does one demonstrate a "tradition," citing texts to show continuity, without implying that those texts are the proof-texts of that tradition, or that one's author knew the tradition, possibly even the very texts, in the same way the historian recording the tradition knows it? There is not, for instance, any sure evidence that Marvell "knew" Bonaventure (or Ficino either,

Paul,[7] pastoral-in-general,[8] libertinism,[9] and many other ample traditions, concepts, and thinkers have been pressed into the service of Marvell's garden of verses, into the service of "The Garden" in particular. At dif-

---

alas!). Intellectual traditions tend to have their *topoi*, just as rhetorical traditions do; to this extent, "Ockham's razor," Descartes' *génie malin*, Locke's blind man, Berkeley's fountain are as much commonplaces as the world-upside-down, the world-as-a-book, or the false modesty commonplaces of classical rhetoric, and themselves become "images" within the philosophical discipline, ready for migration to other disciplines and often found meeting in literary texts.

A given author—Marvell, Sterne, Wallace Stevens—may use such commonplaces systematically, arbitrarily, or accidentally. When he uses such a commonplace with a system that accords with the one we attribute to the host-tradition, we are certainly entitled to assume that he was working consciously within that tradition; frequently, though, he uses such commonplaces in quite independent contexts of his own making, in which case we must assume either that he offers some critique of the conventional system, or that he simply liked the commonplace and transferred it to his own fictional purpose. It is difficult to determine the differences between arbitrary and accidental use, and only the context of the reference and our own literary sense can help us much. For some discussion of the problem, see below, pp. 295-305. For an author's relation to purely literary traditions, see below, footnotes 13, 16, 27, 36, 40.

[3] Stanley Stewart, *The Enclosed Garden* (Madison, 1966), *passim*, esp. 150-83; Wallerstein, pp. 206-11.

[4] Milton Klonsky, "A Guide through 'The Garden,'" *Sewanee Review*, LVIII (1950), 16-35; Wallerstein, pp. 186-88.

[5] Maren-Sofie Røstvig, *The Happy Man*, I, 154-72.

[6] *Ibid.*, pp. 162-63; Røstvig, "Andrew Marvell's 'The Garden,' a Hermetic Poem," *English Studies*, XL (1959), 65-76; L. W. Hyman, "Marvell's 'Garden,'" *ELH*, XXV (1958), 13-22; Harold E. Toliver, *Marvell's Ironic Vision*, p. 142. I fail to see the necessity for an androgynous Adam in the poem; the poet's solitude, chastity, and irony about women seem to me adequately accounted for by the tradition in which he was at work.

[7] Geoffrey H. Hartman, "Marvell, St. Paul, and the Body of Hope," *ELH*, XXXI (1964), 175-94. This interesting article seems to me to exemplify the arbitrary use of learned method (see footnote 2). Hartman's general point can be made from many Scriptural texts, OT as well as NT, and to focus on Paul is to give the impression of genuine textual relevance not in the least manifest from the words in the poem. If "Paul" is simply an "heuristic device," then a more appropriate point of reference to the same thematic material is surely the Platonic epistemology, so clearly indicated in stanza VI.

[8] Frank Kermode, "The Argument of Marvell's 'Garden,'" *Essays in Criticism*, II (1952), 225-41, and "Two Notes on Marvell," *N&Q*, CCXXVII (1952), 136-38; Toliver, esp. pp. 5-56, for a platonized pastoral; Edward Tayler, *Nature and Art in Renaissance Literature*, *passim*, esp. chapter IV; Joseph H. Summers, "Marvell's 'Nature,'" *ELH*, XX (1953), 121-35.

[9] M. C. Bradbrook and M. G. Lloyd Thomas, *Andrew Marvell*, pp. 154-55; Bradbrook, "Andrew Marvell and the Poetry of Rural Solitude," *RES*, XVII (1941), 37-46.

ferent points in this attempt upon the poem, I shall rely on the materials so generously heaped up for my use, although I am seriously considering the proposition that it is the hiatuses themselves, and not their hypothesized "background," that are the most significant thing about the poem.[10]

As scholars remind us,[11] Marvell is among other things a notably playful poet, who knew *serio,* even *sacro, ludere.* One of the things he played with is traditional thought and language; therefore, indeed, it is so important to know something about Bonaventure, Canticles, Plotinus, Horace, Hermes Trismegistus, St. Paul, and now, God help us, Nicholas of Cusa[12] and Descartes.[13] Man does not live by poems alone, and though poems live chiefly by other poems, they draw some of their life from the breasts of theology and philosophy. I follow lines laid down by D. C. Allen and Frank Kermode[14] in reading the seriousness and lightness of "The Garden" against each other; Mr. Allen has taught us a way of reading the Renaissance poetry of civilized grace, and Kermode's exasperation at Marvell's critics has reminded those who tend to forget it that there is a difference in kind between philosophical and poetic utterances. Rather than presenting philosophical and religious traditions systematically,[15] poetry tends to allude to such traditions by means of their particular "languages," their terms of art. Much Renaissance poetry that seems "learned" to us simply asks us to call up associations to metaphysical

[10] In speaking of "hiatus" and "gap," thus of things not said directly in the text, I wish to dissociate myself from the esotericism prescribed by Leo Strauss and so evident a part of the theory of his *epigoni;* here, I try to consider what is not said in this poem in relation to directions given in the poem itself.

[11] Don Cameron Allen, *Image and Meaning;* Frank J. Warnke, "Play and Metamorphosis in Marvell's Poetry"; "Sacred Play: Baroque Poetic Style," *JAAC,* XXII.

[12] Isabel G. MacCaffrey, "Some Notes on Marvell's Poetry, Suggested by a Reading of his Prose," *MP,* LXI (1964), pp. 261-9.

[13] Daniel Stempel, *"The Garden:* Marvell's Cartesian Ecstasy," *JHI,* XXVI (1967), 99-114. Mr. Stempel's method is much like that noted in footnote 7; though it is true that here, as elsewhere, Marvell's capacity to pack his language lends some support to the idea that he was working within the Cartesian systematics, Mr. Stempel's use of the principle of parsimony will not work with a poet whose effort is not to exclude traditions by relying upon a single economical one, but to focus as many traditions as possible within the one work. See footnote 2 for comment on philosophical topoi, and pp. 174-77 for the bee topos.

[14] Kermode, "Argument."

[15] Of course some poetry, and much verse, does just this. In the Renaissance, there is a strong tradition of overtly philosophical poetry (e.g. Bruno, Davies, Greville, More, Pope), following on models believed to have been set by Parmenides and Lucretius. The genre of philosophical poetry needs study, since the enterprise itself poses serious critical problems.

or moral argument which are no longer part of our experience or training and which, therefore, seem to us odd, esoteric, and abstruse. All that such poetry asks, really, is that we resonate to some deep and thoughtful note, not that we reconsider a given philosophical system every time its language appears in a poem.[16]

Literary references within poems are a different matter. Although John Donne may not have entirely understood the structure of the Ptolemaic universe (after all, who could?) or the reasons why the Keplerian schema seemed a better one, he certainly knew what verse epistles were, and satires, and the different forms of the love lyric. Nature influences art, but art influences art even more. Artists, especially Renaissance artists, kept their eye on their mighty predecessors and competitors, and expected their literate readers to know the context of any given literary tradition.[17] When Kermode chides us for accepting the pompous data of various philosophical systems as adequate outworks for "The Garden," he points out that the poet was simply manipulating key elements of philosophical languages to which we are supposed to respond. Oddly enough, he did not follow through on this valuable critical insight, and failed to tell us

[16] We are not, for instance, implored to reconsider the merits of the Reformation when a poet promises his lady "her protestant to be," though we are expected to note as we go to Herrick's smart variation on the love-as-religion trope. Nor are we required to consider the reaches of the doctrine of correspondence everytime we read "A Valediction: of Weeping," or the Ptolemaic system in "A Valediction: Forbidding Mourning," though if we do not know what "protestant" means, or how a woman's body can be "like" a tear from her eye, and both of them like the earth's globe, then we by no means fulfill our obligation to the poem—which is, simply, to understand what the words in it refer to. For our own information, and for our students', we may have to pile up slagheaps from time to time; I do not wish to belittle the results of scholarly excavation, since it is so often the only thing that keeps the past from total disappearance. But scholars often tend to confuse their discoveries with the received opinion of an earlier age, and *vice versa*; just because we are ignoramuses does not mean that, contrariwise, all Renaissance readers were professional experts who understood everything referred to in the verse they read. Like us, they were middling educated, but educated at least in the same terms as their writers, so that a Renaissance writer might fairly expect sensible resonance from his audience.

[17] For the highly compressed materials of the next two paragraphs, I am indebted to much commentary on genre and style, but chiefly to E. H. Gombrich's *Norm and Form* (London, 1966), esp. pp. 1-10, 81-98, 99-106. Leishman's posthumously published *The Art of Marvell's Poetry* provides many analogues to Marvell's practice, some of which can be classified as "sources." In many ways, Leishman's work is an application of Curtius' topical method to Marvell's verse, and as such is essential to any study of Marvell's traditions.

145

(or to show us) how to apply his dictum to the allusive literary language of the poem as well. Earlier I used the word "formalist" about Marvell's verse, meaning to suggest not only his formal elegance, but his use of tradition, convention, and genre as well; to refer to his way of moving in and out of recognized literary habits, in this poem written down in a shorthand that contributes to the poem's many enigmas.[18] From his short-hand comes much of the poem's gappiness, its intellectual caesura, or diaresis.

"The Garden" is by no means Marvell's only poem experimenting in genre, mixing generic allusions. Nor is the poem made remarkable *only* by its generic mixture. *Genera mixta* solves some problems, but it raises others.

In this poem, as in others, the chief difficulties of Marvell's *genera mixta* lie, I think, in the no-man's-land between received meanings and the signs he gives us to those meanings. He has deliberately cut away the immediate conjunction: in "The Mower against Gardens," the poet forces a gap between the elements of the pastoral *paragone*. In "The Coronet," he forces a gap between secular and Christian pastoral, therefore between secular and Christian poetry, and even between secular and Christian living. In "The Nymph complaining," the gap lies at the junction of Ovidian metamorphosis, the garden of Canticles, world-rejecting pastoral-ism, the death of pets, and the ecphrastic power of art; in "To his Coy Mistress," at the junction of various love traditions (*carpe diem, blason,* heroic love, petrarchan conceit, and perhaps, as I recently learnt, *ars moriendi* as well).[19] In each case, not much is made overtly of the par-ticular languages of reference, but without some sense of them the poems are nearly impenetrable.[20]

There are of course different degrees of reference to traditional lan-

---

[18] Leishman, *passim*; and Joseph H. Summers' introduction to the Laurel Series *Marvell*, pp. 12-15, which gives an admirable commentary on Marvell's awareness of generic and formal traditions.

[19] Stanley Stewart, "Marvell and the *ars moriendi*," paper delivered at the MLA meetings in New York, December 1966.

[20] See Leo Spitzer, "Marvell's 'Nymph Complaining for the Death of her Faun.'" This excellent study seems to me to have only the fault of a too-simple dialectic, indicated in its subtitle, "Sources versus Meaning." Arguing against "imagistic positivism" (which the author appears to have attributed to D. C. Allen), Spitzer permitted himself to adopt something like "generic positivism," a critical position subject to his own objections.

guages. Most commonly, a traditional vocabulary is used "straight," as in "Come live with me and be my love." In fact no girl would expect, if someone were to address her in this mode, to bounce out into the fields dressed only in the gew-gaws offered by a generous lover. Such language as Marlowe's, so highly and admittedly artificial, can easily be inverted, as in "The Nymph's Reply," where the irony lies simply in affecting to take the metaphoric language seriously. Or it can be transposed into another dimension, as Donne's piscatory poem, "The Baite," so obviously does. The language itself can become a metaphor for the mode from which it derives, as in "the tangles of Neaera's hair," whereby the poet collects into one quick phrase the themes of idleness, dalliance, love poetry, any distraction from the real job. In "The Coronet," "all the fragrant Towers/ That once adorn'd my Shepherdesses head," suddenly releases anew the meaning of the metaphor, or of the metaphorical meaning of styles. The phrase tells us to think of style itself as metaphor and demonstrates the peculiar metapoesis of this poem, which chooses to define moral and poetic choices in terms of their stylistic relation to each other.

In "The Garden," the poet characteristically strips down traditional languages into brief references, by which the argument of the poem is carried. Such diminution has the advantages of its economies, but it leaves a great deal to the defenseless reader. Too much, I think: the clues have often proved almost invisible hairs to us.

But in contrast to this particular tightfistedness, there is an unexpected largesse in one range of Marvell's technique, where, without violating his principle of aesthetic economy, he gives us much more than at first he seems to do. This is in the area of his puns, on which balances much of the unwieldy bulk of meaning the poet asks us to recognize. Before tackling the larger hiatuses in "The Garden," I should like to look at the way the puns work in the poem. Unlike Donne, who thrusts his flamboyantly duplicitous puns directly at us, Marvell tends to mute his, so that they resonate late in their larger meanings, after the reader seems to have got (or so he may think) safely past them to the next line, figure, or stage of thought. Not only does the poet pun, as in "Toyles," "upbraid," and "Mate," for instance; he also unpuns and unmetaphors in this poem. After Professor Empson's grave analysis,[21] the puns of "The Garden" need only the merest recollection; in the first line, "vainly"

[21] William Empson, *Some Versions of Pastoral*, Chapter VI.

evokes pride as well as emptiness. As we proceed, we realize that the whole *vanitas*-tradition, that celebration of the transience of material things so common in still life painting and openly exploited in "Little T.C.," is developed in Marvell's use of symbolic plants and flowers throughout the poem. But all this realization is to come; at the beginning, we need cope only with the simplest meanings of "vainly," in relation to the activities suggested by "the Palm, the Oke, or Bayes." At the end of the first line, "amaze" involves us in a labyrinth as well as in wonder; both "wonder" and "labyrinth" turn out to be part of the thematic meaning of the whole poem, gathering force as other relevancies develop through the stanzas.

"Toyles" at first seems to be merely the hard work involved in civil, military, or literary endeavors, although the connotations of "amaze" serve to warn us of the trap hidden in the word. In conjunction with "upbraid," the line becomes very complicated, implicated, indeed, like the "braided," plaited garland to which the word also refers. At least four meanings emerge from this double double sound: the narrowness of the shade of one tree is a reproach to men who achieve rewards in only a limited sphere of action; the narrowness of the shade of one tree is a reproach to the temptations such metaphorical plants offer ambitious men; the narrowness of the shade both upbraids (reproaches) and braids up (organizes) garlands as rewards for the efforts of ambitious men; the narrowness of the shade braids up the trailing, catching tendrils and branches of the entrapping metaphorical plants.

All these meanings (and perhaps others) gather behind our immediate choice of interpretation, so that we must shift from one meaning to the next and back again, but are never permitted by the style itself, by the lapidary quality of the couplets, to linger over the problems, or to choose one meaning exclusive of the others. The neat epigrams have their own impulse, so that we go straight through them to the juncture of "all Flow'rs and all Trees," which "close," as garlands do, with some finality to a generous, full garden-shade, where a whole man properly takes his recreation and finds his refreshment.[22] The puns are like the pun involved in the word "re-creation," are, really, like recreation itself: lighthearted, they bring the reader back to awareness of, for instance, the fact that understanding is a less simple operation than at first it seems. "Com-

---

[22] See *Paradoxia Epidemica*, pp. 60-62, for "recreation"; for the notion of garlands as fetters, relevant also in stanza 5, see Virgil, *Eclogues* V, 19.

panies" in the second stanza; "Fond" and "Flame" in the third; "heat," "retreat," "Still," and "race" in the fourth; the notorious "less" in the sixth; and "kind," as well as "transcending," "annihilating," and "green"; "these," I think, also a pun; the thyme-time pun of the final stanza (its clue embedded in "Hortus," the truncated Latin version of "The Garden")—all these make us look again and again at the shiftiness of meanings, moving back and forth across an area bounded, often, by direct contradiction. The shifting back and forth is itself part of the fundamental meaning of the poem; the reader is invited to understand by a metamorphic, even anamorphic process, for which the terms of the poem offer themselves as metaphors.

At first reading, the "sense" seems self-evident, one meaning sufficient, until another emerges from behind it, and perhaps another and another, to suspend us among the alternatives, none unmistakeably sanctioned, all contextually defensible. Sometimes the doubleness is clear-cut—"Toyles," "race"—sometimes penumbral. "Flame" in the third stanza has nothing to do with fire, but is metaphorical at a conventional literary remove, referring to the lover's ardency, or to the woman for whom he "burns"; or (as some think in this case) to the iconographical-metaphorical attribute of Cupid, his brand. "Flame" alerts us to the meanings of "heat" in the next stanza and, in the last, offers some reason for the sun's being "milder"; but "heat" is a wonderful pun, gathering into itself the notion of competition, involving palm, oak, and bays, of burning love, as well as the footrace described. The "warmth" meaning of "heat" complicates "end their race," since the running ends in this poem in trees, thus in plant-rewards, as worldly endeavors and as garlands; and yet the race does not "end," as most pastoral pursuits do, in the pleasures achieved in easing ardency, or in the issue of ardent love. By the poem's assumptions, the race *does* end, in quite another sense.

In the major stanza, "from pleasure less" has displeased as well as puzzled critics.[28] The primary meaning is, surely, "from lesser pleasure," though Empson's "diminished by pleasure" may also be considered, since that interpretation lends cause to "withdraws" in the next line. Contradicting the second meaning attributed to "less," the word "transcending" is both a towering over and a rising above "these"—a plain and unobtrusive word which turns out to be very problematical indeed. "These" can be "all the kinds" as well as the elements of the actual garden, and

[28] Leishman, p. 312.

the worlds and seas postulated in the stanza as "real." "Annihilating" offers a puzzle, since the one meaning it cannot sustain is "bringing to nothing," although the word "all" juxtaposed to "annihilating" inevitably evokes the idea of God's original act of creation, and suggests His final dissolution of the earth.

Creation, re-creation, recreation: from the pleasures of the senses comes both physical recreation (stanza 5) and intellectual re-creation (stanza 6). I have elsewhere talked at length about the relation of recreation to creativity: let me here simply cite Thomas Fuller, "Recreation is a second Creation, when weariness hath almost annihilated ones spirits."[24] Different sorts of creation are involved in the phrase "all that's made," which shimmers between its favorable connotations of divine totality and its derogatory Platonic meanings of material imperfection. *Res creatae* can thus be seen as marvelous because made from God's plan, and as imperfect because of their artificiality and materiality. Indeed, in the many moving meanings of this stanza, we discover that "annihilating" is the mirror-action of "transcending."

"All that's made" can be converted into a single thought—a "green" one at that—can be, then, rarefied to thought, but to lively thought. The phrase, originating in Virgil's seventh Eclogue, endlessly yields its connotations of potentiality, strength, growth, youth, and innocence. The "green Thought" is inside another "green," the protective refreshment of "shade." The doubling of "green" thickens the meaning oddly, by using the word in overlapping but different senses; simply from the combinations, "green Thought" in one case, "green Shade" in the other, we are borne to consider the many possible variations of meaning in this single, simple, common word. In this context, "Shade" is normatively good, as the refreshment of vegetation against the parching sun, but it is also blurred by its connotations of "shadow," the shadow cast by materiality upon the ideal, the shadow also cast by the ideal upon materiality.[25] Within the context of the poem's stricter argument, "green" is of colors the best, "am'rous" in a purer style than the red and white of physical

[24] Thomas Fuller, *The Holy State*, p. 171.

[25] I am indebted to Miss E.G.W. Mackenzie for the reference to Philo, *On the Creation* (LCL, 1962), I, 100-03, 120-25, dealing with the significance of both "green" and "shade"; the passages discuss Adam, sole in Paradise, before the Creation of Eve, in ways that seem relevant to this poem. See also Sir Thomas Browne, *The Garden of Cyrus, Religio Medici and Other Works*, ed. L. C. Martin (Oxford, 1964), pp. 166-67, for "shade" and "adumbration."

love. The doubling of "green" intensifies by the manifold meanings which shift back and forth, metamorphosing thought into thought, as well as thought into shade and back again.

In the penultimate stanza, the eighth, the puns are sharp. "Mate" is the woman, rejected for solitude's sake throughout the poem; "meet" is associated to "mate" by reason of the folkish, analogical formation, by an error, in reading the English Genesis, in the word "helpmeet." "Meet" is also "fit" or "fitting"; logically, solitude is utterly destroyed by any "meeting" with another, helpmate or meet, friend or whatever. What was "fit" is thereby made unfit. In this pun, there is both similarity and opposition of meanings, the two interchanging with one another. "Share" works on the same principle, in its first meaning, "lot," with deterministic implications; in its second, a "sharing," or dividing, partitioning. To put it another way, the first meaning implies *donnée*, what is given from without, the second a giving, an expansion, perhaps even a thinning out of one's self into another.

All words, of course, carry more than one meaning. Fortunately for our reason, they do not come charged with all their meanings at once, but are hedged by the context in which they appear. Puns deliberately concentrate on multiple meanings of a single word, but also, they narrow down the possible meanings very sharply. Marvell's puns are peculiar. Though each separate meaning is self-limiting, clear, sharp, the aggregate punning in the poem results in an atmospheric blur of meanings, to make punning an epistemological device, a device commenting on intellectual perceptions of meaning, particularly appropriate to a poem raising epistemological questions. This poem sets problems of the relation of experience to thought, and problems of thinking itself; it illustrates its critical nature by its peculiar comment on its own, or the poetic, activity; that is, it comments on its own creation and its own meaning even as it undergoes that creation and establishes that meaning. In this poem, one of its subjects, ecstasy, is officially beyond words, so that the punning helps us to see how this experience is, like the words for it, at the limit of meaning.

All the same, though perhaps inadequate to render experience, words are something more than merely adequate. They are somehow magic, creative and recreative themselves; they transcend "these." Words call upon memory and imagination to flesh out the hints and suggestions they supply; they leave room for fantasy, which provides gardens to private taste beyond the blueprints given in garden-poems. Puns have the virtue of playing, at one and the same time, upon both the inadequacy and the creativity of words, *logoi* like green thoughts in green shades, holding in potentiality all that's made, especially all that's made by poets. Puns act out overtly what all words must do, contracting into the limit of their spelling more than conventionally "ought" to fit into such a small space, expanding the one sign into all sorts of relevant and interrelated meanings.[26]

In this poem, the puns transcend and annihilate, expand and contract to afford at the smallest scale within the poem an example, in etymological terms, of withdrawal and emergence, the poem's principal theme. Their doubleness is indeed duplicity, demonstrating the shiftiness of men's perceptions of themselves, of their words, of their own perceptions. The puns move back and forth as anamorphic pictures do, altering with altered angles of vision. These puns teach us—as puns do, of course—to experience the many in the one, rather in the comic than the philosophic mode. Unlike Donne's delineated puns, Marvell's in this poem go on yielding until we find ourselves experiencing not so much objectively separable meanings as shaded meanings along a gamut, sometimes a gamut running between polar opposites. In other words, these puns are not designed to be puzzled out to the limit of their relevant implications, but suggest an endless mirror-world of reflection and speculation upon infinitesimal degrees of differentiation. As our ideas shimmer, oscillate, interpenetrate, even in the puns we can experience something like an understanding which transcends, an understanding in which each particular perception has its own individual clarity and at the same time exists in a shifting interrelation with all other meanings in the poem.

[ii]

FROM THE puns in the poem, I want to move to a parallel range of materials, the stuff of literary convention, tradition, and genre. Like most Renaissance writers, Marvell showed close knowledge of generic literary organization, according to which certain subjects were to be treated in a given decorum, form, style, and diction. To some Renaissance critics it evidently seemed that Greek practice had somehow established *genera* which were confirmed by eclectic, imitative Roman writers; and that the critical treatises of Aristotle, to say nothing of Alexandrian critics, "proved"

---

[26] See *Paradoxia Epidemica*, Chapter 6.

the validity of generic categories in literature. Marvell was fortunate in the time of his birth, after several generations of hard-working literary men had made available to him many alternatives in literary practice. Like many of his gifted contemporaries, Marvell was a great manipulator of *genera*, styles, and modes, sometimes working serially ("The Gallery" and "Upon Appleton House"), sometimes grading generic conventions into each other ("To his Coy Mistress"), sometimes twisting generic elements inseparably together ("The Coronet"). "Upon Appleton House," a poem hospitable to several major *genera*, makes a fine companion-piece to "The Garden," for in the shorter poem generic manipulation is delicate, deft, and understated, and in the longer it is overt, even blatant. Both poems belong to a class of works utilizing different genres both consecutively and in overlap; the poems share, I think, an interest in criticizing the very conventions they exploit. Both are self-critical and metapoetic, poems deliberately about, among other things, poetry itself. Sharing so much, the two poems display quite different solutions to the problem of mixed genres.[27]

In "The Garden," what is so striking is the poet's reduction of such large literary and philosophical traditions to such small verbal units: he applies the epigrammatic method to vast traditions, and manages thereby to compress them into brief but telling phrases. That Marvell arrived at his extraordinarily tacit solution in "The Garden" only after considerable work, is manifest in the apparently fragmentary "Hortus," the Latin forerunner, in which the themes are far more overtly developed than in the English version. There, the poet gave the nymphs names—Neaera, Faustina, Chloe, Corynna, ladies who do not enter the English poem in their full shapes. Instead of "the busie Companies of Men," the Latin version has temples, cities, and palaces of kings. In the Latin, snows give substance to whiteness, the murex to redness; Jupiter, Vulcan, and Mars join Apollo and Pan in finding trees more satisfying than ladies. In the English version, full reference to traditional themes and tales has been

---

[27] A good theoretical and practical article on *genera mixta* is sorely needed; it can be said, I think, that the pastoral mode is, like paradox and picaresque, particularly hospitable to different genres within it. Indeed, because of Guarini's argument and the polemics it aroused, in Renaissance terms, the pastoral could be called *the* mixed genre, the only genre in which mixture was not only permissible but requisite. Marvell's use of several literary forms under a diaphanous pastoral umbrella may be another attempt on his part to explore the implications of "mixedness" in the pastoral mode. (I am indebted to Stephen Greenblatt and Alarik Skarstrom for discussion of this point.)

attenuated; tact and economy have pared down the evocative language needed for all the rich literary reference that feeds the poem. The nymphs have no names—indeed, they themselves are not present in the poem; they have been reduced to colors, red and white. One result of this reduction and compression is hiatus, both between the individual stanzas and within them. The conspicuously diminished images, evoking the traditional ideas which belong with such language, exist in a highly charged emptiness.[28] For the image-structure of the first part of his poem, Marvell had (I think) a particular model as well. This is Petrarca's Sonnet 10, to Colonna, a modern *locus classicus* for the solitude-theme. There Petrarca, punning on his friend's name, contrasts the columns (*colonne*) of *palazzi, theatro,* and *loggia* (Cf. "Hortus") to the columnar trees of the natural environment he has chosen (*abete, faggio,* and *pino*). In that scene, the nightingale sings in the shade as the poet, unencumbered by his usual thoughts of love, reclines on the ground and permits his mind to rise from earth to heaven. Marvell has disposed these elements in another context, greatly enriching his poem thereby. It is interesting, though, to note that Petrarca's scheme, made official in solitude sonnets such as those of Lorenzo de' Medici (*Rime,* XXI), is another of the literary traditions exploited in this poem.

Its title alone suggests that the poem is tradition-rich, and as we progress through it, we realize how much of the garden-past of civilization this poem invokes, always by means of impeccably literary references.[29] Another way of saying this is that the poet decided to see civilization under the aspect of gardens, and in a further *tour de force,* to perceive all literature in vegetable symbols. He had authority for this—*The Garden of Cyrus* is another such imaginative recreation of the universe-as-garden; behind both these delicate literary works lies an encyclopedic garden-world such as that laid out in Benedictus Curtius' *Hortorum libri triginta* (Lyons, 1560), where the historical, archaeological, and mythological

---

[28] For a measure of this contraction, see George Williamson, *Milton and Others* (Chicago, 1964); and William A. McGivern, "The Missing Stanzas in Marvell's Hortus," *PQ,* XLIV (1965), 462-66.

[29] Thomas Browne, *The Garden of Cyrus,* in *Religio Medici and Other Works,* ed. L. C. Martin (Oxford, 1964), is the great seventeenth-century document on the garden-past of civilization. For an excellent analysis of literary gardens in epic context, see Giamatti, *The Earthly Paradise and the Renaissance Epic*; and Comito, *Renaissance Gardens and Elizabethan Romance.*

background of gardens is systematically displayed, together with practical directions to the craft of gardening in both trees and flowers.

In Marvell's poem, though, the gradually thickening meaning of his miraculous planting, never pedantic, never obscure, is not insisted on, such is the lightness of tone stanza by stanza. Only at the end of the poem are all the meanings of "gardens" revealed. Indeed, at the outset, "gardens" are not at issue, as the magniloquent *sententiae* of heroic comment roll out, in their serious stoical dress, so soon and so abruptly to be diminished by themselves:

> How vainly men themselves amaze
> To win the Palm, the Oke, or Bayes;
> And their uncessant Labours see
> Crown'd from some single Herb or Tree.

The grand endeavor impresses—all to be undone by one word, "single," soon followed by the ambivalences of "Toyles" and "upbraid." "Single" unmetaphors a huge tradition of fame, reduces it to an imaginary literal actuality. A warrior cannot expect the statesman's wreath, or the poet's; each achievement, limiting a man's scope, cuts him off from another kind of achievement and is rewarded at best by a meager garland, made of one kind of leaf only (Fig. 14). Among other things, the word "single" points to the fact that professional choice narrows a man, reduces his total potentiality, scales him down from his full self to "a short and narrow verged Shade."

Retirement-literature, of course, must reject the world; in its emphasis both on stylistic diminution and on emotional economy, "The Garden" more than once strikes an Horatian note. It is significant that in one Renaissance Horatian text, Veen's *Emblemata Horatiana*,[30] a visual analogue to the poem's first stanza may be found: there, in one picture (Fig. 15), a man sits in contemplation, rejecting the garlands of palm and oak extended to him by eager *putti*, and evidently having already cast down the garland of bays. In another picture (Fig. 16), a man sits unmoved on his pedestal although threatened by every material discomfort; a garland of bay lies rejected at his feet, and behind him palm trees and ivy-entwined oaks grow.

At this point, the poet turns to his paradoxical argument, elliptical

[30] Otto van Veen, *Emblemata Horatiana* (Antwerp, 1607), pp. 48-49, 82-83.

even by standards of paradoxy: if single plants are good, then gardens, made of a mixed plantation, are better.[31] Gardens are for repose, therefore "all Flow'rs and all Trees" make up the garlands of a retired man, complete in his self-understanding. By a major metaphor, the poet could rely on the world as a mixed wood, the *hule* or *sylva* of experience; translated into poetical usage, this conventional idea provides titles for a mixed collection of poetry, as in Statius', Poliziano's, or Jonson's collections. Here, the move from "wood" to "garden" gentles the mixture, both of experience and of poems, toning down the wilderness without losing the connotations of experience. The variety of experience itself is translated into the language of plants, as these plants conspicuously stand for genres and modes of literature as well as of life. This mixture of experience, mode of life, and literary genre persists throughout the poem, to be clarified only at its end. Among the substantive meanings of "garden," so generously alluded to in the poem—pleasure-gardens, gardens of contemplation, gardens of retirement, gardens of love; the specific gardens of Epicurean, Stoic, and Christian traditions; the Gardens of the Hesperides, of Eden, and of Canticles—lies the cliché literary meaning as well, the garden of eloquence, the paradise of pleasure or of dainty devices, the garden of the muses, its particular beauties, the particular flowers of rhetoric, all gathered into a mixed posie. At the same time, under all these positive meanings, so rich in their evocations, run the qualifications of *vanitas*, the vanity of human wishes and human expectations. Human effort, human fame, human love, all human experience and all things are subject to time and in fact must pass away.[32] Only in a green thought can green shade itself be brought to perfection and permanence.

But to accord with the mystifying diminution so evident in the reduction of literary to plant-traditions, to words and phrases, this garden is never directly named in the poem. It is simply "here," "hither," "this life I lead," "this Dial new." We begin with plants, not gardens, and with specific plants standing as emblems for the traditions to which they have been assigned. In his manipulation of palm, oak, and bay, the poet introduces himself as a *naïf*, examining men's values on their face. The

[31] See Thomas Adams, *A Divine Herball* (London, 1616), p. 49: "What Garden is only planted with one singular Kinde of *herbe?*"

[32] See John Hagthorpe, *Divine Meditations, and Elegies* (London, 1622), pp. 22-23, for a reference to the transience of human beings and plants; and Thomas Nashe, *Quaternio or a Fourefold Way to a Happie Life* (London, 1633), pp. 23-24.

paradoxical defense of solitude is the argument of a *faux-naïf*, since no one seriously questioned the moral and spiritual values of withdrawal, solitary contemplation, speculation, all of them specifics for individual recreation. It is not the argument, contrary to expectation though it is, but the way of arguing that makes this *naïf* so peculiar; his way with figures, not with propositions,[33] permits his bumbling innocence to make a literary revisions of a spectacular kind. Incomprehensibly, the *naïf* has sought quiet and innocence where no one would expect to find them, "in busie Companies of Men"; in a radical reduction, he dismisses all dalliance by claiming green a color more "am'rous" than red or white, traditional colors of pretty women with gardens in their faces, and therefore traditional colors for love. We are led through the poem by a Simplicissimus who sets off his each perception, his each conclusion about the world, from each other, making them unique and "new" by his use of visual and logical disjunction and by his reductive figures of speech and thought. Actually, of course, the *naïf* is a traditional pastoral character, the unspoilt and artless observer whose uncritical comments on what he sees turn out, often, to be very cunning.

The choice of *naïf* as speaker in the poem reinforces our feeling—never quite explicit—of a pastoral underlining to this very mixed poem. Certainly it has its pastoral aspects. It deals with "nature" and with "art," the root-problem of pastoral.[34] Involved in that *paragone* is the argument over active and contemplative lives; involved too is the question of the degree to which any life self-consciously lived can be other than an artefact.[35] In the pastoral debate, the question of artificiality is turned upside-down within the convention itself. The shepherd is always a *faux-naïf*, since the nature which is his nurse and norm is reorganized into an highly-wrought artifice of the creative imagination, a projection of fantastic harmony cast by the poet's mind upon a world really neutral, if not actually hostile, to ordinary men and extraordinary poets. With real sheep the literary shepherd is a dolt; he is a poet, and that is all he is. For such a view of pastoral, the figure of the garden is an appropriate one, since a garden is nature improved by art, cultivated by the imagination, as weed-

---

[33] Kermode, "Argument," and Leishman, p. 296, for Marvell's argument by figure.
[34] Hagthorpe, *Divine Meditations*, p. 6.
[35] Colie, "Castiglione's Urban Pastoral," *Greyfriar*, VIII (1965), 5-12; Harry Berger, Jr., "The Renaissance Imagination: Second World and Green World," 36-78, esp. pp. 72-78.

less and beautiful, as satisfying and nourishing as, in literary pastoral, nature ought always to be.

Marvell's argument for gardens is rooted in the unmetaphored metaphor for ways of life: standing well back from the poem, one must see that to argue for gardens at all is utterly paradoxical, since no one but a few Stoics and Marvell's Mower was ever against them. But logical integrity is of course not at issue here; the games with logic are as light and as critical as the games with puns. The poem examines poetic language and strains at the edges of that language's meaning, by scrupulously literary, not logical, means. Marvell's exercises in logical and tonal disjunction depend on his reducing traditions to manipulable units, which he then can reorganize and reinterpret according to the argumentative dictates of the poem. Polemically, the *faux-naïf* must defend gardens as well as solitude, because for him solitude is conceivably only in a garden-state, a garden-environment.

In stanza 3, the rejection of pastoral and libertine love, of "red and white," follows the solitude-argument, recollected once more, later, in stanza 8. In 3, though, Marvell must get around a literary problem, since gardens are *loci classici* for romantic dalliance, pastoral, libertine, even scriptural. Again, the management is by meiosis, red and white simply written off in favor of green, which thereby reduces the relevant poetical and ethical positions to the emblematic language of colors.[36] Of course,

---

[36] D. C. Allen, "Symbolic Color in the Literature of the English Renaissance," *PQ*, XV (1936), 81-92. The colors of the poem have been discussed, by Klonsky and Hartman among others. I have difficulty with their interpretations of green: first, because I do not find the *color* green to be important in the *Enneads*, although the *subject* of creativity is obviously of the utmost importance in that book. Hartman's argument appears to run like this: since green is the color of hope (—and it is; see Ripa *et al.*), and green is in the poem, then hope is in the poem. But is it? In dealing with iconographical materials, as with mythographic and numerological systems, two other potent sources for Renaissance writers looming large in our "method" of study, one must guard against assuming that all possible meanings, or even *any* possible meaning, associated with a given word, image, myth, or number, must necessarily be present in any given case. Ripa, Conti, Agrippa, and others who explicated these subjects in the Renaissance undertook to do so partly because the subjects were so diverse as to need methodizing. They did not write source books in systematics, but rather handbooks to possible references. For green, see François Tristan l'Hermite, *Les Amours* (Paris, 1652), "Les Loüanges du Vert," pp. 58-60; and Miss Wallerstein's observation on green as the color of *failed* hope. For red and white, Canticles v; 10; for red, white, and green, Marvell, "Eyes and Tears," stanza V; and *Love's Labours Lost*, I, ii, 80-115 (I owe this reference to Daniel Traister).

the triviality of the reduction burlesques the traditional language, since meaning is withdrawn from a whole contextual range to be reinvested in unattached colors. Red and white, secondary qualities, stand for the whole world of love and the flesh; they are also, two, or double, which is in the poem's logic a bad thing; green is single, pure garden-solitude.

With the puns on "Fond" and "Flame," the *faux-naïf* then complains of the way lovers treat trees, carving girls' names on their bark. The metamorphosis of humans into trees is hallowed in epic as well as in the Ovidian tradition, where pain was often inflicted by accident upon the human trees by careless passers-by. The tree-carving in pastoral is conventionally of ladies' names: an illustration for one of Jacob Cats' emblems (Fig. 17) provides a lovely example, complete with quotations from Virgil's Eclogues, of that obligatory pastoral act of homage.[37] Much handy-dandy is involved in the pseudo-logic at this point, for it turns out that in this poem the cruelty lies not in the wounds, as we are initially led to think, but in the fact that the poet carves another's name on the tree. When our poet carves trees, he will carve only the names of his beloved—namely, of the trees themselves. Misled by the normal connotations of "wound" and the general *pathétique* of pastoral, we cannot expect this particular turn: the poet has carried us by this trick into the empty ground between words and things, has collapsed "trees" into their names as in the Body-Soul dialogue he collapsed "fetters" into "feet," the parts of the metaphor into each other. Through the grotesquerie of this conceit, we are brought up sharp against the fundamental oddity of our own naïve assumption that the words we use, the meanings and intentions which, we think, govern our lives, have some intrinsic connection with the things they represent. The poet's occupation is examined at its literal base.

In the fourth stanza, the paradoxical argument continues, now from authority, that is, from Ovid and the case of the gods. Here, literary elements are casuistically used, displayed pseudo-syllogistically in support of the stoical argument that a retired life is better than an active or

---

[37] Jacob Cats, *Silenus Alcibiadis* (Amsterdam, 1622), p. 11. "Crescent illae crescetis, amores," is from Virgil, *Ecl.* X, 54; "Phyllida amo ante alias" is from *Ecl.* III, 78. Ralph Austen, who valued his trees' welfare, is not against inscribing them: "*Also Trees, or Fruits may be with inscriptions, and engravings upon them, by writing with a Needle, or Bodkin, or Knife, when the Trees and Fruits are young, and as they grow greater, so the Letters or figures will be more plaine,*" *Observations*, pp. 26-27.

sensual one. After "Passions heat," love "makes his best retreat." That is, love (i) retires as before a superior force; (ii) withdraws into a woman-free garden, the opposite of conventional pastoral happiness; (iii) makes and (iv) makes up the garden into which he withdraws. It turns out that the gods have behaved just so, though only a *naïf* would think to interpret Ovid—or to motivate lovers' behavior—in just this way. Gods *qua* gods must know the outcome of what they do; gods *qua* gods could not have pursued girls only to be thwarted; ergo, they must have run after the girls knowing and intending them to become plants sacred to the imagination. Jupiter, Mars, Vulcan, all present in "Hortus," have disappeared from "The Garden," leaving only gods of poetry embracing plants that are the numinous signs of their art and the emblems of particular genres of poetry, lyric and pastoral.

The recreative power of plants, celebrated in the ethical literature of retirement and of husbandry, now metamorphoses into the creative power of poetry, as gradually the garden takes on more and more aspects of the *hortus mentis*. Gods turn girls into trees, the trees recompose into lyric and pastoral poetry, symbolized by laurel and reed-pipe. By these unexpected routes we have been returned to a perfectly traditional constellation, of gardens-girls-poetry, and the poetry is precisely the right sort, lyric and pastoral, which should environ and celebrate girls. But with this difference, that the girls have been invoked only to be dismissed, disembodied, into trees. "Trees" are here literally what the poet loves— their asexuality relieves him of the psychological problems laid on by girls, real or imaginary; their mode of procreation, without sex, is the only one contemplated in the poem. Quite literally, this poet can say, "My love is a garden enclosed" and mean exactly that: unmetaphoring.

The stanza carries critical implications, too. The rewriting of the Ovidian story in just this way makes us realize what Ovid himself was about, "making" a world "transcending these," a world in which natural objects are made to derive from human emotions. The pun involved in "end their race" catches up many meanings opening on one another: the heat of passion done, the footrace ended, the gods dying without issue. These gods are in fact dead, fictional, alive only as the imaginative recreations of poetry. Apollo and Pan are figures for ways of life, just as palm, oak, and bay are; the plants, even, have a greater claim on reality, growing as they do in real as well as in imaginary gardens.

The poet enters upon the fifth stanza with solitude achieved. By means of the argument from figure, solitude's alternatives are all cleared away—professional commitment (stanza 1), the "busie Companies of Men" (stanza 2), love and lady-loves (stanzas 3 and 4)—until godlike poets are each left alone with the symbolic plants of their patronized art. If single plants are good, gardens must be better; once again, we realize how much—the different modes of verse, different ways of life—has been reduced to the language of plants. Apollo has only the laurel, Pan only the reed. Our poet has a whole garden, so far constructed out of bits of heroic, pastoral, libertine, and Ovidian traditions, a garden far more "am'rous" and nourishing than the heroes' or the gods' single plants were to them.

In stanza 5, the plants are literally more amorous than red or white, than ladies; they make love to the poet shamelessly, offer themselves, entwine themselves around him, bring him to ground. After the first four stanzas, in which life and love have been simplified to a considerable asceticism, the linguistic shift to the hyper-Epicurean language of stanza 5 is a deliberate shock, the greater because we have been prepared for an unemotional connection between man and the fruits of his orchard.[38] The plants of stanza 5 fulfil the demands of the paradoxical argument, since to prefer plants to women requires the love of plants, not of women; this lush, erotic wish-fulfilment has been dictated by the pseudo-argument. Stanza 5 reports a genuinely climactic experience, culminating in a loss of will in the poet, the plants' beloved, and in his fall. Such an ecstasy is not, after all, uncommon in gardens. As Browne says, in the dedicatory letter to his garden-meditation, "In Garden delights 'tis not easie to hold a Mediocrity; that insinuating pleasure is seldome without some extremity." This fall is "on Grass"; that is, it is a proper pastoral fall into the green grass (whence shepherdesses become "greengowns"), into the shade of the orchard trees, a fall comfortable and soft. "Insnar'd with Flow'rs" recalls the gardens pastoral lovers weave to honor, to entice, and to entrap one another, and also specifically the "Toyles" upbraided in stanza 1. Under this, the recreative tradition of gardens speaks for legitimacy—as

[38] I do not wish to underestimate the importance of the libertine tradition for this poem, favored by Miss Bradbrook and Professor Kermode, but wish to make plain that it is as much parodied, played with, and burlesqued, as the other lyric traditions drawn on by Marvell. The absence of women in this garden is one indication of his upside-downing of this tradition; though, as has been pointed out, the soft fall on grass of this poem may owe something to libertine habits. See also Canticles i:16.

in Bacon's grave essay, soothing to all the senses, calming and restorative. Ralph Austen's serious book about orchards interrupts itself to present *The Spirituall Uses of an Orchard*,[39] in which every sense is satisfied. In the constellation apples-stumbling-melons-grass, Eden is called up,[40] and mortality, though in the barest of references.

Falling on grass—"all flesh is grass"—reminds us that both delight and death take place in a green shade; but the line does no more than hint at *memento mori*. So the stanza shifts between focuses, the lightness shaded by the hints of gravity, the seriousness made playful by the tone and juxtaposition of images. In sheerly literary terms, this stanza outdoes the perfections usually attributed to the earthly paradise, turning the static garden-stage into an erotically active scene, burlesquing then both love poetry and the poetry of paradise. The still life elements, fruits, flowers, plants, and vines, refuse to stay still; in their activity, these fruits and plants are emblems at once of full life and of transience. Beneath the clear pastoral note of falling delightfully on green grass in a golden pastoral world, resonates, as some think, the Christian warning of another kind of fall, as the poet seems to abandon his will to the magnificent gratifications of his *hortus mentis*. But one cannot have it both ways: if the poet "falls" in the Christian sense, then his ecstasy can hardly be so transcendent as it is, by those same critics, felt to be; if he simply falls "on Grass," thereby affirming his own mortality and acting out his own death to come, then what are we to make of the genuine joy of the

---

[39] For the solace to the senses offered by orchards, see Ralph Austen, *The Spirituall Uses of an Orchard*, in his *Treatise of Fruit-Trees*, pp. 35-37. That book offers ancient and scriptural authority for planting gardens (pp. 6-11). See also Walter Montagu, *Miscellaneous Spiritualia* (London, 1649), p. 321; and, for a libertine poem in which the lover likens himself to a vine entwining with his mistress, see Robert Herrick, *Hesperides* (1648), p. 14.

[40] Though I certainly agree with Mr. Stewart that Canticles is important in the background to "The Garden," I find its presence in the poem more ephemeral than he does, because I cannot read the poem as so strongly Christian as he does. Undoubtedly there is a strong pull toward Canticles, though I am certain of only one direct quotation from it: "clusters of the vine" (vii:7), which is in so altered a context that to interpret Marvell's line, as Stewart does, as a reference to the Passion, seems to me to push scriptural parody dangerously far. Though it is true that Canticles was often glossed in relation to the Passion, and the crucified Christ likened to a bunch of grapes in the winepress, not all bunches of grapes are automatically symbolic of the Crucified Christ. In this context, such interpretation would be peculiar in the chronology offered in the poem, such as it is: the Crucifixion then must precede the Fall.

ecstatic experience? One way or another, the stern Biblical meanings of the "fall" seem irrelevant here.

In both physical and spiritual experience, self-abandonment makes ecstasy possible. By another radical linguistic switch, leaving a deep trench across the poem, we move from stanza 5 to stanza 6, from sensuous abandonment to creative ecstasy, in which state the immediate sense-satisfactions are purified by very conventional means into abstractions.

In pastoral, before lovers come to their ecstasy, they must lie down, on the earth's lap, in her bosom, wherever a cave, a hedge, or a haycock offers them opportunity. In dream poetry, the dreamer also lies down to ready himself for his overwhelming vision. Our poet, drawing on both rhetorical sanctions, lies down at one with nature, to enter his experience of fulness and of fulfilment.[41] Withdrawn from his own will, the poet finds that his mind withdraws still farther from pleasure into happiness, from physical rapture to metaphysical ecstasy. At one with nature, the poet is vouchsafed a vision of creativity; or, because we have been shown again and again that the nature of this poem is a radical recreation of nature's ordinary work, the withdrawing of the poet's mind "into its happiness" is a withdrawal into the possibilities of its own creation, its own self. Now at last in the garden of solitude, selfhood can be fully experienced. The operating mind is at one with its operation as, earlier, by metaphorical means, trees had turned out to be at one with their names, or, as the poet had become one with his nature.

This stanza relies on the standard Platonic epistemology:[42] containing an idea of "everything," the mind can therefore recognize, can "know," whatever it perceives. In terms of the image given, the mind is "like" the ocean, containing vast numbers of things unseen; the ocean itself is a kind of mirror-world containing a roster of forms "like" those of the dry earth,[43] so that the mind by this analogy is the mirror of a mirror. The intensification of meaning involved in the idea works as the doubling of the word "green" works, in the last couplet, to give us an image for speculation and reflection without using any of those (metaphorical)

[41] E. R. Curtius, *European Literature of the Latin Middle Ages* (Bollingen Series, XXXVII, 1953), p. 187.

[42] Hence, really, we have little need of an epistemology derived from the Epistle to the Romans.

[43] Browne, *Pseudodoxia Epidemica*, III, xxiv; "That all Animals of the Land, are in their kind in the Sea"; see also Isaak Walton, *The Compleat Angler* (London, 1653), pp. 24 ff. for the same point.

terms for mental operation. The mind turns in and turns out; whichever way it turns, it finds the same thing, "everything" in the external world mirrored in itself, itself projected upon, thus mirrored by, the external world.

As the body loses its will in stanza 5, the mind loses activity, to become passive in the first part of stanza 6. "Each kind" must actively find "its own resemblance" in the still mind. As soon as that passivity is established by the syntax, the mind's activity is at once counterposed; this mind can create into spatial and temporal infinity, "Far other Worlds, and other Seas," can expand to the limit of consciousness. Within its passivity, the mind is active by means of the creative idleness, the *vanitas-*recreation celebrated in literary gardens. This stanza is the crux and climax of the whole poem, an stanza free of tonal ironies though filled with puzzles of another kind, about the nature of intellect, of thought, of creativity, of reality. This stanza presents creative activity firmly within a context of withdrawal and contemplation, both of them justified by the acts of perception and creation which result from such constructive solitary self-absorption. Contraction, expansion; passivity, creativity: "all that's made" reaches infinitely out and is at the same time reduced to one abstracted act of perception.

The phrase "all that's made" is itself magnificently indefinite. It contains the meaning of the created material world, both in its prelapsarian perfections, made as it was by deity, and in its blurred fallen state, marred by man. It is also the world of potentiality, created by man's thought and imagination, these expanded to the limit of conception. Depending upon emphasis, "all that's *made*" or "*all* that's made," it is the world of creation or the world of thought—and it is both. The thought is green, now best of colors, reflecting the "green Shade" that the garden is, projecting its greenness, its creativity, upon the garden. In the poetic world, green is one color for truth, for retirement, for singleness, newness, innocence, and potentiality, as well as the color of finished perfection. The couplet

> Annihilating all that's made
> To a green Thought in a green Shade.

shifts back and forth among the many meanings of "green." The thought is *in* shade, can occur only when protected by trees in the proper contemplative *locus*, a garden, and it is *of* shade. It is green because creative and recreative. Since the thought is also of gardens and of all that gardens mean, it can only be green, shady, innocent, renewing, recreative.[44] Furthermore, Marvell kept decorum in this stanza, too. Instead of the named plants and trees of earlier stanzas—the palm, oak, bay, laurel and syrinx, the mutilated bark of stanza 3 and the passionate vegetables of stanza 5, the plants have been platonized to "thought" and "shade," both of them, properly, green. No specific plants in this stanza, only the idea of all plants.

The expansion and contraction of the mind, as given in this stanza, presents another equivalent, this time in epistemological experience, of the theme of retirement and emergence with which the poem is preoccupied. At one and the same time, the stanza is about self-containment and singleness of vision, from psychological and literal solitude.

The sixth stanza gives us ultimate ecstasy, and is framed by two stanzas in different modes of ecstasy, sensual rapture in 5, spiritual levitation in 7. In stanza 7, disembodiment is made literal: the soul leaves the "vest" of its body, though we are specifically told that it must reassume that garment. This ascent of the soul is in practice for another; however wonderful the vision may be, the soul is not dispatched to paradise within the poem itself, but remains in the garden, preparing "for longer flight." "Like a Bird" it moves into the shade-producing trees above the poet; "like a Bird" it preens and sings in preparation for its heavenly journey, "renewing" its feathers (Fig. 18). This bird is no natural creature: like the laurel and the reed of stanza 6, this bird was created of human emotions, is an artifice, a bird of the mind. Literally, too, this bird "reflects," in an image drawn from the language of optics; "the various Light" finds its own resemblance in the iridescent plumage of the bird.[45]

Stanzas 5 to 7 rely less on literary than on philosophical language, Epicurean, Neoplatonic, theological Platonic. In stanza 7, the state of ecstasy is given in terms both conventional and original; with the merest touch, the stanza is marked by Marvell's idiosyncratic imagination. The preening bird, normal image for the soul,[46] readies itself for its "longer

[44] See Philo, *op.cit.*

[45] Psalm 68, v. 13: "Though ye have been among the pots, yet shall ye be as the wings of a dove covered with silver, and her feathers with yellow gold." See also Joachim Camerarius, *Emblemata*, III, xxxiv, p. 34: "Renovata iuventus," in which a bird renews its plumage in the sun's light. The bird in question is a hawk. See also Johannes Typotius, *Symbola Divina et Humane* (Frankfurt, 1601), I, 11.

[46] Oddly enough, the association of soul and bird, normal for Platonic and Judaeo-Christian traditions, has seemed strange to one or two critics of the poem.

flight" with heaven silently indicated as its destination; but also it preens, a self-referential, self-absorbing operation, in the "various Light,"[47] affirming the different beauties of the creatural world, or of the creatural world as interpreted by the imagination. We note, as we draw back from the poem, that though philosophical traditions are invoked in it, their specifics are not. When all is said and done, though there is a strong thematic pull toward Neoplatonism, toward Plotinus, toward Canticles, we can with difficulty point to phrases specifically linking this garden with those sources. Like much else in the poem, philosophical content is apparent but not actually mentioned; we are (literally) given phenomenal hints, in terms of appearances, adumbrations, shadows, rather than actualities making up this garden's green shade. The garden's name is not mentioned; we are given experiences in "the various Light" of philosophical and literary contexts, pointed by variation, each variation qualifying the last and the next, all counterpointing and also grading into one another.

In stanza 8 the tone shifts again, as the poet begins to emerge into an ironical objectivity, from the selfless and self-confirming ecstasy of the preceding stanza. Once more the *faux-naïf* reinterprets a great tradition, this time of Genesis itself, in support of his paradoxical defense of solitude. The ecstasy of stanza 6 results from total self-sufficiency and self-absorption; such experience is possible only in total solitude. In a place of purity and sweetness, no "Help" can in fact be "meet," since none is needed; in Eleatic terms, only monistic man could have been perfect, and when he split into another, shared his bone and being with another, his singularity became doubleness. Quite literally, Eve was "a Mortal's share," sheared off Adam's side and self, to bring him to his mortality. The poet plays upon division in the last couplet of the stanza, ironic because it acknowledges that Eden's true value can be understood by an experienced man:

> Two Paradises 'twere in one
> To live in Paradise alone.

This time, the doubling obliquely criticized in the poem hitherto is brought up directly, with frank disapproval, since it was by "doubling"

---

[47] The syntax is not quite as expected: the bird "Waves *in its Plumes* the various light" instead of waving its plumes in the light. Again, the drawing of the light into the bird's plumage is an important point in the line of self-reference running through the poem.

into two persons that the paradisal garden was lost at the beginning.[48]
With this stanza, the parodic tone resumes, to add now a scriptural in-
terpretation to the burlesque or parody of heroism, pastoralism, meta-
morphosis, libertinism, Epicureanism. The encomium of solitude is, after
all, foolish too, since stoical and Christian doctrine generally upheld it.
The commonness of the doctrine he defends is one reason for the poet's
search into bizarre justifications of a perfectly legitimate state. In the
tradition of literary paradoxy he has some authority for pseudo-reasons
such as he finds; that tradition also helps to point toward the epistemo-
logical problem touched on, from different angles of entry, through the
whole poem. Paradoxy makes fun of traditions; the most brilliant para-
doxes often turn out to defend the traditions they seem to mock, as in
fact this poem does. The Biblical parody, topsy-turviness, and silliness of
stanza 8 relies on the knowledge of every civilized man, woman, and
child that Adam did not have Eve thrust upon him, but chose to give
existence to her, with the results known to every mortal in Christendom.
Our realization that from Adam Eve was made, also does no harm to
the metamorphic stress of this poem, in which one image turns into
another, one genre into another, one stage of life and of understanding
into another.

[iii]

STANZA 8 looks back at innocence from experience acknowledged, as the
irony testifies. As much as its content, the tone of 8 indicates emergence
from the self-absorbed, self-delighting state of stanzas 5 to 7 and prepares
for the last stanza, with its issuing into the world and its clear implications
of mortality. According to some readings, the last stanza is abruptly shorn
away from the poem by its radically different tone and setting. I find the
tonal shift, as well as the shift in *locus*, of a piece with the general caesural
method of the poem. Given the nature of this stanza, in which the world
is re-entered, some hiatus is required. We move from garden to gardener,
from created things (hitherto given as objects of contemplation) to cre-
ator; we move from the ideal into the real, into a garden planted in the
shape of a timepiece, a garden emblematic of the temporal world and the
temporal universe. Browne provides a gloss for this movement from
timelessness back into time: "For if Paradise were planted the third day

[48] Cf. Cowley's play on number in "Solitude" in *Works* (London, 1681), p. 94.

of the Creation, a wiser Divinity concludeth, the Nativity thereof was too early for Horoscopie; Gardens were before Gardiners, and but some hours after the earth."[49]

The image of the gardener is an important one. As George Puttenham said, speaking not of gardening but of poetry, the gardener is, like art itself, "an ayde and coadjutor to nature":

> or as the good gardiner seasons his soyle by sundrie sorts of compost: as mucke or marle, clay or sande . . . and waters his plants, and weedes his herbes and floures, and prunes his branches, and unleaves his boughes to let in the sunne: and twentie other waies cherisheth them, and cureth their infirmities, and so makes that never, or very seldome any of them miscarry, but bring foorth their floures and fruites in season. And in both these cases it is no smal praise for the Phisitian and Gardiner to be called good and cunning artificer.[50]

God Almighty first planted a garden, as Bacon had said; Zeus set out an orchard of ideas, as Plato tells us. Adam in his innocence worked an orchard; only after the fall did he have to till the ground. For him georgic labor replaced bucolic ease. The world is a garden and can be perceived as such; the gardener may be associated with all kinds of creators, including the poet.

The poem's last stanza offers our last chance to see what the caesural method of this poem is about: by the radical shifts in argument and context, the stanzas are isolated into emblematic scenes, each with its traditional and generic content, each with its ironies and its self-criticism, each with its peculiar elegance. Each stanza is a "spot"—not so much a "spot of time," such as we have been accustomed to expect in recent criticism,[51] as a spot of apperception, a self-contained mental picture. The last stanza is no less emblematic, no less spotted than its predecessors, however different its world of reference may seem from the literary traditions, the ecstasies, the paradoxes by which we have been led up to it. Graphic, visually beautiful, intellectually allusive, the last stanza conspicuously admits the fact of time: in this stanza, love is not made everlasting by names cut in trees, nor are fleeing girls arrested into plants,

[49] Browne, *Works*, p. 129.

[50] George Puttenham, *The Arte of English Poesie*, ed. G. D. Willcock and Alice Walker (Cambridge, 1936), p. 303.

[51] From the work of Georges Poulet and his many *epigoni*, we have in modern criticism considerable comment on literary manipulation of "spots of time."

nor is ecstasy experienced in a timeless "meanwhile." The dial-garden of the last stanza is subject to the rules by which the actual world is governed. But the dial is "new," and renewing, since it is a garden; not only does it keep time by its shape and by the seasonal nature of its plants, blooming in succession throughout the year, but also it renews itself, gives hope for the future even as it marks the passage of time.[52]

In the garden, something moves, a bee computing time. In the "milder Sun" and the "fragrant Zodiack" the bee works, a georgic insect—indeed, *the* georgic insect—to transform the sweetness of flowers into honey and wax, into artifices of nourishment and enlightenment. Pastoral grades into georgic by means of the bee, carefully called "industrious." Man is often enjoined to imitate the bee: as the bee transmutes flowers into a rich distillation through the instrumentality of his own body, so may a man transmute his garden-experience into something "transcending these." A poet may do so too, a poet at least critical of his own creation. With this stanza the literary-critical self-commentary running through the poem at last comes to a peak: the notions variously touched on, creativity in general (6), poetic creativity (3, 4), social creativity (2, 8), all conjoin to make us aware that the poem is written emblematically, not just about ways of life, about styles of thought, about literary genres, but about the relation between ideas and life, about styles as a metaphor for ethics. By this objectification of style into metaphor, the poem itself becomes a huge metaphor, a garden of reflection, the ideal and real worlds reflecting each other, to be reflected upon by readers.

Seen as object, "The Garden" brings into one focus very different angles of literary and ethical vision, collects "all that's made" of traditions into one "green Thought"—that is, into itself. By this means, the boundaries are fused between object and subject, as they are in any self-conscious epistemological activity. Objectively, this poem writes about accepted traditions as "green shades": the poem-garden has its origins in the gardens of dalliance (pastoral, libertine, Ovidian, Epicurean), the gardens of contemplation (Stoic, Epicurean, Neoplatonic, Scriptural) the gardens of the Hesperides, the Garden of Eden; it takes place also in a seventeenth-century formal garden, planted in dial shape.[53] Most important of all, it transcends these.

---

[52] I owe this observation to Stephen Greenblatt; see Pliny, *Historie of the World*, XVIII, xxxi, for gardens as "year-clocks" or zodiacs.

[53] Cf. Bacon, "Of Gardens," for a zodiacal record.

"The Garden"

Made of flowers, emblems of beautiful mortality and of mortal beauty, emblems also of eternal renewal, honey and wax nourish, give light, preserve. Again the time-thyme pun, validated by reference to "Hortus," reminds us how carefully this garden is planted in metaphor: it tells time, warns us to pluck our day as the bee plucks his. Our "sweet and wholsome hours" must be turned into something else, something better, by means of our selective industry. To this extent, the poem is a paradoxical but unmistakable *carpe diem*, the more breathtaking because its argument leads us in a direction opposite to the traditional lyric persuasion's *carpere*, back to the original simple morality of the phrase. The day we are to pluck is the garden-day of solitude, whose *otium* turns into *negotium*, whose *vanitas*—idleness, emptiness, nothing—turns into creation; a day in which "creating" and "annihilating" prove to be two aspects of the same operation. The poet has so managed things that the garden is both a mirror for and a mirror of the outside world, again an inversion of the usual tradition in which retirement-gardens are set into dialectical opposition to "the world."

This garden "recreates," so that a man may easily emerge from it to his worldly calling, strengthened by the recognition that the world to which he returns is a projection of the garden-experience. In this garden, intellect and character are so cultivated, so rarefied, that the spiritual garden, the real garden, the garden of the world can all be identified with the garden of the mind. By the mirror-operation of platonic comprehension, the dialectic between retirement and activity, between nature and art, is destroyed. The Platonic commonplace about the relation of the mind as microcosm to all things in the macrocosm and the world of ideas is neatly assimilated to the pastoral projection of the poet's mind upon a nature he makes up to suit himself.

Somehow, the poet who retired from an unsatisfying world manages by these metaphors to recreate a world into which, in the poem's last stanza, he is ready to emerge. In the world of reflection, a changed person must result in a changed outer world. But as the *carpe diem* imagery so gently reminds us, spiritual ecstasy, with its illusion of timelessness, is as transitory as the commoner sorts of ecstasy, therefore quite as appropriately measured by the conventional symbols of transience, herbs and flowers. By the poet's logic in the poem, furthermore, herbs and flowers have been translated to so high a plane that they are the only proper emblems for an experience as rare and as rarefied as intellectual and spiritual ecstasy.

Even to reiterate meanings, as I have done, is to paw this poem with a clumsy love in a way singularly inappropriate to it, since its method is as delicate as the bee's, which characteristically draws from herbs and flowers without harming them in the least.[54] Marvell contracts and expands his traditions as he contracts and expands metaphors, puns, thoughts; poetic contraction and expansion mirror the themes of withdrawal and return with which the poem is centrally concerned. The poem's mirror-operation keeps working, too, as mirrors reflecting mirrors must. The plant-mixture of the garden reflects the world-mixture of experience, this mixture presented and offered in terms of the poet's craft, in *genera mixta*. Once the reflection is understood, the fusion of retirement and emergence makes sense, although it plays havoc with the tradition in which the poem seems to begin, apparently assuming an irrevocable opposition between active to contemplative life. "All that's made," whether by the Creator God, by great creating nature, or by creative man, is reflected in the mind-garden and in turn projected outward again. The poem, a made thing, is like the whole creation, reflects the whole creation, is in metaphor the whole creation.

Packing so much material and so many categories of thought into itself, the poem can in another, more technical, way be seen as an emblem. The word "emblematic" is one of the trickiest in the Renaissance critical terminology; it is often applied to Marvell's work and to this poem in particular. As the considerable work on emblems indicates,[55] there is more than one way in which poetry may be called emblematic. In its first usage, the word seems to mean a poetic vocabulary that is highly visual, clearly delineated, and often intellectually obscure, conceited, or riddling. From the concrete elements of an emblematic image, the reader is expected to draw a specific abstract meaning, often part of an arbitrary but fixed canon of significance. So a soap-bubble, we may be sure, refers to transience and mortality; a crocodile either to deceit or to moral amphibious-

---

[54] See Camerarius, *Emblemata*, III, p. 93, "Sine injuria."

[55] Mario Praz, *Studies in Seventeenth-Century Imagery* (Rome, 1964); Rosemary Freeman, *English Emblem-books* (London, 1948); Robert Clements, *Picta Poesis. Literary and Humanistic Theory in Renaissance Emblem Books* (Rome, 1960); for Marvell, Kitty Scoular, *Natural Magic*; E. H. Gombrich, "*Icones Symbolicae*," *JWCI* IX (1948), pp. 163-92.

ness; an anchor or a dolphin to hope, and both together become *festina lente*. This habit of mind, reading directly from natural and artificial objects their abstract significance, leads to an emblematic vision, best expressed in Traherne's beautiful phrase, "som thing infinit behind evry thing appeared."[56]

Although "The Garden" is certainly a highly visualized poem, its images like its languages precisely delineated, its wit conceited, arch, paradoxical, it is far less visually emblematic than other poems by Marvell—"The unfortunate Lover," "On a Drop of Dew," or "Upon Appleton House"— and less also than many poems by Donne, Herbert, or Vaughan. Nor is the poem "strained" in the conventional stylishness of seventeenth-century metaphor; the conceits are far from surprising. Daphne and the laurel are perfectly conventional; the oddity of them lies in the poet's interpretation of the image, not in the image itself. The mixed orchard of stanza 5 is eccentric not in its plants, but in what the plants do. The single elements of "The Garden" are not emblematic in ways Signor Praz has taught us to expect; rather, it is in its structure and function that the poem is like an emblem. The proper emblem is a mixed form, made up of picture, motto, epigram, all cryptic, no one element designed as the direct translation of another, or as an exact transference from one medium to another.[57] A complete emblem reveals its significance by the aggregate of hints expressed in the several languages of visual image, motto, and (usually Latin or Greek) epigram. Disjunction is the rule in emblems: the pictorial elements tend to be logically or experientially separate from one another, their juxtaposition designed to surprise, quiz, tease the reader into finding the "solution" to their simultaneous presence. They ask for intellectual effort, but they do not provide blueprints for it. Behind such heterogeneous notions yoked by violence together, a unifying idea was conceived to exist: though the emblem left readers to their own wit, it did not cheat them. Ideally, its accompanying motto and epigram were in different languages, preferably none of them native to reader and writer. Many traditions, many bodies of learning, were drawn on to produce the sharply-focused, impressively reduced emblem: *multum in parvo.*

"The Garden" was, I think, put together on this principle, with its

[56] Thomas Traherne, *Centuries of Meditation*, III, 3.

[57] Henry Estienne, *The Art of Making Devises*, tr. Thomas Blount (London, 1646), pp. 21-22, 25, 27-28, and esp. 40-46.

juxtapositions of cryptic references from different traditions in radically reduced, sometimes riddling, form, which only expose their collective meaning when studied together. Like an emblem, "The Garden" is intellectually designed, to make an extended figure for thought, its peculiar details selected both for what they conceal and for what they reveal. These compacted images, themes, and ideas reveal, among other things, the triumph of the poet's willful intellect, scrupulously assessing, in terms of his craft, the aesthetic, moral, and spiritual possibilities of his civilization, which he has here chosen to perceive and to present in generic literary forms. As such an epitome, the poem is fully emblematic in Traherne's sense, in particular and as a whole: behind it, and behind each part of it, "som thing infinit" appears. Insofar as this is so, the poem works as the emblem works, pointing toward metaphysical and ontological meanings of which it is both indicator and screen. It points at these meanings as if to things outside itself, but it points inwards as well to those same meanings, not as symbolized by poetic elements, but as contained within the whole poem. This poem, like others but more than most, is container and thing contained, a container mirroring what is outside itself and mirroring itself also. Like so many of Marvell's puns, like his syntax and imagery, like the difficult notions of perception and knowledge he dares to tackle, this whole poem works two ways at once, both as a representation of the things it epitomizes and as an identification with those things. So, really, in the poem's substance, mind and matter, thought and world, are presented in two ways at once, from one angle of vision made to seem categorically different and, from another, completely identified. Exploring both difference and identity, separateness and fusion, the poem offers a depiction and a demonstration of coincidences possible only in thought.

One more trick of technique remains for discussion, relevant both to the emblematic effect of the whole poem and to the paradoxical wit deployed by it: the peculiar inside-outing of conventional metaphor. Once the reader has got used to the *naïf*'s unmetaphoring, this poem tends to train expectation away from the customary relations implied by literary figure, so that the total figurative effect of the poem may come as a shock. By exposing the conventional associations of metaphor, the process of unmetaphoring makes us reconsider the function of figurative language, of the idioms developed to answer to needs of communication, of attempts to contain and to transcend different categories of experience.

By the time we come to the bee (Fig. 19), we have learnt to look sharply at meanings. The bee has large responsibilities in the last stanza and, it seems, in the whole poem. He is "industrious," telling time in a pun equating time itself with transient plants. He is a collector and a creator: so a man may gather strength and beauty from his garden-experience and from the world seen as his garden of experience. The bee represents a proper love of sweetness, we are told: "Apes autem quia dulcia tantum gustant, si pascentes pingantur, hominem hieroglyphice significant qui dulcibus tantum rebus delectetur, dulciaque omni cura studioque perquirat."[58] The bee's honey is the honey of eloquence, his industry that required of the poet. Horace's verse is the *locus classicus*:

> . . . ego apis Matinae
> more modoque
>
> grata carpentis thyma per laborem
> plurimum circa nemus uvidique
> Tiburis ripas operosa parvus
> carmina fingo.[59]

The bee is multi-purpose: the creature favors the chaste and pure, properly in a poem ostentatiously arguing for chastity.[60] As Virgil set out in the *Georgics*, by its industry and its power of innutrition,[61] the bee converts its materials first to itself, then to a wonderful artifice, its palace and honeycomb, where its sweetness is to be stored, as sweetness is stored in the cellular, separate stanzas of the poem. The homiletic bee is a literary insect: explaining his cento, his collection from a thousand sources, Robert Burton wrote: "As . . . a bee gathers wax and honey out of many flowers, makes a new bundle of all, *Floriferis ut apes in saltibus*

---

[58] Giovanni Piero Valeriano, *Hieroglyphica* (Basel, 1556), f. 186v.

[59] Horace, *Odes*, IV, ii.

[60] Valeriano, ff. 188r-v, citing Pindar, Plutarch, and Eucherius (who gives the bee as the emblem of virginity). See also Henry Hawkins, *Partheneia Sacra*, pp. 70, 71, 74 for the bee's chastity and for the bee's architectural and engineering accomplishments; Samuel Purchas, *The Theater of Politicall Flying Insects* (London, 1657), p. 20, and many other commentators for the bee's chastity, within and without marriage. For the bee as divine mediator, see Purchas, p. 347. Nicolaus Reusner, in *Polyanthus, sive paradisus poeticus* (Basel, 1569), a book of Latin rhymes about plants and the creatures of a garden, has much to say in praise of bees (pp. 205-06). One section of Julius Caesar Scaliger's *Poemata* (Basel, 1591), is entitled *Apiculae*, a collection of a great variety of subjects.

[61] *Georgics*, IV, 158-69, esp. also ll. 18-20 for the bee's habitat, and ll. 30-31, for thyme and the bee.

omnia libant, I have laboriously collected this cento out of divers writers."[62] Adapting from Lucretius IV, ll. 11-12, the source for Burton's citation, Erasmus puts the bee's function clearly, likening him to a studious man:

> Itaque studiosus ille velut apicula diligens, per omnes autorum hortos volitabit, flosculis omnibus adultabit, undique succi nonnihil colligens, quod in suum deferat alvearium. Et quoniam tanta est in his rerum foecunditas, ut omni decerpi non possint, certa praecipue diliget, et ad operis sui structuram accommodabit.[63]

In the *Ion,* of course, the source for all these likenesses of the bee to the humanist and poet is to be found. There, the poet gathers "*a Musarum viridariis colibus*"; the poet like the bee is light, volatile, even sacred, singing when full of deity, "*et extra se positus, et a mente alienatus.*"[64] I do not want to suggest that Marvell's "Garden" is simply a conceit on Plato's passage, but rather to show of what utterly conventional materials this poem is made up. In the *Ion,* the poet must be both ecstatic and industrious, to do his remarkable duty; Ficino explains the degrees of *furor* possible, fitting nicely the degrees of rapture, the ascent and descent of the soul, as hinted in "The Garden."[65]

The *Ion* combines poetic with holy rapture; Lucretius, Virgil, and the humanists stress the willed industry of bee and learned man. The French sixteenth-century poets particularly took the bee as proper emblem for the poet, rapt or not rapt, in his diligent selectivity and his unforced participation in nature's processes.[66] The bee is a collector. In "The Garden," he is literally as well as figuratively anthological,[67] in another of the etymological puns (here tacit, but obvious) in which Marvell specialized. In Erasmus' image, the bee uses "omnes autorum hortos" for his own purpose, his own "structure." The bee here gathers from the mixed flowers

---

[62] Robert Burton, *The Anatomy of Melancholy,* Everyman Edition, I, 24-25.

[63] Erasmus, *De duplici copia verborum ac rerum* (Lyons, 1535), p. 117. I owe this reference to Barbara Traister.

[64] Plato, *Ion,* in *Platonis Opera, cum interprete Marsilii Ficini* (Lyons, 1567), p. 118.

[65] For Ficino's description of *furor poeticus,* see *Platonis Opera,* pp. 116-17.

[66] Pontus de Tyard, quoted in Grahame Castor, *Pléiade Poetics. A Study in Sixteenth Century Thought and Terminology* (Cambridge, 1964), p. 33; Pierre de Ronsard, "L'Hylas," *Oeuvres complètes,* ed. G. Cohen (Paris, 1950), II, 390-91.

[67] Cf. Laurentius Beger, *Contemplatio Gemmarum* (Brandenburg, 1697), p. 13, for the bee's Ovidian characterization as "Florilegus'.

of rhetoric to make "this Dial new," to renew old tradition, to make old tradition newly relevant, at the same time preserving all their original sweetness in a distillation of his own.

The flowers in this poem are emblematic of the traditions the poet inherited; the poet, like the bee, has gathered from the literary kinds, accommodating what he gathered to his own structure, to the mixed garden of his making, where the literary kinds also "streight [their] own resemblance find," heroic, pastoral, libertine, speculative, ecstatic, meditative, emblematic, paradoxical, gathered into a poem that is, among so much else that it is, also an illustration of the root-meaning of "anthology." The poem gathers flowers, speaks in the language of flowers; the stanzas too may remind us of the regular, clear-cut, separate, but mutually supporting cells of the honeycomb. Their regular, lapidary, unitary qualities have the sharp edge of the cells, and in them is stored the sweetness from the flowers.

Made up as it is of its own literary traditions, the poem is one of the many metapoetic poems of the seventeenth century. Compared with some of those—"The Canonization," "La Corona," "The Flower," "The Forerunners," "The Coronet"—this poem is quite different. Its references to its metapoetic theme are askance and allusive, nor does its own action, its own existence, at once testify that it does what it talks about doing.[68] This poem proceeds by hinting. Not only is there hiatus from stanza to stanza, from tradition to tradition, but there is hiatus between what is said and what is meant by what is said. Quite without saying so, this poem points to the poet's problems with poetry, to the difficulty of his efforts to relate poetry and imagination to experience. Out of experience's mixture, poetry is distilled, to sweeten, to give light, to preserve; but the experience itself is and must be given metaphorically, here in terms of literary and philosophical kinds, these themselves presented in a metaphor at another remove, that of plants. Out of poetry, poetry is distilled. Here as so often, the poem points out and in, out toward the poetic traditions it relies on and lives from, in to itself as a perfection of those traditions. It manages at once to be objective and self-referential, and to make us notice that.

This reading of the poem may make it seem alarmingly diagrammatic,

---

[68] As, for instance, the "short and admirable Lines" of "Upon Appleton House" appear to point to the lines of the poem itself, or as Herbert's "Paradise," "Prayer," and "The Collar" imitate syntactically and formally the poem's substantive content.

its poet too clever by half, as if all there were to this poem were its exactness, its cellular neatness and delineation. But that is not all, by any means: the precision belies itself, produces its own *sfumato*; in that precision, indeed, mystery turns out to lodge.

While seeming precisely to define, the words show the limit of words: "A green Thought in a green Shade" is in fact indefinable. The Chinese-boxing, the mirroring, the inside-outing, the queer fusions of container and thing contained all point in to the epistemological fact that experience *is* beyond words, though only words can do the experience any justice at all. The poem is about hiatus, among other things, about the spaces between flower and flower, the disjunctions between style and style, the gaps between experience and its expression, between living and thinking —the problems with which, somehow, bees, poets, and all men must cope. The pull between the exactness of the style and the elusiveness of the subject of the poem is no accident, but part of the observable fact that human experience and human understanding are finite. As we come to understand the partitions of human experience and understanding, though, for all our sorrow at our human limitations, we are to be cheered by the bee, who in himself, out of his industrious solitude, produces sweetness and light, transforms through himself the mixed garden's gifts and endows mankind with transformations of his own. Like the bee, the poet is industrious in his retirement, ranges through the zodiac of his own wit, makes much of his creative idleness, gathers from the rich, tilled ground of his professional traditions, to make an emblem of the old world recreated, of old time made into a new day.

Part IV

"Upon Appleton House":
A Composite Reading

INTRODUCTION

LIKE "The Garden," which it so resembles in theme and language, "Upon Appleton House" is a puzzling poem, made up of elements in themselves peculiar and in conjunction odder yet. It is unlike "The Garden," though: where the shorter poem is polished, accomplished, at moments even slick, "Upon Appleton House" is frankly irregular. It flaunts its own seams, points to its own joinery, publicizes its own gaps. The transitions from one section of the poem to another, from one theme to another, from one kind of language to another are neither sinuous nor gradual; modulation is not a characteristic of this poem. Though "Upon Appleton House" is full of gaps, the techniques which seemed to help with such hiatus in "The Garden" are not so useful in dealing with the longer poem. We cannot assume the kind of unity for "Upon Appleton House" that the smooth language about a smooth subject allows us to assume for "The Garden" and find we must tackle the hiatus here quite differently. When lapse and disjunction are so apparent in a poem, the poet's silences are strident: it makes some sense to pay attention to them, to hope, by understanding particular lapses and disjunctions, to grasp a principle of the poem's intellectual organization. With just these problems, so ostentatiously displayed in the poem, my reading begins.

The poem has been fortunate in its critics: Miss Wallerstein, Mr. Allen, Mr. Berger, Mr. Leishman, Mr. Summers, Mr. O'Loughlin, Mr. Holahan, and Mr. Wallace[1] have immensely eased our reading of this

---

[1] Wallerstein, *Seventeenth-century Poetic*, pp. 285-318; Allen, *Image and Meaning*, pp. 115-53; Berger, "Marvell's 'Upon Appleton House': An Interpretation"; Leishman, *The Art of Marvell's Poetry*, pp. 221-91; Summers, Introduction, *op.cit.*, pp. 17-25; O'Loughlin, "The Garlands of Repose" and "This Sober Frame," in *Andrew Marvell* (Twentieth Century Views), ed. G. de F. Lord (Englewood Cliffs, 1968), pp. 120-42. Holahan. "The Poet and the Civic Crown"; John M. Wallace, *Destiny His Choice*. There are other readings as well: Røstvig, *The Happy Man*, I, 172-90; Hyman, *Andrew Marvell*, pp. 85-90; Scoular, *Natural Magic*, pp. 120-90; Toliver, *Marvell's Ironic Vision*, pp. 113-29; Tayler, "The Pastoral of the Mind," in *Nature and Art in Renaissance Literature*; Warnke, "Play and Metamorphosis in Marvell's

long and tricky work. Yet difficulties remain, largely because our critical presuppositions tend to favor unity and coherence and this poem challenges exactly those presuppositions. Frontal attacks, however well-mounted, have not proved totally satisfactory. Mr. Summers' all-too-brief sketch comes closest to a wide-angle view of the poem, but his essay is very short; other critics, seeking to illuminate a particular aspect, line, or tradition of the poem, have legitimately ignored its elements that were irrelevant to their particular concern. The criticism suggests how rich, and how madly multiple, the poem is; indeed, it has become, like "The Garden," one self-imposed *rite de passage* for dogged scholars of English seventeenth-century poetry. Aware of the difficulties involved in omission (sacrifice of those aspects which detract from a coherent reading) and in commission (undue annotation of specifics at the expense of larger interpretations), I want to try to look at the poem in terms of the traditions from which it seems to spring, first separating theme, language, and figure into sets or ranges of materials, and after this separation and analysis, to allow recombination in various ways which seem relevant to the text itself. Since by my reading it is precisely in the overlapping, interlocking, and fusion of very different categories of literary and intellectual elements that much of this poem's meaning resides, this method—admittedly unwieldy and often repetitious—seems to me to answer some of the harsher demands made by the text.

Unlike most poems that we admire, this one insists on its brokenness. One reading has divided it into two major parts, another into five, another into six.[2] Its shifts of tone and imagery have been noted; so have its various scenes. Lord Fairfax's country estate is displayed, moralized, and interpreted by a poet figure who instructs us in the meaning of landscape and absorbs both the landscape and meaning into himself. Both the poet figure and the landscapes he passes through in the course of the poem's day are treated in a way owing much to Montaigne's conception of *passage*; in "Upon Appleton House" a personality with no fixed boundaries glides through a series of experiences rendered, and therefore interpreted, in very different contexts, literary languages, and literary moralities. There is something tentative about the way the poet moves

---

Poetry"; H. M. Richmond, " 'Rural Lyricism': A Renaissance Mutation of the Pastoral," *CL*, XVI (1964), pp. 193-210.

[2] Wallerstein, p. 296; Bradbrook and Lloyd Thomas, pp. 33-39; Allen, p. 117.

through his landscape and through his poem, writing as if he were actually living the scenes and experiences that are his subject, as if he were himself uncertain of what was about to happen next, or how an incident will turn out, or how it ought to be understood or interpreted.

Montaigne offers a literary precedent for the problem of tentativeness, managing to present in his *Essais* a psychological world inevitably in movement, change, and flux as a man's (in his case, his own) body, mind, and spirit alter and are altered by the experiences through which he lives. In the *Apologie* in particular, Montaigne presented the physical and historical worlds as unstable, mutable, and shifty, changing even as the world is variously experienced and interpreted. The conceptual world— intellectual, social—in which *l'homme moyen sensuel* and *l'homme moyen élévé* must live—is presented as equally unstable and untrustworthy, this shifting an inevitable result of physical and historical mutability and the necessary psychological mutability of minds attempting to cope with it. From Montaigne, readers and writers could learn that experience is valid only for its moment of happening; that fixed interpretations, of the world, of experience, of man experiencing, are always risky undertakings, to be ventured at one's peril. To be stable, a man ought to be like Montaigne's hanging-balance, which he took as his *impresa*: he must be ready to adapt to a changing environment. This man, this world, this mode of perception Montaigne managed to present in a style forged, as it seemed, of his own personality—a style at least which gave that impression: his flexible syntax altered to match the nature of his subject and the experience recorded, in a style designed to express a thinking and feeling man, a man in process.[3]

However varied the contexts of a man's thoughts, feelings, and experiences, or however similar these might seem to another man's intimate communions with his own personality, Montaigne, the *moi* of his essays, emerges as a consistent personality in spite of and because of his proud mutability and his splendid negligences. One miracle of his accomplishment is that his style, developed to present a highly unorthodox literary figure as well as an individual personality, maintains its peculiar identity through all its diversity. Indeed, it is in that very diversity, that tolerance of deviation in himself and in others, that much of Montaigne's identity

---

[3] Morris Croll, "Attic Prose" and "The Baroque Style in Prose," in *Style, Rhetoric and Rhythm*; see also Erich Auerbach, *Mimesis* (Anchor Books, 1957), pp. 249-73; Imbrie Buffum, *Studies in the Baroque from Montaigne to Rotrou* (New Haven, 1957); Hiram Haydn, *The Counter-Renaissance* (New York, 1950), esp. pp. 139-45.

is taken to reside. "Consistency" is not treated as a formal, structural, or intellectual matter; his consistency is psychological. Montaigne's similarity to himself, over the range of his essays, lies in his characteristic attitude rather than in any classical principle of coherence, structural or formal. The sharp foreshortening of any and all experience from the author's point of view also reapportions meaning from what it is usually taken to be—and, also, alters stylistic priorities as well. Montaigne domesticated a universe he conceived of as untidy, even chaotic, and always anomalous; he tried to teach men to make peace with their insecurities and even to enjoy them.

"Upon Appleton House" presents a world as unstable as that of Montaigne's *Apologie*, but Marvell's means of presenting that instability is altogether different. Where Montaigne canvassed the experiential world to draw from it his authenticated examples of inconsistency, instability, and illusion, Marvell had simply looked back at the world displayed before him and chose fictionally to present the Nunappleton scenes as confused, confusing, and thoroughly problematical. In his *Apologie*, Montaigne rendered the world as confused and uncertain, measured against an assumed reference-world of hieratic order; in "Upon Appleton House" Marvell presented a world with no fixed reference-point, no text like Sebonde's against which to measure the world under scrutiny, so that its shiftiness and its peculiarities seem in Appleton's nature, intrinsic to it rather than the result of a particular astigmatism or particular perspective.

At least, so it seems: but the confusion is so artfully managed that, in spite of the apparent absence of measuring-rods, the reader is always aware of conventional canons of stability, and of consequences depending upon this strange world's condition. In "Upon Appleton House" the confusions are manipulated to point directly to the artifices and conventions by which they are expressed; like "The Garden," this poem plays with self-reference, makes no bones about its self-regard and self-criticism.

Here, as in so much of Marvell's poetry, traditions of literary expression are singularly examined; here, as elsewhere, the poet stretches conventions and traditions to their limits, examines their reasons for existence. This poem is pointedly like and unlike its generic companions ancient and modern. Like "The Garden," this poem deliberately speaks in several literary languages, several generic vocabularies, several moral styles. It deliberately stretches the limits of the country-house (or great house) poem,[4] and also inverts the usual thematic import of such poems, so that although this poem certainly praises the perfect microcosmic order of an ideal moral ecology, it also presents the elements of that ideal ecology in so disorderly a fashion as to force attention to the problems involved in consciously living *any* life, even one of happy retirement. In the quiet of Nunappleton, the poet presents to his patron and to his readers a life in fact both like and unlike that of Horace's happy man,[5] Virgil's old men in the first Eclogue and Georgics,[6] or Claudian's old man of Verona.[7] Crowned by oak and palm, Fairfax in retirement might hope to achieve the bay and all the garlands of repose. His little country seat (smallest of his several holdings) was neat and sufficient in the way Horace and the Protestant moral economy prescribed; having achieved success in war, he might turn, as Virgil had exhorted patriotic Romans to do, to replant a depleted countryside.

To withdraw into such a seat was to withdraw from the untidy, unpredictable world of men—in this instance, of men at war—into a controllable, tidy empire of one's own, a world designed and manned by one's self, according to one's own standards and wishes. A man's home, honored in English law, was his own, and ought to be just that. As Henry Wotton put it, in his *Elements of Architecture*:

> Every Mans proper *Mansion* House and *Home*, being the *Theater* of his *Hospitality*, the *Seate* of *Selfe-fruition*, the *Comfortablest* part of his owne *Life*, the *Noblest* of his Sonnes *Inheritance*, a kind of private *Princedome*; Nay, to the *Possessors* thereof, an *Epitome* of the whole *World*. . . .[8]

By Wotton's standards, the country house should be actually self-sufficient, not merely symbolically so, as in poems such a house is usually presented. It should be "well watered and well fewelled," as Nunappleton

---

[4] See G. R. Hibbard, "The Country House Poem in the Seventeenth Century," *JWCI*, XIX (1956), 159-174; and O'Loughlin, "Garlands," as well as C. E. Ramsey's unpublished dissertation (University of Florida, 1967), on country-house poems.

[5] *Epodes*, ii. [6] *Georgics* II, 490-512.

[7] Claudian's poem about the happy old man of Verona was translated by Thomas Randolph (*Poems*, London, 1688, p. 32), as was Horace's second epode; Cowley also translated Claudian's poem, as well as Horace's "Beatus ille" and Virgil's "O fortunatus nimium" (*Works*, London, 1678, pp. 135-36, 105-07, 107-08).

[8] Henry Wotton, *The Elements of Architecture* (London, 1624), p. 82.

was; it should be on "some navigable *River* or *Arme* of the *Sea*," for ease of access and provision. It should not be too large, so that the master can enjoy *"Lordship* of the *Feet"* as he perambulates his estate, enjoying its various prospects; it should be varied, of course, to the eye, since "there is a *Lordship* likewise of the *Eye* which being a raunging, and Imperious, and (I might say) an usurping *Sence*, can indure no narrow *circumscription*; but must be fedde, both extent and variety."[9] Wye Saltonstall's description of "A Gentlemans House in the Countrey" shows the habitual charity associated with a well-run, self-sufficient estate.[10]

In the case of this house, its master was also its designer; the older house had been altered for the comfort of the Lord General and, evidently, altered according to the modern taste. Fairfax called his "New-built House" an "Inne," where he would lodge for his short sojourn on earth; actually, his retirement lasted for twenty-one years of his life. This little house was peculiarly Fairfax's own work; perhaps Marvell's poem was written, as Fairfax's short poem surely was, to celebrate the rebuilding of the house, an intimate occasion which may account for some of what seems to be the private references within the poem.[11] As the poet at once points out, the architect of this house is English

> Within this sober Frame expect
> Work of no Forrain *Architect*;

and, in the ninety-fifth of the poem's ninety-seven stanzas, he turns to praise Appleton House against the huge pleasure palaces of imperial and Catholic Spain. The poem's patriotism is by no means blatant, but it is constant: the style in which Fairfax erected his "house" is indigenous. Though the point is only once touched on, the estate's architect chose this particular small job of reconstruction when he might have undertaken a larger task of reformation and rebuilding; he might, indeed, have undertaken to rebuild the nation itself (stanza 44), but chose instead to retire, to concentrate on small things, to construct within finite limits. After the death of the King, Fairfax was forced by circumstances and his conscience to make do with his houses and gardens, or, as the poet sets out

[9] Wotton, pp. 4-5.
[10] Wye Saltonstall, *Picturae loquentes, or Pictures Drawne forth in Characters* (London, 1631), "A Gentlemans House in the Countrey."
[11] Thomas Fairfax, "Upon the New-built House att Appleton," *The Poems of Thomas Third Lord Fairfax*, ed. Edward Bliss Reed (New Haven, 1909), p. 297.

his patron's life in this poem, with a small house and a fit estate. "Reconstruction," architectural, georgic, political, is all undertaken at Nunappleton, but on a small scale.

The figure of the architect points to the establishment of a functioning order; the architect was often likened to the creating deity, drawing with his compass upon chaos to bring forth "all," or the material universe. Marvell begins his poem with a compliment to his patron and his patron's house with the very image of architecture, as he contrasts, in England's and Fairfax's favor, the styles and moral aims of the native with the foreign designer.[12] The poet began with the concept of the house, its design, its *disegno*, and discusses intention and aesthetics entirely in moral terms (stanzas 2-9). It is perhaps worth noting another example of a "perfect" architect, the one referred to by Hawkins in his *Partheneia Sacra*, who designed another house to be set in an emblematic garden of perfection. Hawkins' spiritual and metaphorical "house" has both body and soul; its architect is skilled in many arts—painting, geometry, perspective, arithmetic, history, philosophy, astrology, and physics:

> This is certain, that al art is then in truest perfection, when it may be reduced to some natural Principle or other. For what are the most iudicious Artizans, but the Mimiks of Nature? This same in our *House* is seen, comparing it with the fabrick of our natural bodies, wherin the high *Architect* of the world hath displayd such skil as even stupifies the human reason to enter into it. . . .[13]

These commonplaces are all also carefully worked into the texture of Marvell's poem, a covert praise of Fairfax's domestic and moral economies.

To be virtuous, however, an estate need not be dull; "extent and variety" are necessary to keep the economic balance steady, as well as to please the owner's eye. Such a practical criterion, found in georgic writings of different sorts, is also an aesthetic one; in the *Natural History*, Pliny speaks of landscape painting in a way which relates it to this poem and the literary genre to which it belongs, as well as to types and topics prescribed for landscape painting:

> . . . Ludius [Spurius Tadius] . . . first devised to beautifie the walls of an house with the pleasantest painting that is in all varietie;

---

[12] See Holahan, pp. 117-21, for an excellent statement of the architectural background of Marvell's argument.

[13] Henry Hawkins, *Partheneia Sacra*, pp. 166-68.

to wit, with the resemblance of manours, farms, and houses of pleasure in the country, havens, vinets, floure-worke in knots, groves, woods, forrests, hills, fishpools, conduits, and drains, rivers, riverets, with their banks, and whatsoever a man would wish for to see: wherein also hee would represent sundrie other shews of people, some walking and going too and fro on foot; others, sailing and rowing up and downe the streame upon the water; or else riding by land to their farms, either mounted upon their mules and asses, or els in waggons and coaches: there a man should see folke, in this place fishing and angling, in that place hawking and fouling: some hunting here, the hare, the fox, or deere both red and fallow; others, busie there, in harvest or vintage.[14]

Ut pictura poesis: so Jonson gives us the Sidneys' Penshurst, so, later on, Pope gives us Lord Burlington's house, or Lord Bathurst's.[15] Marvell is a poet particularly alive to visual convention and technique; in this poem, filled with images and conceits paralleled in the visual arts, exploiting also optical tricks of enlargement and reduction, the poet borrows also from different sorts of landscape painting practiced in his time, much of that painting relying, as the passage from Pliny indicates, upon ancient canon. But as we shall see, in this range of materials Marvell is not bound by canon; he mixes these modes, genres, and sub-genres to give us a sense of disorder, mixture, and prodigality, as well as a sense of the idyllic ethos upon which all country-house pieces, poetic or visual, fundamentally rely.

Though Appleton House was "an *Epitome* of the whole *World*," a perfect and perfectly guarded refuge from the turbulence outside its boundaries, Marvell conspicuously does not praise the estate in these terms, without qualification of the terms themselves. Stressing the conventional reasons for praise due in such a poem, he manages all the same to turn the patron's traditionally ordered world upside down, to give patron and readers—to say nothing of "himself"—an experience of disproportion, instability, and topsy-turvydom. To do this, he plays fast and loose with conventions and genres, visual as well as literary. One might say—indeed, critics do—that accord-

---

[14] Pliny, *Historie of the World*, xxv: 10. For an extraordinarily suggestive study of the relation of landscape painting to other genres in painting, see E. H. Gombrich, "The Renaissance Theory of Art and the Rise of Landscape," *Norm and Form* (London, 1966), pp. 107-21; for the connection between pastoral and landscape painting, p. 112.

[15] For this subject, see Lee, "Ut pictura poesis," *op.cit.*; Hagstrum, *The Sister Arts*.

ing to modern categories, this mixed poem is well within the canons of baroque aesthetics.[16] I have, it is true, gratefully borrowed from some critics of the baroque some concepts and terminology, although I am too oppressed by the term's contradictions to tack the label "baroque" upon any single work of art, *pace* Wittkower, Hauser, Friedrich, Rousset, Sypher, and the rest,[17] more secure in their knowledge and theory than I could ever be in mine. (As for mannerism, in spite of the contemporary critical favor the term enjoys, I am not at all convinced that the *style* ever existed.[18])

There is no doubt, though, that whatever one may call it, in this poem there is more flux, metamorphosis, illusionism, *trompe l'oeil*, transformation, and alteration than is customary in Marvell's poetry, and no doubt also that these qualities are remarkable in the poem even when it is compared, say, to the work of the notoriously baroque Crashaw, or Benlowes, or Cleveland or other extremists in seventeenth-century style. One theory is that such an emphasis on incongruity, raising it almost if not altogether to an aesthetic principle, is designed to match the randomness and unpredictability of brute experience. Morris Croll's brilliant analyses of the various shifting styles in seventeenth-century prose brought out the sense of immediate experience that such a style attempts to convey, as it too plays fast and loose with syntactical, linguistic, and structural patterns. Usage of this sort tends toward informality—Montaigne, Browne, Donne, Burton are all cases in point, in which the author seems often to be directly conversing with his reader; such practice does not mean, of course, that writing is not at the same time highly composed, stylized, even mannered. Donne's sermons, as well as some of his poems, show considerable grammatical looseness, which is coupled with extreme control over and

[16] See *inter alia*, René Wellek, "The Concept of the Baroque," in *Concepts of Criticism* (New Haven, 1966); Lowry Nelson, *Baroque Lyric Poetry* (New Haven, 1961), 1-10; Odette de Mourgues, *Metaphysical, Baroque, and Précieux Poetry* (Clarendon Press, 1953), pp. 67-102; Jean Rousset, *La Littérature de l'âge baroque en France. Circe et le paon* (Paris, 1953).

[17] See *inter alia*, Rudolf Wittkower, *Gian Lorenzo Bernini, the Sculptor of the Roman Baroque* (London, 1955), and *Art and Architecture in Italy, 1600-1750* (London, 1958); Arnold Hauser, *The Social History of Art* (London, 1951); Carl J. Friedrich, *The Age of the Baroque, 1610-1660* (New York, 1952); Roger Callois, *Au cour du fantastique* (Paris, 1965); Wylie Sypher, *Four Stages of Renaissance Style* (Anchor Books, 1956).

[18] E. H. Gombrich, "Mannerism: the Historiographical Background," *Norm and Form* (London, 1966), pp. 99-106; my apologies to Peter Schwenger.

reliance upon conventions in ranges outside style which provide another sort of order to balance the stylistic disorder.[19] Asymmetry may be deliberately induced in one range of language or imagery, as a writer chooses to look upon his material with an uncorrected astigmatic vision which necessarily distorts expectations of order and design. The danger in this sort of work is that too much looseness, too much astigmatism makes a poem fall apart: confusions cannot be carried too far, but must allow of some regulation, invoked or implied, to make bearable for readers aesthetic disorder and negligence.

In "Upon Appleton House," vision is always at least bifocal, requiring different settings for close and distant vision. Scales shift, and as we alter our views to pass through the poem, the shifts themselves begin to take on meaning too. Into the gordian knot of baroque scholarship, so devoted to shifts and astigmatism, I cut with diffidence: Marvell's work cannot be limited to the qualifying term "baroque," but since the term is an international one, it may suggest that there are affinities between Marvell's practice and that of poets and artists of other countries and other linguistic traditions. From a background of conventions literary, philosophical, and moral, Marvell's originality stands out in high relief. Against his own literary traditions, of which he was so conscientious a student, Marvell's essays in poetic form and meaning demonstrate his idiosyncrasies and his craftiness. The more one knows of Renaissance poetic prescription and practice, the more one can understand what Marvell was up to. By looking at this curious poem according to different ranges of literary and intellectual convention and idiom, I hope to see what ties it together, what controls the great variety of episodes, genres, styles, and scenes of this long poem—a poem which, like all examples of *genera mixta*, challenges readers by its disparateness, its brokenness, and also by its mysterious powers of cohesion.

Like "The Garden," "Upon Appleton House" turns out to be a poem of remarkably mixed genres. Like "The Garden," it is a poem with its own reserves and preserves, its own privacies and secrecies. But where "The Garden" has seemed, for all its mysteries, to offer some kind of coherent poetic experience to a reader conscious that there may well be "more" to the poem than he can at the moment understand, "Upon Ap-

---

[19] See Joan Webber, *Contrary Music. A Study of John Donne's Prose Style* (University of Wisconsin Press, 1963), as well as her *The Eloquent "I"* (University of Wisconsin Press, 1967).

pleton House" has not appeared so self-evidently a single poem. Of course, ninety-seven stanzas must make up a long fiction; "The Garden" has after all only nine stanzas. In poems of this sort, length is an important factor: some of this poem's quality is indeed related simply to quantity. Length permits just the richness of allusion which seems in this poem to offer such peculiar problems; it permits also the serial presentation of scenes and landscapes, of activities and lyric tones, which nowadays make the poem seem so recalcitrant *qua* poem. But a poem of this length is not, after all, characteristic of Marvell's compact mode of writing his lyrical poems; though the political poems and satires were often very long, this poem is an anomaly among its fellows.

The following essays on the poem are all partial, that is, they try to isolate ranges of technique, topic, and theme for analysis, to disentangle elements which are gloriously intertwined in the poem itself; at the end, I try again to permit them to intertwine. Beginning with a study of Marvell's use of visual traditions in this poem, I consider the effect of new techniques in optics, by which Marvell makes exact and new the traditional *adunata* upon which for centuries poets had relied to present the problematical and even the impossible. From this study of point of view, single and multiple, I turn to some of the perspective applications in the poem, examining the themes of "within" and "without," of inwardness and involvement, of retirement and emergence, of contemplation and action. From some of the oppositions set by the languages of private and public life, I pass to some of the literary devices to present the flux, mutability, and metamorphosis so evident in this poem's universe. Next, I try to consider the poet's role in the poem, as well as his means of relating his experiences to each other; finally, I turn to his use of generic form and language, particularly considering the moral implications of generic cliché. As in the analysis and interpretation of "The Garden," I hope to read this wayward poem in terms, intelligible to its author, of Renaissance intellectual habits, trusting that such a reading will not violate but may enrich the poem's meanings for readers even today. This attempt is offered not so much to solve the problems of "Upon Appleton House" as to identify the place of problematics within the poem as a whole.

⊄ 2 ⊅

VISUAL TRADITIONS

i. Landscape

U PON APPLETON HOUSE" is a poem about a house and the estate crowned by the house, mutually supporting and honoring each other. From very different perspectives, the poet provides us with different views of the topography: we see the house itself, as a study in architecture; the ruins of an earlier "house," still visible as a pile of masonry on the estate, seen in the poem as a "quarry" and even a "chaos"; the formal gardens next the house; the water-meadows by the river, with the rural activities appropriate to such a scene; the wood, cut by a straight alley; the river in its bed and out of it. Nunappleton offers just such a landscape as Pliny laid out as the proper sort for a painting, with considerable differentiation and variety in both view and function. The estate satisfies its master and its master's poet with *"Lordship . . .* of the *Eye,"* its landscapes seen in accord with mood and moral (Fig. 20).

As one runs through the standard topics of seventeenth-century landscape painting, both fantastic and actual, topothesical and topographical, one discovers that the locales of this poem can be classified according to recognizable and accepted visual genres of landscape depiction. In the repertory, there are many pieces showing individual buildings, painted both as a record for their owners and as a form of praise to his greatness. Some were large enough to show the estate's principal activities taking place around an architectural center. Ruins-pieces form a genre, often designed to induce melancholy or nostalgia;[1] there are many examples of bucolic scenes of sheep, cattle, and mowing; and georgic scenes of sowing, reaping, harvesting, and gleaning.[2] There are forest-pieces with many

---

[1] For discussions of types of landscape pictures, see Harry V. S. Ogden and Margaret S. Ogden, *English Taste in Landscape in the Seventeenth Century* (Ann Arbor, 1955); and Wolfgang Stechow, *Dutch Landscape Painting in the Seventeenth Century* (London, 1966); both have been particularly helpful. For ruins-pieces, see Ogden, pp. 43-44.

[2] For bucolics, see Ogden, pp. 48-50, and Stechow, figs. 37, 45, 62.

variations, some not unlike Marvell's different views of his variegated enchanted wood;[3] there are river-landscapes,[4] often with angler or anglers; there are panoramas or prospect-pieces[5] which present many of these elements in one picture (Fig. 21).

According to visual tradition, pastoral and georgic scenes, with human figures going about their natural activities, were regarded as stressing the prosperous nature of a given countryside, as the browsing cattle, the mowers, or the fishermen in this poem demonstrate the balanced economy of Fairfax's estate and the benevolence of local Nature. Figures were, we discover, generally deliberately included in a landscape to increase its mood of well-being;[6] well-being did not always extend to ecstasy, as in this poem it happens to, but neither was it uncommon for a figure in a woody landscape to be beside himself with one rapture or another. Different activities suit different sorts of well-being, as in Ruisdael's magnificent "Grainfields,"[7] or his pictures of linen bleaching across wide fields (Fig. 22). In Adriaen van de Velde's "Farm by a Stream,"[8] the house, the cows, the sheep, and the horses all make up a small but sufficient unit, the prosperity of which is evident; in the same painter's "Summer," many elements gather to show the varied richness of that season (the season of "Upon Appleton House")—mowers, haycocks, sheep, and shepherds, horsemen and footmen are all present, as well as a ruin and a town in the background.[9] As for the wood-scenes, there are many lovely ones in the repertory of Dutch seventeenth-century landscape—entrances to forests,[10] some showing a dark and mysterious wood, some a light glade within the gloom, the sun brightening a particular spot or dappling the floor of the forest. Most forest-landscapists are inclined, like the poet in this poem, to note some specifics of their wood—as Wolfgang Stechow pointed out, on the whole they painted woods, not trees,[11] and some, like Gerard David and Altdorfer, painters in an earlier tradition closer to miniature, went so far as to paint leaves, not trees. Had he been a painter, Marvell's foliage-style would doubtless have taken after theirs, since he

[3] Ogden, pp. 40-41. [4] Ogden, p. 50.
[5] Ogden, pp. 48-49. [6] Ogden, p. 51.
[7] Stechow, fig. 37 (Metropolitan Museum).
[8] Stechow, fig. 45 (London, Nat. Gall.); see also fig. 66: Jacob van Ruisdael, "View of Naarden," Lugano, Coll. Thyssen.
[9] Stechow, fig. 62.
[10] Ogden, pp. 40-41; Stechow, fig. 133: Simon de Vlieger, "Entrance to a Forest" (Boymans).
[11] Stechow, p. 64.

was careful, he tells us, to note each leaf in his environment. It is not wholly a surprise, then, to discover that he had access to an important book on miniature-painting: Ralph Thoresby the antiquarian, who acquired many of Fairfax's books and manuscripts, had a manuscript copy of a major book in the miniature-tradition, Edward Norgate's *Miniatura*, "dedicated to the Lord's Daughter Mary,"[12] which Marvell may well have known. This book is a professional study of "the art of limning" small: Norgate's subject ranges over pictures "by the Life, Landskip, and History," with directions for perspective drawing and for mixing colors. In view of Marvell's famous tendency to miniaturize, this book may have some importance in his education as well as that of his little pupil; it may even have something to do with this poem.

Forests were variously depicted: some painters favored very dense forests, as Vroom did; others favored open paths through a wood, even lanes and alleys of the formal sort which, as Marvell tells us, divided Fairfax's wood as the Red Sea was divided. Hackaert's picture in the Rijksmuseum[13] shows a road passing a pond, with woods on the far side; there is a similar picture in the Wallace Collection. Hobbema's "Road into a Forest"[14] might be an analogue to Marvell's wood at Appleton, the wood, edged with arable, dark from without but light within. There are, also, dawn-pieces in the repertory of landscape-painters, to which the poem's garden-scene offers an analogue; and evening-pieces, the last, like Marvell's river landscape, often with a still sheet of water to show the day's final piece.[15] In Aert van der Neer's evening pictures in the Mauritshuis and in the Boymans Museum (Fig. 23), just as in Marvell's poem, the water's stillness helps give the evening its mysteriousness and fulness.[16]

Such topical scenes are often related—in Marvell's poems are overtly connected—to specific historical or mythological events. Landscapes as

[12] Ralph Thoresby, *Ducatus Leodiensis* (London, 1715), p. 525. Norgate was concerned also with the Bermuda venture, and made the beautiful map of the islands (see my "Marvell's 'Bermudas' and the Puritan Paradise," *Ren. News*, X, 1957, 75-79).

[13] Stechow, fig. 160: J. Hackaert, "The Alley" (Rijksmuseum).

[14] Stechow, fig. 151: M. Hobbema, "Road into a Forest" (Washington, Nat. Gall.); cf. also figs. 139, 141, both by Ruisdael, "Forest Entrance," (Rijksmuseum and Vienna Akademie).

[15] Stechow, figs. 358, 363, 369: A. van der Neer, "Evening" (The Hague, Brussels) and A. Cuyp, "Evening" (The Hague, Bredius Mus.).

[16] Stechow, fig. 358; this picture is remarkable in showing a brilliant sunset, the landscape saturated with red, as Marvell's evening is saturated with blue.

settings for biblical scenes and Ovidian metamorphoses[17] are common enough: Marvell's poem offers analogues to both subjects. By means of imagery, the mowers metamorphose into Israelites crossing the Red Sea, later miraculously gathering food in the desert. The poet turns into a Noah, then a Solomon, in the retreat of his wooded ark. In late sixteenth-century paintings, a small biblical scene was often "planted" in a landscape, so subdued and understated as to be hardly noticeable at first glance. In Alexander Keirincx' painting, what seems a wooded landscape with river and roads, turns out to be a Temptation of Christ.[18] The wilderness and woods seemed to be the appropriate setting for saints and hermits:[19] like such a holy figure, the poet becomes in his wood "some great Prelate of the Grove," in Marvell's magnificent conflation of Christian with pagan imagery. Though the "prelacy" is consistent with one iconographic tradition, the poet blends it with others; he takes advantage of the wood as the proper habitat for ecstasy, and assumes many other roles in that passage, finally allowing himself to metamorphose into the very landscape. As such a Proteus, he descends from an Ovidian rather than a meditative source.

Though the traditions of generic landscape-painting lie in the middle-ground of Marvell's poem, the poet draws on many other visual conventions as well. Indeed, it would be difficult not to: the more one knows of poetic description, the more frankly ecphrastic it turns out to be, closely related to visual renderings schematized by tradition. It was as difficult for poets to write a pastoral wholly independent of visual traditions, for instance, as for painters to show a pastoral scene without recourse to verbal sources. Pliny's descriptions of ancient pictures set models for later imitations in both painting and poetry, for which Horace's tag could always be cited in justification. Homer's description of Achilles' shield gave ecphrastic exercises their respectability, and parallels in minor genres, for instance from the Anthology, were common also.[20]

---

[17] Ogden, p. 23; Stechow, p. 25.

[18] Stechow, fig. 128 (München, Bav. State Coll.).

[19] Ogden, p. 52; cf. Raphael Sadeler's prints of hermits, anchorites, and solitaries, with such titles as "Solitudo," "Sylvae sacrae," etc. These pictures were dedicated to Clement VIII; I used the Bodley copy (Douce Prints e.6). See also Gillis van Coninxloo's picture, "Forest" (Stechow, fig. 122, Vaduz), of a deep wood with a man lying beneath a great tree.

[20] Cf. Lee, "Ut pictura poesis," and Hagstrum, *The Sister Arts*; also Miner, *op.cit.*, and Osborne, *op.cit.*

One can, then, see "Upon Appleton House" as no less a gallery-poem than Marvell's lyric "The Gallery"; the house-poem is a coherent series of pictorial descriptions, this time not of a lady in different symbolic poses, but of a landscape seen from different perspectives. The Appleton gallery contains many variations upon the theme of topography, as biblical scenes (Exodus, the Flood, Solomon, a *pentimento*-Crucifixion) and classical scenes (the pyramids, a Roman camp, Roman tumuli, the Nile) are interspersed among more conventionally representational views. In one image, Sir Peter Lely is introduced (stanza 56); shortly after that, an ecphrastic passage from *Gondibert* is recalled.[21] But not only are large-scale views introduced with their suggestions of epic painting; the poet also provides lovely miniatures: the nuns embroider pictures, taking Isabella as their model for the Virgin; Mexican feather-pictures are referred to; and emblems occur as well. In these ways, the exotic is set in contrast to the standard, the sacred or near-sacred to profane and profaning notions.

ii. Miniatures and Emblems

CRITICS noting Marvell's "miniaturism" have found examples in "Upon Appleton House." Kitty Scoular's finds have been most valuable in this respect.[22] As her work suggests, Marvell's visual imagery drew from the rich resources of moralized picture, and as we examine these in this poem, we recognize not only his remarkable skill in diminishing, but also his ability to underscore the themes of his poem by the intellectual meaning of the traditional images he used. The texture of his poem turns out to be very closely woven, as his emblematic images demonstrate. The tortoise, for instance, appears in the emblem literature in various ways relevant to Marvell's themes. Miss Scoular gives us Wither's tortoise,[23] whose modest and sufficient house is his shell; one could add Henry Peacham's sensitive creature (Fig. 24),[24] or Rollenhagen's, Typotius', or Camerarius' to the list, all of them used to symbolize qualities for which Marvell honored his patron.[25] In the wonderful illustration to Zacharias Heyns'

21 William Davenant, *Gondibert* (London, 1651), II, vi, stanzas 44-45, 53-66.

22 Scoular, *Natural Magic, passim*; see above, pp. 118-23.

23 George Wither, *A Collection of Emblemes* (London, 1635), p. 222.

24 Henry Peacham, *Minerva Brittana* (London, 1602), p. 178.

25 Gabriel Rollenhagen, *Nucleus Emblematum* (Arnhem, n.d.), pp. 74, 64; Jacobus Typotius, *Symbola divina et humana* (Frankfurt-am-Main, 1601-1603), II, 19; III, 13; Joachim Camerarius, *Symbolorum et Emblematum Centuriae*, III, xci. Cf. Pliny,

"Vivitur parvo bene," though, is the very finest analogue to Marvell's tortoise-imagery, as well as to his theme of containment and proper occupation;[26] there, on the authority of Pliny, a picture is presented of the tortoise-shell put to various uses: "There be found Tortoises in the Indian Sea so great, that one shell of them is sufficient for the roufe of a dwelling house. And among the Islands principally in the red sea, they use Tortoise shells ordinarily for boats and wherries upon the water."[27]

Heyns' emblem shows a man in a boat on the sea, evidently made of a tortoise-shell, and another emerging from his tortoise-shell "house," propped up so that it seems to be the shell of the man himself, borne on his back as the fishermen carry their coracles in Marvell's poem (Fig. 25).

Other images have their emblematic analogues: Miss Scoular prints Beza's neat geometrical emblem of the cube within the circle: the stability of the cube, as well as the perfection of circle and sphere, are endlessly attested in other sources.[28] In Freitag's emblem book, the stork sacrificing its nestling obviously relates to Marvell's heron who sacrifices its first-born to the Lord, so curiously letting it drop from the high nest in Appleton wood (Fig. 26).[29] Emblematic storks, cranes, and herons turn out to represent a cluster of qualities relevant in the thematic structure of this poem: the stork is a conspicuously good provider, the parent-birds of their young and the young in turn of their parents (Figs. 27, 28).[30] The mar-

---

ix.:10; G. P. Valeriano, *Hieroglyphica* (Basel, 1556), p. 200, where the tortoise's scorn of fortune and its guardianship of virgins are mentioned.

[26] Zacharias Heyns, *Emblemata Moralia* (Rotterdam, 1625), pp. 6-7.

[27] Pliny, *Historie of the World*, ix.:10.

[28] Scoular, Pl.VIII; for the cube, see Guy de Tervarent, *Attributs et symboles dans l'art profane 1400-1600* (Geneva, 1958, 1959), I, 137-38, citing Bocchius' cubic stone: VIRTUTI MERITO SEDES QUADRATA DICATUR; the Metayers' printer's mark: RECTUS UBIQUE; Rollenhagen, II, 70; Whitney, p. 228; cf. also Valeriano, p. 286 (*De Circulis*) and p. 290 (*De Quadrato*); Vitruvius, *De Architectura*, ed. Daniele Barbaro (Venice, 1567), p. 90. See also Rudolf Wittkower, *Architectural Principles in an Age of Humanism* (London, 1962), esp. pp. 22-23; Marjorie Hope Nicolson, *The Breaking of the Circle* (New York, 1962); and Puttenham, pp. 100-101, for the relations between the "square" stanza, in which the number of lines equals the number of syllables in a line, and *homo quadratus*.

[29] Arnoldus Freitag, *Mythologia Ethica* (Antwerp, 1574), pp. 250-51, given also in Scoular, Pl.IX.

[30] See Freitag, p. 243; Camerarius, III, xxvii, xl; Geoffrey Whitney, *A Choice of Emblems and Other Devices* (Leyden, 1584), p. 73; Andreas Alciati, *Emblematum libellus* (Paris, 1535), p. 9; and Tervarent, I, 97; Nicholas Reusner, *Emblemata* (Frankfurt-am-Main, 1581), pp. 74-75.

ried storks are, also, images of fidelity.[31] Storks, herons, and cranes are all provident; Camerarius shows us the heron, like Lord Fairfax, flying above the storm (Fig. 29).[32] The stork's and heron's sacrifice may be a way of referring to the Fairfax's earlier loss of a child, since Thoresby records the burial of another daughter, Elizabeth, "ob. inf." beside the heiress Mary.[33]

In the case of the stork, Marvell has provided the nearest equivalent in native British birds to the classical emblem: his stock-doves too are local, though their qualities are assimilated to those of the emblematic dove. Doves are religious, faithful in marriage, chaste in widowhood, and good providers (Figs. 30, 31).[34] They are, also, sensible retirers (like the tortoise); according to Camerarius, when threatened, doves take refuge in woods. His picture shows a pair flying thither,[35] as one assumes Lord and Lady Fairfax, honored in the poem's stock-dove reference, made their retreat to the country (Fig. 32). The halcyon, used in the poem to praise Mary Fairfax, shares some qualities with the dove: she nests on the sea, of course, but also finds her needed solitude there, as the dove finds hers in the wood; the halcyon is also a faithful mate and a provident parent. Its floating nest was, in an earlier seventeenth-century poem, likened to the island England.[36] Miss Scoular reproduces Camerarius' lovely nesting halcyon, but the bird is in most emblem books, and descends from Pliny and Ovid.[37] Another provident parent is the woodpecker (Fig. 33); according to Pliny, the "spight," or woodpecker, goes catlike up a tree, carefully placing its stroke, as Marvell's bird does;[38] in Jacob Cats' woodpecker emblem, the woodpecker, like a lover aiming for the beloved's

[31] Typotius, *Symbola divina*, II, 159; IUGALIS FIDES.
[32] Camerarius, III, xl, xlii; cf. Archibald Simson, *Hieroglyphica animalium* . . . (Edinburgh, 1622), pp. 6, 12, 84; Pliny, x:23.
[33] Thoresby, *Ducatus Leod.*, p. 68. Kitty (Scoular) Datta, "Marvell's Stork: The Natural History of an Emblem," *JWCI*, xxxi (1968), pp. 437-38.
[34] Cf. Alciati, *Emblemata latinogallica* (Paris, 1584), cxciii; Camerarius, III, lx, lxiv; Peacham, pp. 92, 110; Simson, pp. 40-46.
[35] Camerarius, III, lxi; Peacham, p. 110; cf. *Aeneid*, VI, 11.
[36] Giles Fletcher, *Christs Victorie* (Cambridge, 1610), Canto IV, St. 10.
[37] Alciati (1535), p. 23 (with nestlings); Rollenhagen, p. 78; J. G. Zincgrefius, *Emblematum ethico-politicorum liber* (Heidelberg, 1681), p. 24, gives two halcyons on the nest and notes their excellent training of their young; Reusner, p. 93; Whitney, p. 236; Pliny, x:32; Camerarius, III, lxvii; cf. Erasmus, *Parabola sive similia* (Lyons, 1528), p. 137, in which the halcyon brings calm not for herself but for others' good.
[38] Pliny, x:18, "Of the Spight, or Woodpecker," a bird presaging good.

heart, pecks firmly through the hard tree (Fig. 34).[39] Like the heron's, the hewel's sacrifice in the poem is reverential; the tainted oak falls without hatred or bitterness, to keep the forest clean. The bird is, in an archaic technical term, a "holt-felster," in charge of the health of the health-giving wood.

The nightingale too is prominent in the emblem repertory, chiefly as an educator of its young, training them in their remarkable birthright. Pliny's description of the nightingale's traditional tuition is often illustrated in emblem, most sweetly in Camerarius' version, given here in Fig. 35.[40]

I can find no rail in the pictured emblems, although the characteristics of other low-nesting birds seem to have been assimilated to Marvell's local bird. The usual emblem-equivalents are the lark and the quail, with the last of which Marvell specifically associates his little bird. Peacham shows the careful partridge-mother teaching her birds to fly the nest as the mowers approach, and Camerarius' lark does the same thing (Figs. 36, 37).[41] Valeriano notes that the rail is precocious and provident, two qualities notably absent in this poem's rails; and Pliny calls the little bird "amphibious," which ties in to another major theme of the poem. In "Upon Appleton House," the humility and innocence of the bird are stressed, as are its failures to adapt rather than its powers of accommodation. The rail is not here used to demonstrate moral adaptability, although the theme is otherwise stressed in the poem before its clear enunciation in the last stanza. The tortoise and the crocodile offer hints that the poet to some degree approves of moral amphibiousness, a necessary quality for life in the human world.[42] The emblem books offer many models for amphibiousness; frogs, tortoises, and especially crocodiles, are all approved, not reproved, for their adaptability.

Birds and animals do not provide the only emblematic parallels to the imagery of this poem: Camerarius' systematic emblem book stresses the meaning of grass and mowing, to reinforce the biblical and classical implications clearly legible in the poem. When grass is cut, it waxes richer—

[39] Jacob Cats, *Silenus Alcibiadis, sive Proteus* (Amsterdam, 1622), p. 13.
[40] Pliny, x:29; Camerarius, III, lxx.
[41] Peacham, p. 131; Camerarius, III, lxxiii; Whitney, p. 75.
[42] For amphibiousness, see Scoular, pp. 33-35; Pliny, viii:25; Beroaldus' annotations to Columella, *Enarrationes . . . de re rustica* (Paris, 1543), ddiv; Camerarius, I, xcvii; Reusner, pp. 58-59, on the crocodile; Typotius, I, 75-70 (frog). The crocodile is typically malign: e.g., Rollenhagen, p. 100, Erasmus, *Parabola*, p. 112.

"Surget uberior" (Fig. 38); haycocks reward labor ("Non metentis sed serentis," Fig. 39). Following Paul's great image, grain is the emblem of the Resurrection: "spes alterae vitae" (Fig. 40).[43] The emblem from De Jode's *Microkosmos* (Fig. 41), showing a hamadryad in a hollow tree, illustrates the notion that man is an inverted tree;[44] Cats' river-god, with sedge on his head and his body fusing with bank and river,[45] has his analogues in classical and neoclassical art as well as in Ovid (*Met.* ix.3) and Virgil (*Aen.* viii, 31-35).

In general, the emblem books provide interesting corroboration for the themes of the poem as well as analogues to Marvell's graphic vignettes; but in this range of reference, as in so many others, Marvell alters his traditional sources in favor of problematics. The birds in this poem do very odd things, after all: why should the stock-dove, so clearly associated with his lady patron, weep *before* experiencing widowhood? What is the heron's attitude to its sacrifice, or the woodpecker's? There is an unexplained element to many of these scenes, whose emblematic language of reference was perhaps more intelligible to the circle in which the poem was written than to more general readers. When one consults the emblem books, particular obscurities about these birds seem somewhat to be cleared up, but not altogether. Though the cryptic emblem literature offers some straightforward help in filling in the hints made in the poem's imagery, no "source" seems to provide an exhaustive gloss to Marvell's intentions. His meaning is elusive, even with these useful aids.

Marvell's miniature scenes offer a scalar contrast to the set of large landscape pictures of which the poem is chiefly built. His gallery holds great and small, each kind of picture observing the conventions of its genre, and complementing other kinds. For all their obscurities, the emblems are noticeably exact, as the tradition demanded. Marvell's mysteriousness is well within the emblem tradition, though, which notoriously combined an exact observation with an esoteric thought or generalization: part of the test, in emblem-writing, was to puzzle or trick the reader as well as to enlighten him. Emblem pictures, of course, shared some content with the ordinary, undidactic landscape: Lebei's emblem, "Eunt anni more fluentis aquae," for instance, with its two fishermen, river-god with

43 I Cor. 15:35-38, 42-44; Camerarius, II, lvi, lxxviii, xcix.
44 Geerhardt de Jode, *Microkosmos, Parvus Mundus* (Antwerp, 1589), p. 35; see A. B. Chambers, " 'I was but an Inverted Tree': Notes toward the History of an Idea," *Studies in the Renaissance*, VIII (1961), 291-99.
45 Cats, *Silenus Alcibiadis*, p. 45.

sedge and urn, might as well point to well-being as to transience; one needs the motto to read the lesson as the writer intended.[46]

Comparing Marvell's imagery to its emblematic analogues shows that he made use of two opposed tendencies in emblem-technique, utilizing both the precision and the fixedness on one hand, and the ambiguousness and mysteriousness of the tradition on the other. Nor was his manipulation of landscape conventions merely standard or routine, even though his descriptions do fulfil the criteria for such genre-scenes. Indeed, the standard element of Marvell's scenes is the least remarkable thing about them: it is their deviations which command our chief attention.

iii. Deviations in Perspective, Metamorphoses, and Anamorphoses

IN VISUAL and intellectual ambiguity, the poet could and did find particular resources for his own presentation of the fluidity of both material and intellectual worlds. In *adunaton*, rhetoric offers a standard mode of inversion, on which the poet certainly relied, as in his stanza 60, about the Nunappleton flood:

> Let others tell the *Paradox*,
> How Eels now bellow in the Ox;
> How Horses at their Tails do kick,
> Turn'd as they hang to Leeches quick;
> How Boats can over Bridges sail;
> And Fishes do the Stables scale.
> How *Salmons* trespassing are found;
> And Pikes are taken in the Pound.

This is the familiar commonplace of the world-upside-down, a classic literary signal of topsy-turvydom, of handy-dandy, of a morally upset universe in which things do not keep their accustomed or assigned places, but waywardly rearrange themselves in ways disruptive to conventional thought. The tradition has its long history, this particular image occurring (also with stress on its literal truth) in Ovid's *Metamorphoses*; (with stress on the overwhelming nature of love) in Virgil's eighth Eclogue; (with stress on its figurative element) in Horace's Odes, II, ii and IV, vii, there to suggest the disaster attendant upon civil war. As Mr. Allen

---

[46] Denis Lebei, *Emblemata* (Frankfurt-am-Main, 1596), emblem ii.

has pointed out, this kind of imagery was regularly associated in Latin poetry with the chaos produced by civil war in a country, especially the countryside. An even more relevant storm, also metaphorically connected to the disastrous effects of war upon the agrarian economy, is that of Georgics I, when the reapers face the rain-flood sweeping away their harvest. From this storm, the heron escapes by flying above the clouds and the cranes by flying into the valleys.

In Marvell's poem, the facts in the end reverse the function of this upside-downing, modify the frightening references to civil war. If this world-upside-down, this world in flood, is designed to invoke the civil war raging outside the boundaries of the estate, it retracts its utterance too: the disasters suggested by the imagery turn out not to be disasters at all, but simply the seasonal observance of georgic providential behavior— commended by, among others, Pliny.[47] This flood-after-reaping restores the proper relation between harvest and replenishing, prevented in the Georgics by the disastrous natural flood. At the same time, though, the image is not simple: the landscape is made into a double scene, the high seriousness of its biblical and classical references dissolving into the happier context of the real episode, merely seeming catastrophic but in fact beneficial. The original disproportion of the scene sinks back into normality, as we learn that what would be a world-upside-down, in another and more ordinary context, is here simply regular and beautiful. The poet plays with his and our own literary expectations, ultimately to empty the great *adunata* of their paradoxical meanings.

Marvell's way with this standard *topos* for inversion should give us pause, since his manner in this stanza is a model for much else that he does in the poem. The more one studies it, the more the poem's use and abuse of order demands attention, most obviously in the many images of inversion. For in this poem, there are many worlds-upside-down, many men-upside-down: in the wood, whither the poet retires to escape the flood, he experiences an extraordinary identification with the birds and plants of that thick landscape, an identification which involves his own metamorphosis. To himself, and to us forced to observe with his eyes, the poet's form and nature, his real "being," seem fully to merge with the elements of his environment. Had he wings, he would fly, he says; inverted, he would be a tree.[48]

---

[47] Pliny, xviii:28.　　　　　　[48] Chambers, *op.cit.*

Yet, although the imagery inverts so much, and so strikingly conveys the poet's sense of freedom from the gravity even of himself, and all the cares the self must bear in the ordinary world, we discover that the man in the poem is in fact never turned upside down: he stays upright through everything. However high his raptures, he walks upon the ground, moves from here to there; even when he seems prone in ecstasy he is mysteriously on his way to somewhere else. It is true that in one sense nature's order is inverted in the wood-ecstasy, but that inversion is intellectual, not actual. Attributing high powers to nature, this man wishes to be turned into bird or tree, elements on the scale normally regarded as lower than a man. But even in the poem's fiction, we learn that the scale of creatures can be altered only in imagination: the poet throughout remains a man, simple and complex. He does not fly; he is not a tree. Only in his imagination can the rules of nature be altered to suit a passing psychological need.

In the meadow scene, the poet sees the mowers as inverted men: they "dive" through space, through the meadow as if through a sea, losing their sense of spatial relation, losing their sense of themselves. In the final stanza of the poem, the fishermen are inverted, "rational *Amphibii*" appearing on the scene like Antipodeans, in a multiple image of inversion. On Cleveland's authority at least, men on the other side of the world were deemed to wear their shoes on their heads;[49] the Yorkshire fishermen habitually carry their coracles on their heads, or backs. Both behave peculiarly, wearing on their heads what they ought to have beneath them, shoes or boats; but, in the normal way, Antipodeans are antipodal to Yorkshiremen walking right side up. One pair of feet is, from the other's perspective, always upside down. This pairing is not a mirror-reflection, though: Antipodeans, even with shoes on their feet, are not mirror-images of Yorkshiremen with boats on their heads.[50] Only when men upside

---

[49] John Cleveland, "Square-cap," *Poems,* ed. Brian Morris and Eleanor Withington (Oxford, 1967), p. 44; I have been unable to find a source for this notion of the poets. For a plainer version of the *sub sole,* mirror-image notion of the Antipodes, see *Parnassus Biceps* (London, 1656), p. 33: "Upon some pieces of work in York House":

> Almost too dear for man to tread upon,
> A floor all diaperd with Marble stone,
> Feet to our feet. This mystery beguiles
> Philosophy with many thousand wiles.
> Nay to increase the miracle; with ease
> We here become our own Antipodes.

[50] Following A. Alvarez (*The School of Donne,* London, 1961), Mr. Holahan

down oblige by wearing shoes on their heads can the images mirror one another. Then, if they do, the men are twice antipodal, doubly upside down: their feet against one another are antipodal, and their pseudopoda in the air make them seem antipodal to themselves. They are doubly topsy-turvy, and since this is so, they are not topsy-turvy. They mirror each other, but only by verbal sleight-of-hand. There are too many possibilities in this image for readers to keep straight, or to interpret as they read—the salmon-fishermen and the antipodeans are grotesque, decorative figures thrust into the poem to remind us, at its peaceful end, that things are simple nowhere in the world, that all men are sometimes, in some perspectives, upside down. In contrast to the diving mowers who emerge from the meadow to stand up straight in the poem, the figures in the final stanza retain some degree of mystery, of oddity, as they move offstage and out of view, trailing their ambiguity behind them, leaving readers at the poem's end aware of the mystery even in daily occupations.

For somehow, it is not as comforting as it ought to be that most of the things inverted in this poem are not in fact inverted; readers' stability is not increased by the righting of the men and worlds upside down. Even when right side up, these figures do not behave conventionally: in the abracadabra of their positioning lies their peculiar meaning, pointing to the world's instability, the illusion in all perspectives, even those taken from Appleton, upon the multiple lives of men. Gradually, though, the conventions of upside down and right side up cease to matter as much as they normally do in the world. These topsy-turvydoms come to seem artifices and constructs like anything else: the river floods the land, the fish swim through buildings—but the flood is an artful one produced to georgic prescription. The mowers are not divers, even if the meadow is later flooded; but in the mowers' lives some uncertainty comes, as they must question their occupation after the death of the baby rail. The poet is not a tree, but he understands the book of nature written on the leaves around him, and is the better for it.

To say all this, though, is to speak after the riddle has been set and studied, after the effect of the bizarre images has come to seem normal, and the grotesque naturalized. In the developing poem, readers certainly think and feel catastrophe as the flood comes up over the land and the

suggests that the association of canoes and shoes results from the local Yorkshire pronunciation of "boats" and "boots" as homonyms.

fish swim in the stables. It is somehow disturbing to realize that all this is *not* crucial, or that our emotional reactions to the evident meaning of the words used are continually undercut and undermined by what the poet does next, by the shifts of context and tone from one passage to its successor. By such stratagems the poet works to involve his dutiful readers in the very unbalancing of which the poem speaks.

iv. Scalar Shifts and Optical Illusions

SHIFTS provide one kind of puzzle for the reader expecting, from his acquaintance with other house-poems, an orderly cosmos displayed for his admiration and edification.[51] Scalar disruption contributes to the muddle, as when, for instance, grasshoppers are seen to contemn the men "beneath" them. This seems an inverted world, in which grasshoppers are larger than men; but it turns out, only, that the grasshoppers are sitting, in their usual small shapes, on top of the grass grown taller than men. Inverted, but not inverted; and the poet involves himself in this scene as a figure wandering in this world. As he enters the meadow scene—in the first person, now: "to the *Abbyss* I pass"—he seems to see the haymakers from a great distance, themselves mere grasshoppers in the tall grass. At that point, the grasshoppers are introduced as "Gyants there": to a cinematic generation, such a shift from distant prospect to close-up is familiar enough, but such switches were rarer in Marvell's time, though some analogues can be profitably cited.[52]

Among the visual analogues is the curious painting in Hartford, attributed to Ruisdael, an extraordinary view of thistles and other weeds, seen from such a perspective as to dwarf the postulated beholder with respect to the towering plants (Fig. 42).[53] In the poem, the grasshopper shift turns out to be deceptive itself: the creatures are not giants at all, and as we realize that, an element of sanity returns to the meadows that they had seemed conspicuously to lack.

There are other shifts of focus in the poem. We are shown the mowers at a considerable distance, but the rail killed by the scythe moves instantly to the foreground as "bloody *Thestylis*" seizes it to convert it into lunch. Rubens' great landscape in London, where the partridge hide in the clearing, and are enormous compared with the actually more imposing

[51] See Hibbard and O'Loughlin.   [52] For instance, *PL*, I, 777-782.
[53] In the Wadsworth Atheneum, Hartford, Conn.

landscape elements depicted in the distance, may be compared to this (Fig. 43). One thinks too of emblem conventions, where illusionistic perceptive is so often abandoned in the interests of thematic emphasis, and small things bearing heavy symbolic weight are seen as monumental.

In the famous image of the grazing cattle sent to crop the stubble-fields, the same movement occurs from small to great.[54] At first we see the cows from afar; they are like fleas, or like stars in the night sky. The flea image is turned inside out: the fleas emerge from a subsidiary position in the original metaphor to be transformed into something huge, as if seen through a microscope. And what huge things are they seen to resemble? Cows, of course, so that the total circularity of the image is established. "Multiplying Glasses" are the means used to telescope tenor and vehicle of this image: we are made to consider the fleas through a microscope, where they appear disproportionately large—like that classic page tipped into Hooke's *Micrographia*, where the flea is depicted as enormous (Fig. 44). We then turn to look up, not down, at the stars; through a telescope, not a microscope: the image itself works in reverse, too. Unlike fleas, constellations are made up of huge bodies which look small to us who are so distanced from them. By the many kinds of opposition exploited here, all scale is somehow obliterated. We are made to lose our measuring-rod, so that the cows lose their reality between the very small and the unbelievably huge.

Marvell's incisiveness in describing small objects calls up another kind of art, the minute precision of the still-life painter. That artist consistently used magnifying glasses and microscopes to observe and render his subjects; for his art, fleas could be on the bovine scale of Hooke's engraving.[55] Normally, the still-life painter does not falsify the scale of his picture, but maintaining the illusion of a fixed perspective, strives for a highly developed representational illusionism.[56] Marvell's details are the result of exact vision: in the "Hazles thick," for instance, the poet sees not the whole thrush upon her nest, but its "shining Eye," distinct from the surrounding leaves, a sharp eye which in its own right catches and holds the sharp

[54] Leishman, pp. 222-23, cites Theocritus, *Idyll* 35, on the Cattle of the Sun.

[55] Robert Hooke, *Micrographia* (London, 1665), "The Flea"; cf. also "The Louse," an even more impressive enlargement of a minute creature.

[56] See Charles Sterling, *Still Life Painting from Antiquity to the Present* (New York and Paris, 1959); Max J. Friedländer, *Landscape, Portrait, Still Life* (New York, 1963) pp. 272-84; E. H. Gombrich, "Tradition and Experience in Western Still Life," *Meditations on a Hobby Horse* (London, 1963), pp. 95-105.

eye of the poet. Montaigne and his cat; Marvell and the thrush—who plays with whom, who observes whom?

In his communion with the wood, the poet knows all nature, even down to the individual leaf:

> No Leaf does tremble in the Wind
> Which I returning cannot find.   (stanza 72)

Like the still-life painter, the poet seems to accord each thing the attention due it as itself, to honor the individuality and individuation of each bird, each leaf—and of each element, whatever it may be, of his scene. This attention, however, is in the poem quite inconsistent, notably selective. Only now and again can the poet demonstrate his sense of the autonomy of each individual thing in the environment: in the wood episode, as in the sixth stanza of "The Garden," the poet's revelation of nature's unity does not prevent him from recognizing nature's separate elements. The greater his absorption into nature, the more precise, apparently, his appreciation of its particulars. From intense awareness of individuals the poet's cosmic identification emerges; in turn, the cosmic identification brings understanding of the value of individuals.

Later in the poem, in the evening, a panoramic still life is rendered as a miracle wrought by Maria. Again specific elements are honored; each fish in the river is, somehow, separately delineated:

> The stupid Fishes hang, as plain
> As *Flies* in *Chrystal* overt'ane;   (stanza 85)

What had fluctuated is brought to stasis, as the halcyon-girl stills the fluid scene; the rapidly changing elements of earlier passages, the lapping, relaxed particulars of the river scene just before Maria's entrance, are at this point all arrested, frozen into a moment of still life, caught at an instant of immobility as a painting catches its shifting actuality.[57]

Though optical instruments were at first considered to be clarifiers of sense-experience, isolating and distinguishing new facts about the natural world and, by extending the sense of sight, making possible great advances in the taxonomic effort of the Renaissance, in Marvell's hands optical techniques are used to very wayward ends. Seeming to sharpen a reader's perceptions, so that with the poet he sees for a moment the

[57] E. H. Gombrich, "Moment and Movement in Art," *JWCI*, XXVII (1964), 826-49.

thrush's black eye, in fact these devices are confusing and puzzling. After all, the grazing cattle are neither constellations nor fleas, but by these similes, the poet expressly prevents us from more than a fleeting glance at the cattle plain. In the wood and stream, the opposite is the case: the details are plain enough, but their aggregate is confusing: "the hatching *Thrastle's* eye," the separate leaves, "the stupid Fishes" are all so separated from their environment that we have difficulty in piecing their world together. Here, pieces are missing from the picture-puzzle. An analogue to this technique is, for instance, a plate by Hoefnagel, to which E. H. Gombrich has drawn attention. Each element in the picture is shown for itself, detached from the others, some flying, some sitting on a flat ground, some casting shadows in one direction, some in another, some casting no shadows at all.[58] In the wood passage, some of the poetic elements are so distinct and detached from environment that they seem entirely without context. Though the thrush sits on her nest—and nests are clearly important in this poem—the poet leaves us to work out where the specific nest may be, and indeed what the connections are from nest to nest. Disjunction is of course typical of many ranges of this poem's operation: the cattle are detached from scale, the bird's eye is detached from the bird, the hewel's curiously hierophantic, unexplained activity quite detached from the usual forest-behavior of that bird.

There are other devices borrowed from optical techniques in this poem beside the microscopic separation of an element from its accommodating background. Of the cattle, the poet says they

> seem within the polisht Grass
> A Landskip drawn in Looking-Glass.

that is, the cattle seem to be elements of a picture drawn on backed glass, so that when someone uses it as a looking-glass, he sees the cattle on his own reflection, "As Spots, so shap'd, on Faces." By this means, the poor cattle are again transported from context, this time into a double picture of a sort not yet met in the poem, in which a rural landscape is transposed into a face. To read the landscape-face picture as one, the beholder must see the cattle as disfiguring facial spots. In this passage, the poet refers deliberately to anamorphosis: somewhat earlier, in stanza 56, he had achieved an anamorphic effect simply by verbal means, without invoking

[58] E. H. Gombrich, *Art and Illusion* (London and New York, 1960), p. 230.

the visual arts at all, when he gave us at once "A new and empty Face of things" and a full depiction of an active rural scene.

Mirrors characteristically repeat pictures, repeat what is before them: the "mirror" at the poem's end, the still river reflecting the scene outside it, has its double function too, something like the looking-glass of the cattle image. This time, though, instead of two pictures interpenetrating one another, the river presents a picture of the world to the world, a picture so perfect that the things reflected in the river seem to lose their identity in their reflections, or in the reflection of themselves. Therefore, all things "doubt/ If they be in it or without." And if they *are* in it, of course they are antipodean. Even in his image of perfect stillness, serenity, and rest, the poet cannot resist raising questions of ontology and epistemology, so that things themselves are for a moment animated to question and to doubt, along with the readers working their way through the poem.

Visual imagery—and mirrors, of course—provide the vocabulary in classical as in modern languages for understanding and perception. With the systematization of linear perspective, the problem of point of view, both as an organizing device and as a limiting one, became paramount in the visual arts and lent its language to that of epistemology, too. To see things "in perspective" requires that things be organized and rendered in specific relation to each other; the perceiver must have a fixed viewpoint, a rooted stance, must have taken a decision about his place in relation to the world. It may, though, be something else, the indication of a decision not taken, for any given perspective implies only a limited view of things; and a picture or drawing may suggest that there is much more than can be shown, just out of the viewer's range.

Perspective itself is an honest illusion—a deceit, as some Renaissance critics wrote[59]—by which things are made to look true, even though their actual relation may be something quite other than what the eye from a given point can perceive. In a picture, perspective implies a conventional, expected falsification, even as it observes the illusionistic "truth" of phenomenal vision. Perspective is, then, a severely limiting device; the

[59] For the quarrel over perspective, see *Italian Art 1500-1600, Sources and Documents,* ed. Robert Klein and Henri Zerner (Basic Books, 1966), pp. 106-11. For an excellent discussion of critical "perspectivism," see Claudio Guillén, "On the Concept and Metaphor of Perspective," *Comparatists at Work,* ed. Stephen G. Nichols, Jr., and Richard B. Vowles (New York, 1968); pp. 28-90.

beholder of a perspective view must reorganize his "picture" whenever he shifts his position, since with each shift on his part, perspective relations also shift. As Jurgis Baltrušaitis pointed out in his fascinating book,[60] once one has learned to present visually "true" perspectives, it is but a short step to producing deforming perspectives, manipulating the science of optics to heighten the illusion not of proportion only, but also of disproportion, deformation, and irregularity. "Anamorphic" pictures, which broke up conventional forms and relations by geometrical means, insisted upon the relativity implied in the rules of perspective, but by using at least two points of view to organize a picture, brought to the beholder's attention questions of irregularity normally unasked, at least in pictorial form. In order to compose a picture of this sort, its beholder had to discover the exact position from which the various pictorial elements would fall into place in a "normal" perspective. In some pictures, of which Holbein's "Ambassadors" is the most famous example, no single position can bring the different elements into one focus. Still other pictures manipulated pictorial scale so as to preclude the possibility of a fixed point of view.

Such pictures are rarely important as works of art, though Holbein's picture is an exception. Normally, they are intellectual exercises rather than pleasing pictures, which have involved a great deal of careful planning on the part of their designers. They force questions upon beholders willy-nilly. There are other kinds of double or multiple pictures, of which the human landscape is one of the most common sort. Other kinds of displays were possible in the seventeenth century, such as the catoptrical instruments which showed, in rapid succession, several different tableaux. After these had been shown serially, all could be composed into one grand final synthetic picture of an officially important subject.[61] In metamorphic and anamorphic pictures, several perspectives are offered; some mental energy is required of the beholder in putting the disparate elements into a consistent context. In catoptric displays, the beholder stays in one place, as it were, watching the set scenes metamorphose without having to solve them himself. "Upon Appleton House" offers analogues to both kinds of display. Sometimes perspectives must be forcibly arranged by the viewer; sometimes he can stand passive before shifts of scene which

[60] Jurgis Baltrušaitis, *Anamorphoses* (Paris, 1955); for double pictures, see William Drummond, cited Freeman, *English Emblem Books*, p. 16.

[61] Jean-François Nicéron, *La perspective curieuse* (Paris, 1638), p. 116.

do not demand his attempts to control them, as in magic lantern performances.

v. Magic Lantern and Masque Devices

THE meadow scenes seem much like a catoptric or magic lantern performance; Marvell may have known the magic lantern device, for as early as 1618 such a performance had been put on at the English court by Cornelis Drebbel,[62] and others had tried the trick subsequently. Drebbel had projected pictures of himself in different costumes from beggar to king, one figure metamorphosing into the next through the social scale. As the poet enters the meadows, he pauses as if to focus on his view, trying out several perspectives, in the first of which men seem like grasshoppers, and then grasshoppers are seen as giants. After a time he achieves a "normal" focus, in which the haymakers' progress is seen, presented in diminutive form (i.e., like a magic lantern performance) and as a highly stylized, choreographed formalization of reality (i.e., as a masque):

> No Scene that turns with Engines strange
> Does oftner then these Meadows change.   (stanza 49)

After many "turns" of mowing, rail-killing, and triumphal dance, the players withdraw to leave the stage empty for another series of changes, in a different mode altogether:

> This *Scene* again withdrawing brings
> A new and empty Face of things;   (stanza 56)

By moving ungraded from one operation to the next, all the bustle of horses, haycarts, pitching and tossing has been avoided, so that the accomplished mowing brings us naturally to a "Table rase and pure," a blank canvas ready for the painter. This blank canvas is also the world empty on the First Day of Creation: for a moment, the painter is like the deity, with all creation in prospect. Onto this set, the "Villagers in common chase/ Their cattle": the animals enter as if from nowhere, on Creation's Fifth Day, or into the bullring at Madrid. The one is nature plain and pure, the other manifest artification, the subtle arts of a highly developed civilization, in which the primitive behavior of bulls has been subjected to rigorous and ritualized control. In this stanza there are

---

[62] Royal Library, The Hague: Kon. Akad., Ms. Huygens 47, f. 207.

other switches: the tempo, at first nervous and quick, slows down utterly as the cattle's movement becomes imperceptible:

> They feed so wide, so slowly move,
> As *Constellations* do above.   (stanza 58)

The cattle vanish from the poem as the stars vanish in the morning, again without fuss or explanation; and the last meadow scene begins:

> Then, to conclude these pleasant Acts,
> *Denton* sets ope its *Cataracts*;   (stanza 59)

This language of staging and scenery recurs in the poem, as for instance the poet dresses for his priestly part in the wood, and in the final scene at the riverside, where

> . . . Men the silent *Scene* assist,
> Charm'd with the *Saphir-winged Mist*.   (stanza 85)

until, at the very end, the professional fishermen lead in the night and lead the principals off the stage.

Magic lantern performances exploit scalar shifts, projecting a tiny original as unbelievably huge; masques, too, are lifesize presentations of a series of emblematic scenes. In magic lantern presentations, one scene can be made to melt into another, as the anamorphic body-landscape melts from scene to human shape. In such pictures, a natural scene is characteristically converted into a reclining man or a huge human head: conversely, a human figure can be seen to be made up of animal or vegetable elements, as in the many arcimboldesque paintings of the sixteenth century (Figs. 45, 46).[63] In various ways, the poet makes use of the body-landscape trick, as when he makes himself metamorphose into wood-elements and into the stream: he uses even himself, in this poem, to call into question the principles of definition, limitation, and boundary. The superposition of forms points to forms' ambiguities: nothing seems to be itself, or itself alone.

Devices like those used in masque and magic lantern performances permit the poet to shift from one scene to another without gradation or transition, to alter sharply differentiated episodes into one another. Focus

---

[63] For Arcimboldo and arcimboldesque pictures, see Benno L. Geiger, *I dipinti ghiribizzosi di Giuseppe Arcimboldo* (Florence, 1954); Francine-Clair Legrand and Felix Sluys, *Giuseppe Arcimboldo et les arcimboldesques* (Aalter, Belgium, 1955).

once achieved, the poet could maintain a single perspective for a time; he could shift perspective radically too, by shifting his own apparent focus. Drebbel made himself his own subject in his magic lantern entertainments; Marvell presents himself as a character in his invention, too.

In the meadow scene, the poet begins as an observer, well outside the action he observes. As critic and commentator, he is clearly separate from the mower-masquers,[64] whom he seems to manipulate according to his fancy, as the inductor does. His little world is very much his theater: by his highly stylized framing of the scenes, the simple behavior of simple men, even down to their sweating, is raised to the level of courtly entertainment. What could be more detached from the actual activity of mowing than this graceful pastoral? Lest we take it as only that, though, a radical disjunction jars us into realizing the artificiality of the artifice: one of the actors refuses to be manipulated by the poet, and turns on him, to expose him to our view. The poet's previous metaphors, addressed to the readers who overhear his inventions, ought to have been inaudible to the *farouche* Thestylis, who has nonetheless caught his drift and herself imaginatively extends the poet's metaphor by her reading— counter to the nostalgic tone he then affects—of the events taking place. By this trick, scale and perspective both shift, and with them the psychological or tonal angle. Though the poet has indeed called the mowers "Israelites," by the time Thestylis burst into the poem, he had abandoned that image and become absorbed in the small tragedy of the rail's death. Thestylis irrupts upon the language of pastoral sentimental identification, the lament for a creature dead ere its prime. Her speech calls attention to the very *writing* of the poem: she carries the poet's biblical metaphor to an area into which he had not planned to take it, and we realize, suddenly, that another imagination might have gone another way, that the poem might, in another poet's hands, have been quite different. Her untimely comment also has the effect of calling into question not just the limits of the poet's aesthetic attention and thus the limitations in this kind of poetry, but also the whole process of figural reading, mocked in her speech. More important, she effects a major reversal of role, the poet becoming for a moment an actor in *her* drama. Hitherto effaced and neutral, although in fact manipulating the whole scene, the poet finds himself rudely recast, forced into evidence in the poem he writes, his scale suddenly dwarfing

---

[64] Mowers are not uncommon masque-figures; see *Tempest*, IV, i.

the mowers', even as Thestylis' seizing the little rail dwarfs that tiny bird, till then so much in the foreground.

The poet's apparently involuntary intrusion into the scene has affinities with the painted self-portraits in which the artist seems almost accidentally to be a part of his picture. More important, though, is the poetical self-criticism involved in the behavior permitted Thestylis: the poet, intent on "creating," on finding his many various figures for the scene he presents, has forgotten, as it were, the "Israelites" of a few lines before, gone on in his prodigal versatility to quite another range of reference, when he is sharply recalled to his tonic, the metaphor, which of all those given, finally dominates the mowing scene. His sympathy for the rail is cut off, as Thestylis forces back on him the providential implications of his metaphor from Exodus. Pastoral sympathies must be abandoned before the providence of the Lord; one language must give way to another, one theme to another. Extended to refer to the state of England at large, the metaphor forces both poet and readers to count the cost of passing from bondage to the rule of saints.

In the wood, the poet-director frankly takes on the role of actor in his "mask" there, but he is at the same time an audience for scenes displayed for him, in magic lantern sequence, by the wood environment. Nightingale, doves, thrush, heron, and woodpecker go through their gestures for him. According to his imagery, he becomes first a Solomon who knows every leaf and feather of his world, and who understands the language of its creatures. At this point, the poet assumes the costume appropriate to his part:

> And see how Chance's better Wit
> Could with a Mask my studies hit!

that is, he wears a mask for his part, takes his place in a masque of nature. The poet becomes the landscape, ceasing simply to be a figure enhancing the landscape to turn into the elements themselves of that landscape:

> The Oak-Leaves me embroyder all,
> Between which Caterpillars crawl:
> And Ivy, with familiar trails,
> Me licks, and clasps, and curles, and hales.

The still-life elements, even to the caterpillar, absorb him into their decorum. Although he does not stay "still," as he ought if he were pictured, he moves in a garb appropriate to a picture of a wood:

> Under this *antick Cope* I move
> Like some great *Prelate of the Grove,*   (stanza 74)

The word "antick" manages semantic references both to miming and to antiquity; the player plays at a natural priesthood, in the shape of a druid, identified as the *numen nemoris.*[65]

In yet another way, the imagery tends to gather the poet cryptically into the several habitats of the wood. He himself asks to be covered with woodbine and vines, "chained" and "nailed" in a natural crucifixion, gentle if prickly, by "Brambles" and "courteous Briars." By these small chains, he requires nature to gather him into its artifice, that he may maintain his rapture as long as possible—longer than he can expect it naturally to last. In his piscatory experience, the poet once more fuses with nature, this time with another landscape, as he becomes one with the riverbank, crowned with ("vocall") reeds:

> Oh what a Pleasure 'tis to hedge
> My Temples here with heavy sedge;
> Abandoning my lazy Side,
> Stretcht as a Bank unto the Tide;   (stanza 81)

These alterations of scene are very different from the abrupt, dramatic changes of the meadows. There, the scenes changed so rapidly as to affect balance as well as sense of dimension and proportion, whereas in the wood and stream scenes, the poet melts in and out of the landscape, loses and finds "himself" in the nature he contemplates. Once again, as in "The Garden," the poet has managed to bring literary figures to life in his poem; before our eyes, he shows himself becoming one with nature. This absorption of the poet into his scene is in radical contrast to his jutting-out when Thestylis interjects him into the meadow scene. In the wood, the poet is enchanted and shares his enchantment with us, while Thestylis had made the audience turn to laugh at the poet, so brutally exposed to ridicule just as he was most absorbed in his poetizing, most secure in safe stage management.

What has happened is that by these devices, especially because he was willing to use them against "himself," the poet raises questions of place and of volition fundamental to the theme of the poem. On the one hand, the magic lantern devices and the masque episodes involve activity on

---

[65] See Berger, pp. 22, and Allen, p. 146.

the poet's part, who manages them for us, and activity on the reader's part as well, who must make sense of context and reference; on the other, poet and reader seem both to lose their volition as they watch the effortless metamorphoses taking place. In the wood and stream episodes, we are invited to share the poet's delicious languor, to abandon mental activity, to "let be" with nature herself.

Visual devices are used to many ends in this poem, not the least of them their stress on the world's instability, on the fluidity of material things, and the relativity of human perception. In the contrast between activity and passivity, even between styles of activity and passivity, we can perceive the differences between voluntary and involuntary commitments to one's situation as given; we can perceive, further, the difficulties involved in what is "voluntary" and what is not. Choice and destiny are recognized as the problems they are for any responsible man, although in these scenes neither choice nor destiny is more than the fleeting subject of the poem.

In the wood episode, for instance, the poet subdues his claims upon human rights to aspire (if one can say that for a "downward" wish) to wood and stream ecologies. Or, he subdues his own personality to the demands of the landscape—reversing thereby our normal expectations of literary *pathétique*—and thereby relinquishes some of the privileges of his humanity. By becoming "one" with these scenes, the poet illustrates in himself the amphibiousness with which the poem is concerned; he demonstrates man's need to be part of more than one environment, more than one ecology, more than one world. Though the nature into which the poet is absorbed, or permits himself to be absorbed, is traditionally lower than his own, he is by no means diminished by that absorption. Rather the opposite: as in "The Garden," the poet is recreated by his days' recreation, having given himself wholly to nature divinized at Nunappleton. Interestingly enough, as we examine this absorption of the poet into landscape, we find it working both ways. The poet, like the pastoralist, makes nature reflect his wishes and objectify his fantasy, but he bends to its powers as well. The wildwood will not submit to pastoral, then, but works its own poetic enchantment on the poet, earlier an enchanter himself. In yet another way, not wholly unlike his treatment by Thestylis, the poet allows himself to seem manipulated by the elements of his own poem.

There are many other kinds of connection one might make with this episode: in his passive descent into nature, the poet does not recapitulate, though he does recall, Isabella's passive descent into the cloister. She was absorbed for a time in the life "within," and thus forced her manly lover to strenuous activities of reclamation. Isabella was victimized by art; Marvell asks to be drawn into eternal nature itself, both of them "suckt in" by very different means, to very different moral contexts. The poet must be reclaimed too, we find: another Fairfax is required to free him from his delicious relaxation by the streamside to a more strenuous posture, to a less passive life. At the end of the stream episode, another metamorphosis takes place, as the kingfisher flies across the scene to transfix the Wharfe landscape as the halcyon stills the sea. Isabella's will had been sucked out of her by the art and will of someone more sophisticated than herself; this bird permits its hallowing color to be drawn out of it, to infuse and transfix the landscape. Like the poet, the bird "becomes" its scene:

> The viscous Air, wheres'ere She fly,
> Follows and sucks her Azure dy;
> The gellying Stream compacts below,
> If it might fix her shadow so;
> The stupid Fishes hang, as plain
> As *Flies* in Chrystal overt'ane;　　　　　(stanza 85)

The halcyon fuses with Mary Fairfax, as the two enter the scene together and jointly arrest the landscape in a convention familiar in masque-production, where, for better or for worse, players and dancers were often immobilized, as in *The Tempest*, or *Comus*. This enchantment, to stillness and perfection, is just the opposite of the enchantment with which the nunnery episode had ended, with the nunnery vanishing like a false castle (stanza 42). Again, the proper masque-ending serves to put to rights an unpleasant episode and to crown a lovely one.

At the stream, natural things achieve stasis in an educative moment in which things are transformed from what they are to what they ought to be. With this stilling, we return to human scale: the poet and his pupil walk lifesize through their landscape, to meet the recessional fishermen bringing the day's labor to a close. Now, the figures are not diminished, as the mowers and cattle had been, nor grotesquely enlarged, as the grasshoppers and the rail had been. This evening light does not deform, as for instance, Charles Cotton's evening had done:

> The Shadows now so long do grow,
> That Brambles like tall Cedars shew,
> Mole-hills seem Mountains, and the Ant
> Appears a monstrous Elephant.[66]

As night comes down on Marvell's scene, things are in their proper proportion; the poet and his charge can go "in" quite naturally although, as we watch them go, their "in" is "out" to us, as their figures follow the choral procession offstage.

[66] Charles Cotton, *Poems on Several Occasions* (London, 1698), p. 241.

THEME AND THEMATICS:

MEANINGS FOR

"WITHIN" AND "WITHOUT"

ROM HIS remarkable use of many different kinds of visual tradi-
tions, it is plain that Marvell wanted to emphasize the problem-
atical in "Upon Appleton House." In this poem, itself directed
to questions of choice and of self-definition, definitions themselves
are continually called into question, and point of view comes to take an
overriding importance. Officially, the poem praises retirement, the country
life, the pastoral-georgic existence in a mutable world. The more it is
examined, however, the less straightforward this "praise" turns out to
be, the more peculiar and qualified life on the perfect estate seems. Re-
tirement has its problems, too, and its own involvements with "the world."
Simply said, in this poem, the problem of what is "in" and what is "out,"
though endlessly pursued, is never fully resolved. What are definitions for
"within" and "without"? What is retirement, and from what does a man
retire? What is active participation in the public world, and in the private
one too? The devices discussed in the preceding sections are not present
in the poem only to show the poet's virtuosity, though they do that, cer-
tainly; rather, they are some of the technical means by which the poet
returns us to the thematic heart of his poem, the question of moral choice.

"Upon Appleton House" is addressed to a great warrior who had served
his cause and country with distinction, and who had publicly chosen to
retire from further service to the state, either in council or in the field. In
spite of the poem's compliments to the Lord General, implicit throughout
and explicit in stanzas 31, 44 and 45, "Upon Appleton House" has re-
markably little of Fairfax himself in it. Of course, there are manifest
references to Fairfax's public career: Marvell's mild disapproval of the
Levellers (stanza 57) may reflect his patron's more extreme distaste;
Fairfax's suppression of the Levellers at Burford in 1649 was, as he felt,
the proper procedure for dealing with anarchic elements in both common-

wealth and army.[1] Marvell's stress on the reforming soldierly virtues of the Fairfax family, who fought "through all the *Universe*," in *"France, Poland*, either *Germany*," reflects history: Fairfax's grandfather and father fought abroad for Protestantism, as did the Lord General himself, who married into another such family of Protestant soldiers, the Veres. Two of Fairfax's uncles died in the Palatinate, a third at Montauban, still another in Turkey.[2] The Veres were distinguished in the service of international Protestantism; Marvell's passage about the pedigree-oaks "shooting to heaven" honors both Vere and Fairfax families, as well as the long connection between the two, brought to its climax in the marriage of *"Fairfax* and the starry *Vere."*[3]

On the whole, though, as befits a retirement-poem, attention has been shifted away from the General and his exploits in war and peace to something less personal—to his setting in time and place, his background, his history, his occupations; has been shifted, then, from the man to his context. The estate is the world, but the world in little, its each part emblematized into some significance beyond its "mere" self. The house, the building (of which Fairfax was the architect), is itself something "reformed," that is, it was built from the ruins of, and it replaced, a building in the old style and the old religion. The house, or family, looks backward to Isabella and forward with Maria the heiress. As Isabella's marriage-choice was praised, so is the General's; his indomitable wife, the present lady-mother, has her proud place in the poem. Fairfax, who must descend in a single daughter, is seen in terms of the extraordinary women in his family, seen in terms of a wife (the marriage-partner traditionally more withdrawn) and of a daughter not yet "out," although on the verge of

[1] Thomas Fairfax, *Short Memorials of Thomas Lord Fairfax* (London, 1699), p. vi: "But after that [i.e. battles in the field], they broke into Factions, and were overrun with Enthusiasm, chose their own *Agitators*, and were managed by Men of the deepest Dissimulation and Hypocrisie: by whose fair but treacherous Promises, some greater than Himself, were deceived to their own Ruine."

[2] *The Fairfax Correspondence*, ed. George W. Johnson (London, 1848), I, xxviii-xcv.

[3] Cf. *A Catalogue of the . . . Library . . . at Leeds Castle . . . of the Lords Fairfax* (Christie's, 1831), p. 137, item 149; "A Shorte Discourse of the Descent of the Right Hon. prudent and pious Lady Anne Vere, wife of Thomas Lord Fairfax, illuminated with arms in colours, in two parts." For the use of the words "shield" and "scutcheon" to indicate a type of grafting of trees, see *The Country-mans Recreation, or the Art of Planting, Graffing, and Gardening* (London, 1640), p. 34. Cf. "Upon the Hill and Grove," stanza 6.

maturity and marriage. An odd way, one might think, to present a warrior-hero, so domestically and cosily among his womenfolk.

In other ways, too, Fairfax is domesticated. As critics of the poem have noted, there seems to be much private reference in the poem. An examination of Fairfax's own poems, both in his holograph copy[4] and in the (not very) fair copy made for him,[5] shows some evidence of private reference, as if Marvell knew his patron's efforts in verse. The Fairfax men were, it seems, given to verse, although only Fairfax's uncle, Edward Fairfax, can properly be called a poet. Both Ferdinando and William wrote verse as well, Ferdinando metrical psalms (Thomas Fairfax tried these too),[6] and his father odds and ends which appear not to have survived. In Marvell's poem, there may be a compliment to Edward Fairfax's romantic epic world in the nunnery-episode; certainly the heroic Protestant warrior-hero is praised in stanzas 32 and 33. In Lord Fairfax's own work, there are trivial parallels to "Upon Appleton House," and perhaps the length of Marvell's poem is a play upon the extreme brevity of Fairfax's poem on his "New-built House at Appleton."[7]

Other, minor, points in the poem may indicate Marvell's deftness in complimenting his employer's interests and talents: the adaptation, in stanza 80, of Saint-Amant's image of water so still that the things reflected in it were unsure of their own identity may owe something to Fairfax's translation of "La Solitude";[8] Fairfax's strictures "Upon a Patcht Face,"[9] may have an echo in stanza 92; in 96, the "rude heap" is a *topos* in Fairfax's account of the chaos re-ordered by the Nativity. The imagery of the Red Sea may bear upon Fairfax's poem, "Moses his Songe,"[10] where a description of the Exodus is given. It is possible that "Upon Appleton House," among so much else that it does, attempts to epitomize the family's literary interests, offering a domestic intellectual record as well as a set of more conventional domestic scenes and themes.

In the "Discipline severe" by which Maria was raised, we may see some compliment to the strong religiosity of her father and mother, and of their backgrounds. Many of Fairfax's poems are on scriptural subjects, as are those preserved of Ferdinando; Ralph Thoresby records in his collection the possession of various notes on sermons made by the Lord General,

---

[4] Bodleian Library, MS. Fairfax 40.   [5] Bodleian Library, MS. Fairfax 38.

[6] *The Fairfax Correspondence*, I, lxxxiii; cf. MS. Fairfax 38, ff. 475-85.

[7] MS. Fairfax 40, f. 593.   [8] MS. Fairfax 40, ff. 562-63.

[9] MS. Fairfax 38, f. 317.   [10] MS. Fairfax 38, f. 33.

his wife, and his daughter.[11] Marvell's playful and abbreviated history of the world, as interpreted by the "Prelate of the Grove," may owe something to Fairfax's interest in ancient chronology; equally, the references to Romulus and to Roman history may compliment his patron's interest in Roman antiquities.[12] The witty use of military idiom in the garden passage may also be in some part compliment to Fairfax, who naturally wrote his *Short Memorials* in the terminology of his chief art. Fairfax was skilled in languages (his patronage of the Walton Polyglot Bible may be recorded in stanzas 72 and 73, where "the learned Original" of *"Natures mystick Book"* is so clearly understood by the poet); and it seems that the poet compliments his pupil in praising her linguistic skill in stanza 89. Further, the long nunnery episode, though it is certainly important in the poem's thematics, may owe something to Fairfax's antiquarian interest, manifest in his patronage of Roger Dodsworth, who continued the great work begun by Dugdale.[13]

A domestic event which caused some difficulty within the Fairfax family is directly referred to in the poem: Fairfax's breaking the entail in favor of his only child, the poem's Maria. The old Lord Fairfax, greatly disturbed by his son's effort to this end, expressed to another son his views on the ambitions of Thomas's wife, which he regarded as the cause for such a move.[14] In 1671, at Fairfax's death, Appleton and Bolton came to Mary and her issue male, if any; the other properties remained in entail. In the poem, we can read the intimacy of the poet with his patron's family by his natural assumption of their concerns and in his brief but familiar references, in stanza 91, to this controversial family issue. All these references are very slight: they do not obtrude from the poem but merely demonstrate the alliance of the poet with his patron's interests. The major subject remains the estate itself.

The estate is beautiful and peaceful—the garden, the meadows, the wood, and the stream all offer habitats of quietude. Because of the stillness, the withdrawnness, the self-sufficiency of the estate, it is the more remarkable that so much of its activity is rendered in terms of warfare

---

[11] Thoresby, *Ducatus Leodiensis*, p. 541.

[12] Cf. *A Catalogue of the ... Library ...* , p. 96.

[13] See Dugdale's *Monasticon. Additamenta* (Vol. III) (London, 1673); William Dugdale, *Monasticon Anglicanum* (London, 1693), esp. p. 107, for the rules governing the nuns' behavior at Nunappleton. For the same, see also John Burton, *Monasticon Eboracense* (London, 1758), pp. 276-79.

[14] *Fairfax Correspondence*, I, cvii-cxv, 314-16.

and often in genuinely epic figures. Having drawn himself back from the actual war, the master of Nunappleton is nonetheless consistently presented by his poet as living amidst battles in embattled landscapes, although most of these are symbolic battles and masque-wars.

Fairfax's withdrawal from active participation in the war is by no means unequivocally praised. In stanza 44, there is more than a hint of regret at Fairfax's choice to retire:

> And yet there walks one on the Sod
> Who, had it pleased him and *God*,
> Might once have made our Gardens spring
> Fresh as his own and flourishing.

The terrible nostalgia for pre-war England which pervades stanzas 41 and 43 leaves the reader in no doubt about the poet's feelings toward current disasters; his regret extends to the comment on what Fairfax "might have made" of the country as a whole. Still, with the passage on conscience, in stanza 45, the tone returns to the steady moralizing which honors the patron's choice; the poet makes his own resolve to see that choice, which he cannot help lamenting a little, as the General's destiny. Had God and Fairfax been willing, a garden-England might have been restored, but since God and Fairfax willed matters another way, the country and the poet must for a while remain "unhappy."

Fairfax as architect and as gardener, then, has the attributes of a constructive hero, suggested also in the reference to Romulus. He might have redesigned England, now in its travail resembling the chaos, the "quarries," the "rude heap" of the poem. Though the Lord General himself did not undertake the patriotic task of replanting the island as the paradisal garden it had once been, and which his estate has managed to remain, nonetheless he can husband his estate to offer it as a model for the island's ultimate reformation.[15] "Georgic life," traditionally a retired one, was not after all a total retreat from reality, not a total rejection of *res publica*: Virgil's poems were a plea to restore Italy to its proper cultivation after the destruction caused by civil war; Horace's Sabine regimen, too, was no life free of care, but had its own severities and rigors. To achieve *otium* on a country estate involves a great deal of planning, as well as hard labor; Epicurean enjoyment of nature was virtually impos-

---

[15] Cf. Browne, *Works*, p. 86: "But the Earth is the Garden of Nature, and each fruitfull Countrey a Paradise."

sible except in vacations from serious georgic life. In a georgic context, so to speak, the pastoral affords such a vacation. So Fairfax's life in retirement was one of planning, building, and cultivating, including human cultivation, too, the education of the heiress to the estate suitable for her.

In the public life of Marvell's time, furthermore, what might be called a georgic policy was in the process of developing. The war increased the nation's agricultural difficulties,[16] and projectors concerned for the commonwealth addressed themselves to agricultural recovery. From the late forties through the mid-fifties, there was a stream of books and pamphlets arguing that the swords must be beaten into plough-shares,[17] the helmets turned to beehives;[18] many such arguments were directed to the most powerful men and groups in the country. It was no accident, after all, that the name given the state after the King's death was "Commonwealth"; Commonwealthsmen[19] were proud of their inheritance from Rome (Fig. 47).

[16] Christopher Hill, "The Agrarian Legislation of the Revolution," *Puritanism and Revolution* (New York, 1964), pp. 153-96; and relevant bibliography, esp. Joan Thirsk, "The Sale of Royalist Land during the Interregnum," *Econ. Hist. Rev.*, NS V, 188-207.

[17] Samuel Hartlib was responsible for several such works: *The Reformed Husband-Man* and *His Legacie* (both London, 1651), about improvements; *A Discourse for Division or Setting out of Land* (London, 1653), in which among much else he offers a plan for an estate which is designed as a segmented circle fit within a square; *A Designe for Plentie, by an Universall Planting of Fruit-Trees. Tendred by some Wel-wishers to the Publick* (London, 1652), of which he was editor. Walter Blith's book, much quoted by the georgic reformers of the time, *The English Improver*, went into several editions. The third edition (title page reproduced Fig. 47) has various prefatory epistles: to the Lord General Cromwell, to the Industrious Reader, to the Nobility and Gentry, to the Inns of Court and the Universities, to the Soldiery, to the Husbandman, Farmer, or Tenant, to the Cottager, Laborer, or the Meanest Commoner. Ralph Austen's work may be cited in this connection, in particular his *Treatise of Fruit-Trees*, Epistle Dedicatory. After the Restoration, the agricultural problem continued to attract attention: Moses Cook's and John Evelyn's works, among many others, testify to the need to replant the island. Evelyn's *Sylva, or a Discourse of Forest-Trees* (London, 1664, later much enlarged) argues for the literal replanting of the nation. He was as concerned about the depopulation of forests as others were about human depopulation. With this as background, Fairfax's "retirement" may be seen as a less private withdrawal than it has been taken; georgic activity in the service of England was a public duty, too. For plowshares to swords, see Virgil, *Georgics* II, 500.

[18] Alciati, *Emblemata Latinogallica*, clxxviii, "Ex bello pax," bees hiving in a helmet; Rollenhagen, p. 78, for the same picture.

[19] See Caroline Robbins, *The English Commonwealthman* (Cambridge, Mass., 1959), *passim*.

Theme and Thematics

As Appleton House seemed an island of relative peace in the swirl of destruction and disorder which the poet saw outside it, holding in its balance the memory of the garden that England had once been,[20] so it holds a temporal balance as well, between past and future. The "now" experienced at such variety and length throughout the poem, is continually dissolved into its interpretative history and its expectations of what is to come. The mock-heroic, mock-romance of Isabella Thwaites, who descended in "offspring fierce," and the prophecy about Maria reiterate the same theme: retirement has its place in any life, as a preparative for future emergence into the social world of duty and custom.

The long narrative of the nunnery provides an example of false retirement and proper emergence. Isabella is "suckt" into a world of fallacy and deceit, a world of peculiar topsy-turvydom, where rhetorical trickery entirely unbalances the girl. The nunnery is, after all, an attractive place: Mr. Berger has pointed to its affinities with the epicurean delights offered by Created Pleasure. In the nunnery, in "holy leisure," the nuns pray, weep with pleasure—and with that penance, they clear their complexions as well; they read "holy Legends," embroider saints' pictures in needlework, preserve fruits which purify (as they think) nature for religion's sake:

> ". . . through the mortal fruit we boyl
> "The Sugars uncorrupting Oyl:
> "And that which perisht while we pull,
> "Is thus preserved clear and full."   (stanza 22)

The nun's language, of course, is full of peculiar, slanting exaggerations, set to warn us of the unnatural and irregular character of her house. Her attack on men (stanza 13) and the sexual undertones of stanza 24, for instance, argue an emotional distortion which in a "natural" environment would be set right. Still more important, in the nun's persuasion of Isabella, the proper relation of morality to metaphor is inverted, showing thereby the inversion of the nun's moral ideas. Isabella's face, she says, will serve as a model for that of "our Lady"; the girl herself is described by the nun in an apotheosis more appropriate to the Virgin than to any mortal virgin, no matter how well-born:

[20] England as a garden, even as the Garden of Eden, was a familiar *topos*; the political georgic writers cited above make the comparison regularly, and see Mildmay Fane, "Anglia Hortus," *The Poems of Mildmay, Second Earl of Westmoreland*, ed. A. B. Grosart (n.p. 1879), p. 133.

"I see the *Angels* in a Crown
"On you the Lillies show'ring down:
"And round about you Glory breaks,
"That something more than humane speaks." (stanza 18)

The Virgin is likened to Isabella, as if to the Virgin's advantage; a similar inversion of values is evident in the nun's assurance that heaven will be drawn down to the cloister by the attractive powers of Isabella's voice (stanza 21). The girl is promised things which, to the Protestant, betoken the falsity of conventual life: for instance, the nun assures the coy postulate that should the Cistercian rule prove too strait for her taste, it can be made to "bend" to her wishes or convenience (stanza 20). Isabella's personal beauty, the nun assures her, is "at such a height" that she must be "consecrate" for it, so that her loveliness can work miracles for the convent (stanzas 19, 21). In these lines, there is no humility; although elsewhere in the poem "height with a certain Grace" is said to "bend," the moral context of this vainglorious cloister points to just the opposite view.

The falsity of both the nun's rhetoric and the cloister's values is exposed when the young Fairfax, Isabella's promised husband, sues for her release and, when denied, snatches her away by force. At this point, the nun's true nature emerges, and all the nuns are exposed:

[They] guiltily their Prize bemoan,
Like Gipsies that a Child hath stoln. (stanza 34)

Fixed in their cloister, the nuns are likened to the social strays of the world. The poet looks forward to the time, reached shortly in his narrative, when the nuns shall be cast out altogether.

In a fusion of times which, in the history of the Fairfax family, actually lasted more than a generation, the poet in one stanza dissolves the nunnery's fabrics as Britomart demolished the House of Busyrane in *The Faerie Queene* (II. xi. 43):

Thenceforth (as when th'Inchantment ends
The Castle vanishes or rends)
The wasting Cloister with the rest
Was in one instant dispossest. (stanza 34)

At the real Dissolution, the emptied buildings were granted to Fairfaxes of the next generation, sons of William and Isabella:

Theme and Thematics

> At the demolishing, this Seat
> To *Fairfax* fell as by Escheat.   (stanza 35)

but the poet behaves as if the redistribution happened immediately upon the liberation of the stolen Isabella from her captors. For the purposes of the poem, all Fairfaxes are fused into a single generic heroic figure.

Isabella, who had gone "in" to a deceptive retirement, comes "out" to real security, in marriage and in the world. Subsequently, by the poet's time, the very building in which she had been held imprisoned was itself entirely "without," a great pile of masonry, formless and chaotic, a folly, a topographical feature of the Nunappleton landscape, a mark of the historical development of the house of Fairfax from the false to the true religion. In the nunnery episode, the poet permits no nostalgia for a time past, as one might expect in a ruins-piece such as this; there is no hint in the tone that when the priests walked the land, times were better. Quite the contrary, in fact: the poet's version of the ruins episode is a foreshortened version of the Reformation struggles. Appleton, he says, was "no Religious House till now."

In the next episode, set in the garden, the poet's regret for a lost world is made poignantly clear. In the nunnery episode, all thoughts of gardens —which might be, after all, appropriate similes for cloisters—are eschewed; this foundation was no garden enclosed, there was no Solomon's Song for Isabella's near-marriage to a superseded worship. But the Lord General's strange little garden *is* enclosed, its perimeter planted like a fort to protect what is "within" from external dangers. The rearrangement of conventional landscape association, this time the fusion of a garden of retirement with the outworks of military defense, is another means of surprising readers into reconsidering cliché notions of retirement and activity.

From the Isabella episode, one can read some of the ambiguities involved in "in" and "out" in this poem. As we look back to the beginning, it is evident in the first stanza:

> Within this sober Frame expect
> Work of no Forrain *Architect*;
> That unto Caves the Quarries drew,
> And Forrests did to Pastures hew;
> Who of his great Design in pain
> Did for a Model vault his Brain,

227

"Upon Appleton House"

> Whose Columnes should so high be rais'd
> To arch the Brows that on them gaz'd.

The whole poem, the Fairfaxes, the House are all somehow to be understood "within this sober Frame"—a painter's frame, to demarcate rational limits. But just what *is* "this Frame," and what does it "frame"? Of that we are never quite sure, although we understand, after the extravagances at the end of the stanza, that within the frame—the house, the estate, the ethics of house and estate, the aesthetics of the poem, the poem itself perhaps—all is English.[21] The moderation, fitness, and understatement on which Englishmen pride themselves is the norm for Fairfax's house and his life. This particular house is the smallest of his holdings, fit for his most "human" needs, as the nest is fit for the bird's needs or his shell the tortoise's. This house was, as it were, secreted to hold its master,[22] who was, in fact, its architect. Shell and house are "cases fit" for their possessors and tenants. The self-sufficiency of the tortoise is an emblematic *topos*, the creature's economy famously imitated, according to Vitruvius, by the ancient Colchians, in their domestic architecture.[23] The images, traditional and frequently emblematic, with which the poet characterized proper domestic architecture—beasts in their dens, birds in their "equal nests,"[24] "the low-roof'd Tortoise" in his shell—are all images of a proper place of withdrawal, a "within" of private economy. Beasts retire to dens for their private purposes, among which is the rearing of their young; birds build nests precisely for their eggs and young. The tortoise "is" his own dwelling; his house is his body, fitting him as the proper house fits its owner. The tortoise is also the classic retirer of the created world, withdrawing whenever he is threatened by elements "without" into his house, there to await disruption.

But the tortoise's shell is in fact quite rigid. This house of Lord Fair-

---

[21] See Holahan, pp. 117-21, and Davenant, *Gondibert*, II, vi, 96:

> The Arched Front did on vaste Pillars fall;
> Where all harmonious Instruments they spie
> Drawne out in Bosse. . . .

[22] Berger, "Marvell's 'Upon Appleton House,' " p. 10.

[23] See Vitruvius, *De Architectura*, ed. Barbaro, II, 49, for the *testudo* of the Colchians; and cf. Wither, *Emblemes*, p. 86 ("Omnia Mea Mecum Porto"); Camerarius, "Domus Optima," both with tortoise-emblems.

[24] Pliny, *Historie of the World*, x:33; and Vitruvius, II, i, on the origins of dwelling houses as imitations of birds' nests.

228

fax, on the contrary, is unbelievably flexible, a magic house that, upon its master's entry, alters its proportions to accommodate his greatness:

> Yet thus the laden House does sweat,
> And scarce indures the *Master* great:
> But where he comes the swelling Hall
> Stirs, and the *Square* grows *Spherical*;
> More by his *Magnitude* distrest,
> Than he is by its straitness prest:
> And too officiously it slights
> That in itself which him delights.   (stanza 7)

By this point, the images are so extreme as to seem much like the "great Design" of the "Forrain *Architect*," given to exaggeration and irregularity. The strict house, sufficient and austere in its neatness, has become animate; it sweats, swells, stirs, "grows *Spherical*" in a pregnancy-image, enlarges itself in honor of its great-hearted master. That is, this house, already a miraculous solution to the circle-square problem, becomes even more miraculous in its alteration of its own proportions, its metamorphosis from one regular solid, the cube, into another, the sphere. By its self-aggrandizement, this house seems to deny its earlier excellence, to "slight" the quality most appreciated by its master, its smallness. Into this metamorphic wonder, many images and ideas are gathered: first, the animation of the inanimate; second, the Vitruvian idea that "these . . . *Mathematicks* can/ In ev'ry Figure equal Man"—or, that man is properly the measure of all things, especially of architectural proportion. The cubic hall of the actual house was topped by a cupola, which "proves" to the poet that circle and square, or sphere and cube, can be simultaneously proportional; but even these architectural achievements are too little for a man like Fairfax. For him, the house performs its own subliming magic, transforms itself from one figure, the solid and reliable square, into another, the sphere, traditionally the perfect form.[25]

[25] See Nicolson, *The Breaking of the Circle*; Wittkower, *Architectural Principles*; Vitruvius, p. 90, for circle and square; Wither, p. 228, for the stability of the cube:

> This *Cube*, which is an equall-sided-square,
> Doth very well, in *Emblem*-wise, declare
> The temper of that vertuous minded man,
> Whose resolutions nothing alter can.

See also Erwin Panofsky, "The History of the Theory of Human Proportions as a

At the same time, however much circle and sphere may be regarded as regular, or even as perfect figures, the image in which they occur is conceited and grotesque, an image of great irregularity. The shifting of the house from one shape to another is of a piece with other kinds of shifts within the poem—optical shifts, scene-shifts, metamorphoses and anamorphoses governing so much of the poem's mood. This time, we are asked to believe that the house actually changes its own shape, not that our perspective upon the house has altered, although it can be argued that all this is a fancification of something quite ordinary. The cube could be experienced as the entrance hall, the sphere as the dome above the hall, and all that is happening, in this elaborate stanza, may be that the poet is coming into the house.

But the effect of the stanza is to make the house seem less and less clearly established on a site: is it, merely, in the mind of the architect? Something *is* in an architect's mind, but not, it turns out, Appleton House—rather, a grandiose plan, a foreign hypothesis, a house of which the arches are so high that they swell the head of their designer and raise the eyebrows of their beholders. All these vaultings are made, somehow, to fuse, and thus to confuse the reader: whose "Columnes" these are, is never quite clear. The architect's elevated conceit makes everything disproportionate, even human faces; the extravagance of the imagery demonstrates the absurdity of the architectural extravagance, of marble crusts built "T'impark the wanton Mote of Dust" that a man is. The house of the poem is not such a house: it is, and is in, a "sober Frame." This first wild image echoes through the poem: the swelling skull of the first stanza relates to the swelling house in the seventh, the one a false conception and the other a real one; the unnaturally arched brows in the first stanza are recalled in the "arching Boughs" and *"Corinthean Porticoes"* of stanza 64, the first distorting a man, the second restoring him to the proper frame of himself. To call the trees of the wood *"Corinthean Porticoes"* is a pretty image, and an unmetaphoring, since Corinthian columns were designed to remind one of a tree or plant; the image also "artifies" nature, as so many of Marvell's images do. In this Jan Vredeman de Vries, a "forrain" landscape architect, was master. His formal gardens were planned in the "orders," Doric, Ionic, and Corinthian: the Doric based on square and

---

Reflection of the History of Styles," *Meaning in the Visual Arts* (Anchor Books, 1955), pp. 53-107; Vitruvius, III, i; Wotton, *Elements of Architecture*, p. 7.

rectangle, with some ellipses and spades; the Ionic busier than the Doric, with smaller geometrical units and a wider variety of curved lines; the Corinthian labyrinthine and complex, apparently irregular in spite of its regular patterns. Vredeman de Vries' "Corinthian" gives an impression of copiousness, compared with the relatively simpler and more austere Doric and Ionic.[26] By making us remember the arching brows of the arty first stanza in the arching boughs of the artified wood, Marvell forces his contrasts upon us.

There is much art, even in nature, in this poem, and in the House we are never quite sure how much of its force is imaginative, how much is natural. When we come right down to it, what we are asked to believe about Appleton House is even more extravagant, even more unlikely than what we are asked to believe foreign architects can do. The foreign design deforms human beings, as such extravagance might be expected to do. Fairfax's effect on his house is to make it refit itself to his moral span. The difference between the pretentiousness of foreign architects and the excellence of "holy *Mathematicks*" is that the "short but admirable Lines" of the house can indeed hold more than themselves. As in Leonardo's Vitruvian figure, a man could measure out geometrical figures "larger" than himself; he could, also, be contained, however great his mind and spirit, as Fairfax was, in a geometrical figure.[27] So Fairfax not only measures out circle and square in the house-plan, but finds his cube becoming a sphere. In stanza 1, human features are geometrized; in stanza 7, geometrical figures are animated. Simply by going "into" his house, Fairfax enlarges it, makes it greater: we may assume the same for the whole estate, made great by the General's retirement into it. That house and grounds are somehow sacred is implied by Marvell's image of the "Pilgrimage" "in after Age": as visitors cannot imagine how a man of Romulus' stature fitted into "his Bee-like Cell," so will they wonder how Fairfax fitted into his little house.[28] The house and the landscape are made great; no wonder, then, that they are so often dealt with in heroic terms.[29]

By her going in and coming out, Fairfax's ancestress had brought the

[26] Jan Vredeman de Vries, *Hortorum Viridariorumque elegantes et multiplis formae* (Antwerp, 1583).

[27] See Vitruvius, III, i; Panofsky, *op.cit.*

[28] Vitruvius, II, i, for Romulus' cell; and Fuller, *Holy State*, p. 156, for "a faire entrance" to a house, "not (as in some old buildings) where the doores are so low Pygmies must stoop, and the rooms so high that Giants can stand upright."

[29] See below, section 4, pp. 239-45.

earlier, false house to the ruin it deserved, a destruction presented in terms of magic and enchantment. The false nunnery dissolves and ceases to exist: by her leaving of it, Isabella made it vanish, so that the new edifice could be reformed, a far more truly religious house than under the nuns. Fairfax had left England, also transformed, but not into something greater than it had been, rather into something less. England had been a garden; now it is waste, and Fairfax can find a proper garden only on his estate. There, the private garden has or is a self-enclosed, self-defended fortress—but there too we find some confusion about "in" and "out." At first the garden seems to "attack" its own inhabitants, aiming at their senses (stanza 36), overpowering them with its manifold beauty.[30]

As in stanza 5 of "The Garden," this garden is strenuous, though its exercise is military rather than amatory. An epitome of the paradisal garden that England had been, the Nunappleton garden excludes the world, concentrating on the private sense-experiences which a resolved soul may permit himself—though in this passage, the language pulls somewhat against the sense. It is customary to indulge in the legitimate and harmless pleasures of the senses when one has retired; pastoral and libertine poetic traditions, even the grave temperament of Bacon, all exploit the recreative powers of gardens. Religious meditation was properly engardened, as *Partheneia Sacra* and many other works show.[31] Such pleasures are usually described in languorous language, in the rich sensuous traditions of, say, Canticles; the last thing one would expect in a garden of retirement is a military metaphor carried through with military precision, so that even bee and tulip have a proper place in the warlike discipline of this garden. This garden is a camp, in which the soldiers rise to the "Dian," are drilled and reviewed, go through their functions at the ready for a real engagement.[32] But suddenly, the garden is, as it were, turned inside out. The enclosing, delighting garden, whose five bastions aimed inward at its inhabitants' five senses, directs its aim, now less playfully, outward against the world, beyond it, at a neighboring episcopal holding. The garden is a garden of retirement and a military garrison because no garden can be fully enclosed: "in" must always be protected from "out."

The poet perambulating the estate is always, literally, "without," or

---

[30] See Hawkins, *Partheneia Sacra*, p. 5, for the garden's proper appeal to the senses.
[31] Hawkins, *Partheneia Sacra*, pp. 11-12; Stanley Stewart, *passim*.
[32] Pliny, *Historie of the World*, xi:6, for the military bee.

outside in the open air. After watching the mowing and "wandring" in the river, he is forced to go "in," or to take refuge from the rising waters within the wood. The house might have sheltered him, too, but he seeks its natural equivalent outdoors, a temple-wood in which he becomes a mock-priest, or, perhaps, a real priest. The wood is his "green, yet growing Ark," an ark which turns out to be even better than Noah's, a place of protection against every kind of danger. Here, the literary cryptography to which the images obliquely refer works very efficiently: as Fairfax had retired from the actual Civil War, classically represented as a flood, so the poet now retires from the rising waters of the estate. Fairfax and the poet are linked in the reference to Noah, whose "house" had been made of wood, and had preserved his family—in his case, therefore, the family of mankind—whose carpentry and architecture had saved civilization.[33]

The wood in this poem is unlike the usual poetic wood, the mixed wood, the *hule, sylva, selv' oscura* of confusing experience,[34] where, for instance, the Nymph's Sylvio dwelt, or fauns and satyrs, or Circe and her son, or madmen driven wild. Literary woods tend to carry the connotations of darkness and uncontrol: not only do Dante and Redcrosse lose their way in woods, but Hercules, Lancelot, Orlando, and others struck mad automatically run back into the woodland where, like primitives, they threaten civilization with their fierceness. Poetical woods tend to be dark.

So at first glance this one seems to be:

> When first the Eye this Forrest sees
> It seems indeed as *Wood* not *Trees*:   (stanza 63)

Kitty Scoular has pointed to Peacham's emblem of a dark wood, stand-

---

[33] See Vitruvius, II, i, for the equation of carpentry with civilization.

[34] For *hule* as material, see *Timaeus*, Dante, Spenser, Milton, etc.; for *hule* as the general material of poetry, see Julius Caesar Scaliger, *Poetices libri septem* (Heidelberg, 1581), II; for *sylva* as experience, see Francis Bacon, *Sylva Sylvarum*, whose title manages to combine the ideas of "collection" and of "the vast *Wood of Experience*," as his editor, William Rawley, points out. For *Silva* or *Sylva* as the title of an anthology, collection, or miscellany, see *inter alia*: Statius, Angelo Poliziano, Ben Jonson, Dudley North, John Dryden, *et al., et al*. Poliziano's *Silva* is doubly useful in this context, since the work was a collection of poems on georgic subjects, a critique of Virgil and Hesiod. I am indebted to Alarik Skarstrom for his list, much truncated in my version.

ing for the chaos of human experience;[35] but Marvell's wood is not after all impenetrable. Once inside, the poet sees that

> Dark all without it knits; within
> It opens passable and thin; (stanza 64)

The wood is a true sanctuary, its "light *Mosaick*" informing the poet of far more than his own safety; in the ark of the wood he can ride out catastrophe, become (in a pun) at one with the nature of the place:

> . . . my self imbark
> In this yet green, yet growing Ark; (stanza 61)

The wood alters the poet's role, and releases him from his earlier critical self: alone, he permits himself fantastic visions and identifications.[36] The book of nature is spread before him, and he can read it, until like Solomon he finds that he has full communication with the creatures:

> Already I begin to call
> In their most learned Original:
> And where I Language want, my Signs
> The Bird upon the Bough divines;
> And more attentive there doth sit
> Then if She were with Lime-twigs knit. (stanza 72)

The poet is a Solomonic kingly priest, aware of nature's secrets; his ark, filled with pairing creatures, is both Noah's and that of the Temple. Like Noah, he notes the birds singly and in pairs; like Solomon, he knows the speech of natural things. The wood is only a fraction of Fairfax's total retreat, but for the poet, this wood opens upon the imaginative prospects of all nature and all history. There, he can read from "*Natures mystick Book*": the leaves, the birds' feathers, and the birdsong tell all that is worth telling:

> What *Rome, Greece, Palestine*, ere said
> I in this light *Mosaick* read. (stanza 73)

The phrase "light *Mosaick*" is one of the richest in the poem: the light by which the poet "reads" all this is like that of Moses, who chronicled

---

[35] Peacham, p. 182.

[36] See Berger, "Marvell's 'Upon Appleton House,'" pp. 13-14, 21-22, where the notion of comedy is very firmly stated: I tend to find his reading at this point extreme.

the beginning of all created things, who gave the world its geography, its cosmography, and its morality. Also, the light on the forest floor makes a mosaic from which the "one History" can be read, the character of truth cast before the poet in the mixed wood of his experience. The wood is a great grove, numinous with classical connotation and with his own celebration of Fairfax's other grove at Bilbrough; it is a sacred place, an ark. As in some painted forest-scenes, a numinous human figure is present: the poet, becoming the "prelate" of grove and ark, moving in a ceremonial cope made up of natural elements (oakleaves, caterpillars, ivy). Even in that image, an anamorphic one, customary expectation is reversed; the embroidery on vestments is usually of stylized natural elements, and this cope is made of "real" ones.[37] These Corinthian columns are real trees, this cope is made of real plants.

"Mosaick" suggests something else, borne out in the imagery of this section of the poem. The word "emblem" has its etymological connection with a mosaic stone, the *tessera* of which mosaic pictures are made.[38] It is hardly accidental that in this scene there are so many emblematic passages, all read by the "light *Mosaick*." The emblems themselves are interesting, too; none is wholly explicable with the data the poet affords us, but as we begin to puzzle them out, their relevance to the poem's main themes becomes more and more obvious. What happens in the emblem vignettes is unbelievable: the nightingale finds that the thorn-bush somehow retracts its prickles, while nearby "list'ning Elders prick their ears" at her song; the doves, though apparently happily situated, mourn; the heron casts her chick down from the ash tree's top; the little woodpecker by itself brings down a huge oak.[39] Like an emblem, each of these scenes seems to imply more than it says outright, in particular the hewel episode.[40] All connect with one another, to form that network of thematic references running through the poem, this time to nesting and raising children. Strangers to this imaginative mode, we have to work hard—unduly so,

[37] See above, Part II, 3, pp. 39-40, on artification in Marvell's poetry.

[38] See Freeman, *English Emblem Books*, p. 37, citing Whitney and Andrew Willet, and, for a more careful examination of the "mosaic" meaning of *Emblema*, Hessel Miedema, "The Term *Emblema* in Alciati," *JWCI*, xxxi (1968), pp. 234-50.

[39] Pliny, x:18; and see Allen, pp. 144-46 for the kingly and priestly functions of the woodpecker; also Virgil, *Aen.* VII, 191.

[40] Mr. Allen and others take the oak to be a royal oak, symbolic of Charles I and his execution; I am disinclined to accept the interpretation. See Cats' woodpecker (Fig. 34) for the determination and singlemindedness of the bird.

probably—at these emblematic incidents, unravelling their meanings with difficulty as the poet does not: he seems to understand them totally, to be quite unaware of the ambiguity or incompleteness of the episodes. For him in his magic wood, all knowledge has become obvious.[41]

In the wood, the poet recognizes his own safety from the siege of experience available to him in the world outside: he is well within, tucked into his concealing and revealing wood, dark to those without it, light to him within it. The world outside is, of course, part of the estate, and therefore itself set within the real world, in turn "without." The poet is at the heart of things, but protected fully, so that neither can conventional beauty touch him, nor can the world strike him with its shot. Quite the opposite: his mind, "incamp'd" "behind these Trees," makes sport of the dangerous world, "gauling" its "Horsemen" at will. For all the poet's playfulness and delight in this particular fortress against the world, he is unable to free himself entirely from the world, however: battle-imagery sounds in stanza 76, and he has fears of leaving the permissive wood, of having to abandon its visions of purified experience. Against the danger of his prospective ejection from the wood, he asks to be imprisoned, to prolong by this paradoxical means his experience of freedom. The bondage he asks for, though, is hardly severe: he himself calls it "silken," his crucifixion by briars is to be "courteous." The poet asks to be pegged down by day in the wood of enlightenment, though let out at evening to lie under the open sky by the stream. There, he fuses anew with his environment, abandoning himself, pouring himself out in self-delighting languor as the wind dies, the sun sets, and quiet comes over the world.

At this hour, as in the early morning, "*Maria* walks": and nature behaves this time in a way quite different from the way it had behaved during her morning constitutional. Then, Maria was so much a part of the garden that the flowers mistook her for one of themselves and forgot to perform their military duties due to the Fairfax family; discipline lapses for Mary's coming. In the evening, she restores discipline, as the elements of "loose Nature" (among them the poet) "start" and "recollect" themselves from their languorous pleasure in themselves. Like the poet on the arrival of his pupil, nature ceases to play; she puts herself in order,

---

[41] Cf. Nathanael Culverwell, *Spiritual Opticks* (London, 1651), p. 17: "Adam in innocencie . . . could read the smallest print, the least jot and tittle in the book of nature. See how quickly he tumbles o're the vast volume, and in a name gives a brief glosse upon every creature, a concise epitome of their naturale histories."

stands in her best clothes as for inspection. In the phrase, *"Bonne Mine,"* nature is seen to artify herself, literally to "redress" herself. Nature, like the garden at the day's beginning, is at the ready. Looking back across the poem, we can realize from the last incidents how much "readiness" is involved in all the episodes. The military garden is at the ready; young Fairfax readies himself for his venture; the mowers ready the fields for next year's crop; the poet "recollects" in himself all history and all nature, ready for fullness as a man. Withal, it is the problem of readiness rather than the condition of readiness that the poem concerns itself with: things *get* ready rather than *are* ready. Nowhere are rules given for total preparedness, nor do we learn what to be specifically ready for. We know only that the man engaged in living must be ready for what comes, however unexpected it may be.

And though what is to come may be very dangerous indeed, it turns out that what happens at Appleton is not so bad as it looks: in the end, the floods simply make the meadows "redress" themselves, in a green finer than before. As the poet emerges from the wood, the meadows appear to be

> . . . fresher dy'd;
> Whose Grass, with moister colour dasht,
> Seems as green Silks but newly washt.   (stanza 79)

Nature, then, primps as in a glass, until "every thing" is "whisht and fine," a tidying operation in radical contrast to the cosmetic repairs of a "Fond Sex" that places all its "useless Study" on its face, a mere "Black-bag" of mortal flesh. Nature at Appleton House becomes, in Maria's presence, "tame," georgic, cultivated, cultivating, a model then for all places, any place:

> *You Heaven's Center, Nature's Lap.*
> *And Paradice's only Map.*   (stanza 96)

At this moment of revelation, night falls and the tableau breaks. The salmon-fishermen break off their day labor, light denied, to go "in" under the hood of their canoes, or, under the burden of their occupation. In the pageant, these "rational *Amphibii*" have indeed vaulted their crania by putting their coracles on their heads, under which they walk *"Tortoise like,* but not so slow." The tortoise must walk under the vault on his back; in the stanza, the three hemispheres, the dark, the canoe, the tortoise-shell, all fit into one another in formal iteration as the poet and his pupil, like the day, the fishermen, and the creature in the metaphor, go "in" under the vault of their house. As tortoise and fishermen carry their houses on their heads—that is, bearing their protection and their occupation with them wherever they go—poet and pupil go in, too, to a place of retirement that is a place of preparation for further activity. Nothing is ever entirely "in" or entirely "out" in this poem, but is now the one, now the other, in some contexts the one, in others, the other. A deeper inwardness is always possible, no matter how retired one's position is; from the most profound communication with the self, extraordinary freedom may derive, as the poet in the wood demonstrates for us. Penetrating deeply into himself, he loses that self in his environment. Understanding the meanings of Appleton and its House, he can stay out or go in, confident that he will find protection and preparation wherever he is.

3. The Soul encaged ("Dialogue of the Soul and the Body"). Hugo, *Pia Desideria*.

2. The Soul imprisoned in the Body ("Dialogue of the Soul and the Body"). Hugo, *Pia Desideria*.

1. The High and the Low, the Great and the Humble ("The Hill and Grove at Bill-Borrow"). Camerarius, *Symbolorum et emblematum . . . centuriae*.

5. Holy Lovers ("The unfortunate Lover"). Hugo, *Pia Desideria*.

6. Holy Lovers ("The unfortunate Lover"). Hugo, *Pia Desideria*.

4. The Snake in the Grass ("The Coronet"). Camer-

11. The Lover assailed by Love's Thunder and Lightning ("The unfortunate Lover"). Veen, *Emblemata Amatoria*.

7. Playful Amorini ("The unfortunate Lover"). Veen, *Emblemata Amatoria*.

8. The Ship of Love in Travail ("The unfortunate Lover"). Veen, *Emblemata Amatoria*.

9. The Lover assailed by the Winds of Love ("The unfortunate Lover"). Veen, *Emblemata Amatoria*.

10. The Lover with his self-consuming Torch ("The unfortunate Lover"). Veen, *Emblemata Amatoria*.

12

13

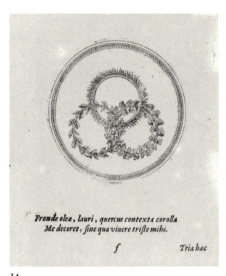

Fronde oleæ, lauri, quercus contexta corolla
Me decoret, sine qua viuere triste mihi.

f   Tria hæc

14

12. Salamander in Love's Fire
("The unfortunate Lover").
Veen, *Emblemata Amatoria.*

13. The Lover wounded in the Breast
by Love's Arrows ("The unfortunate
Lover"). Veen, *Emblemata Amatoria.*

14. The Olive, Oak, and Bay
("The Garden"). Camerarius,
Symbolorum et emblematum . . . centu

15. The steadfast Man rejecting Garlands
("The Garden"). Veen,
Emblemata Horatiana.

16. The steadfast Man beset by Temptation
the Bay with Oak and Palm in the
Background ("The Garden").
Veen, *Emblemata Horatiana.*

15

16

17

Exuviis vitii abjectis, decus indue recti,
Ad Solem ut plumas accipiter renovat.

17. Love written on Trees ("The Garden").
Cats, *Silenus Alcibiadis*.

18. The preening Bird, Symbol of
"Renovation" ("The Garden"). Camerarius,
*Symbolorum et emblematum . . .
centuriae*.

19. "Th' industrious Bee" ("The Garden").
Hawkins, *Partheneia Sacra*.

19

20. Mixed landscape, with human activities. Rubens, *Castle at Steen.*

Figures 20 to 47 relate to
"Upon Appleton House."

21. Figures demonstrating
well-being. Koninck, *Landscape*.
National Gallery, London.

22. Figures demonstrating well-being. Ruisdael, *View of Haarlem.*
Mauritshuis. The Hague. P. A. Dingjan.

23. The mirror-calm of dusk, with fisherman. Van der Neer, *Evening.* Mauritshuis.

SO quicke of fenfe as hath experience taught,
The *Tortoife* liues within her armed fhell,
That if wee lay the lighteft ftraw aloft,
Or touch that Caftle wherein fhe doth dwell,
Shee feeles the fame and quickly doth retire,
A worke of Nature we do moft admire,

So many men are in theire Nature prone,
To make the worft of matters vaine and light,
And for a ftraw will take occafion,
In choller moou'd to quarrell and to fight,
Then meddle thou the leaft for feare of wrong,
But moft of all beware a lavifh tongue.

Bb3.   Negatur

Genefis.   Ick wil u een bete broods geven, daer na fult ghy
18.5.   voort gaen.

*Ie t'apporteray vn morceau de pain, puis apres vous
paßerez.*

24. The sensitive, retiring Tortoise.
Peacham, *Minerva Brittanica.*

25. The Tortoise-shell as Boat and as House.
Heyns, *Emblemata.*

Iuſtitia omnibus partibus abſoluta.

...cum timẹ, & mandata eius obſerua: hoc eſt
enim omnis homo.   Ecclef. 12, 13.

26. The Stork sacrificing its Young.
Freitag, *Mythologia Ethica.*

SEE heare the ftorke prouides with tender care,
And bringeth meate, vnto her hatched broode:
They like againe, for her they doe prepare,
When fhee is oulde, and can not get her foode:
Which teacheth bothe, the parente and the childe,
Theire duties heare, which eche to other owe:
Firft, fathers muft be prouident, and milde,
Vnto theire fruicte, till they of age doe growe:
And children, mufte with dutie ftill proceede,
To reuerence them, and helpe them if they neede.

Aelianus lib. 10.
cap. 16.
Idem libro 8.
cap. 22. vbi de
natura Ciconiæ
mira fabula.

*Defeſſum fertur portare Ciconia patrem,
Hinc illa pietas fanſta notatur aue.*

Paradifus poſti-
cus.

K   Anaritia

27. The Stork feeding its Young.
Whitney, *A Choice of Emblems.*

ACCEPTVM RED.
DIMVS OFFICIVM.

O rara illustris pietatis imago, parentem
Quando humeris gestat filius ipse suis!

28. The Stork feeding its Young in mid-air.
Camerarius, *Symbolorum et emblematum . . .*
centuriae.

NATVRA DICTAN
TE FEROR.

Je vais don: l'ordre de la
nature

Prospicit atq. fugit fortunæ flamina prudens,
Ceu fugit imbriferos Ardea celsa notos.

voli: au denc: des mes
Ja providence et le

29. The Heron, flying above the Storm
Camerarius, *Symbolorum et emblematum .*
centuriae.

FIDA CON-
IVNCTIO.

Castæ persistunt æterno in amore columbæ,
Quo sint humani regula conjugis.

30. Doves, Symbols of nuptial Love and Fidelity.
Camerarius, *Symbolorum et emblematum . . .*
centuriae.

NON, NISI NVPTA, VIGET.
I.

Lucret.
Omne adeo genus in terris, hominum-
que, ferarumque,
Et genus aquorum, pecudes, pictaque vo-
lucres,
In furias ignemque ruunt.

Montagn. lib. 3 des Essais cap. 5.
Tout le movement du monde se re-
& rend à cest accouplage; c'e,
matiere infusée par tout, c'est un Cent
toutes choses regardent.

31. Nuptial Doves, in nuptial Palms. Cats,
Silenus Alcibiadis.

VNDE AVRI
PER RAMOS AVRA
REFVLSIT.

elle et repennte vere et
ramum

Auricomum geminæ ramum monstrate columbæ,
Vt nobis sancti fulgeat aura DEI.

misu drone non.
morio a Dieu

32. Nuptial Doves retiring to the Woods.
Camerarius, *Symbolorum et emblematum . . .*
centuriae.

MERCES HÆC
CERTA LABORVM.

Spernit humum picus, petit ardua : sic quoque virtus
Appetit excelsis sacra reposta locis.

33. The Woodpecker feeding its Young.
Camerarius, *Symbolorum et emblematum . . .*
centuriae.

REPETE.
VI.

VERS.
VVLGAR. **N**on amet, aut discat duros tolerare labores,
Optati compos qui velit esse sui.
POLYB. LIB. 10.
Vlla re utili abstinendum est , propter apparentem difficultatem : sed comparan-
dus habitus, quo cuncta bona mortalibus comprehensibilia redduntur.

34. The Woodpecker's Persistence. Cats,
Silenus Alcibiadis.

MELIOR DOCTRI-
NA PARENTVM.

La meilleure education
est celle des parents

Vt canere alma docet pullos philomela tenellos,
Sic genitor gnatos formes & ipse pius.

Le rossignol apprend à
chanter à ses petits

35. The Nightingale teaching its Young to
sing. Camerarius, *Symbolorum et*
emblematum . . . centuriae.

36

36. The Partridge preparing to evacuate her Young from the Nest.
Peacham, *Minerva Brittanica*.

37. The Lark preparing to evacuate her Young from the Nest. Camerarius, *Symbolorum et emblematum . . . centuriae*.

38. Grain, Pauline Symbol of the Resurrection. Camerarius, *Symbolorum et emblematum . . . centuriae*.

39. Grain gathered together in Harvest. Camerarius, *Symbolorum et emblematum . . . centuriae*.

40. Grain, Symbol of the Resurrection. Camerarius, *Symbolorum et emblematum . . . centuriae*.

NEMO QVI-DEM MELIVS.

Cum sua quis rectè curare negocia possit,
Alterius stulte pendet ab arbitrio.

37

SVRGET VBE-RIOR.

Luxuriem segetis castigat falce colonus.
Ingenium præcox reprime: sic sapies.

38

LXXVIII.

NON METENTIS SED SERENTIS.

Pigra far esse manus, plenam ne collige messem:
Commoda frumenti qui petit, ille serat.

39

SPES ALTERA VITÆ.

Securus moritur, qui scit se morte renasci:
Non ea mors dici, sed noua vita potest.

40

41. Man as inverted Tree.
Jode, *Microcosmos*.

42. Perspective: small Things
seem great. Ruisdael,
Thistles and Dunes. Wadsworth
Atheneum, Hartford.

43. Small Things seen as great. Rubens, *Castle at Steen* (detail).

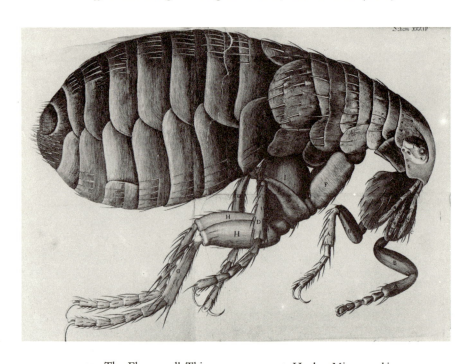

44. The Flea: small Things seen as great. Hooke, *Micrographia*.

45. Anamorphic figure. Zucchi, *Spring*. Wadsworth Atheneum, Hartford.

46. Anamorphic figure. Zucchi, *Summer*. Wadsworth Atheneum, Hartford.

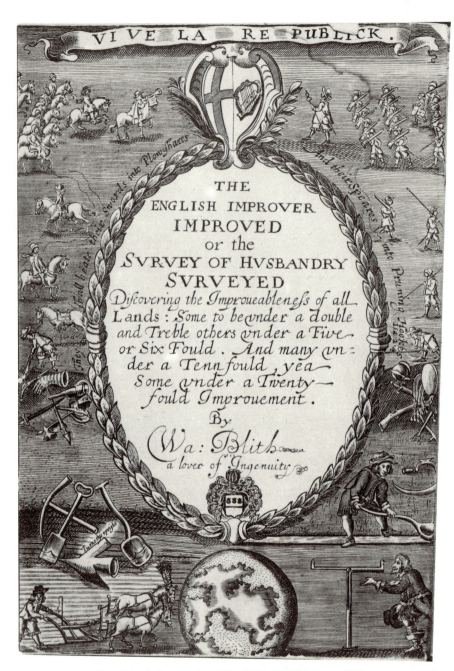

VIVE LA RE PUBLICK.

THE
ENGLISH IMPROVER
IMPROVED
or the
SVRVEY OF HVSBANDRY
SVRVEYED
Discovering the Improveableneſs of all
Lands : Some to be under a double
and Treble others under a Five
or Six Fould . And many un=
der a Tenn fould , yea
Some under a Twenty
fould Improvement .
By
Wa: Blith
a lover of Ingenuity

47. The Swords beaten into Ploughshares. Titlepage, Blith,
The English Improver Improv'd.

FIGURES FOR THEME:
WAR AND PEACE, WITHIN AND
WITHOUT

POET AND pupil, then, go properly "in," retiring to a house designed as a fixed point at the center of the swirling instability outside it. They go in without fanfare, because it is night: so Lord Fairfax went in, because the political world was benighted, and men were in the dark. But Appleton House, though in so many ways a model of goodness and proper economy and thus a model from which England might well be redesigned, is at the same time no earthly paradise untouched by time, disorder, and disaster. On the estate, catastrophes seem to take place, although they turn out to be emblematic or adumbrated rather than actual, consequential disasters. In literary forms, the contrast between "in" and "out," between an active and a retired life, is by means of landscape: the retired man lives in the country, in a garden, perhaps even in the woods; the public man lives in "busie Companies of Men," in a world really or figuratively engaged in struggle or in battle. The language of "Upon Appleton House" takes care to mix these categories, these modes, these themes. In every episode, there is some battle-imagery, incidents given in terms of violence and disorder. The static house is itself not besieged by anything specific, although the garden's behavior suggests that the ambitions of the *"Prelate* great" extended to Nunappleton; and the poet does choose to introduce us to the house in terms of a battle between aesthetic moralities, between extravagant, conceited foreign styles of art and the simplicities of the native designer, a battle of ideas with considerable implications for men's souls. In the Isabella episode, the generic "Fairfax" is presented as a universal knight and a model of behavior to his posterity (stanza 36), a defender of due rights, of manliness, and of the true religion; like a medieval hero, he storms the nunnery to free his promised bride. His battles, though, are also more ideological than real: the *"Virgin Amazons"* fight with such weapons as wooden saints, holy-water brushes, beads, and their sharp tongues (stanza 32). Like a masque figure, Fairfax rises as *deus ex machina* to win against no real opposition; like magic, he "through the Wall does rise," to carry away the cloister's only genuine jewel, the "truly bright and holy *Thwaites*," from the relic-decked altar. The ladies' defenses are trivial before the force of Fairfax's *virtù*, which bursts through the nunnery-wall as through a stage-property barrier. It was easy enough for those without to get into this cloister, and we know that its warfare was emotionally and ideologically rather than physically violent, a parodied battle, a ridiculous struggle.

In the next section, the garden is entirely militarized. This is and is not normal: the armed bee and the military bee occur in the Anthology, in Pliny, and in the Georgics; and in the vocabulary of sense-warfare, especially the figurative war-games of love, militarization of the gentlest things regularly takes place. Here, though, the conceit is carried to extremes: the Dian, drum, ensigns, pans, flasks, volleys, firemen, reports, colors, regiments, patrols, sentinels, passwords, garrisons, towers, "the *Switzers* of our *Guard*" (Protestant substitutes for the Papal Guards), soldiers, magazines, winter-quarters, ordnance, powder, trenches, bastions, artillery are all involved in this garden's daily round. This garden of retirement, then, is devoted also to "warlike Studies," and, appropriately to those contemplations, is rendered in a vocabulary least suited to such a topic.[1] The war-games theme runs through the poem, recurring in the mowing-triumph and the wood-siege.

Yet the garden of the estate, and the estate which is a garden, are both praised in terms of paradise-gardens, of which the poet adduces two others, Eden and England. England as a paradise, or at least a demi-paradise, is a national commonplace: we need look no farther than to Shakespeare for several famous examples. According to the implications of this poem, England had evidently remained an unfallen garden longer than most of the rest of the world, perhaps because of her island situation. As an island, England could exclude the fallen world, remaining an area blest and sainted, withdrawn from the normal turmoil of a lapsed society. Indeed, the suggestion is present throughout this poem that England did not altogether participate in the original Fall, but is experiencing in the present wars a more recent fall of her own:

[1] Another example, then, of Marvell's stretching the possibilities of style to the limit.

Figures for Theme

What luckless Apple did we tast,
To make us Mortal, and The Wast?   (stanza 41)

After that incident, a gardener's talents are especially called for, to restore the island which is now planted with ordnance and sown with powder, breeding only war and warriors. Fairfax, as the poet suggests, would have been the man for such responsibility, but was led by his prickly conscience to renounce both ambition and the accompanying responsibilities of public life.

In his private life, however, the struggles continue. The mowers massacre the grass and kill the fledgling rail.[2] There is much more than simple mowing going on here, although what this "more" is exactly, is very difficult to say. The mowers seem to relate to Marvell's private poetic world, where mowers have had so much to say, so much to do:[3] they call up biblical reference, then, "All flesh is grass"; they may reach out to the mowing angels of the Apocalypse as well. As Mr. Allen has indicated,[4] soldiers were regularly figured as reapers; Mr. Holahan notes the use of the figure in the *Iliad*. When swords are beaten into scythes, then something of swordship remains; here, the mower kills a baby rail, even though it was as hidden in its low nest, as humble as it was possible to be, as unassuming as befit its place on the scale of creatures. Nonetheless, the bird comes in the scythe's way and is wantonly killed. The mower has much of the pastoralist in him, and sympathizes with the little bird; indeed, he goes farther, and detests his act. That his view of the incident is peculiar to him, the joy of Thestylis makes plain, as she seizes the baby rails to roast for lunch. There is a breath of tragedy here, breathed out and breathed back in before the effects of tragedy can be felt.[5] That incident past, though, the pastoral scene is converted into a battle:

The Mower now commands the Field;
In whose new Traverse seemeth wrought
A Camp of Battail newly fought:

[2] See above, pp. 199, 205-6.   [3] See above, Part II, 5, p. 35.
[4] Allen, pp. 130-31; see also Thomas May, *Virgil's Georgicks, Englished* . . . (London, 1628), introduction: ". . . crooked sicles turn'd to swords, so late/Had drunke the blood of Romes divided State."
[5] Cf. *Georgics*, IV, 510-12, for the killing of the baby nightingale by the ploughman, an analogue to the rail's death by mowing. It is worth noting that this Thestylis fulfils her proper role of cook for the reapers: cf. *Eclogues* I, l. 11.

"Upon Appleton House"

> Where, as the Meads with Hay, the Plain
> Lyes quilted ore with Bodies slain:
> The Women that with forks it fling,
> Do represent the Pillaging. (stanza 53)

All flesh is grass: the metaphor becomes fact, as grass and rails go down together before the same rhythmic, seasonal operation. As the grass is a body, so is the rail: though in fact these are the only victims, of a warfare not internecine but truly civil, their death seems to point to something far more momentous than the end of hay, or of baby birds. With the death of the rail, the deaths of the Civil War are reduced to minute scale: an emblematic war-piece is given, with its reflections in the lowly innocents' suffering, although they mind their business and keep within. The language of this passage, the moralizing on the rail, the prosopopeia of the rail's "Orphan Parents" (another inversion of a normal relation between parent and child), the battle and sepulchral imagery all serve to deepen this pastoral to the heroic and tragic; but the occasion for all this language is of course trifling. The mowing of grass, the death of a tiny bird: the discrepancy between the event and its language is too great; one feels the trickery involved in anyone's caring so deeply about the bird. The poem borders on the burlesque at this point, borders, but does not overbalance into it. The mower's self-disgust at his killing the bird, the "creaking note" of the parent birds bear a deeper sorrow than the event can justify, but sound a note heard earlier in the poem, as the poet lamented the loss of England's innocence in the garden passage. Just as we realize the disproportion, even the silliness, of the mower's sorrow and of Thestylis' bloodthirsty greed, the sad vistas of tragic reality behind the emblematic scenes open out to turn the near-comic into near-tragic once more. In England, not so far from Appleton House, after all, the "Soldiers Obsequies" had been performed.

Near-tragic only: the poet turns away again and again from expressing deep emotion, as the pastoral reasserts itself in stanza 54, for example. A celebration not of bloody victory but of innocent toil accomplished concludes the massacre of the meadows:

> And now the careless Victors play,
> Dancing the Triumphs of the Hay;
> Where every Mowers wholesome Heat
> Smells like an *Alexanders sweat.*

242

> Their Females fragrant as the Mead
> Which they in *Fairy Circles* tread:
> When at their Dances End they kiss,
> Their new-made Hay not sweeter is.   (stanza 54)

But this sweet vision, with the faithful pastoral fairies somehow in their place, gives way to qualification in the very next stanza, as dangers and fears of danger arise. The haycocks are seen as rocks in a sea, threats to sailors; as pyramids, tumuli of great kings; as the tombs of Roman soldiers dead on the field. Hay becomes its own tomb, inevitably cut down, as men inevitably are cut down, especially men professionally violent. These are funeral games as well as victory celebrations, properly epic in one sense, properly pastoral in another. The kiss of peace that ends stanza 54 is framed by two stanzas of oblique reference to war and death.

In the wood passage, the poet is "within" great protection (stanzas 61-78). He "incamps" his mind behind the trees, evidently immune to assault by love and by the harsher aspects of the world, brave enough to take his own potshots at the world. Evidently "troopers" pass by even this wood of retirement, for the poet seems to have no difficulty in sighting his "Horsemen" to "gaul." Even more than that of the meadow episode, the wood-warfare is playful at best, mental at most: there is no question of bloodshed here, save perhaps in the ritual sacrifice of the baby heron. In the stream scene, the battle imagery is as little serious, relating as it does simply to the hypothetical assaults made on Mary Fairfax by her insufficient suitors, assaults she has no trouble in parrying. Against their metaphorical trains, shot, and cannon by which she is ambushed, she is in her chastity proof. Like the poet and like her father, Mary "scap't the safe, but roughest way."

At other points, particular epic details strike one: Mr. Berger pointed out that the lines about

> . . . that more sober Age and Mind,
> When larger sized Men did stoop
> To enter at a narrow loop;
> As practising, in doors so strait,
> To strain themselves through *Heavens Gate*.   (stanza 4)

refer to *Aeneid*, VIII, 362-365, when Evander tells Aeneas of Hercules' stooping to enter his poor palace, as well as to Matthew 7:13-14; and to *The Faerie Queene* (I.x.5), when the Redcrosse Knight must stoop to

243

enter the House of Holiness. Mr. Holahan noted the similarity between
the model Troy Helenus built, with its dry brook, to the model England,
with its half-dry trenches, which occupied Fairfax's attentions;[6] and the
doves in the wood, showing Aeneas the way, may have something to do
with the stock-doves in Marvell's numinous grove.[7] In Christian epics,
the hexaemeron is a principal subject, also hinted at several times in this
poem (stanzas 1, 56, 96). Across each of the poem's sections, the shadow
of warfare lies, to give the whole poem an epic undertone;[8] not, I think,
more than that, but not less than that either. War is involved in what
happens on the estate as it is involved in what happens outside the estate;
the actual warfare from which Fairfax retired is adumbrated on the
estate in psychomachic terms. The nunnery skirmish was fought in terms
of religious symbols and of the law; the garden engagement has to do
with a man's relation to his senses. Both poet and Mary easily overcome
threats to themselves, nature offering protection to the poet, her nature
and nurture to Mary. Only the mowers' battle language reaches the depth
of genuine pain—in the place where generically such pain least belongs,
so that for a moment the fledgling's death can stand for all the iniquities
inevitable in war. Although we are not allowed to take the incident seri-
ously, we are also not permitted to dismiss its implications as trivial, pre-
cisely because its language of grief and mourning pull so strongly toward
darker reflections and more threatening possibilities than those literally
present in the poem.

The flood language relates to the war language, as has been mentioned.
Even without the authority of Lucan and Horace, readers can sense the
dangers of any flood: the purifying Flood of Noah left, as does this flood
on a smaller scale, spectacular disruption behind it. In terms just of this
poem, the war imagery on land and the flood imagery on the river
demonstrate the instability of the elements' relation to each other: at
Nunappleton as in nature, nothing gold can stay, and the Golden Age
is constantly threatened by mutability. Further, in the metaphoric ecology
of the estate, we find that the four elements conventionally celebrated in
country-house poetry,[9] each represented as a major aspect of this poem

[6] *Aen.* III, 349ff.; and see Wallace, *Destiny his Choice*, pp. 242-43.

[7] *Aen.* VI.

[8] Mr. Wallace takes the view that "Upon Appleton House" is an epic: for reasons
laid out principally in Part IV, section 7, below, I do not, although his association
of this poem with *Gondibert* is very interesting.

[9] Hibbard, *op.cit.*

(earth, the mowing; water, the flood; air, the birds, especially the king-fisher; fire, the warfare), tend to flow into each other, as the water flows over the land to make actual the paradox of stanza 60. The mixed elements, the chaos, the abyss: these references keep us alive to the complexities of life, even here.

The miniature flood is, in terms of the poem, by no means a surprise, since there are so many earlier hints at flooding. Fairfax seems to be assimilated to the patriarchs, who habitually walked with God, in stanza 44; of these, Noah is conspicuous as a reformer of the defective world. The poet's first reference to the meadows is in terms of the primeval sea—"And now to the Abbyss I pass/ Of that unfathomable Grass" (stanza 47)—the image calling up notions both of the deep and mysterious sea and of the watery chaos. Through this "sea" the mowers are seen as divers, who lose all sense of themselves and of their activities as they abandon themselves to the water. That loss of self-control is picked up later in the poet's very different self-abandonment in the wood. In the case of the mower-divers, they are men upside down, men loosened from their customary moorings, literally at sea in their world:

> As, under Water, none does know
> Whether he falls through it or go.   (stanza 48)

Having sounded the depths of the meadow, the divers come up with flowers; in short, they remain pastoralists, who pluck the day with their gentle labor: therewith, the sea becomes land again.

In the next stanza, though, the meadows metamorphose again into a sea, the Red Sea making a lane for the Israelites to walk across; the abyss is made a "lane" by divine miracle. This passage, beautifully worked through the poem, may be a compliment to Fairfax's own Exodus; it is likely too that it relates to one of Fairfax's own poems, in which he dwelt on the difficulties of the departure from Egypt, and the horrors of the Egyptians' drowning.[10] The fields continually shift back and forth between land and sea imagery, until the metaphor becomes reality as the floodgates open and the meadow becomes "(What it but seem'd before) a Sea" (stanza 59). At this point, the poet replaces Fairfax as a patriarch, and in his turn reconstitutes a world, this time a mental world of extraordinary fantasy.

When the poet emerges from his wood after the flood which had

[10] Thomas Fairfax, "Moses his Songe."

frightened him away, he discovers the world fairly restored, improved over what it had been. In this new world, as if answering the questions raised about fallen England in the garden section, it is made plain that there is no chance of a fall's taking place:

> No *Serpent* new nor *Crocodile*
> Remains behind our little *Nile*;
> Unless it self you will mistake,
> Among these Meads the only Snake. (stanza 79)

The river has, though, its own deceptions, its reflections so exact that "all things" doubt their own identities, their limitations, their places, doubt then whether they or their images are real. The mirroring river is an abyss, but a gentle one, holding "all things" within it without paining them. As the river deceives the things "without" that are mirrored in it, the poet deceives things naturally in the river, as he tries to lure the fish "out" of it. His is a gentle deception, though: it is unclear whether he in fact contrives to capture any of the fish. He fishes childishly: his lures are "Toyes." Gradually, the scene comes to a standstill, with the halcyon and Maria. All chaos, all disturbance are brought to a halt with the entry of the bird and the girl; another tone rules the poem to its end.

Though there is no serpent and therefore no guilt, all things are conscious of propriety, even of relative proprieties. When Maria comes, loose nature behaves better: the sun falls asleep more modestly; modest Maria draws the wood about her as a screen.

The stillness of this scene makes us notice anew the poem's characteristic swirling. Maria comes onstage a little goddess, a supernatural figure controlling and quelling the forces of disorder in the poem—like the halcyon, the girl calms storms and causes peace.[11] Like Britomart, too, or Milton's Lady, she can walk through all temptations undisturbed, safe in her sunclad power of chastity. In contrast to her ancestress, Maria is not "like" the Virgin; she is a separate, independent virgin Mary, an aspiring maiden dedicated to her delightful duty, fulfilment of her destiny as a Fairfax. Instructed in the "Discipline severe" of her parents, Mary has access to true wisdom (stanza 89); she knows "all the Languages"— but how matter of fact, how unself-conscious is she in this knowledge,

---

[11] Mr. Allen and Mr. Wallace both see Mary Fairfax as Heavenly Wisdom, her behavior like that of Sophia in the Book of Wisdom; I find this association unconvincing.

as compared with the poet's reveling pride in his understanding of the birds' speech! Evidently Mary Fairfax, like her father, was a good linguist; this compliment stretches reality into hyperbole.

For the little girl is also "real." She is no grand substitute for Sophia, Solomonic or Panathenaic; she does not tower heroically in or over the poem. Like much else in this poem, she is a diminutive figure, a young girl in a blue prospect: she walks through the landscape as if unaware of what she does to it. The poet watching her sees her miracles happen, as the halcyon's miracle simply happened; Maria herself seems unconscious of the effect she creates. The theme played in so many variations through the poem, "things greater are in less contain'd," comes to its tonic in Maria, the "sprig," the "bud" in whom the Fairfacian virtues are concentrated and by whom they will be borne into the future. Bred of a happy marriage, she is bred for a proper marriage of her own, to continue the virtues and hopes of her great house. One epic significantly ends on a marriage, the *Aeneid*, when the hero marries the dignified heiress to make her lands his own, to cultivate them with the virtues he brought from his destroyed civilization as well as with the native strengths of the land itself.

Andrew Marvell was Mary Fairfax's tutor, an assistant in the severe discipline applied by her parents. For the important fledgling, Appleton House was the nest. However modest the proportions of the house, though, we know from the rail's fate that happiness and security cannot be guaranteed even by the the most careful retirement. There is much nesting in this poem: the nightingale is traditionally taught by her elders, and here evidently her music-making is overseen; the stock-dove is, in Marvell's poem and out of it, an emblem for married fidelity; the "thrastle" hatches its young as the poet catches its eye among the cryptic leaves; the heron sacrifices its first-born, as the Fairfaxes have dedicated theirs, to God; the carpenter-hewel seeks worms for its young. The halcyon is distinguished for its remarkable nesting-habits: for the span of its brooding, the sea is still, as the landscape is still when Maria walks through it. Bred in the paradisal environment her parents designed for her, Mary, it is hoped, will continue her halcyon-course, extend her identification with the miraculous bird, herself to nest on still waters and to bring up her children in a peaceful, georgic world.[12]

[12] Sadly enough, her marriage was in fact very troubled.

All this is very domestic, very simple, very private: the poem deals constantly in diminished images, diminished meanings, in the psychomachia of retirement and emergence, of withdrawal and activity, all these things merged into the pursuits of one peaceful estate's commonwealth, a microcosmic ideal condition, in which fighting is mock warfare, the flood is beneficent, the poet's crucifixion an image for joyful, not painful, rapture. In this world, though, accidents take place: the rail is killed, Thestylis is violent, the heron drops its chick from an incredible height. The disproportion between language and topic, the extremity of fantasy and conceit, qualify the estate's halcyon perfection and force recognition that even within its orderly and secure confines, small injustices and fatalities may occur, diminished images of the great injustices and fatalities of the world. Appleton House is an ideal microcosm, but it is a real one too: it tenders the same difficulties, scaled down, of interpreting life that are encountered in the world without.

One reason the rail episode is so curiously gripping, in spite of its obvious overstatement, is that it points directly to the problems besetting any man committed to his life: in even the most innocent contexts, like mowing the grass, a man may blunder severely at the expense of another's life. The woodpecker knows that the tree is corrupt from "the *Traitor Worm*," and contracts, as it were, with the tree to bring it down. That pruning is not given to us drenched with sorrow or grief, as the rail episode was: if all public duties could be fulfilled by contract, with victim and executioner evenly recognizing the need for sacrifice, then public life would not be the problematical, unreliable, unrewarding thing that it is, and men like Fairfax would not have to retire. The nostalgia for a lost paradise, when even rails were safe from the mower's scythe, when oaks were without taint and England without sin, is what makes the rail's and the mower's grief so serious; distant as it is from its referent, the rail stands for the unwitting cruelties of public responsibilities. And Mary Fairfax stands to correct the rail, so rudely "exprest" from its nest: like the tortoise, she carries her heritage with her, her house on her back, both Appleton and the traditions of her heroic family. In the last scene, when things are arrested at a perfect moment, they still "doubt" whether they be in or out—within or without a sheltering protection, within or without a man's mind. Maria brings to the world a moment of stasis in the constant flux, gives it a standard, then—but even that moment has its inevitable puzzles, not very different from those of the flux. The metaphysical and ontological doubts that plague the whole poem are asserted here too. Just for a moment, though, those doubts hang at equipoise, the poet's mind balancing with them, not caring if he is, or they are, "in" or "out." The nesting-place is a place of retirement and of preparation, a place where the young are legitimately withdrawn from the world they are made ready for by "list'ning Elders" who know the world and can teach of it. "In" and "out" are natural parts of that preparation. As night falls, the confusing mirror-picture which the mirror offers is erased, and the questions it poses must be put aside, for the night leaves no room for doubt. At night, sensible people naturally go "in."

⚛ 5 ⚛

LANGUAGE AND FIGURE:
INTERPENETRATION IN TIME
AND PLACE

IKE so much else in this shifty poem, "in" and "out" shift their boundaries, interchange with one another, interpenetrate one another. The poet has learned much from Montaigne's method of working, although compared with Montaigne's essays, Marvell's work is far more indirect, offhand, mysterious, noncommittal; Marvell never tells us directly what his subject is, only circles around it, alludes to it, builds it up by inference, reference, and tone. One must abstract from what Marvell says in "Upon Appleton House" to understand what he is doing. In the *Apologie*, Montaigne is far franker: he takes mutability as his subject, faces its problems with a panache and aplomb designed to embarrass the nervous and insecure; Montaigne, one feels, enjoys not only the personal risks of disequilibrium, but also the fact that others do not share his confidence in the face of reiterated uncertainty. There are degrees of disequilibrium: Montaigne seems a frank charlatan in the ending to his *Apologie*, unfairly tricking the audience struggling to keep up with him. Marvell is even trickier, though his game is to make "himself," the poet in the poem, appear the victim of the same confusions, shifts, and paradoxes imposed on his readers. Montaigne's *Essais* are a set of tracts, instructions, *exempla* upon how to come to terms with the inevitable variability of our lives. Marvell had profited, certainly, from the excellence of Montaigne's teaching and no longer had to regard Montaigne's message as surprising, difficult, or particularly paradoxical; he could take it for granted that mutability had become domesticated, in part as a result of Montaigne's work, so that he had no need to preach its threatening lessons. And yet, of course, "Upon Appleton House" *does* teach lessons: the poem *is* moral, instructive, fundamentally educative, dealing with problems of training and education. Inward as it is, it nonetheless leads one into larger and larger considerations. Its repeated imbalances, its

250

conceits stretched to the limit of fantasy, its metamorphoses and anamorphoses force reconsideration and reassessment of values and assumptions—and, as Montaigne's work does not, the poem forces that reconsideration by purely literary means.

For it is by allusions, metaphors, figures, linguistic uses that the poet manages to present his significantly unstable world, to set in such strange juxtaposition elements from such disparate contexts. The shifting from large to small, the transforming of large into small and small into large, the forcing of metaphor and emblem into arrogant, demanding conceits, the interchange of figure with fact and fact with figure—all are done to point implicitly to the moral and ontological questions at the poem's heart. From the study of optics, from various graphic and theatrical conventions, the poet adapted means to further his poem's confusions. Just to maintain his consistent inconsistency, he also wrote passages of total clarity and simplicity. The last episode in the poem, an untroubled instant between a troubled past and an uncertain future, is carved to crystal perfection out of the flux and change of the rest of the poem. We know the moment's value by what it issues from, and we know that the moment must itself be lost before the coming on of night. Whatever the poet's hopes for his well trained, well balanced Mary, he can promise her a future of halcyon security only in the invocations of verse.

That static moment, isolated from the flux of past and future time, is, however, deeply connected to the other moments, other times of the active, swirling day of the poem. In the poem as a whole, time-schemes are peculiarly disturbed; time itself is pleated, skipped, metamorphosed, fused in various ways. In the time-schemes as in the spatial metamorphoses, one thing continually turns into another: some such fusion takes place by typological hints, as the poet acts out his variations on the roles of Noah and Solomon. Fairfax walks in Appleton straight from a patriarchal age, and the poet himself plays in the woods as Solomon, if his Song is to be trusted, allowed himself to play in the countryside. Fairfax's house is like the creatures' natural dwellings and like the modest houses from which great civilizations sprang (Romulus' cell, Evander's tiny palace). His garden is like paradise and like a paradisal primitive England; his meadows are like the world at its creation, like the Red Sea parting for the Israelites to return to their inheritance, like the tumultuous Flood. His woods are an Ark and a Temple. Nature and art, sacred and profane, provide models for Fairfax's commonwealth, and the streams of sacred and profane writings have their confluence in his Wharfe.

Maria is a typological figure as well as a real person; first of all, she recapitulates her ancestress' life, as the virgin bride Isabella becomes distilled into the perfect Maria, immune to nuns' or young men's flattery. She is blessed by nature, is the mistletoe on the sacred oak, hallowed by both the prelate of the grove and the Christian priest. She is her father's fulfilment, performing miracles as great as his and far more beautiful; she can alter the landscape, while her father could only alter the construction of his house. She is a Fairfax, heiress to courage, decision, and integrity. Past, present, and future are epitomized in this young girl, seen against the prospect of her estate, topographical and moral. The estate is an epitome too, of the unfallen world, of paradise, of a garden-England; at the same time it is the particular holding of a particular master. From the Fairfaxes Nunappleton took its form and meaning, and the Fairfaxes were confirmed in their condition by the estate's excellence. "Things greater are in less contain'd": the smallest of Fairfax's holdings and the smallest Fairfax contain all these miraculous powers and benefits.

Though it is not by any means totally clear, the tense-pattern of this poem is far less complicated than, for instance, that of *Lycidas* or even of the "Nativity Ode," both so subtly analyzed by Lowry Nelson.[1] Marvell largely uses the present tense in the poem, but now for one purpose, now for another. The poem begins outside time, and often reverts to a timeless present during its actual narrative time, of a full day, from dawning in the garden to nightfall by the house.[2] Narrative sequence is often interrupted; most incidents are told in a continuing present, and require a considerable number of clear transition words; "now" (stanzas 52, 53, 54, 71, 79, 95, 97) and "then" (stanzas 33, 37, 40, 43, etc.) and "yet" (stanzas 7, 8, 30, 44, etc.), mark a sequence of rapidly succeeding scenes and events. But these simple words are not unambiguous in themselves; in the final stanza, for instance, "now" occurs twice, once in the last line, as night enters on the heels of the fishermen. The effect of that final "now," after so many others, is to diminish our sense of finality, to suggest that there will be another and another "now," that the performance is over only for this particular summer's day.

From the varied uses of the present, one must read several kinds of

---

[1] Nelson, *Baroque Lyric Poetry*.
[2] See Curtius, "Topics of the Conclusion."

"presentness": an immediate present, a narrative present, a continuing present, and an aphoristic present, about conditions timeless and unalterable, as in the epigrammatic passages:

> No Creature loves an empty space; (stanza 2)

> But He, superfluously spread,
> Demands more room alive then dead. (stanza 3)

> So Honour better Lowness bears,
> Then That unwonted Greatness wears. (stanza 8)

This use of the present tense may be called the philosophical present, used for choral or epigrammatic statements of reliable truth and unalterable fact, against which the bewilderments of experience may be measured.

The tenses shift a good deal, usually to arrange the events in some logical relation to the dominant present. Such are the stanzas about Fairfax's conquest of the nunnery which, though told in the present tense, is in fact long past to the poet's present of his ideal day. In stanza 31, a complicated shifting keeps the temporal levels of action straight:

> Is not this he whose Offspring fierce
> Shall fight through all the *Universe*;
> And with successive Valour try
> *France, Poland*, either *Germany*;
> Till one, as long since prophecy'd,
> His Horse through conquer'd *Britain* ride?
> Yet, against Fate, his Spouse they kept;
> And the great Race would intercept.

"Is," "shall fight," "[shall] ride," "kept," "would intercept": the stable point in these tenses is Fairfax, what he does is given in the present. His issue naturally is "prophecy'd" in the normal way, that is, in the future tense; as the poet returns to the events present in his narrative, he shifts to the past tense, the final verb prophesying, but only conditionally, the nuns' unsuccess. Two stanzas later, Fairfax's activity is in the present, the nuns' action in the past:

> But, waving these aside like Flyes,
> Young *Fairfax* through the Wall does rise.
> When th' unfrequented Vault appear'd,
> And superstitions vainly fear'd.

253

The *Relicks false* were set to view;
Only the Jewels there were true.
But truly bright and holy *Thwaites*
That weeping at the *Altar waites*.   (stanza 33)

Isabella weeping at the altar requires a verb—we obediently supply "is,"
as the false altar of the nunnery fuses with the altar of her own marriage-
service. "Waites" reliably establishes the present tense, as if Isabella were
designed always to wait for her deliverer, who also acts in the present
tense.

The next two stanzas shift tense considerably. The active events are
put in the present—"the glad Youth away her bears"; "to the *Nuns* be-
queaths her Tears"; they "guiltily their Prize bemoan"—their prize and
their loss put into the last tense, "Like Gipsies that a Child hath stoln."
But it is not the metaphor-verb which invariably goes into the past, to
show its dependence upon the actual facts of the poem—"Th'Inchantment
ends," a false "Castle vanishes or rends," while the actual fate of the
cloister is put into the past, "was dispossest," a finite, unchangeable event.
The cloister, then, in its own future, "To Fairfax *fell*"—at which point
in the poem, the tenses intertwine to mingle events which in fact took
several decades to work themselves out:

And what both *Nuns* and *Founders* will'd
'Tis likely better thus fulfill'd.
For if the *Virgin* prov'd not theirs,
The *Cloyster* yet remained hers.
Though many a *Nun* there made her Vow,
'Twas no *Religious House* till now.   (stanza 35)

Except for "is fulfill'd," these actions are all cast in the past tense; though
the last verb is imperfect, the action described in that line continues into
the present ("now"). In this stanza, historical time is radically pleated,
since the actual dissolution of the cloister took place in the generation
after Isabella's and Fairfax's. The same pleating takes place in another
fusion of Fairfax heroes; in stanza 36, the sense leads us to believe that
the Lord General was responsible for the design of the garden-fort, but
in fact, as Marvell and his patron knew, the military garden was laid
out by Guy Fairfax, a predecessor of the present owner.

Sometimes tense-shifts manipulate several ranges of reality, as in stanza
56, the *tabula rasa* stanza:

> This *Scene* again withdrawing brings,
> A new and empty Face of things;
> A levell'd space, as smooth and plain,
> As Clothes for *Lilly* strecht to stain.
> The World when first created sure
> Was such a Table rase and pure.
> Or rather such is the *Toril*
> Ere the Bulls enter at Madril.

The present tense dominates, but there are two presents, that of the meadow incidents taking place, and that of a distant place, Madrid, where evidently habits are deemed not to change, where the *"Toril"* is, where bulls can confidently be assumed to be entering it. But the verb forms of the middle lines are in the past—the world was so at the Creation, and Lely's canvasses *have been stretched* for him, in the future, to "stain." The shifts here manage to present a tumble of times past, present, and future, all given at once: in the longer passage of which this is a part, the time from the Creation to the Flood, all given by types of metaphors, is cramped into five stanzas.

Often, as in stanzas 34 and 35, the tense shifts involve the typological history of the house of Fairfax. In stanza 62, biblical typology is translated into natural terms: the narrative present has to do with the poet's un-folding experiences in the wood, but it stretches out to include a longer existence, that of the oaks that are heraldic symbols of the houses of Fairfax and Vere:

> The double Wood of ancient Stocks
> Link'd in so thick, an Union locks,
> It like two *Pedigrees* appears,
> On one hand *Fairfax*, th' other *Veres*:
> Of whom though many fell in War,
> Yet more to Heaven shooting are:
> And, as they Natures Cradle deckt,
> Will in green Age her Hearse expect.

Trees are, as Evelyn said, "the nearest emblems of eternity"; these trees outlast nature and outlast time. "Fell," "are shooting," "will expect": like their oaks, the Fairfaxes continue across time, green and growing. There are other fusions here besides tense fusions; it is not quite clear to what "Of whom" refers—to the heroes of the two families, or (unlikely) to the trees under discussion. Nor does it greatly matter whether the poet speaks here of Veres, Fairfaxes, or oaks, but only that the one means the other. Men and trees are fused in the poet's view of things; and, we note, here both men and trees, so solidly fused, are upright, not "turned," as the poet later asks to be.

Sometimes the past tense indicates a finite action entirely done away with, as in the nuns' attempt to intercept the great race of Fairfax; sometimes the past tense is used to indicate a model situation now past. An example of the first is the passage about the foreign architect's treatment of landscape; he

> . . . unto Caves the Quarries drew,
> And Forrests did to Pastures hew;   (stanza 1)

This stanza echoes the sentiments of the mower in his poem "against Gardens," and of the unhappy soul, in the "Dialogue between the Soul and Body"; the artifices of civilization are attacked from a position labeled "nature." Near the poem's end, the poet returns to this theme in his attack on the great pleasure-palaces of grandiose, showy, and, of course, Catholic Spain, Aranjuez and Buen Retiro. The use of the past suggests that such aesthetics belonged to a time now outmoded, now replaced by the present-tense economies displayed at Nunappleton. Nature's above art in this respect: as the poem goes on to show, woods are sanctified, the tree-columns of the wood temple more beautiful and more functional than the high columns of foreign designs, which deform those who conceive and those who perceive them.

Sometimes the past tense refers to something lamentably lost, as in the stanzas about a past paradisal England. Within the estate, though, and in the present tense, the garden condition is restored, the economy, "orderly and near," recapitulating that of a "more sober Age and Mind," when Hercules willingly stooped to enter Evander's palace, and pointing to a future when men will go through the strait gate to salvation. The poem has a great deal of the future in it, even before the overt prophesying about Maria: Appleton House, the poet promises, will become the object of pilgrimages, as Romulus' house on the Capitol had become. The spiritual hope lying behind the prophecy that the humble and meek shall be exalted informs the early passages on proper humility, against which, later, we are to measure the morality of the nun's urgings to Isabella. In her false promise, the nun speaks in the future tense, offering the girl what she ought never to desire, either in her life (" 'The Rule it self to you shall bend' ") or as heavenly reward (" 'Your voice, the sweetest of the Quire, Shall draw *Heav'n* nearer, raise us higher' ").

As befits a poem involved in problematics and conditionals, there is extensive use of both subjunctive and conditional forms. Contrary-to-fact constructions occur:

"Ah, no! And 'twould more Honour prove
"He your *Devoto* were, then *Love*."   (stanza 19)

"Were there but, when this House was made,
"One Stone that a just Hand hath laid,"   (stanza 27)

Or turn me but, and you shall see
Man is but an inverted Tree.   (stanza 71)

The passage of verb forms from stanza 19 to stanza 21 illustrates the insinuating skill of the nun's rhetoric. Beginning in the subjunctive and conditional, she passes into the future, then returns to subjunctive and conditional:

"How soft the yoke on us would lye,
"Might such fair hands as yours it tye!"   (stanza 20)

By stanza 21, the situations stated earlier as conditional have turned into accepted fact in the nun's rhetoric, the future tense indicating her conviction that she will be successful with her dupe:

"Your .Voice, the sweetest of the Quire,
"Shall draw *Heav'n* nearer, raise us higher.
"And your Example, if our Head,
"Will soon us to perfection lead.
"Those Virtues to us all so dear,
"Will straight grow Sanctity when here:"

To quite different ends, young Fairfax, deep in the problematics of will and duty, also deals in conditions and contraries-to-fact: "Yet would he valiantly complain." (stanza 26); "Small Honour would be in the Storm"; "What should he do? He would respect/ Religion, ..." In stanzas 32-35, the tense states Fairfax's ultimate victory; having been resolved in history, Fairfax's problems can also be settled in the poem. His descendant's situation, at the moment of the poem's being written, is less easily determined. Concentrating on the Lord General, stanza 44 locates him clearly at his own moment of choice, between two worlds, a rational amphibium between one mode of life and another, between his glorious past and his problematical future. To have abandoned the active life meant that he had left undone something which, "had it pleased him and *God*" he might have done well—that is, to reform the "luckless" and "Wast" island into a new-springing garden. The poet's dissatisfaction with accomplishment cut off emerges in his verb forms—"had it," "might have made," "might command"—although in the compliment of stanza 45 he comes to terms as resolutely with his employer's choice as that choice was resolutely made:

> For he did, with his utmost Skill,
> *Ambition* weed, but *Conscience* till.
> *Conscience*, that Heaven-nursed Plant,
> Which most our Earthly Gardens want.
> A prickling leaf it bears, and such
> As that which shrinks at ev'ry touch;
> But Flowrs eternal, and divine,
> That in the Crowns of Saints do shine.

In this stanza, the tenses shift from the past, denoting accident, to present, denoting essential truth. That the poet accepts his patron's choice of integrity over ambition the garden passage confirms, as in the next stanza, the "fenced" garden protects its master from "proud" Cawood. Small, neat, efficient, unpretentious, Appleton House is a proper bastion against ambition, wherever that threat occurs.

"Seems," in the passage just cited, is a recurrent word in the poem, reinforcing the tentative nature of all experiences and the tentative nature of the poet's assessment of them. In the nun's rhetoric, Fairfax only seems a proper rival to heaven; the rule, the nun assures Isabella, should it seem strict to the girl, can be liberalized to suit. Maria seems to be a flower; the leaves seem to be ensigns; the mowers seem to be Israelites; the meadows seem a sea; the forest seems a solid mass; the oak seems to fall content; the sun seems to sink more modestly in Maria's presence. The frankness of the poem's illusionism and *trompe l'oeil* is manifest in this simple verb substitute for similitude. The use of "seems" has another effect too: it permits the similes to act semi-prophetically, so that when they become facts of the poem—the meadows turning into a sea, the rails serving as quails—we have been prepared by the poet's double perception.

The same dubiety, the same sense of unreality, is conveyed by the several "as if" constructions. "Free" nature, in stanza 10, shows her graceful sweet wildness as far more beautiful than the regular accomplishments of art— "as if," the poet says, "she said leave this to me." Particularly in the passages where there are especially daring conceits, "as if" conjoins with "seems"—in the flower-bed/artillery passage, or the wood/tree-trunk passage, or the woodpecker's "tinkling" to fell a huge oak.

Such forms increase our sense of the poet's tentativeness, of the sliding nature of reality with which he finds himself unable to cope. In stanza 56 this comes to its extreme, as the poet corrects himself and his image, from the "*Table* rase and pure" to the "*Toril.*" However outlandish the "*Toril,*" it turns out nevertheless to make sense, as the Nunappleton herds are chased on the scene, to combine the idea of Creation with the crude notion of the bullring.[3] Sometimes images which in these stanzas are protected by "seems" or "as if" are presented without a screen, as if they were entirely normal, entirely factual. One instance is the brain-vaulting, brow-arching design of the first stanza, another is the swelling hall of the seventh, both presented as if such events simply happened before our eyes. The fanciful battle between Fairfax and the nuns, the military order maintained in the garden, the grasshoppers scornful of the men beneath them—all these are given without benefit of "seems" or "like." The diving mowers are assumed to dive—the "as" clause describes their sensations, not their actions; both poetic events are the poet's invention, not the visual facts of the poem. It is as if the poet did not care to distinguish actual from poetic truth in this poem, actuality from imagination, fact from figure, but permitted now the one, now the other to dominate, without particular consistency.

In such a context, it seems only fair that the poet be mistreated within his own poem by a character of his own invention, that the energetic and aggressive Thestylis force him out of his inductor-role to take for granted the poet's function as part of her fiction, as he presents her functions as part of his fiction. In the wood episode, we are not supposed to question what the poet says he sees enacted before his eyes: a heron tossing its young from a great height; a woodpecker tapping down a great oak. Such conspicuous oddities are made to seem normal in an environment which invests the poet with expanded consciousness

[3] See Davenant, *Gondibert*, II, vi, 60, where "The universall Herd" appears on the Fifth Day of Creation.

of the meanings of every thing, every creature, every act. The poet's woodland sensibilities are so heightened as to permit him to take for fact what would in the ordinary world—even in the ordinary poetic world—be purest fantasy.

The interpenetration of the world of evidential fact and the world of the imagination makes Thestylis' irruption less peculiar than it might have seemed in a more conventionally organized poem: what she does, after all, is to actualize metaphors, as the Wharfe actualizes the flood trope. Sometimes the metaphorical elements, in both cases fantastic, turn inside out, as in the case of human beings and architecture; in stanzas 1 and 4, architecture deforms human beings; in stanza 10, this process is reversed, so that architecture is deformed by a human being. Man is the measure of all things—and if things do not fit that measure, poetry can find means to make them do so.

These fantastic elements and scenes, though, are not mere conceits drawn from the poet's uncontrollable creativity. The small house always means something specific, something moral; the relation of the house to its master bespeaks a moral economy of which architecture is simply a symbolic sign. The heron, the hewel, the stock-doves, the nightingale, the halcyon all have their conventional symbolic meanings which, although varied somewhat from the norm in Marvell's usage, they share with other poems and other references. The poet plays with his materials, the stiff elements of his craft, to see how malleable they can become in his hands. Fairfax could turn a cube to a sphere. Marvell could do the same and more.

The rail episode is a case in point. The largest British rail, or crake, is eleven inches long, the nestlings correspondingly smaller. One rail, even for Thestylis' lunch, is a skimpy prize to elicit such ferocious joy as hers—or, for that matter, such dire self-disapproval as the inadvertent murderer shows. Only if the fundamental reference is inverted, and all grass becomes flesh, does the rail's significance, so much greater than the creature is itself, begin to emerge: much has been packed into that tiny frame. The mowing angels of Revelations thrust in their sickles to cut down the human race; all this is reduced to the accidental killing of a tiny bird, whose death reverberates so far. The rail is innocent, but is nonetheless rudely "exprest" from its nest to die. Another inversion: it is the parents who are thereby "Orphan," as war turns the world upside-down.

The rail's death, the heron's sacrifice, the felling of the oak all emphasize the disconcerting undertones of sadness and threat in this so playful poem. The oak must fall because of the *"Traitor-worm*, within it bred," which like the original sin in our flesh, destroys its host. The oak is "content" to be laid low by the priestly, pruning woodpecker performing his "Saxon" function of cleaning the woods. It is as if there were a ritual pre-arrangement between executioner and victim: assigned their parts, they understood what they were doing. Compared to the language of the rail episode, that of the oak episode is curiously neutral, as if indeed the two figures understood this foreordained behavior and its significance—which is, actually, more than the reader is ever told. Throughout the wood episode, the poet, elated in his rapture, seems to know very well what is going on; he knows all languages and thus, *"easie Philosopher,"* knows he need waste no tears over the oak's fall. The woodland crisis is radically understated, as the rail crisis was radically overstated. "Massacre," "carves," "bloody," "detest," "black," "greedy," "Orphan," "funeral," "Death-Trumpets"—all this for the death of a tiny bird, cut off before its prime. The horror parodies itself by its overstatement, but because of the implications of the death itself the parody is checked, so that we realize how deeply the poet deplores the hazards and brutalities of war, even as we realize how detached he is from the actual war, in this universe of privileged freedom.

One problem of this poem lies in its handling of the present events of its time. The narrative of the poem covers, in a major topic inherited from antiquity, an ideal day—although this ideal day is very peculiar indeed. First of all, though the day turns out to have been a very good one, it is presented as if fraught with dangers, disasters, and discomforts: the most one can say of a day so highly charged as this is that it needs men of strong nerves to regard it as ideal. Second, it is obviously "ideal" in the literal sense, since it is an imaginary day: the events described as taking place would take the better part of a week to perform in fact, and a particularly lucky week at that. Mowers cannot mow meadows, cattle cannot graze the stubble, rivers cannot flood and recede, all in the space of one day. Time is compressed and pleated here, too, much as the catoptric or masque devices otherwise serve to foreshorten tedious reality. Literally speaking, all those birds cannot nest together, except in poetry; they are as organized as the garden is, to play their parts of traditional compliment in a poem which tries to bracket all nature into itself, not to lend verisimilitude to a deliberately unconvincing narrative.

Beyond the poem's present, arranged with such love and such license, lies also the present state of England, the warfare in which the whole country was somehow involved. Stanzas 41 to 43 point directly to what is happening in the world Fairfax has chosen to leave: there is no doubt that the poet knows what is going on beyond the range of his own sight. And yet very little else directly refers to the war, although there is much oblique reference to it: the *"Levellers,"* who enter only once, in stanza 57, offer one direct comment on public affairs, clearly unfavorable to them, though complimentary to Fairfax, responsible for their reduction at Burford in 1649. Levellers, in a metaphor, intended to "level" the country to an "equal Flat"—which is at the same time, in the poet's opinion, "naked." Here again, he literalizes and trivializes an important political metaphor. There may be a further reference in the next line to the futility of radical economic proposals, as the poet points to the customary use of common ground for grazing; Diggers, for instance, wanted to turn that back to arable. The mowers in the poem also have to do with soldiers—Christopher Hill points out that soldiers went into battle armed with scythes, sickles, and pitchforks; the flood has to do with civil war, the rail with the sufferings of the lowly innocent, trying to keep out of harm's way. The hewel's Saxon function may refer to the notion of reformers that in Saxon precedents might lie some deliverance from the "Norman Yoke," the burden of laws applied by another kind of "Forrain *Architect*" to English polity.[4]

The poet makes none of these equations explicitly; all are allusive, all must be filled in from material external to the poem itself. Such interpretations are always risky, but the pattern of these seems to me to substitute for a deeper fear, unrealized fully but palpably present in the poem. The poet's preoccupation with a kind of half-defined trouble, which he deliberately tries to put from his mind, echoes through all these strange, deep images, to keep the notion of war trembling behind this landscape of bucolic well-being. Fairfax is not the only retired man in this poem; the poet is in flight from the harsher conditions of his world as well. I say this because of the ways in which we are given the experiences of

---

[4] See Hill, "The Norman Yoke," in *Puritanism and Revolution*, and J.G.A. Pococke, *The Ancient Constitution and the Feudal Law* (Cambridge, 1957), for discussions of "Saxon" liberties and "Norman" impositions.

the poem, its games, its ecstasies, its delights, the idyll always qualified by images or emblems of another decorum. The darker world insists on itself, in spite of the games, in a way because of them: in the very artificiality of these scenes, the evident causelessness of events, the continuity of experience regularly broken up and broken into, there is a sense of the idyll's psychological unreality, or of the idyll as dream. The odd temporal fusions and extensions by which sometimes events jumble each other in overlapping happening, or an event seems endlessly drawn out, match the curious spatial metamorphoses to give the whole poem an air of being not totally experienced, not totally grasped. The disjunctions of this world suggests its habitation by a being distracted, a being whose mind was not wholly free to control and order the experiences offered him, but who was doing a pretty good job of trying to control them in spite of his own preoccupations. The poet's unspoken awareness of the nation's crisis comes through the way he sees and makes us see the events in this perfect microcosm: if Fairfax's Nunappleton was a retreat from the war, the poet's Nunappleton was not, as the images of warfare and destruction penetrate his appreciation of private peace.

6

"MORE DECENT ORDER TAME"

WHEN Maria transfixes the natural scene into its still-life, the irregular flux of this long poem is for a time checked: in the poetic language, the flowing river, the actual *fluvius*, is hardened to glass, the creatures in and around it arrested to a perfect stillness. Against the background of metamorphosis and anamorphosis, this moment forces attention, as the poet also redresses himself, puts away his "Toyes" in obedience to his strict pupil's appropriate decorum. From that moment to the end of the poem, the poet addresses himself to a proper chronicle and moralization of what is and should be in the world of Nunappleton. All the same, one cannot say that the poem therewith settles into the river's crystalline clarity, even though it is so unequivocally proclaimed that Mary Fairfax is the most perfect of girls and the estate the most perfect of estates:

> . . . as all *Virgins* She preceds,
> So you all *Woods, Streams, Gardens, Meads.*

But just at the point when the poet announces the wonders of Nunappleton, he does so in a stanza of which, as Mr. Berger has pointed out, the syntax suggests several different interpretations:

> 'Tis not, what once it was, the *World*;
> But a rude heap together hurl'd;
> All negligently overthrown,
> Gulfes, Deserts, Precipices, Stone.
> Your lesser *World* contains the same.
> But in more decent Order tame;
> *You Heaven's Center, Nature's Lap.*
> *And Paradice's only Map.*   (stanza 86)

The world is not what it once was, that is, a mass of chaotic material, later organized into pattern; or, the world is not what it once was, that is, a paradise, but has degenerated into a chaotic mixture of elements. In either case, though, it is clear that Appleton House is, or has preserved, the model for created perfection. It is an epitome of good, and Mary Fairfax is the epitome of it. She is entirely "decent," thoroughly "ordered," herself an ordering principle within her small and beautiful world.

The relations of order and disorder in the poem are very important: Kitty Scoular's study tackles the problem very well, laying out the problems involved in cramping *multum in parvo.* The final chapter of her study deals with this poem, concluding that its disparate, jostling elements are successfully "tamed" into order, that the poem is an aesthetic success. Excellent though her study is, it does not altogether settle one's vexations and tensions about this poem's structure and organization; no matter how often one reads it, this poem seems unbalanced, awkward, disparate, and disproportionate in many of its parts. There is no getting away from its disorders: nor, one may assume, from the ubiquity and obviousness of disorder in the poem, are we supposed to argue it away or turn the poem into a solidly composed and conventionally constructed literary work. And yet a poem about a new-built house, about a well ordered estate, a poem which insists so extravagantly upon the values of order, cannot be supposed to have jettisoned all structural principles only to show how chaotically a man could write about subjects traditionally handled with an eye to architectonics.

The poem has its solid framework, obviously, parts of which show plainly enough through the dressings at the surface: the "estate" is geographically divided, to show its various parts properly, house, ruins, gardens, meadows, wood, and stream, each section properly landscaped, properly peopled, properly functional, properly in style. Save for the ruins passage, "To Penshurst" shows the same topical structure: what is clearly *not* the same is the relative weights assigned to the different parts of "Upon Appleton House," the kaleidoscopic events of almost every section of the estate, and the peculiar metamorphic, abrupt relations of one part to another. A genuine difficulty in the poem is the ruins section, dramatized in the long historical nunnery episode, stanzas 12 to 35, an incident interesting in itself but weighing heavily on the poem. It is easy to read "Upon Appleton House" without that episode, and easy to read the episode alone, but its peculiar mode and style seem more out of line with the other parts than they are with each other.

Thematically, however, the section is both important and integrated with the rest of the poem. It is in this episode that the morality of the retired and active life is most clearly argued out, even to debate and drama. Here, the cheating presumptuousness criticized in the architecture section is given actuality and drama, as the nun describes the life she leads and advocates. The poem is in many ways a religious poem throughout, in its references and the underlying values it expresses; this section is the only one overtly cast in religious terms, however upside down, the only one tackling the emotional problems involved in defining a truly religious life. The mock battle of moralities and religious styles in this section points to the difficulties in living religiously in an age in which authority carries no special sanction and responsibility is squarely laid upon each man, woman, and child—upon general, poet, and girl ungrown.

The theme of individual choice is of course a cliché of western morality and its literature; Marvell does not handle it in the terms most freely given him of the stoic or *beatus ille* traditions, although there are certainly traces of both in the poem. His presentation of experience in this poem's world, so jumbled and confusing from point to point, is not one in which choices are made obvious—the possibilities of life are presented out of expectation and category, out of the norm and out of true; from the *trompe l'oeil* of this poem's day, we are somehow to see how to pluck days; yet nowhere in the poem are we given specific directions for that task. In this respect "The Garden" teaches a far more explicit lesson than this poem ever does.

Among the ways in which the poet keeps us off balance is his treatment of himself, now as presenter, now as actor, now as spectator; and his treatment of us, his audience, his readers. We are forced to see things his way; we accept his visions distant and close, clear and blurred, exact and astigmatic. We have a sense of his private associations therefore, under, over, and around what he actually allows us to see; the sense, then, of entering the structure, however unstructured, of this poet's mind. We are let in so intimately on the private workings of his sensibility that he seems to recognize no intrusion on our parts, to feel no need to explain to strangers what he has no need to explain to himself.

Some of the exclusive, obscurantist intimacy critics have felt in the poem, attributing it to a world of private references shared by the Nunappleton inhabitants, is the result of this trick played on the audience, made to overhear the poet's uncensored, unordered reveries and reactions, to come "in" to his interior world.[1] That world is Chinese-boxed, of course: we are in England, a war-torn container for a properly organized Appleton; within Appleton, we are within the idiosyncratic, fantastic mind of a poet, whose person perambulates the estate and whose mind races across history from the chaos to the Apocalypse, across space from the tiniest point to the constellations and the crystalline sphere.

The poet scans surfaces intently and penetrates essences with equal ease, and as he does so, "we" are well and truly manipulated, at the beginning enjoined conventionally, given the ground rules for our expectations, set on our meditations: "Within this sober Frame expect. . . ." That these ground rules do not hold is part of the poet's sleight-of-hand, but it takes a while to realize that among the elements the poet manipulates is precisely his readers' expectations. At first, reader and poem seem identified: together, "we" accept the dimensions of a sober frame; "we" survey "these," the "fragrant Gardens, shaddy Woods,/ Deep Meadows, and transparent Floods" of the estate. In the romance episode of the nunnery, "we" are abandoned as the poet concentrates on the unfolding narrative; the ancient incident is imagined with utmost immediacy, its dialogue and exciting battle action, so fanciful and stilted, given great intensity. In the gardens, the poet is once more the presenter, pointing out the patron and the members of the patron's family walking across the scene in the strange, disciplined little garden; in stanzas 41-43 he moralizes upon the state of England, and of the estate, and on Fairfax's place in both.

In these stanzas, "we" are again involved, with the poet drawn into one overriding concern for England's real plight. With the mowing scene, the poet begins to speak in the first person—"And now to the *Abbyss* I pass"—an introduction filled with ominousness, as by entering the meadows he seems to go straight into the war. Oddly enough, it is in this pastoral section that the vocabulary of violence is most extreme; with no overt reference to the war, we are nonetheless forced to consider it most deeply. The poet joins the mowers in this section, with them insolently towered over by grasshoppers. In the next stanza, "we wonder," "we" see the flowers brought up from the meadow-floor; but "we" disappear from the rail scene, from the mowing, the dancing, and the haycocks, these presented impersonally with no reference to anything but

[1] Berger, "Marvell's 'Upon Appleton House.'"

themselves and their thick metaphorical associations, in a series of self-significant vignettes. But "we" return to consider the mowing accomplished, joining the poet in boats on the river; we see from a great distance the cattle slowly grazing across the nipped surface of the water-meadows. As the flood rises to force the poet into his wood-sanctuary, he refuses to treat that event passionately, but passes it off with a shrug— "Let others tell" the paradoxes of the deluge.

In the wood, "we" are left ignored once more; the poet is at once himself and another, but concerned entirely with these. "I . . . / Take Sanctuary," he writes, normally enough; but the reflexive "I . . . my self imbark" in the trees shows his "other" self. He leaves himself out of the stanza celebrating the oaks of Fairfax and Vere; in stanza 63 he does not refer to himself but to "the Eye," a neutral, single organ concentrating entirely on its single function, to look, to perceive, to see, to define. In the passages following, most of the incidents are presented in and for themselves, as if the eye were automatically performing its function, undirected by a whole personality; the "other I,"[2] the first person, does return from time to time with its own life, preferring the stock-doves' music to that of the nightingale, catching the thrush's eye in the leaves, noting the heron's behavior. With great exactness, the poet notes the woodpecker's actions, in terms of carpentry; the woodpecker is an architect and a Noah, measuring "the Timber" as Noah had done, numbering "the good" trees and marking them, choosing the hollow oak, "That for his building he designs," the last word a lovely pun which sends us back to the strange design in the poem's first stanza. After these emblems have been recorded, with such total clarity and objectivity that their extended meaning is implied in the very exactness of their description, the poet alters his tone and in his own person begins to indulge himself, letting himself go even out of his own control, into that of nature. Interpretation, even of the truncated sort offered in the bird scenes, is altogether abandoned. In the mosaic and the Mosaic light of his wood, he can read all history at once, sacred and profane; he can rest on his swelling moss and forget even to think. If he likes, he can amuse himself by "gauling" the world from his tree-house, his place of refuge, retirement, rest, recreation, and creation. He is free, in his protective wood, to talk to plants and birds—"Bind me, ye *Woodbines*";

---

[2] See Joan Webber, *The Eloquent "I"* (Madison, 1968).

"Here in the morning tye my Chain." He is free even to lose control of his own actions until we find him, he finds himself, slowly melting away into the river.

There, too, the scene is presented immediately—"now"—he sees anew the river's loveliness, a Nile quite free of noxious beasts. There he languishes, fishing halfheartedly as one does when one is too happy or too fulfilled to work at it. To fish seriously is to compete with nature, not to be as the poet is, entirely at one with her.[3] In the stream episode, too, there are two selves in the figure, the languid fisherman and the poet noting him, commenting on his pleasure in the libertine formula: "Oh what a Pleasure 'tis. . . ." Undone with the rest of nature, he too "starts" when "young *Maria* walks tonight"; he too must put away his toys and behave as a responsible man or tutor ought to. Inversion again: the tutor puts away childish things when his pupil surprises him, not the other way around. The poet then watches the girl as from a distance, reading from her actions how interpretations should be made. She simply "comes," and he watches her miracles: the vocabulary hints at apocalypse—"flames," "vitrify'd"—but in contrast to the apocalyptic hints of the mowing stanzas, this eschatology is entirely calm. The world turns to crystal, becomes clear, pure, transparent, translucent, without the dust-up and untidiness of the scarifying final fire.[4] Things take their places within the moral hierarchy of poem and estate:

> 'Tis *She* that to these Gardens gave
> That wondrous Beauty which they have;
> *She* streightness on the Woods bestows;
> To *Her* the Meadow sweetness owes;
> Nothing could make the River be
> So Chrystal-Pure but only *She*;
> *She* yet more Pure, Sweet, Streight, and Fair,
> Then Gardens, Woods, Meads, Rivers are.   (stanza 87)

Maria becomes the central figure, a tiny hieratic figure acting magnetically on the scene. We see her ceremonially acting in relation to her

---

[3] In general, in lyric poetry fishing involves deceit: a standard sample of the attitude is Donne's "The Baite."

[4] Browne, *Religio Medici* (*Works*, p. 48): "Philosophers that opinioned the world's destruction by fire, did never dreame of annihilation, which is beyond the power of sublunary causes, for the last and proper action of that element is but vitrification or a reduction of "a body into Glasse. . . ."

world, the estate taking from her and giving back to her again. The meadow is her carpet, the gardens provide her virgin-wreath, the brook is her looking-glass, the wood her screen. Appleton is her house, inside and out; all nature is domesticated into her dwelling-place, and the river is both her mirror and her fish-pool. The *"She"* of stanzas 87, 88, 89, 93 and 94 is considerably more than mere girl, as she fulfils her ancestry in the poem. The nuns had promised Isabella, falsely, that she should work miracles; Maria does so in fact. She is wiser than her tutor, knowing more languages than he; she steadies the balance of the shifting world in which he has treated himself as an unstable element. Order is precisely epitomized in the girl, whom "we" see exposed as on a morality stage, untouchable, going through the ritual of her function not as a part of the sociable world but as a model for proper behavior displayed to educate us.

From the objectification of the girl into a principle, the poet returns to the estate, addressing the streams, gardens, woods, and meads he has so scrupulously surveyed for himself, for his patron, and for us. Each of these elements at Appleton moves to the head of its category: "That, as all *Virgins* She preceds,/ So you all *Woods, Streams, Gardens, Meads.*" Aranjuez and Buen Retiro, Tempe, the Grove of Ida, Elysium itself are all inferior to this perfect place.

Just at the poem's end, in the last two stanzas, the ordered, stable tableau is blurred by the ambiguous syntax of stanza 96, and by the enigmatic fishermen of stanza 97: after the crystalline vision, we come upon "the *Eben Shuts*" of night. The juxtapositions are once more radical, perfect order next to chaos, clarity next to hooded dark. At the very end, then, as at the beginning, we are faced with enigma; the poem is framed with questions; the questions are left hanging. That such enigmatic treatment relates to the underlying theme—the problematical nature of moral choice and of epistemological certainty—by no means solves the structural problems of this poem, however. It is not enough to rely upon a notion of imitative form, of a neat parallelism between content and its vessel, to award this poem some claim upon structural virtue. That explanation of imitative form may have some application, but as a notion it is after all only self-confirming; in this case, clearly, sense and language, theme and figure do not always "imitate" each other but as often, if not more, pull against each other.

All the same, there are connections to be made in this work, through the pattern of images and figures of speech, which in turn direct us to the thematic unity of the poem's preoccupation. *Pre*-occupation is the word: this poem seems highly schemed, the patterns of its surface carefully designed and carried through. Some themes are very obvious. The poem is called "Upon Appleton House": "housing" is an obvious example of theme, handled in figures large and small, beginning with the birds-nests and tortoiseshells of the second stanza, picked up again in the hemispheres in the last. The tortoise stands for self-sufficiency and intelligence about retirement and emergence; in the poem, by a chain-stitched connection of images, he is related to bees and to Romulus himself. When the tortoise crawls across the scene in the last stanza, we meet him in his self-sufficiency and also as an amphibian actualizing at last the meaning of the amphibious images in the poem. Even the rail, according to Pliny, is amphibious, as is the crocodile: the tortoise provides a benevolent substitute for the usual deceits of the smiling crocodile. Both rail and crocodile are unsuccessful in the poem, the rail killed in one environment when he ought to have taken refuge in another, the crocodile denied a place in the reconstituted Eden of the estate. Other amphibious creatures are benevolent, like the tortoise; chiefly, the halcyon, between day and night. The principal environment for an amphibian is presented by the flood-meadow, the sea-land, requiring flexibility of its habitants, lest they be killed like the rail, limited to land, or the Memphian cavalry inundated by the Red Sea.

The tortoiseshell is like the cupola of Appleton House, the miraculous sphere grown from a cube; it is also like the boats of Antipodeans, which, if they are made of tortoiseshells, also form Antipodeans' lodgings. Its shell is then the tortoise's occupation, the place he occupies and the function he fulfils. And, as *"Antipodes"* reminds us, since this subject is always linked to the hemispheres in the cosmographies, those half-domes covered the world, one dome the day, the other the night. There is an amphibiousness of time as of place, and of occupation as well: Fairfax is a warrior in the field and, by conciliar responsibilities for the Cinque Ports, a commander of the sea; the sea in turn is epitomized in his half-dry trenches at Appleton. Further, his participation in the governing of the Cinque Ports is made to overlap with his government of his own senses, those five ports of knowledge for every man.[5] Man is amphibious

---

[5] Cf. Sir Thomas Browne, *The Garden of Cyrus, Works,* p. 174.

simply by his condition, whether he likes it or not. He lives in divided and distinguished worlds by necessity; as a rational amphibian, his occupation is to distinguish them from one another. The geometrical, natural, and economic imagery all fuse in the cluster of the last stanza, to gather the threads lying loosely across the poem into a net holding it all tightly together. In the domestic scene all space is enclosed, as the "dark *Hemisphere*" hoods the house; the fishermen are all men and any man, Antipodeans by turns going in when the dark comes upon them.

Again and again, the themes and images repeat, with variations: the judicial, warlike Fairfaxes fuse into the figure of the poet's patron; Isabella Thwaites and Mary of Nazareth, two virgins curiously compared and opposed in the nunnery episode, manage to fuse in Mary Fairfax. Fairfax is patriarchal, and builds a house of God in Yorkshire; the poet is Noah and Solomon in Fairfax's wood. In that wood, a "lane" offers a strait way through it; a "lane" had opened for the mowers in the meadow, as for the Israelites in Exodus, as the poet in his daring makes the green one red. The arching brows and tall columns of stanza 1 are recapitulated and reformed in the arching boughs and natural Corinthian columns of the wood. The marriages of Isabella and William Fairfax, of Anne Vere and Thomas Fairfax, and the symmetrical marriage-in-prospect for the heiress are all gathered into the family trees of that wood, emblems of continuity and strength.

Appleton House was properly low-built, as opposed to the "ambitious" seat of the Archbishop of York, Cawood Castle, across the river. Opposed to that proud prelate's office is the poet's function as a natural priest, "coped" in a weave of real plants. The false security of the cloister, too, is contrasted in one way with the solid virtues of new-built Appleton and in another with the protections offered by the wood.

As housing, so is habitat important in the poem—each person, each creature, establishes some relation with his place: "No Creature loves an empty space;/ Their Bodies measure out their Place." Fairfax makes his house, walks in his garden; Maria turns the estate into her apartment; the poet fits into the wood; the nuns live in what became a ruin; the birds are in their nests. The poem concerns a nestling, Maria; from the counter example of the rail, we know that danger can come even to nestlings. On the whole, though, "nesting" is a favored natural activity in the poem's universe. The bee builds his cells; he nestles in the flowers at night; thrush, nightingale, heron, and hewel all care for their young.

The rail's parents are "orphaned" by the loss of their chick; the heron surrenders its baby to the Lord. Maria's parents lose her with pride, making "Destiny their Choice" as she goes into marriage and her own *oikos*.

Though lowness is generally good and height generally bad in this poem, the rail's low nest is proof of uncertainty within that rule, and the birds otherwise nest high and safely. Lowness and height are everlastingly played against each other in the poem, not always consistently. Little Appleton House is far better, morally and aesthetically, than either Cawood or Spanish pleasure-palaces; tortoise, rail, and crocodile all keep low, but are variously admired for that. The nun urges Isabella to "aspire" too high, which is bad; Fairfax "rises" through the wall, which is good. The rail does the proper thing and suffers nonetheless; the grasshoppers lord it over men but do not visibly come to grief therefore. When fish "scale" the stables, they turn out not to be so out of place as at first we think; trees properly "shoot" to heaven, grow as tall as they can. Not all ascents, then, are clownish, nor are descents fatally bad. A little bird brings down a huge tree, but his reasons for such odd behavior are good ones. Music, both high and low, is fitted into the lowness-height pattern, too. Isabella's singing is to draw heaven down to earth; the nightingale sits low, but "adorns/ With Musick high the squatted Thorns," and the oaks stoop to hear her, as the undergrowth of elders "prick the Ear."

The language theme recurs, beginning with the military "Word" for which the bee does not wait, running through the poet's gift of tongues in the wood, culminating in Maria's familiarity with all languages, subsumed under *"Heaven's Dialect."* The knowledge of languages helps to establish the difference between creatures that are amphibious and "rational *Amphibii*": men must know how to live in different habitats, must speak different languages to accommodate themselves to experience. Also connected to this notion of amphibiousness is the synesthesia, noted by Kitty Scoular and others,[6] of some of the images, particularly in stanzas 39 and 64; this kind of image affords a linguistic parallel to the constant metamorphoses and anamorphoses of the poem.

Puns are another example of such categorical mix; in this poem, there are several sorts of play on words. Sometimes, as in the fettered/feet play of "A Dialogue between the Soul and Body," a word is used metaphorically to point to its primary meaning, as in the line "The *Nuns* smooth Tongue has suckt her in"; sometimes a second idiomatic meaning is

---

[6] Scoular, pp. 163ff.

quietly exploited beneath the first and most obvious one, as in the reference to parturition in the line "For *Virgin Buildings* oft brought forth." Sometimes a single word is used, in which many relevant meanings are gathered up, as in the simple line "That live without this happy View": the word "without" suddenly makes the rather uninteresting line come into sharp life. The word "Traverse" in stanza 53 fuses two senses, the mower's path across the field he cuts, and the Israelites' crossing the Red Sea. The "Elders" pricking their ears are both the bushes and the child-bird's parents. This kind of playing on words is unostentatious, especially as compared with some of Marvell's virtuoso performances in other poems. Much of the double meaning is latent, emerging only after a reader is quite familiar with the themes and the image-pattern of the poem. The punning, like everything else in the poem, however, helps a reader to realize the tremendous strategy that went into this apparently haphazard piece of work. To keep a poem going with all the imbalances of this one, is in itself a considerable intellectual achievement.

The shifting of category which so marks this poem, where microscopic and telescopic vision are invoked in one image; where an insect is now taller than a man, a tree now brought low by a small bird's beak; where images of worlds upside down and men upside down abound; where a rail comes into focus as imposingly as a whole house does; where the commentator in the poem is elbowed out of his directorial role by one of the characters in the poem and is made to play a character part—all this is the work of a considerable planner, too: as we work through these images, we see that almost nothing happens twice the same way.

The flood brings a dominant metaphor forward into reality; entanglement with briars is turned into a mock crucifixion. The poet scouted his various alternatives to try as many as possible, to exercise himself and us in the *sylvae* of miscellaneous figures, shifting from one poetical technique to another even as focusses and categories shift in the poem. Not only does he present an unstable world, but he presents many points of view upon it as well: he is aware of the personal interpretation of each different person's view of the same world. The garden at Nunappleton, therefore, seems to turn inside out, first training its artillery on its owners, then on a neighboring estate; the cloister at once barred men out and women in; the wood was a shelter from the dangerous world, but opened inward upon a rampant imagination playing over universal history. Things are not what they seem; what they are is unpredictable.

As time and space, times and spaces interpenetrate, so do inwardness and outwardness, withdrawal and emergence. Amphibiousness is the rule: the more "rational" a man can be about his divided and distinguished worlds, the better he can hope to deal with them. Maria is prepared "within" her georgic environment, within the house, within her own mind, but prepared for coming out in order to prolong her family in that biological eternizing that oaks symbolize in the poem. Her parents can rejoice in her going out, in their own expectations of more buds from their "sprig." Since she has been so thoroughly trained in the Nunappleton world, "within," she must take with her wherever she goes "without" the inwardness that is her heritage. In several senses, the girl is the proper heiress of Appleton.

For Maria, destiny and choice appear to be yoked together; for her father, as the poet presents him, they finally come to seem as thoroughly yoked. For the poet, however, we may assume that life was not so simple. His vision was always dual, so that he could see the problems in Fairfax's choosing which, in the poem, he spares Fairfax himself. To the poet, the tortoise's life seemed simpler than that of "rational *Amphibii*," who, if the poet is an example of the species, consistently remembered the war-world even as they celebrate the peace-world. There are degrees and styles of emergence and of inwardness: to cope with the flood, the poet had to retreat into the wood of experience, and in that wood, deeper into himself. The poet in his own psychological and professional terms, "retires" as Fairfax had done for his reasons—and, like Fairfax, is the better for that withdrawal. Even in his idyll by the stream, things tended to fall apart for him, delightful though that relaxation of tension was, until the tidy heiress came to set them straight. Crystal gives way to night: from the beautiful, exciting, varied world "without," in which the poet had spent his long day's living, he must retire "within" before what he cannot control. The hint of chaos in the penultimate stanza picks up the earlier hint in the first, to remind us of mysteries before and after time; the poem itself demonstrates the mysteries of daily experience in the illusions of the perceptual world.

The poet's response to this world and these experiences is to experiment with his own relation to them. Thestylis' behavior shows him failing in his own efforts at controlling experience. Maria shows him the limitations even of total naturalistic absorption. Art alone is not enough; nature alone is not enough. The poet searches for himself and finds rapture in the wood, when paradoxically he experiences simultaneous ecstasy and total understanding: all nature serves his particular psychic needs. That wood-madness was simply poetic fury, which like any other rapture cannot stay. The poet has to ask for imprisonment to enjoy this liberation, a request which marks his awareness that such freedom is only conditional. Imagination can reshape the world for a time, but there is a dark hemisphere for every dome of light: fantasy can rule at best only by turns with reality.

But since the poem's dark hemisphere is the night, we know that it must pass, that there will once more be a time for going out into the delightful world of the estate, into the less delightful world beyond the estate. One condition gives upon another: night and day, dark and light, world and estate are all mixed conditions; in the poem, experience is always qualified, ambiguous, illusory, defiant of interpretation, resistant to classification. Insofar as possible, the "Discipline severe" must instruct that there is no fixed protection either without or within, that within may at any moment be turned inside out to become without. "In" and "out" depend upon perspective, after all, by a perspective of illusion designed to fit our experience and to save the phenomena.

7

SYLVAE, OR A MISCELLANY OF
MODES AND KINDS

O N THE largest scale of literary elements, "Upon Appleton House" manages to express its author's attitude to the world by still another means, the peculiar manipulation of languages, subjects, and themes associated with different literary genres. We have become accustomed to the notion that as soon as Renaissance authors learned to observe the strict definition of literary kinds, they immediately began to trespass across the generic boundaries; in seventeenth-century English literature, for instance, we find *genera mixta* self-consciously and self-confidently displayed in some of the very greatest works of the period. By strict standards, very few authors adhered for long to generic rules: Jonson maintained a relatively schoolmasterish allegiance to the kinds, but his disciple Herrick, for instance, cheerfully reduced the Ovidian metamorphosis to epigrammatic size. There are many different ways of working across generic boundaries, which the happiest ignoramus may do as freely as the learned man: some works, which seem to us now more self-consciously involved in problems of genre than others, are interesting to analyze. For all its sub-genres, passages in various styles, sometimes as much as a book long, *Paradise Lost* is unmistakably an epic, and an epic in the official mode; though astonishingly flexible, its style is fundamentally "grand." Donne's *Anniversary Poems*, though, are more difficult to classify: to call them "anniversaries," which they certainly are, is to beg the question; as we understand the duties of that sort of poem, Donne's pair of poems bursts the limits Scaliger sets for the anniversary form. We can call the first poem an "anatomy," as its author did, assuming with Northrop Frye that many different elements are thus obliged to be displayed; but the term does not help us notably with the second poem, called a "progress" although constructed on much the same generous lines as its predecessor. Burton's *Anatomy of Melancholy* displays its intent, literary as well as medical, in its title: we are not surprised to find many different kinds and styles occurring across the book's great length. What is often more difficult is to determine where one sample leaves off and another begins: occasionally, the author makes his divisions quite plain, but at other times, the kinds flow into each other, or are cushioned from one another by passages so indefinite that we distrust our efforts to mark the edge of any specific generic exercise.

In "The Garden," Marvell exercised himself in the genres of literature, I should say, really, in the *idea* of literary genre, constructing an anthology of his own preference, himself planting a garden of the flowers of rhetoric whose distinctions he so remarkably understood. Throughout the poem, his extraordinarily compressed references seem to maintain generic autonomy, even though the poem itself opts for no single rhetoric, no single generic point of view. Genre implies a given "fix" on the world, as perspective in drawing an organization of materials according to specific conventions which, for literary purposes, reader and writer contract to accept for the duration of the work.

In "Upon Appleton House," however, it is just this set which the poet questions. Because his subject involves "exercising" and "choosing," his choice of literary styles is importantly involved in his dramatization of the problem of life choice. In the poem, the poet is both apprentice poet (as he had presented himself in "An Horatian Ode") and apprentice adult, finding his range, making his tentatives towards choice. To match this theme, literary modes, literary conventions are taken to be deeply involved in moral styles, modes, and conventions, so that the poet experimenting with them can at the same time test out the limits of the life-styles they represent, can try himself as poet and as critic, of life as of literature. In this poem, there is not the same sense of literary sufficiency, or totality, as a reader feels in "The Garden," which appears a far more controlled, even pointed, poem, a tighter exercise in every way. There, the kinds are kept radically separate from one another, whereas in "Upon Appleton House" they are jumbled in many ways, sometimes juxtaposed hard-edge, again so fused and intertwined that separation seems impossible. "Nobis placeant ante omnia sylvae": itself also an anthology, a *sylva*, or miscellany of forms, "Upon Appleton House" manages to anatomize literature as it anatomizes the estate; the major generic sub-divisions match the landscapes they represent, with many echoes, hints, and undersongs, more or less audible, many counter-themes playing against, beneath, and for the major themes of the poem. By the generic shifts, as by so many other kinds of shift, the reader is kept off balance through the poem—but from those shifts, too, he can take readings of the poem, can "sound" it, can find some measurements for the Nunappleton universe. The poet perambulating the estate is its surveyor, and meanwhile, also a surveyor of the forest of forms.

> Within this sober Frame expect
> Work of no Forrain *Architect*;

the poem begins, proudly proclaiming its Englishness. In spite of the nationalistic disclaimer, there is much that is very "foreign" about the design and materials of this poem, related as it is to a host of poems and poetic traditions from antiquity to Marvell's own time, whose motifs were freely adapted by the poet to suit his idea of the Yorkshire landscape.

Though it seems hardly necessary to point out that "Upon Appleton House" fulfils one major criterion of Renaissance literary excellence in its determined but lighthanded uniting of classical with Christian elements, still a short digression on Marvell as *pontifex* between these two traditions may not be entirely amiss. Primarily, the sources approving a busy, cultivated, constructive private life lie in classical literature, in Horace's wonderful celebrations of his sufficient Sabine life and in Virgil's exhortation to responsible farming. From Virgil also come many of Marvell's delicate, attenuated, half-joking references to the heroic life, to Evander's house, to the small model of Troy, and so on, as well of course as the poetical laments and praises of pastoral life. Thestylis is a standard pastoral name, in Virgil the reapers' cook (*Ec.* II, 10-11), though, as Mr. Allen points out, the girl in this poem is more like Bellona than like a gentle shepherdess.[1] Roman soldiers' obsequies occur in the poem; Alexander appears for a moment. The flood makes its references to Latin literature as well as to scriptural source; the poet learns in the wood all there is to know of ancient history, sacred and profane. Narcissus appears in a simile, to comment in a minor key on the self-absorption and self-delight which form one theme of the poem. The halcyon flies out of Ovid, to emerge in other environments and to merge with them; Romulus and Aeneas are invoked, both the founders of a state; the nostalgia for peace in the poem owes something to the idea of *pax Romana*, the absence of an English equivalent to which causes so much grief in the poem and out of it.

[1] Allen, pp. 136-37.

As for Christian elements, these are everywhere in the poem: the constant reference to Christian virtues, charity, humility, conscience, the last a prickly plant which, growing within a man, produces its sharp *ayenbite*. The Crucifixion is hinted at, though in an entirely lighthearted mood and environment; the lamenting doves owe as much to the standard image for the Christian soul as they do to Virgil's first Eclogue. Again and again, as in biblical pictures of the Renaissance, scriptural scenes are set in landscapes the painter knows: at Nunappleton, the Israelites leave Egypt and gather their providential food in the desert. The Flood, Solomon, are all set somewhere in the familiar local scenery.

Simultaneously, the poem invokes a peculiarly patriotic past, an England regarded as long free from the taint of the first sin; the druids, the oaks, the mistletoe, call up a local sanctity unforgotten. References to Fairfax's achievements and to prophecies of his family's further heroics project that national pride into the future. In the awful reference to the war, the Cadmus myth is brought up to date. The georgic reversal of the line "We Ord'nance Plant and Powder sow," implies the terrible self-perpetuation of these wars, involving the death of many soldiers and many "rails," innocent bystanders trying to keep free of the battle itself. The term "holt-felster" has been mentioned, with its possible compliment to the political theory revivifying a Saxon past from which England's true freedoms derive; the reference to "Levellers" brings the political problems up to the minute. Classical and biblical traditions meet in Marvell's contemporary world, accommodated and composed within Fairfax's microcosmic polity and within the poet's domain as well.

Chiefly, as Mr. Allen has taught us, the poem is a praise of a patron and his "house," the edifice in which he lives, the family of which he is representative. In English, there were several major examples in the genre.[2] As an estate-poem, or great-house poem, "Upon Appleton House" is necessarily also a topographical poem, demonstrating the excellence of a given spot. The "places" of the estate tend to fall into particular sections which are, as it happens, generic locales as well: gardens, meadows, woods, stream are all necessary to a well-managed estate and part of its self-sufficient economy. The genres provided Marvell with language: so we find in this single poem traces of pastoral, piscatory, and mowing eclogues,

---

[2] See Hibbard, *op.cit.*; the doctoral dissertation (Gainesville, 1967) by C. E. Ramsey, which he was kind enough to let me read; and O'Loughlan, "The Garlands of Repose."

as well as georgics and *sylvae*. Since it is a poem in praise of a family, this one has its genealogical episode, as well as an adumbrated prothalamion and a near-epithalamion: by these means, harking back and looking forward in a family's history, the poet manages to deal in the past, present, and future, by purely literary devices. A poem in praise of a patron, this one celebrates a general, though hardly in a conventional military way, since the poet's most unqualified language is reserved to praise the general's child.

The poet makes a place for himself in the poem, as country-house poets (especially Jonson, in English) often did: his place, however, is a very odd one, in a different decorum from the poetry of praise, either of a public figure or of a promising child. The lyric self-indulgence of the wildwood of the imagination comes more from the so-called libertine tradition of solitude-poetry, continental and English—although, when one examines the work of Saint-Amant and Théophile, of Stanley, Lovelace, Herrick, and the translations of Katherine Philips, Marvell's astonishing simplifications seem obvious at once. Other lyric themes, especially the pastoral, are quoted, criticized, and mocked in this poem. The genealogical episode is an epyllion, a mock saint's life, a passage from a romantic or mock-romantic epic; through the whole poem, now seriously, now mockingly, epic references recur, to convince at least one student of the poem that the whole poem is to be understood within the epic genre.[3]

Dominantly, though, the poem is one of the retired and active life, to that extent both polemical and dialectical, though the life surveyed is so equivocally presented that neither polemic nor dialectic emerges clearly. It certainly presents the contrary moods of *l'allegro* and *il penseroso*,[4] figures of both types presented in enigmatic landscapes decorated with natural elements pointing to emblematic interpretation. The happy life is by no means so clearly separated from the thoughtful one as in Milton's paradigm it may seem to be; just as epic language interpenetrates pastoral, so moods of contemplation overlap and intrude upon those of activity and involvement. The imagery touches on history from the hexaemeron to the apocalypse, lightly brushes in a theodicy, hinting at the origins of evil, disposing of the snake in his natural paradise regained after the local flood has receded. The poem openly praises simplicity while indulging in prodigal fantasies; it is full of masque scenes, monologues, and

---

[3] Wallace, *Destiny his Choice.*
[4] See Richmond, " 'Rural Lyricism'," pp. 203-6.

emblematic insets, the last never wholly interpreted, although their general lessons are made clear. It has its still life pictures and its *memento mori*, themes closely related in visual tradition; again and again, it brings its meanings to a point in a moral epigram. As is customary in emblem and epigram, where compression is the rule, the poem remarkably manages to contain great things in small; but it is worth noting in this poem that small things are also vastly enlarged, often to the point where that enlargement seems mockery or even burlesque. The nunnery scene, where the argument over an heiress' person suddenly swells into a full-fledged battle, is a case in point, though the inflation is as sharply punctured when the actual battle is presented as taking place. Throughout the poem there are metamorphoses, brief, sleight-of-hand, impermanent, but always somehow moral. Like Herrick, from whom he may indeed have learned the trick, Marvell could compress Ovidian accomplishments into very small space.

By the very mixture of genre and voice, language and tone, simple categories are always questioned, positions undercut. In the very first stanza, the plainness of the native writing-style is contorted in just the conceited "foreign" way that the doctrine there decries. In the nunnery episode, the falsity of the spokeswoman nun is reflected as much in her syntactical and argumentative styles as in the luxurious conventual life she describes, where the nuns' only self-denial was rejection of sexual love. The embattled garden seems to change its normal ecology because of a single, small literary insect, the bee: he is set in a landscape entirely militarized, of flowers which salute their master and mistress, keep military hours, and generally guard the house and its inhabitants. The mowing bucolic is interrupted by the rail's death and Thestylis' general bloody-mindedness; the sweet pastoral dance of the dutiful mowers, triumphant lovers after their toil, is set between two stanzas on death, the rail's and Roman soldiers'. Boundaries shift constantly.

From the chaos to the creation to the Apocalypse, history is enclosed in Fairfacian frames: typology helps to pleat times together and to draw connections between present, past, and future. In the poem, "history" is often typological, or unhistorical; it is temporal and contemporary as well. Appleton is "like" paradise, but it is also like the England of the Civil War. Though Exodus, the Flood, and the Crucifixion all have their dumb-show versions in the poem, these emblematic events make a comment on present affairs and point to future fulfilments.

Sylvae

What sort of poem can so jostle elements cheek by jowl? What is one to make of these genres and modes? How can their presence be understood in this poem? By looking at them, one by one, I should like to tackle these questions, and begin therefore with the major genre in which the poem is cast. Primarily, "Upon Appleton House" is a house-poem, an estate-poem, a family-poem. That Lord Fairfax wrote on his new-built house makes the poem at hand at once more private—we may expect more allusions to interests of the Earl and his family—and more public, since the poet could write of the house in terms far grander than those its builder could use with decorum. Martial's praise of Faustinus' bountiful sufficiency (*Epigrams*, II, 58) set the thematic decorum for the type; his contemporary Statius' house-poems, on the villas of Manilius Vopiscus (*Sylvae*, I, 3) and Pollius Felix (II, 2) confirm the complimentary style. Martial's poems stress the activities of a house's economy, Statius' stress the structure and decoration of the building itself. Both styles involve the poet in conscious perambulation, which forces him to pay attention to the literary order of his discussion. In I, 3, Statius writes,

> quae rerum turba! Iocine
> ingenium an domini mirer prius? haec domus ortus
> aspicit et Phoebi tenerum iubar. . . .   (ll. 44-46)

In Sidonius' "Burgus Ponti Leontii" (*Carmina*, XXII), written in the fourth century A.D., a myth of past worship is told to explain the particular qualities of the site under discussion as in both the ruins episode and the wood episode the poet cites the past to understand the present. Topical variety is inevitable in such poems, cataloguing as they do the delights of an estate as lovingly and carefully as other poets catalogue the delights of a lady's person. In Statius' epithalamion for Aruntius Stella and Violantilla (I, 2), a house-praise is included within the longer poem; in Martial's house-poem, a prophetic marriage song finds its appropriate place. Jonson's "To Penshurst" is rich, abundant, and not ostentatious. Like Appleton House, Penshurst is not an architectural showplace designed to aggrandize its builder:

> Thou art not, Penshurst, built to envious show,
>   Of touch, or marble; nor canst boast a row
> Of polish'd pillars, or a roofe of gold:
>   Thou hast no lantherne, whereof tales are told;

Or stayre, or courts; but standst an ancient pile,
  And these grudg'd at, art reverenc'd the while.[5]

Though both poems celebrate what is called a "great house," the houses in question are neat, tidy, sufficient edifices whose aesthetic economics have more to do with Horace's villa and farm than with Audley End, Hatfield, or Burleigh House. Just the same, both Penshurst and Appleton were clearly *loci amoeni*, naturally abundant (at Penshurst, the fish leap out of the water to be taken by hand; the fruit hang within reach of any child) and georgically provident as well. Penshurst was governed by the bounty of its generous master: house-poems of the masculine type fall into this category; the second Penshurst poem, by Waller, belongs to the feminine type. There, the poet's Sacharissa is the genius of the place, cultivating in it a beauty even greater than its original loveliness:

> Had *Sacharissa* liv'd when Mortals made
> Choice of their Deities, this Sacred shade
> Had held an Altar to her power, that gave
> The Peace and Glory that these allays have:
> Embroidred so with Flowers where she stood,
> That it became a Garden of a Wood:
> Her presence has such more than humane grace,
> That it can civilize the rudest place;
> And beauty, too, and order can impart,
> Where Nature ne'r intended it, nor Art.[6]

The feminine house-poem takes its major conceit from the pastoral compliment to a lady who is said to improve nature by her presence in it, a thematic commonplace (Cf. Virgil, *Ecl.* VII, 45-48) Leishman has called simply "pastoral hyperbole."[7] Cleveland's "Upon Phyllis Walking in a Morning," Robert Hookes' "To Amanda walking in a Garden," Lovelace's "Amarantha," and several other similar poems present the natural world sprucing itself up as "loose Nature" does when Maria walks in upon it at Appleton. Even this complimentary formula, though, is altered in Marvell's hands, for his lady is not a mistress but a pupil, a young girl

---

[5] Ben Jonson, *Works*, ed. Herford and Simpson, VIII, 93; cf. Carew, "To my friend G. N. from Wrest," *Poems*, ed. Dunlap, pp. 86-89.
[6] Edmund Waller, *Poems* (London, 1680), pp. 96-97.
[7] Leishman, p. 238 ff.

of whom he specifically states that she is still unready for conventional love-compliment.

In Lovelace's "Amarantha, a Pastoral," there is no precise locale; the poem takes place simply in "the" pastoral landscape. In the poem, though, there are motifs present also in many estate-poems, for the lady makes her promenade through garden, meadow (where she breakfasts directly from a "rev'rend lady cow"), and wood. Her perambulation is much like that of Marvell's poet, though less specific and emblematic than his: "Amarantha" simply exploits the sentimentality implicit in pastoral, as landscapes answer to the girl's mood and need. There are many other house-poems, lady-in-nature poems, and promenade-poems whose topics are much like those of "Upon Appleton House." The house-poems of Tristan l'Hermite and Théophile de Viau display many of the commonplaces of such poetry, Théophile's in particular sharing qualities with Marvell's poem.

Even from this cursory catalogue, it is clear that Marvell was remarkably eclectic in his poem, managing at once to praise the sterner bounties of a masculine patron, in properly Horatian style celebrating sufficiency, neatness, and discipline, and to have the advantages of a spontaneous nature of overflowing beauty and bounty. Neither aspect is unequivocal or exclusive: the greatest discipline is achieved in the garden, described in the language of flowers; the "Discipline severe" of her parents has developed a maiden pastorally hyperbolical. Maria is like Phyllis, Amarantha, and the rest in that her nature transcends its natural boundaries to transform nature itself—though in this poem, nature does that transforming by curbing itself to an ordered neatness in keeping with the fundamental moral aesthetics of the whole poem. As in the universe of a more primitive condition, at once the hard primitivism of "Romulus his Bee-like Cell" and the softer version of the wood's sympathetic magic, rigor and abundance intermix to modify and balance each other's potential excesses.

"Balance" is at issue in the house-poem generally, dedicated as it is to the praise of orderly richness, sufficient abundance. "To Penshurst" overtly mentions the elements, in balance in that blessed place:

> Thou ioy'st in better markes, of soyle, or ayre,
>   Of wood, of water; therein thou art faire.   (ll. 7-8)

Carew notes the four elements at Saxham, too:

"Upon Appleton House"

Water, Earth, Ayre, did all conspire,
To pay their tributes to thy fire. . . .

In his poem, Marvell does not refer directly to any of the four elements as elements, although we may assume that the episodes refer, among other things, to each one. The only element directly named in the poem is in stanza 63, in which by a grammatical figure of some ambiguity, the trees seem to fuse into a fifth element. Usually, the elements are seen as intermingling and interfusing, in accordance with the poem's characteristic alchemical physics. The meadows are an abyss, then a sea; the poet changes his locale from land to water and thence to higher ground; air and water combine in the birds ("tuned fires"); air and water fuse in the halcyon's flight; air and stream "compact"; the sun (fire) shrouds himself in clouds (air) as he sets. Day and night fuse, too; quite without expecting it, the poet finds that evening has come, and as he watches Maria in the blue evening air, night comes up to surprise them both.

This kind of fusion points to the significance of the "amphibiousness" discussed earlier: men go about their business in a world which does not keep to conventional barriers either, a world which must be reordered to suit each man's pattern of public and private value, public and private need. Amphibiousness—ambivalence, accommodation, mediation—must alter the clarified microcosm of conventional house-poems, so that not just one world, that of the house, but adumbrations and aspects of other worlds, come to be included in what had seemed at first a formally exclusive cosmos. The Nunappleton universe is anomalous, and men who live there must recognize the power of anomaly and govern themselves accordingly. But in some things, even Appleton is quite normal: day is for work, and when night falls, men go in.

The poet figures variously in house-poems. In this one, he is more uncompromisingly present in the poem than in most ancient analogues. From the beginning, this poet paces out the estate, surveys it, presents and inteprets it to his patron and his readers; he is engaged in reassessing its values. The patron does not, in the poem, accompany the poet—nor, we feel, does he sit at home waiting to read the full poem when it is done. Fairfax moves about the estate, too, now miraculously appearing to alter the construction of his house, now in stately review of his military gardens. As subject, though not in his own person, Fairfax appears at the end of the garden episode, to be praised from a polite distance as a model of integrity. If the poet speaks to anyone at that point, it is not to Fairfax but to an unseen audience of readers confused about how to interpret Fairfax's retirement from active public life. Emblematically, the Fairfaxes are present in "the double Wood of ancient Stocks," also probably in the "list'ning Elders" and the stock-doves. At the end, the elder Fairfaxes enter for a moment as at the end of a hymeneal masque, as the poet speaks his prothalamion for their daughter. The scene-shifts are manipulated by the poet, who either moves from one sight to the next or imagines one scene superimposing upon another; sometimes he gives up art and simply drops one scene to plunge into the next. The poet himself takes the pastoral promenade in this poem, and although Maria enters at the end to take over his neglected duties toward the landscape, only the poet has completely surveyed the estate. In his perambulation, he often pastoralizes, in the mowing scenes and others, perceiving and presenting the landscape before him in terms of his own preoccupations and inward feelings. It is worthwhile noting variations from the norm in his walk, too: when he finds his full emotional or sentimental satisfaction, it is not in garden or meadow, normal habitats of pastoralizers, but in the shelter of the wood, where his excitement peaks in acts of climactic imagination and creative understanding. There, alone and at one with nature, he produces his dithyramb. By the stream, he is overcome with languor and barely able to keep himself from "being" the brook.

The poet's view of garden and meadow is colored by his preoccupation with war, which "all this doth overgrow." The mowers are seen as warriors, massacring the grass, in a reversal of the usual direction of the image, which likens warriors to mowers. If the biblical implications of the flesh-grass metaphor are fully carried out, then the angels of Revelations with their sickles belong here too. The *adunata* of the flood bring us back to the war; outside the magic wood the "Horsemen" can be seen.

The perambulating poet is doing something more than taking a literary walk; he is also on a mental near-heroic quest, attempting to interpret from the various landscapes his own intentions and directions. Though the poem's plot concerns a life of retirement, and its most engaging episode is the self-delighting solitude of the wood, life is throughout seen as warlike, its moments of peace qualified and tinged by warfare. It is not only that civil war surrounds the ideal island estate at Nunappleton; it is that any life, even the most retired, is involved in some kind of struggle, actual or metaphorical, physical or spiritual. Isabella Thwaites was the subject of a metaphorical war, a war rendered in language which points to the serious struggles of the Reformation; the retired Fairfax takes his recreation in a garden, but his garden is built as a fort, to be the gentler mirror of embattled England as well as a shadow of the garden that primal England was. Both gardens have been turned into military scenes; both the garden, defending its inhabitants from the severe sieges threatening from without, and the wood, defending the poet from the world, are fortresses helping virtue in its endless psychomachia. Not, surely, an epic, this poem—but as surely not mock epic either. However ridiculous its conceits, the language of yearning for a snakeless Eden is too passionate, the nostalgia for a garden-past too strong, to permit one to laugh at them. Psychomachia offers a thematic form for struggles not quite physical in nature.

The poem is certainly about the psychomachia of an embattled and besieged personality. There are elements of the body-soul debate in the nun's speech; the local gardens, with their handling of sense-temptation, take both parts in a different kind of psychomachic paradigm. Like "A Dialogue between the Soul and Body," this poem does not permit conventional opinions about the senses, the body, and the world to go unchallenged. The senses are now dangerous, now restorative in the Nunappleton world; context determines their function. Chiefly, though, this poem celebrates the senses in its catalogues of delights; the poet's wood-ecstasy is at the very least a sensuous experience.

Here again, the poet, manipulating with one hand the moralistic traditions of psychomachia, with the other manipulates the traditions of libertinism. Marvell certainly is not an unqualified libertine, either in program or in style. The raptures of Saint-Amant and Théophile rely on a range of classical mythology and circumlocution almost wholly absent from "Upon Appleton House"; in the Yorkshire estate there are no dryads, naiads, and so on which regularly throng the French house-poems; no satyrs dance, nor fauns with cloven heel. Such presences as there are in the landscape seem to be Yorkshiremen and women—Fairfaxes, the poet, the mowers, the fishermen. Classical names are rare at Appleton—the nightingale is not Philomel, nor the sun Apollo: when the poet likens the sun to a classical figure, it is, atypically, to Narcissus. The only nymph in Appleton is the daughter of the house, "blest" by more than a classical *numen.* The raptures of this poem, like those of "The Garden," reject physical love; unlike Carew's famous rapture-poem or Saint-Amant's odd house-poem, "Le palais de la volupté," Marvell chooses to take his ecstasies alone: not even Théophile, although he called his poem "La Solitude," did that. In *libertin* poetry, there is much of the fantastic, the apocalyptic, the macabre, as well as an occasional dank breath of the gothick; such things are only hinted at in "Upon Appleton House," although both "The unfortunate Lover" and "The Gallery" do contain them. Here, the ruin is merely a "quarry" where stones for the new "Religious House" can be gathered; the apocalypse is entirely calm. Appleton's hospitality to friends and the poor does not extend, like Saint-Amant's, to "*honnestes Yvrognes*" and "*Débauchez vertueux*." Though his vocabulary of images, especially his conceits, share something with the *libertins*, Marvell's fantasies are in a different mode from theirs; such libertinism as he expresses is of the spirit only. In Appleton, the body has liberty for self-expression, but no license. Even the poet's pleas for languor are rationed, first by the poet himself, then by Maria, come to stiffen his resolution.

An underlying theme of this poem, never so overt as in other poems of Marvell, is the pastoral *paragone* of nature and art. This estate and this house are composed on nature's plan, "orderly and neat": "Art would more neatly have defac'd/ What she hath laid so sweetly wast." In a program contradicted by their language, the *libertins* also characteristically speak out against artificiality, in manners, social customs, conceits, and constraints; usually, they do so in conceits of great sophistication. Marvell of course praises simplicity at the expense of fancification in the first stanza; he makes plain that natural temples are more satisfactory and more beautiful than ornate architectural ones; nests and tortoiseshells take moral precedence over Aranjuez and Buen Retiro. But in this poem art is so artful as to be almost natural, the idiom in which the poet must speak. He admires the significant artifice of the formal gardens planted in Fairfacian metaphor, he admires the newly achieved proportions of Appleton House, he admires a supernaturalized natural scene at the poem's end.

Nor is nature always pure, or always perfect, in contrast to a vitiated art; thoughout the poem, nature cries out for reordering. All the same, one major theme is the art-nature debate, here given in terms of plain and ornamented styles in art as in life; the sufficient is set against the grandiose, the economical against the wasteful, the art of limitation against the art of prodigality. But the debate cannot be resolved, of course, in the terms the poet sets for it: this too is a problematical matter, for empirical solutions. Although sufficiency is clearly seen to overcome extravagance, nature herself often turns out to be virtuously prodigal and wayward, literally "wild." In different contexts and in different terms, this debate is carried over to deal with fancy and fantasy. Even at the end, when "loose Nature" is organized by Maria, the categories are far from clear, since it is by supernatural means, a miracle, that nature has been steadied and brought back to rights. At the very last moment of the day and the poem, we go in against a fantastic, unexplained frieze of men upside down, men parading offstage with their shoes on their heads. At Appleton, we early learn, "Nature here hath been so free/ As if she said leave this to me." That is, the neatness of art, so unequivocally praised in the early stanzas, turns out to be the same economy for which Aristotelean nature is famous. But also, in this passage and elsewhere, nature is "free," even to the abandonments of wood and stream. We return to straitness, of course, and prodigal nature is set within a frame of straitness, beginning with the fantastic discipline of the gardens and ending with the recollection of nature into Maria's still life. The mowers adjust nature, tidy her, by their mowing; their fields are by their work reduced to a *tabula rasa* inviting recreation; the flood swallows up the barbered surfaces in what looks like chaos but turns out to be another recreation, as the meads are made to seem "as green Silks but newly washt." The hewel trims the dead wood out of the forest; an allée divides the wildwood for the family's convenience.

Sometimes nature, passive, needs to be washed, trimmed, or repaired; sometimes she does the restoring and the recreating. Sometimes nature seduces, sometimes she protects against seduction. At her beginning, nature was a "rude heap" not unlike the disintegration of present-day England; beyond the Appleton confines, one feels, chaos is come again. Only within can nature achieve her "more decent Order tame," and even then such order is the joint achievement of nature and art. Both categories, loosed from their pastoral struggle with one another, are seen exercising their legitimate claims upon judgment and upon life.

Another way economy works in this poem, as well as art and wit, is in the epigrams, always a strikingly rational literary form which notoriously tames recalcitrant materials. In "Upon Appleton House," the epigrammatic passages serve to generalize, to summarize, even to halt the headlong movement for a moment into some permanency and some shape. Such couplets as

Sylvae

Height with a certain Grace does bend,
But low Things clownishly ascend.

These *holy Mathematicks* can
In ev'ry Figure equal Man.

Thrice happy he who, not mistook,
Hath read in *Natures mystick Book*.

And *Goodness* doth it self intail
On *Females*, if there want a *Male*.

can be extracted, without undue loss, from the poem; they make sense detached from the content they sum up. Their tidiness, their stasis, does not check the headlong rush of the poem for very long—the "*holy Mathematicks*" is at once followed by one of the most peculiar metamorphic passages of the poem, when the laden, pregnant house changes its shape from cube to sphere. Epigrams, finally, seem to reinforce the poem's general fluidity, by the contrast in tempo which they offer. Stasis can be—in this poem, it is—achieved in other ways as well, in the near-ecphrases of the garden stanzas and in the passages about vitrification, both of which arrest the poem's movement and force the poet too to an intent stillness. From the vitrified landscape to the end of the poem, all movement dies slowly down. The fishermen move faster than tortoises, but with a slow tread, to bring the day's restlessness to a close.

Almost until the end, the restless poet is the commanding figure. He demands attention: he stages and dissolves the scenes, interprets the set-pieces, the dances, the tableaux. He intrudes his long anecdotal mock-romance-saint's-life-psychomachia into a perambulation of the estate. Save for Thestylis' victory over him, he passes from one section to another at his own rate, until he resigns his command to his pupil, who takes over and perfects his duty, while he muses on her significance as nymph of the place he praises. At the poem's end, things tend to be boxed up: the beautiful estate is enclosed from the world and by the night; Maria, who epitomizes the estate, enters the house to be enclosed by it. The poet, presenter, interpreter, explicator of this world, in whose head the whole meaning of it is summed up, also goes in with his pupil-mentor, carrying his image with him. They go in under a hemisphere, the house's cupola, itself beneath the cupola of night; outside, the tortoise goes in under his hemisphere and the fishermen go in under theirs. They go in, because of the night, simply, and because of the larger symbolizations of night, as Fairfax himself had gone "in" to his estate, "out" of the world's doings.

Though he is its commanding figure, his intelligence and sensibility guiding us through poem and place, the poet-figure is not a simple one, and the guidance he gives us is not clear. He too is both "in" and "out" of the poem. In the Thestylis incident, his apparent detachment was just what permitted his own created figure to manipulate him as he manipulated his puppets: just as he seemed most personally effaced, the poet turns out to be made part of the scene. In his sylvan rapture, where he presents himself as wholly given over to his experience, his body and mind so fully felt as to lose his sense of their separateness, we realize that, like the nightingale, the woodpecker, and the rest, the poet has simply become another example to teach himself and us. He stages himself, turns himself into an emblem at precisely the moment which seems to be his profoundest self-commitment. He manipulates himself as he had had Thestylis manipulate him earlier.

But the lesson remains all the same: as in the garden ecstasy of the shorter poem, the wood ecstasy teaches that spiritual freedom can be achieved after release into the natural world, as the poet realizes himself as part of his environment. The liberating wood becomes his home, his cope, his ark, his den, his integument: like the dens, shells, nests, cells of the other animals, the poet has for a moment found his true domicile, one which "expresses" him and him alone. But this ecstasy will not be prolonged, either; like stasis, ecstasy can only be prolonged in memory. One capacity of ecstasy is to realize the limits time lays on sensation. As he knows himself, the poet must return or be returned to society, via the ideal maiden and the ideal house. Exhausted by his wonderful experiences, he languishes by the stream until he is once more recollected to his task of praise. The post-sylvan scenes do not seem noticeably less delightful than the wood scene; the poet's happiness does not diminish by his return to selective society. For him, in reality as for Fairfax in metaphor, Appleton is an "Inn." The poet is not a Fairfax and not a mower; his stay is limited in this demi-paradise, from which, when he is ready, he too must emerge.

As with the generic landscapes, the generic modes lapse into one another, the poet seeming to pass with psychological ease from one to the next. Literally, and literarily, these landscapes offer experiences for mastery; when he knows his little world from inside, he can safely venture into the greater world without. The different settings offer him different modes of interpretation, different roles to take on as man and poet. He tries out each in turn, fitting himself to his literary task as the creatures fit into their nests, cells, and shells. Within the literary genres morally interpreted, he exercises his skills, within their limits playing to achieve what freedoms he can, striving to acquire experience and control, accustoming himself to challenge and to change. Exploring his literary alternatives, he admits alternatives in life: though no overt choices are made in this poem, it is about the problems of choice. Like Maria and her parents, the poet prepares to accept his destiny as his choice, to give himself to his role and to order it as well, to teach the lessons of his mixed environment to, among others, himself. So the experiences at Appleton, where each trivial event stands for so much more than itself, are enormous in their implications. The cultivated nature and art of this place cultivate those living in it; pastoral, georgic, and sylvan episodes, all instruct, educate, lead outward from within. Even in retirement, as the poet learns, crucial moral activities continually go on, and paradise can, for a time at least, be regained. Leisure, idleness, self-enjoyment turn out to be cultivating, recreative, instructive, to be georgic in all its meanings. Public and private life interpenetrate to express the complications in living, and in understanding how one lives. Over and over again, worlds are turned upside down in the poem, and men too; seen from some perspective, the poet seems to say, all men sometimes have their feet in the air.

Seen from different perspectives, the fixed genres cannot stay still. Seen from different perspectives, life "in" and life "out," retirement and activity, cannot be maintained in dialectical opposition. A man's position, upside down or right side up, is fundamentally problematical, so that Fairfax's choice to go in cannot shield him altogether from the very discomforts which drove him in upon himself, although in this poem the difficulties are withdrawn from the public to the private world, reduced from national to personal scale. When the poet retires to the innermost depths of his being, within the protection of a magical wood, he is at once most withdrawn into and most outside himself, "ec-static." In his new-found expansiveness, he understands the speech of birds and "everything" else beside—"What *Rome, Greece, Palestine*, ere said," all gathered into "one History." But such moments of total insight are rare: it is to illustrate the problems facing an assessing intelligence that the poet so unceasingly mixes and shifts his rules, scales, emphases, points of vision, so mixes logic, style, generic convention. The reader is led into the poet's problematical world, to question himself, his world, all generalizations; but withal he is never permitted to lose hope in the face of confusion and multifariousness.

Precisely by such shifting and such fusion, the poet challenges human intelligence and human courage. The poet demonstrates, now in one context, now in another, that the limits of security cannot be finally set for anyone, but that anyone can use his powers of perception and organization, can choose his points of perspective, as Fairfax had chosen Appleton, from which to take the measures of himself and of his world. From the perspectivism of experience and the pluralism that perspective teaches, order somehow can be derived. Order so achieved, however, must be constantly revised and reconsidered. Fears of disorder can be allayed only by the practice of living with disorder; as all amphibia learn to distinguish their environments, choosing now one and now another, so men and women too must learn that same lesson: when to go in, when to come out. For a man learned in that, retirement is as demanding as public life, contemplation as taxing as fighting at Marston Moor, solitude as complicated as living in the busy companies of men. If one knows one's "within," then one can go "without." When a man's negative capability is sufficient to let him live at ease with the doubt whether he "be in it or without," then he may say without fear, "Let's in," knowing that virtue is neither cloistered nor fugitive merely because it is "within," whether within an estate, a house, or a human being.

The poem begins with a staggering conceit and ends, surprisingly, with a sudden, gentle "Let's in," addressed to anyone in the poet's hearing, his pupil, his readers. The understatement, the matter-of-factness, of that ending makes going "in," retirement, seem a natural and human thing. That final vernacular touch is itself a relaxation from the high conceits of the poet's working imagination, for the last stanza began with the salmon-fishermen and all they call up for him about all men on earth, beasts, and the cosmos, coming to its quiet conclusion: "let's in." The complexity of the poem is asserted throughout, until that last stanza; but the poet can live with complexity calmly and naturally—and expects us to live with it, too.

AFTERWORD

IN SPITE OF the clarity and frankness with which Marvell uses his literary resources in both "The Garden" and "Upon Appleton House," he consistently mutes his references to traditions, presenting only obliquely his peculiar modifications of them. With so much expressed in these poems, the wonder is that so much is *not* said as compared, say, with Milton's practice: Milton's references to sources and to traditions are usually clear, while Marvell's are sidelong, more often than not concealed. Marvell manages to make uneasy very alert and learned readers by his hints and insinuations of further meanings just beyond their grasp. By his uses of counter-themes, counter-styles, or even counter-genres, he allows levels normally distinct from one another in verse to interpenetrate and qualify one another in his poetry. Often his means of achieving this are very slight: in "Upon Appleton House," for instance, it is not easy to find evidence of an overt Christianity in the poem, although few readers escape at the end without having felt its strongly Christian undertow. When it is compared to other poems somewhat like it—for instance, Théophile's "La Solitude" and Saint-Amant's "La Maison de Sylvie"—this is the more remarkable; both these poems, although officially "libertine," end on a frankly Christian note for which little in the body of the poems has prepared the reader. Such endings seem to honor some poetic obligation, to make a gesture toward conformity, whereas in "Upon Appleton House," although the poet nowhere speaks in terms of didactic Christianity, the reader is quite aware of the Christian assumptions under the poem; this in spite of the fact that by far the larger number of traceable references to ethics are to sources in the classical repertory.

"The Garden" is as difficult to locate squarely within a Christian tradition, although more than one critic has made the attempt. If one feels the poem to be Christian, then it is by other than the customary means that one is drawn to the assumption. Of course, we are continually set off balance by the strategies of this poem: we are not, I think, quite prepared for the bee's industry, or any industry at all, in the last stanza; we have so far left time behind that the resumption of the zodiacal calendar comes as a surprise. When we have taken in the real world of industry and time, however, such explanation and justification for that notion must be found, not in the poem's argument or in the previous figures so much as in the poet's tone throughout the stanzas. Hence, when "industry" moves out from behind the trees and flowers of "The Garden," one must understand why this is so in terms of the sub-argument of the poem, of the poem's drift and strategy.

It is possible, I suppose, in view of the poem's attitude to contemplation and action, to read from it a Benedictine, Franciscan, or Calvinist lesson; but such a moral is certainly not dictated by the language or the thematic structure of the poem. Even the references to Scripture are too playful to be trustworthy evidence of the poet's doctrinal orthodoxy; if we want "The Garden" to be Christian, we must accept simply that some patterns of Christianity underlie it. "Upon Appleton House" is a different matter: there, the biblical imagery requires consideration of the poet's religious "opinion." Certainly that is not plain—as, for instance, in such religious poems as the two Dialogues, "The Coronet," and "On a Drop of Dew," where the religious content is clear; or, as in "Bermudas," the Scriptural paraphrase *is* the major part of the poem. There is in fact quite a bit of Scriptural imagery, curiously foreshortened, in "Upon Appleton House," the Israelites crossing the Red Sea, Noah, "the first Carpenter," the messages to be read in and by "the light *Mosaick*." Other references are less overt—though Solomon seems clearly implied in the poem, he is not in fact mentioned.

Other elements point toward religiousness, perhaps even to a particular brand of religiousness, but they are far from direct. From the satire of Romanism in the nunnery episode one must deduce the fundamental Protestantism of the poem's set; in stanzas 44 and 45, where the poet discusses Fairfax's destiny, one might read some hint of the predestinating deity prominent in Fairfax's thought, if not in Marvell's. Otherwise, our impression of the poem's underlying religious morality comes from such curious and oblique phrases as *"holy Mathematicks,"* "blest Bed," and the *"Religious House"* that Nunappleton, under the Fairfaxes, finally became. The estate has its near-religious rituals (the heron's *"Tribute* to *its Lord"*; the serpentless purification of the fields by the local flood; the "light *Mosaick*" of the wood). The daughter of the house is a nymph, but she is "blest"; her life was conducted under the *"Discipline* severe" of a *"Domestick Heaven"*; one result of that tuition was that she easily understood *"Heavens Dialect."* These phrases indicate, however, religious assumptions rather than religious doctrine: linked, they support the fundamental ethics of this poem, that of the sufficiency, modesty, and retirement which is more overt in the house-den-shell-nest imagery running through the poem. In the *"holy Mathematicks"* and the "light *Mosaick"* we have hints of religious miracle; otherwise, the language is more modest and workaday, tending to support the stoic Horatian values approved throughout the poem.

This use of figure is marked by economy. By means of compact and epigrammatic phrases, sometimes made "fuller" and ambiguous, "fuller" of implication by their very brevity, the poet manages to cast a thin net of connectives across his poem, so that we come out knowing what his values were, if not what his value-system was. The hints are clear enough, but the way they are given is not always so apparent: for instance, without knowing something about the Vitruvian correspondences, it would be difficult to accept the assertion that "These *holy Mathematicks* can/ In ev'ry Figure equal Man"; we are not told in what the *"Discipline* severe" of the Fairfaxes consisted; if it was their firm Presbyterianism, the poem does not say so. In both cases, the poet assumes that we have a ready rationale for his references, that we will fill in the gaps inevitably left by poetic shorthand. Phrases like these leave an echo in the mind, and as the overtones gain in volume, we acknowledge accumulated meaning to make conclusions to which the poem directs us. But not always at the time— so the crookedness of the architect's foreign design is not made straight until the poet finally enters his natural cathedral-temple-wood: this technique of separating connections from one another has its parallel in another range, in the late-realized puns in "The Garden." The technique works, somehow: we recognize that in "Upon Appleton House," a house is deformed-reformed by a man; this "fact" corrects the image, three stanzas earlier, of men stooping to enter a small door; Fairfax's recreative military garden is both like and unlike the garden that England was, now destroyed by military disorder. The tortoise appears briefly at the poem's beginning; when he crawls back at its close, he gives the poem a frame and acts himself as a refrain. His "hemisphere" finds its counterparts in human life and in the universe itself: all kinds of domes crown and enclose the poem. Then, the domes grade from the contracted tortoiseshell to the great hemisphere of heaven, so that by mere juxtaposition of images, Marvell reminds us of the themes of withdrawal and emergence, contraction and expansion, with which the whole poem deals.

Tricks of this sort recur in Marvell's poetry, among them the communication to readers of "ideas" and "philosophy." Compared to many other Renaissance poets, Marvell cannot be said to be overtly philosophical —we can find more philosophical *substance* in Greville's work, or Davies', or Milton's, or Pope's. Nonetheless, it is interesting that so many critics have turned naturally to philosophical traditions to get help in reading Marvell's verse: Neoplatonism, Bonaventurism, and so on have all been called in to help with explication. It is difficult, really, to associate Marvell with a particular philosophical system, although someone detected a brand of Spinozism in Marvell's attitude to the numinous, Plotinus has been called in as gardener of "The Garden," and Descartes has recently popped up as a contributor to Marvell's philosophical instruction. Philosophical systematics does not help us with the delicate problems of Marvell's poetry, although this poetry certainly manages to suggest philosophical questions and to force consideration of philosophical matters. If Marvell is "something" philosophically, then I think he is simply a generalized Neoplatonist of the sort most seventeenth-century poets were, half conscious of the implications of such "system" as that belief had, half reliant upon its empirical usefulness to poets of any philosophical allegiance. It was easy, then, for the middling-thoughtful man to be Platonist: in fact, it was difficult for him not to be. But in Marvell's poetry there is certainly a preoccupation, as Mr. Hyman has said, with "ideas," and to this subject I wish to turn.

In spite of his failure to write about philosophies or about philosophical ideas, there is a way in which Marvell might well strike readers as a more philosophical poet than Davies or Greville, concerned though both were to set down the doctrines of their metaphysics and epistemology. Marvell plays with what might be called the affective aspect of philosophy—for instance, in the limpid relaxation-ecstasy of "The Garden," where the poet effortlessly annihilates all that's made and creates new worlds and seas, or in the ecstatic realizations of the wood episode in "Upon Appleton House," where readers are let in on the extraordinary psychological freedom of creative inspiration. It is the *experience* of understanding, not its processes, which is presented to us: we are allowed to experience how inspiration works to transform the commonplace into the significantly rare; we feel with the poet both the separate wonder of each individual element of creation and its beautiful harmonious interconnection with all else. The poet turns from perceiver into creator, and we are allowed to share the experience. As Mr. Berger has said, the poet "stages" himself in these scenes, gives us the privilege of watching how it's done: with him in the wood at Appleton, we become "easie Philosopher" too, reading the secret messages of the Creation, *"Heavens Dialect"* as written in the Book of God's Works. Literally, we see this particular poetic universe becoming animate and didactic, as its elements catch and command the poet's creative attention. Such extraordinary communication of an experience both rare and private may tempt some to think that, according to some modern versions of poetic psychology, Marvell accords us a vision of unmediated perception. Whoever thinks such a thing about the passages in "The Garden" and "Upon Appleton House" that deal with heightened consciousness, has been victimized by the poet's illusionism. These passages, with their singular selectivity and their extraordinarily self-conscious uses of the language and habits of traditional intellection, are as "mediated" as it is possible to be. In stanza 6 of "The Garden," for instance, the choice of words must give us pause: all the nouns are abstract; no single element can be felt with sensuous precision—"Mind," "pleasure," "happiness," "Ocean," "kind," "resemblance," "Worlds," "Seas," "Thought," "Shade." The verbs do not help much either: "creates," "transcending," "annihilating." Such consistently abstract language can only come from a very self-conscious and controlled man, a man who, even by the intellectual standards of this sort of poetry, strains affective language to its utmost, radically shifting from the stanza before, with its gay sensualism, to the notional elevation of this one. Even the sense associations of that normally visual word, "green," are erased as the particular color ceases to give distinction to landscape elements but rather pervades all that is, in the material as in the ideal world. Before our eyes, so to speak, "green" loses its color, as it is translated from a sensuous to an intellectual plane.

This trick is remarkable, but it is achieved by purely literary means. A glance at the phrase's literary ascent is helpful in letting us see how Marvell manages to endow his line with a generality which may be called philosophical. In the seventh Eclogue, Virgil speaks of *"rara viridis . . . arbutus umbra,"* and in the ninth, of the green shade around fountains. In "Hortus," Marvell had tried his hand at perfecting the notion and its expression, still in Latin: "Celarant Plantae virides, et concolor Umbra." *"Concolor"* is fine strategy, but the "green Thought in a green Shade" raises the notion to a higher power, transcends "these" that went before it. In the associations of "Thought" and "Shade," both of them adumbrations, is called up the neoplatonic epistemological theory, with no need of its direct mention. Even in the vernacular, the word "green" provokes connotations linked to epistemology, since creativity in nature characteristically partakes of "greenness." When to all this, the mirror-effect is added by the doubling of the word "green," readers have been maneuvered into a philosophical frame of mind without having been conducted to such a mood by the usual disciplinary steps and stages. The Many-in-One and the One-in-Many are suddenly there, in the poem, in our minds; naturally, it seems. Similarly, though this poem has some elements, as Mr. Martz has defined them, of the formal meditation, it actually merely sketches out those stages, bringing us to full contemplation without having seemed to be arriving there.

Quite a different kind of "philosophical" effect is achieved in stanza 6 of "Upon Appleton House," which also offers a simulacrum of intellectual discipline:

> *Humility* alone designs
> Those short but admirable Lines,
> By which, ungirt and unconstrain'd,
> Things greater are in less contain'd.
> Let others vainly strive t'immure
> The *Circle* in the *Quadrature*!
> These *holy Mathematicks* can
> In ev'ry Figure equal Man.

The stanza has a pseudo-logical structure, seeming to "prove" that short lines can contain an undefined "more," that man can equal both circle and square, and that (somehow) circles can be squared. The difficulties of the logical identification are all left unresolved—the lines are short *but* admirable, although that conjunction is never explained; they are short but also "ungirt and unconstrain'd"—that is, they are neat *and* loose, economical *and* prodigal. By some miracle, attributable to Fairfax's superhuman nature, something which human intellect cannot achieve—i.e., the squaring of the circle—can and does come to pass. The couplets seem rational enough, with their occasional connectives (but, by, which) and their careful exceptions ("Let others vainly . . ."); the final couplet seems to bring the whole thing to a conventional solution.

But all this is sleight-of-hand, really; the conclusion is no more normal in logic than in Euclidian geometry. Only by reference to the intellectual origins from which the phrases come, can we supply the steps the poet skips. Only in rhetorical manuals, not in physics, can things greater be in less contained; only by stretching the mystification of Vitruvian correspondences can circle and square, sphere or cube, be thought to "equal Man." When, in the next stanza, plane geometry turns into solid, the only normalizing reason one can adduce for this is the habitual disciplinary progression which every schoolboy takes for granted. So with "hemispheres" in the last stanza; in cosmologies, hemispheres and the Antipodes characteristically go together, so that to a seventeenth-century reader, whose knowledge of geography and cosmology came from such schematized books, the association of the two was natural, if not logical. Upon such disciplinary frames Marvell relies, counting on his readers' familiarity with the schemata of the intellectual world and acceptance of the associations such schemata imply.

The image of the Antipodes in "Upon Appleton House" is not all that easy, though; cosmographical association does not fully "explain" its presence in the poem. Reality no doubt has something to do with it—Marvell had seen the local fishermen with their coracles on their heads. The boats could be seen as huge shoes (with or without Cleveland's image to direct one) or "boots" (as Mr. Alvarez thinks "boats" was pronounced in Northern speech): those associations pick up the important themes of world-upside-down and man-upside-down, and when one can add to it the hemispheric dome, the cosmic setting of the poem, suggested in the Pole passage in the garden episode, can be re-established to suit an ending.

In its first meaning, "antipodes" is merely a literal description—these men have their shoes on their heads. More than once, I have noted Marvell's etymological punning: by his punning and unpunning, he seems to return to questions lying at the heart of language and thus at the heart of all representation. His use of puns and unpuns manages to point up not only the inevitable ambiguities involved in any use of language, but the particular difficulties of the realist position about words. By deducing from one aspect of a thing named its logical linguistic consequence, he can point to the peculiar irrationality and untrustworthiness of linguistic conventions. Sometimes he extends a metaphor prettily: "the vigilant *Patroul*/ Of Stars walks round about the *Pole*"; sometimes he makes nonsense of linguistic associations, as in the captivating/ chaines association in "Eyes and Tears." At its richest, his plays point to the mystery at the heart of analogy (fetters/feet), raise questions about priority and primacy of thing and idea. Such playing with names, though hallowed in antiquity and made an official clerical habit by its dignification in Isidore of Seville's great work, does not mean that Marvell was (like Isidore) a "realist" in this matter. Rather the opposite: by behaving as if he were a realist, Marvell shows the limitations of the position, directs us to a nominalistic position which he does not seem overtly to affirm.

This way with language is consistent with Marvell's generally problematical approach to his craft: though careful to speak in the language of received ideas, he was really engaged in examining the validity of both the ideas and their appropriate languages. Certainly the impression one gets from Marvell's work is of a very skeptical mind at work, prying into difficult questions without seeming to do so. In many ways Marvell is a systematic poet—one can see, in his handling of the thematics of love poetry, or of pastoral, how carefully he planned his experiments; and in one sense, he was encyclopedic, drawing his imagery from many ranges of the natural world and the world of ideas. Compared to a genuinely encyclopedic poet like Du Bartas, though, Marvell's encyclopedism turns out to be very haphazard—we assume that he knew the system, but he picked and chose among its examples at his own will, for his own purposes.

So with his strong concern for epistemology and psychology: compared with the verse-treatises of Greville or Henry More, or the speculative poems of Giordano Bruno, Marvell's poetry is clearly outside the official genre of philosophical poetry running from Parmenides' fragments through Lucretius to the Renaissance. Like Donne's *Anniversary Poems*, Marvell's "Garden" and "Upon Appleton House" are too blatantly poetical to be called philosophical: at all points of choice, philosophical system is sacrificed to poetry.

Nor is doctrine the chief concern of these works, although a good deal of teaching undeniably goes on in them. Primarily, they deal with affective experience, appealing to the understanding by means of sense-experience rather than by means of the reason. Withal, the reason is by no means untouched by these poems. First of all, one has to work with one's head to follow the author's implications or to solve the puzzles he sets. Since these are so often set in terms of literary convention, they demand reconsideration of literary practice and of literary experience, "received" and personal. Since, too, Marvell does not hesitate to compare his fictional worlds with an undescribed, assumed world of common sense, necessarily in his poems the world of literary myth and convention comes into conjunction with the "real" world. When the two worlds conflict, the poet points to that fact; when he can, he reconciles the oppositions he finds; when he cannot (as in the Body-Soul dialogue), he leaves the problem to us. Unlike Milton, who so unhesitatingly affirms the great literary and philosophical traditions he sums up, and unlike Shakespeare, whose light-handed use of highly traditional literary themes and conventions open up enormous prospects of further possibility, Marvell's verse seems self-enclosed and self-referential. He turns back on his tradition, and he turns in on it; even when he questions or rejects one or another received opinion or received language of his craft, he accepts poetry's traditional directives and works from within them.

By his critique of his art, Marvell's verse brings readers back to what we had always taken for granted, returns us by unexpected routes to the monumental commonplaces of western thought—which, since they are that, are also the proper topics of poetry or of any serious expression. Among other things, Marvell deployed his techniques to open poetry upon questions usually limited to philosophical discussion—but he sets such questions in terms of criticism and aesthetics. Any critic ends up in philosophy, finally: where questions of expression are concerned, the relation of words to things is inevitably dealt with; where the morality of literary form and style are concerned, questions of ethics must arise. Since Marvell was concerned to make a poem express more than it was properly expected to, he therefore examined the tensile strength of language and form; he occasionally imitated philosophical "grammars," both of logic and of intuition. Again and again, by purely poetical investigations, we are brought up against philosophical questions and problems—and we are not given much help in solving them.

For, in such an enterprise, a poet is entitled to protect himself, both from other poets and from philosophers. His subjects may be serious, but he himself can choose to play with them. Marvell's poetry is the work of an "easie Philosopher," who played as fast and loose with the rules of disciplined thought as he did with the rules of poetical expression. By his various techniques of reduction, verbal analysis, juxtaposition, conceit, and so on, Marvell managed to play with ideas in several ways. He played at catching an important notion in a short or witty phrase; he juggled with his idea-bearing phrases to make all kinds of shifting patterns of them; he skirted metaphysics and ontology, all without overcharging readers with his grave burdens. Indeed, he went further: he discouraged us from concerted and disciplined thoughts about a given problem, even a literary one; he gave us no chance to linger, no chance to contemplate, even when the subject of the poem is contemplation. Poetry offers a kind of solution to philosophical problems—or, rather, the affective experiences poetry offers can be exploited to gain, without readers' awareness of the goal, intuitions usually called philosophical. Marvell used his own heightened common sense to bring him and us to terms with problematics. Mercurial, unsystematic, irreverent, fantastic poet that he was, he nonetheless relied upon the fundamental good sense of his readers to piece together from his hints, images, scales and tricks some defense against mysteries often too difficult to bear thinking on.

To make readers think of philosophy in the middle of demanding poetic games is no trivial accomplishment. Altogether, Marvell seems to have looked for the unexpected precisely where one should not expect to find it, in expected and received traditions and conventions; his intransigent examinations of those traditions earned him his freedom surely, so that when he presents problems of history, theology, ethics, ontology, or epistemology in lyric poems, always in terms of poetry itself, we must honor him for the thoroughness of his achievement. True, these things are the subject-matter of the poetic tradition; but they are presented normally as definite topics, not concealed under the arts and artifices of poetic craft. His confident attitude toward his intellectual world, rare in any poet, and especially rare in a poet examining questions in so tentative a way, is one mark of the personal style of this poet that I may have seemed at pains to deny. For, of course, he was committed: though certainly his examinations of literary techniques and topics— literary love, the pastoral mode, *genera mixta*—show the masterful flexibility of his craftsman's art, a single and fundamental devotion to that art underlies his investigations.

At all times, Marvell was a critic, and his critic's view informs the least as well as the greatest of his works, sometimes shaking the foundations of a tradition, sometimes stripping it of excess, sometimes reforming it and making it stronger than before. Like many critics, he is not so concerned to solve as to explore the problems he sets: since my own interest is in what I call the moral aspects and implications of literary technique, I am inclined to think that he knew, sensible man that he was, that the problems he explored were basic and therefore not subject to final solution. He was not, though, irresponsible: one way and another, he consistently offered some new way of thinking about a problem, either by defining it, or by redefining it, or by altering its context. For all his chameleonic adaptability, Marvell was not simply an apprentice poet working out the possibilities of his craft, in imitation of great predecessors in his profession; his verse is far too strong for such a judgment. Nor can one say, in spite of its modes of detachment, that his verse was impersonal; compared, say, to the work of Thomas Carew, another poet extraordinarily true to his traditions and singularly absent, in autobiographical persona, from his poems, Marvell's verse is marked by his peculiarly quizzical attitude to his material, his subjects, and his technical means.

Marvell stood up to his traditions, treating with them as an equal, subjecting them to test and examination, trying one tradition against another, trying himself against one and another tradition, exploring the possibilities of traditional expression from the smallest scale, of a single word, to the largest, such as the cosmic, profound setting of "Upon Appleton House." The refinement, reduction, and minute exactness of his poetry seems its peculiar characteristic, until we realize how generous, inclusive, even prodigal he could be, how open to the challenge of his art. Marvell's objectivity, manifest in the evident detachment of his attitude, honors the received conventions of a long and authoritative past; with that, he nonetheless forced an immense revision of the schematized world of his inheritance simply by his idiosyncratic insistence on professional responsibility. His intransigent selfhood made itself felt on the very traditions of his art, from which he drew his strength and which he felt obliged always to question and to test.

INDEX

activity, 17, 22–23, 24–25, 29, 65–66,
  104, 141, 152, 157, 170–71, 185,
  191, 216, 219, 225–27, 239, 248,
  266, 271, 275. *See also* retirement;
  paragone.
adunaton, 55, 191, 201, 287.
Agrippa, Henry Cornelius, 158n.
Alciati, Andrea, 112, 112n, 137, 197n,
  198n, 224n.
Allen, D.C., ix, ixn, 144, 144n, 146n,
  158n, 181, 181n, 182n, 201, 215n,
  235n, 241, 241n, 246n, 279, 279n, 280.
Altdorfer, Albrecht, 193.
Alvarez, A., 203n, 301.
amphibiousness, 171–72, 199, 271–73,
  275, 286, 294.
anamorphosis, 149, 152, 201–05, 208–10,
  230, 235, 251, 264, 273.
anthology, 21, 92, 106, 137, 175–76, 289.
Anthology, Greek, 105, 110, 195, 240.
Apocalypse, 35, 241, 267–69, 281, 282.
architecture, 98, 122, 186, 187, 223,
  228–31, 260, 333.
Arcimboldo, Giuseppe, 212n.
argutia, 84–85.
Aristotle, 152.
astigmatism, 184, 190.
Attic style, 80, 81, 88. *See also*
  style, plain style.
Auerbach, Erich, 183n.
Austen, Ralph, 23n, 27, 27n, 37n,
  38n, 159n, 162, 162n, 224n.

Bacon, Francis, 37, 37n, 162, 168,
  169n, 232, 233.
Baltrušaitis, Jurgis, 210n.
Baron, Hans, 62, 62n.
baroque, 86, 188–89, 190.
Beger, Laurentius, 175n.
Benlowes, Edward, 189, 298.
Bennett, Josephine Waters, 141n.
Berger, Harry, Jr., ix, ixn, 26, 26n,
  31n, 61, 61n, 92n, 130, 130n, 131,
  157n, 181, 181n, 215n, 225, 228n,
  234n, 267n.
Berthoff, Ann E., 58n.

Beza, Theodore, 197, 197n.
Blith, Walter, 224n.
Bonaventure, St., 142, 143n, 144.
Bonaventurism, 298.
Borroff, Marie, 101n.
Botticelli, Sandro, 108.
Boyle, Robert, 18.
Bradbrook, Muriel C., 13n, 144n,
  161n, 182n.
Brooks, Cleanth, 62, 62n.
Browne, Thomas, 80, 150n, 154n, 161,
  163n, 167, 168n, 189, 223n, 269n, 271n.
Bruno, Giordano, 18, 144n, 302.
Buffum, Imbrie, 183n.
Burckhardt, Sigurd, 95n.
Burton, John, 222n.
Burton, Robert, 174, 175n, 189, 277.
Bush, Douglas, 62, 62n.
Butler, Samuel, 20.

Caesar, 65, 86.
Callois, Roger, 189, 189n.
Camerarius, Joachim, 23n, 165n,
  171n, 196, 196n, 197n, 198, 198n,
  199, 199n, 200n, 228n.
Canticles, 102, 142, 146, 160, 162n,
  166, 227, 232.
Carew, Thomas, 75, 284n, 285, 288, 305.
Carscallen, J.A., ixn.
Castor, Grahame, 175n.
catoptrics, 210, 211–12.
Cats, Jacob, 159, 159n, 198, 199n, 200,
  200n, 235n.
Catullus, 21, 55.
Cézanne, Paul, 95.
Chambers, A. B., 200n, 202n.
chaos, 93, 192, 234, 245, 267, 275,
  282, 290.
Charles I, 63, 64, 66, 67, 68, 69, 86,
  87, 99, 133, 142, 186, 235n.
Charles II, 63.
Claudian, 185, 185n.
Clements, Roberts, 171n.
Cleveland, John, 17, 64, 75, 76, 189, 203,
  203n, 284, 301.
Columella, 199n, 236n.

Index

Comito, T.A., 14n, 154n.
conceit, 49, 82, 85, 111, 125. *See also* concettismo.
concettismo, 49, 75–76, 82, 85, 189, 230, 251. *See also* conceit.
Coninxloo, Gillis van, 195n.
Conti, Natale, 158n.
contraction. *See* diminution.
Cook, Moses, 224n.
Coolidge, John C., 62, 62n, 65, 70.
correspondence, doctrine of, 43–44, 49, 118–20; pastoral, 32–34, 49, 89–90, 122, 297.
Cotton, Charles, 217, 218n.
Cowley, Abraham, xi, 24n, 64, 98n, 167n, 185n; *Davideis*, 20.
Crashaw, Richard, 17, 43, 75, 116, 124.
Creation, 150, 255, 259, 282, 299.
criticism, xi–xii, 5–6, 79, 96, 213, 278, 303, 304–05. *See also* metapoesis.
Croll, Morris, 80, 80n, 81, 87, 91, 183n, 189.
Cromwell, Oliver, 21, 25, 63, 64, 65, 66, 68, 69, 70, 86, 87, 98–99, 104, 133, 142.
Crucifixion, 196, 215, 236, 248, 274, 280, 282.
Cruttwell, Patrick, 63n.
Cudworth, Ralph, 64.
cultivation, 36–37, 104, 223–24, 237. *See also* georgic.
Culverwell, Nathanael, 236n.
Cunningham, J.V., 92n.
Curtius, Benedictus, 154.
Curtius, E.R., 145n, 163n, 252n.
Cuyp, Aelbert, 194n.

Dante Alighieri, 233n.
Datta, K.S. *See* Scoular.
Davenant, William, xi, 196n, 228n, 244n, 259n.
Davies, John, 144n, 298.
David, Gerard, 193.
Davison, Denis, 13n, 58n.
Davison, Francis, 27n.
Descartes, René, 143n, 144, 298.
Diderot, Denis, x, xi.
Diggers, 262.
diminution, 3, 22, 34, 61, 103, 106,

118–23, 137, 147, 154–55, 172, 191, 247, 258, 282. *See also* Horace; sufficiency topos; *multum in parvo*.
disjunction, 3, 61, 158, 172, 177, 181–82, 190, 208, 213, 263. *See also* hiatus.
Dodsworth, Roger, 222.
domestication, 270; Charles I, 68, 87; Cromwell, 68–69; Fairfax, 220–21.
Donne, John, 17, 43, 75, 76, 80, 124, 145, 147, 152, 172, 189, 269n, 277, 302.
Drebbel, Cornelis, 211, 213.
Dronke, Peter, 130n.
Drummond, William, 210n.
Dryden, John, 64, 64n, 233n.
Du Bartas, Guillaume Salluste, 302.
Dugdale, William, 222, 222n.

Ecclesiastes, 30.
ecphrasis, 22, 50–51, 100–01, 106, 113, 118, 119, 127, 146, 195, 291.
ecstasy, 27, 56, 61, 123, 161–63, 165, 166, 168, 169, 170–71, 193, 195, 203, 216, 292.
Eden, v, 36, 61, 166, 240, 271, 288. *See also* paradise.
elements, 244–45, 285–86.
Eliot, T.S., ix, ixn.
emblem, 53, 75, 95, 106, 110–13, 116–17, 118, 123, 128, 137, 156, 160, 171, 196–205, 235, 235n, 251, 268, 282, 292.
emblematic method, 53, 103, 171–73.
emergence. *See* activity.
Empson, William, ix, ixn, 13n, 147, 147n, 149.
Epicureanism, 78, 161, 165, 167, 169, 223.
epistemology, 18, 119–20, 151, 163, 165, 167, 169, 177, 209, 270, 300.
Erasmus, Desiderius, 16, 175, 175n, 198n, 199n.
Estienne, Henri, 172.
etymology, 84, 94. *See also* pun.
Eucherius, 174n.
Euclid, 59n.
Evelyn, John, 23n, 24n, 224n, 255.
exemplum, 22.

Index

Index

Index

Index

Virgil, xi, 8, 28, 28n, 68, 77, 104, 137, 148n, 150, 159, 174, 174n, 175, 185, 185n, 198, 198n, 200, 201, 202, 223, 223n, 233n, 235n, 240, 241n, 243, 244n, 279, 280, 284, 299.
Virgin. *See* Mary, the Virgin.
Vitruvius, 197n, 228, 228n, 229n, 230n, 231n, 233n.
Vlieger, Simon de, 193n.
Voltaire, 20.
Vredeman de Vries, Jan, 230, 231, 231n.

Wallace, J.M., ix, ixn, 25n, 62, 62n, 66, 181, 181n, 244n, 246n, 281n.
Waller, Edmund, 64, 64n, 284, 284n.
Wallerstein, Ruth, ix, ixn, 142, 142n, 181, 181n, 182n.
Walton, Isaak, 163n.

Warnke, Frank J., ixn, 144n, 181n.
Webber, Joan, 30n, 189, 268.
Wellek, René, 188n.
Whitney, Geoffrey, 112n, 197n, 198n, 199n, 235n.
Willet, Andrew, 235n.
Williamson, George, 154n.
Williamson, Karina, 61, 61n, 131n.
Winters, Yvor, 75, 75n, 83.
Wither, George, 196, 196n, 228n, 229n.
Wittkower, Rudolf, 189, 189n, 197n, 229n.
Wotton, Henry, 63n, 185, 185n, 186n, 230n.

Yates, Frances A., 107n.

Zincgrefius, 198n.